P9-CFQ-739

Interactive Writing

WITHDRAWN

INTERACTIVE WRITING
How Language and Literacy Come Together, K–2

Andrea McCarrier
Gay Su Pinnell
Irene C. Fountas

TOURO COLLEGE LIBRARY
Kings Hwy

HEINEMANN
Portsmouth, NH

KH

Heinemann
A division of Reed Elsevier Inc.
361 Hanover Street
Portsmouth, NH 03801–3912
www.heinemann.com

Offices and agents throughout the world

© 2000 by Andrea McCarrier, Irene C. Fountas,
and Gay Su Pinnell

All rights reserved. No part of this book may be
reproduced in any form or by any electronic or
mechanical means, including information storage
and retrieval systems, without permission in writing from the publisher, except by a reviewer, who
may quote brief passages in a review.

The author and publisher thank those who gener-
ously gave permission to reprint borrowed material.

**Library of Congress Cataloging-in-Publication
Data**

McCarrier, Andrea.
    Interactive writing : how language and
literacy come together / Andrea McCarrier,
Irene C. Fountas, Gay Su Pinnell.
        p.   cm.
    Includes bibliographical references and
index.
    ISBN 0-325-00209-6
    1. English language—Composition and
exercises—Study and teaching (Early childhood).   2. Language arts (Early Childhood).
I. Title.   II. Fountas, Irene C.   III. Pinnell,
Gay Su.
LB1139.5.L35 M35   1999
372.62'3 21—dc21
                                    99-045057
                                         CIP

Editor: Lois Bridges
Production: Melissa L. Inglis, Renée Le Verrier
Cover and text photos: Tom Dubanowich,
    Columbus, OH, and Mark Morelli,
    Cambridge, MA
Cover design: Darci Mehall/Aureo Design
Manufacturing: Louise Richardson

Printed in the United States of America on acid-
free paper

06 05   ML   10 11 12

12/13/05

We dedicate this book to the memory of our friend and

colleague Moira G. McKenzie, whose pioneering work in

early literacy learning has inspired us for many years.

Her development of shared writing is the basis

for the work described here.

Contents

Acknowledgments

This book is filled with the work of children and teachers. Their learning, their energy, their thinking, and their creativity radiates from the pieces of interactive writing and art we have included here. This strong work from real classrooms is the foundation for the conceptual models we have created and the procedures we describe. Not only does this work provide practical guidance for the implementation of interactive writing but it represents data to spark our thinking. Examining the work of teachers and children stretches our powers to analyze the process and to look for evidence of learning. The wonderful examples given here are drawn from the classrooms of Kate Bartley, Amy Davis, Sharon Esswein, Nancy Kelly, Karen King, Flo Metcalf, Toni Newsome, Ida Patacca, Pat Prime, Stephanie Ripley, Kate Roth, Joanne Sabik, Tammie Silvia, Pat Slater, Susan Sullivan, and Kristen Thomas; teachers who are leaders in the education of young children. We want to thank Julie Edwards, Alma Escamilla, and Carmen Ramirez for providing examples in Spanish. Every day, we appreciate the generous contributions of these teachers.

We work with a group of educational leaders who provide us daily models of commitment to the improvement of literacy education for young children. We express thanks to all our colleagues in the Literacy Collaborative and especially to the teams at Ohio State University and Lesley University, for their teaching, their research, and their spirited engagement in teacher development. We thank the Lesley team, including Sue Hundley, Diane Powell, and Sandra

Lowry for their strong contributions to our work. For their collegiality and their ongoing development of these approaches, we are also grateful to the team at Ohio State University, including Lisa Brandt, Diane E. DeFord, Mary Fried, Paige Furgerson, Peg Gwyther, Justina Henry, Carol Lyons, Denise Morgan, and Joan Wiley. We want to thank Jane Williams for her precise and detailed examination of the data that indicate the effectiveness of interactive writing. We acknowledge the wonderful contributions of colleagues in Reading Recovery, Mary Fried and Rose Mary Estice, who have demonstrated so much commitment to helping young children become literate, and of Katie Button, Texas Technological University, who has contributed over many years to this work.

For their original development of interactive writing, we express appreciation to Charlotte S. Huck and the original teacher study groups, beginning in 1989. Charlotte is a leader who has brought national attention to children's literature; in this ongoing research project, she extended literature through writing. The first study group included Sue Hundley, Connie Compton, Melissa Wilson, Stephanie Hawking, Ann James, Bette Coles, Carole Spahr, Paula Connor, Diane Powell, Synda Slegeski, Julie Wittenberg, Melanie Murnan, Mary Ann Penzone, Jean Westin, Tennie Tyler, and Robin Holland. Members of the kindergarten study group were Ida Patacca, Beth Sherwood, Francee Eldredge, Connie Jones, Elizabeth Sturges, Laura Locke, Hope Perry, Dody Brooks, Traci Michalek, Grace Wiley, and Mary Ann Ewert. We also express appreciation to the primary team at Memorial Spaulding School in Newton, Massachusetts, and their highly committed leader, Principal Bunny Meyer. We have learned from all of you.

The pioneering work of Moira McKenzie inspired twelve years of effort in the development of interactive writing. As we looked at the examples in this book and reconsidered interactive writing, we realized again the power of the shared writing model as described by McKenzie. The combination of shared and interactive writing puts effective tools in teachers' hands. The pioneering work of Martha L. King also contributed significantly to the development of shared writing. Her unparalleled research on children's writing and her understanding of children's language learning have informed and inspired us and we thank her. We also thank our special friend, Mary Ellen Giacobbe, who constantly inspires us to learn more about children's writing.

We appreciate the hard and detailed work of Polly Taylor, Jennifer Gleason, and Heather Kroll in bringing this book into existence. We are also grateful to Sharon Freeman for her assistance in so many ways.

We thank the team at Heinemann, including Renée Le Verrier, Melissa Inglis, and of course, Mike Gibbons, who provides the leadership that makes things happen. It is a measure of our respect for our editor, Lois Bridges, that we waited with such expectation to hear her opinion after sending our completed manuscript last spring. She liked the book, could see its possibilities, and then gave it her own special touch, which so greatly increased its value. Thank you, Lois, as always.

We thank Ron Melhado and Ron Heath for their love, patience, and kindness during the preparation of this book, and we especially thank John McCarrier for assistance of just about every kind—from proofreading to providing feedback to computer work. And we express our deepest love to our families, especially Elfrieda Pinnell, Catherine Fountas, Esther Miller, John McCarrier, Meghan McCarrier Harding, and Rebecca McCarrier. Meghan and Rebecca made some of the original videotapes that provided examples for this book and they have always supported this work in a multitude of ways.

Introduction

Young children want to be writers. Witness their enthusiasm as they make marks on paper, frosty car windows, and any other surfaces available to them. Revel in their joyful excitement and deep satisfaction as they experience the power of making those first written signs and symbols. As teachers we want to keep that excitement, interest, and confidence alive while at the same time introducing young children to the way written language works.

We want children to become writers whose voices radiate from paper, who can capture their ideas in cogent written statements, who understand both the constraints and possibilities of written language conventions, and who can organize and structure various kinds of texts, texts that serve multiple purposes—everything from a poem to celebrate the birth of a new sister to a business letter requesting information about a new video game.

But writing is a complex process, and as teachers we must find a way to help children begin the journey. We believe that the most effective instructional support for doing just that is *interactive writing*. Simply defined, interactive writing is a dynamic, collaborative literacy event in which children actively compose together, considering appropriate words, phrases, organization of text, and layout. At points selected by the teacher for instructional value, individual children take over or "share the pen" with the teacher. In this book we illustrate and describe how teachers can use interactive writing to involve children in spelling the words they need to express meaning. In the process, teachers draw children's attention to spelling patterns and letter-sound relationships within words so that they can learn how words "work."

The Purpose of Interactive Writing

We are familiar with children's first attempts at representing letters and approximating the spelling of words. These initial attempts reveal both their knowledge of written language and their eagerness to discover how it all comes together to convey meaning. While recognizing and celebrating young children's linguistic competence as early writers, we need to find ways to help them move beyond approximation. We want them to notice the details of written language and to understand that conventions such as proper spelling and grammar not only support them as writers but also support the readers of their written work. Interactive writing provides powerful demonstrations of writing that help young children make progress in their own writing. Using interactive writing, teachers not only show children how writing works but invite them to participate, with support, in the act of writing.

How Interactive Writing Works

In interactive writing lessons, the teacher serves as guide and often as scribe supporting children in an "apprentice" role. That means that both teachers and children negotiate the meaning and the structure of the text as they compose the message together. Above all, interactive writing sessions are a time when teachers and children share the joy of expressing meaning as they collaborate to produce a written text. Among the many examples of writing we showcase in this book, we describe a science project in which children learn about plants and write about their experiments. We also include a grocery list that children create for a cooking project, an "original" Little Red Hen story, and instructions for making a peanut butter sandwich. We collected the examples, created in real classrooms, from the primary teachers with whom we work, including teachers who are teaching literacy in Spanish and those who work with English learners. Note that interactive writing is an instructional strategy that works well for children of all linguistic backgrounds and is particularly helpful for those transitioning into English literacy. Many of the examples we share clearly demonstrate a sequence of instruction that covers days or weeks. These examples reveal that writing is an accessible and delightful entry into the rich complexities of written language and an endlessly fascinating tool for expression and learning. Furthermore, since examining children's writing is the most effective way for readers to learn about interactive writing, we have included numerous photographs of classroom work, including samples from a bilingual classroom in which the children are learning to read and write in Spanish.

We see interactive writing as a transition tool to help children move forward in their development as writers. They come to us in kindergarten with some knowledge of literacy and, perhaps, the ability to write their names, a few letters of the alphabet, or letter-like forms. Interactive writing is an instructional format that allows children to learn a great deal more about writing. As a group, the texts they compose and write are beyond those that they could write or read alone.

These powerful opportunities for writing are embedded in the daily exploration of interesting topics in the classroom. The teacher helps children to find reasons for writing across the curriculum. Additionally, she shows them how they can use writing to extend the meaning of their favorite literature books. Polished and completed drafts of interactive writing are treasured and read again and again.

Interactive writing is a superb tool for working with children who are just developing an awareness of reading and writing. As a support for early writing development, interactive writing is designed for children in prekindergarten, kindergarten, and grade one, but it is also very useful for teachers working with small groups of second and sometimes third graders who need stronger support in early writing skills.

We have been working with teachers in interactive writing for more than fifteen years. Each year, we have been newly impressed by teachers' reports of their students' growth as writers. Interactive writing enables students to transfer the strategies and skills required for competent writing to their own independent writing. We describe the ways that teachers can document student learning and we provide, as examples, some summary data. Even more important, we include the work of teachers and children as evidence of the learning that is possible within interactive writing.

The History of Interactive Writing

The term *interactive writing* was coined in 1991 by a research group comprised of faculty members from The Ohio State University and teachers from Columbus, Ohio. All members of the group were literacy teachers who were accustomed to using their thoughtful observations of children as a teaching guide. They were concerned about helping young children, especially those who had limited experiences in literacy, to understand how words work. The group examined Moira McKenzie's work in shared writing and enthusiastically adopted the approach as a powerful instructional prompt to help children understand the writing process. They varied the approach with a "share the pen" technique that involved children in contributing individual letters and words to the group writing.

The research group spent a great deal of time talking about the place of interactive writing in the curriculum and the ways it differed from the traditional language experience approach, shared writing, and independent writing. Language experience, as we had used it previously, involved writing for the children as they expressed their ideas verbally. It was used to document their language and demonstrate the writing process. Shared writing, on the other hand, entailed greater planning, as the goal was to create a readable text. In both language experience and shared writing we teachers acted as scribes. While we did not stop using language experience and shared writing, we began to involve children in sharing the pen. Later, we discovered many ways to combine shared and interactive writing. The interactive nature of this experience revealed ways to make our teaching examples even more powerful.

Within a rich literacy curriculum, a child will have many connected writing and reading experiences. Interactive writing has a key role within this curriculum because it

❚ can be used for many different purposes, from creating stories that the children can read to making labels to writing directions and informational pieces
❚ can be used at any time during the instructional day and in any content area
❚ provides a context within which the teacher can provide explicit instruction in conceptualizing and composing text, using the conventions of written language and learning how words work.

Our research team found that much can be accomplished in just a few minutes of interactive writing because the teacher draws children's attention to powerful examples selected from a text in which they are heavily invested with meaning. The high engagement present in interactive writing lessons and the lively pace it requires create an ideal setting for helping children keep the meaning of a text in mind while focusing on the details of print.

The work of the research team has continued over the years by teachers involved in the Literacy Collaborative, a university-school partnership for implementing classroom literacy programs. The teachers with whom we work have found interactive writing to be an essential component of a rich primary literacy program. We wrote this book to support their efforts in refining their practice as well as to engage more teachers in the conversation about young children's acquisition of effective writing skills. Several books have emerged from these efforts.

In our book *Guided Reading: Good First Teaching for All Children*, we focus on teachers working intensively with small-group reading instruction in grades K through 3. That book emphasizes the contribution that writing can make to helping children become literate, but provides only a brief description of interactive writing. In the companion volumes *Word Matters: Teaching Phonics and Spelling in the Reading/Writing Classroom* and *Voices on Word Matters: Learning About Phonics and Spelling in the Literacy Classroom*, we and our colleagues provide more in-depth information about interactive writing. This book, *Interactive Writing: How Language and Literacy Come Together, K–2*, however, is a comprehensive examination of all aspects of this instructional approach, from the initial start with children's own names to interactive written inquiry in literature, science, social studies, and mathematics. We describe how teachers adjust interactive writing to meet the varying needs of learners across the grades. Through examples, we also demonstrate that when young children are involved in this highly successful, satisfying process, they see themselves as writers who can represent their ideas and understandings about their world. For beginning writers, putting together and talking about ideas, negotiating the text with others, and sharing the pen to write it, propel them toward grasping the power of producing the written word.

Organization of This Book

This book is organized into five sections, each of which highlights a different aspect of interactive writing. Section 1, "Learning to Write in a Quality Literacy Program," presents four chapters that define and describe interactive writing and place the process within a broad language and literacy learning curriculum. We also offer practical ways to organize space and materials so that interactive writing can be used efficiently in the classroom, and a comprehensive chapter on the nuts and bolts of getting started with interactive writing, including communication with parents, colleagues, and administrators.

Section 2, "Sharing the Pen with Young Writers," includes four chapters that provide an in-depth description of the essential elements of interactive writing. We discuss how the teacher works with children to compose a readable text with high learning potential. We describe the process of constructing a variety of texts—a message, story, or the like—word by word. We provide examples and detailed descriptions of how interactive writing can be used to help children learn about letters, letter-sound relationships, the conventions of the printer's code, and the "inner workings" of words.

In Section 3, "Young Writers Engage in Literacy," we describe and discuss exciting classroom work in writing both narrative and expository texts and focus on learning about literature through interactive writing. Using interactive writing in small and whole-class groups, we explain the process of teaching children how to remember, summarize, and construct meaning from a text as well as how to extend meaning by interpretation or innovation.

We extend the discussion to the important area of expository text. Writing is a tool for living, and interactive writing is a good context for involving children in using written language to accompany and enhance their daily activities. Like adults, children can work together to make and use lists, label things, write letters, and tell stories. Expository text can also be used to describe a sequence of events over time and to explain phenomena. As we show by example and illustrations, interactive writing is also a tool for helping children engage in inquiry. Like scientists, they can use expository interactive writing in many ways as a tool for investigation and reporting.

In Section 4, "Young Writers Engage in the Literacy Journey," we focus on knowing learners as a foundation for effective teaching. We describe ways of observing and assessing children's knowledge of written language, and we discuss how teaching decisions are tailored so that no time is wasted and the interactive writing lesson is effective. We also describe a gradient of difficulty that will guide teachers in varying the interactive writing lessons to suit learners over the primary years.

Section 5, "The Foundations of Effective Writing Practice," presents the research base for interactive writing, providing a comprehensive answer to an important question: *Why* should I use interactive writing with young children? We address the many underpinnings of interactive writing—the powerful rationales for this highly effective tool.

The appendices to this volume provide useful lists of books, organized by theme and genre, that we have found to be excellent resources in supporting children in interactive writing. We include directions for making an easel that is especially suited to interactive writing. We also provide a useful self-assessment rubric so that you can reflect on your own professional growth over time.

Teachers—both those who are new to interactive writing and those who are experienced with it but want to refine their instructional practice—will discover through our book that teacher decision making is the critical factor in interactive writing lessons. Accordingly, *Interactive Writing* will help all teachers learn to make effective instructional decisions that enable their students to grow as competent, creative writers and readers.

Together with our colleagues, we have devoted ourselves to a study of interactive writing and its instructional potential for many years. We invite you, our readers, to join our learning group. To assist in the process, each chapter features suggestions for professional development that will support you and your colleagues in learning more, not just about interactive writing but about the language and literacy development of children.

As primary teachers, we have always taught young children to make the critical connections between oral and written language required to become skillful readers and writers. National standards have confirmed the value of good first literacy teaching in the early years and raised public awareness of its importance. Helping young children make an early, meaningful, and joyful entry into literacy is of paramount importance. And, in our journey toward that goal, one tool we find indispensable is interactive writing.

Interactive Writing

Learning to Write in a Quality Literacy Program

In Section One we define interactive writing. While a powerful tool for helping beginners, it is only one component of a dynamic and interconnected language arts program. Interactive writing is most effective when there are connections between this group writing activity and the other parts of the curriculum. Two important questions are: What materials do I need? And, how do I get started? We provide information about organizing materials and using space. Efficiency is essential for effective use of this instructional approach. We also provide some practical suggestions for getting started, establishing routines, organizing materials, communicating with colleagues and with parents. We include two step-by-step ten-day plans.

CHAPTER ONE

What Is Interactive Writing?

Children enter school with a variety of experiences. Some come from homes where they are read to every day; others arrive with few book experiences. Some love to chatter about everything; others are virtually silent, preferring to observe instead. Each child needs specific support structures to develop the essential skills and knowledge for literacy. The great challenge for us as teachers is to provide the right support for each child, support that acknowledges diverse backgrounds and needs. We must understand how to help children with the learning process. What can we show and tell them about writing? What must they discover for themselves?

The Writing Process

The process of writing involves far more than putting letters and words on paper.

■ A writer needs a *purpose* or reason for writing, and purposes arise from all circumstances of life. We take notes for later reference, convey information, correspond with others, record our experiences, even try our hand at writing as art.

■ A writer thinks about the *audience*. Who will the readers be? What is their point of reference? What do they need to know?

■ Based on purpose and audience, a writer selects a *form* for the writing—say, a list, a sign, a story, a letter, or a set of directions.

■ A writer decides on a *message*—what to say and how to say it. We call this process *composing*.

■ A writer constructs text to express the message. The process of *constructing* involves forming letters, arranging them into words, working from left to right and top to bottom, and separating words by spaces on the page. To begin writing the message, a writer has to think about the first word and start writing the first letter of that word, then move along to the rest of the letters. The writer pays attention to the details of written language while keeping in mind the message, constantly referring to the larger message when writing the individual words.

■ A writer reflects and evaluates during the process. If the text is longer than a few sentences, the writer continually rereads as he or she goes along, thinking about each sentence as part of the larger text. *Editing* and *revising* are an important aspect of the craft.

■ A writer considers text *layout*. Punctuation, paragraphs, and other visual conventions help to make a text clear to the audience.

Above we have described, in general, what writers do. But this brief description does not capture all the complexities of the writing process. Helping children become writers means helping them become skilled and knowledgeable about all aspects of this process. No wonder primary teachers can find the teaching of young writers to be a daunting challenge.

Helping Children Participate in the Writing Process

Interactive writing is an instructional context in which a teacher shares a pen—literally and figuratively—with a group of children as they collaboratively compose and construct a written message. We want to help children learn how written language works so that they can become independent writers.

As we observe children's behavior we need to remember that all children develop differently, along a continuum of learning. In other words, they are individuals and we need to treat them accordingly. Who loves to answer questions out loud in class? Who is shy about speaking up? Who can recite the alphabet? Who knows all the Margaret Wise Brown stories by heart? Recognizing children's individual traits, behaviors, and skills helps us determine a starting point for their learning process in school. We want to support children in using what they know to get to what they do not yet know. In this way, we keep each of our children working "on the edge" of their learning.

Emergent Writers

Most students enter prekindergarten or kindergarten as *emergent readers and writers*. Emergent readers and writers are just beginning to develop the idea that what we say can be written down and what we write down can be read by others and ourselves. As they engage in shared reading—reading together from a single text—and as they try out writing for themselves, they begin to discover some relationships between the easy-to-hear sounds of the language and the symbols that represent those sounds. They may know how to write a few simple high-frequency words and how to write their names or parts of their names. They may know the names and/or sounds of a few letters. They are beginning to develop control of left-to-right directionality and word-by-word matching while rereading their written products. Often they form large letters that are irregularly proportioned, because they are just beginning to achieve control of the motor coordination needed for writing. They are beginning to achieve control of the use of space but need support in using space to define words and lines as they write a text.

Interactive Writing with Emergent Writers

In the lesson described below, Ida Patacca, a kindergarten teacher in an urban school, is working with a class of children, most of whom are emergent writers. Daily participation in interactive writing is especially critical for children in kindergarten, their first year of school.

This interactive writing lesson was based on Ida's reading of *Peanut Butter and Jelly* by Nadine Bernard Westcott as well as children's natural interest in the everyday activities of shopping, preparing food, and eating. Each day for several weeks, Ida brought children together to create shared experiences on which they could base their writing. In this case, the subject area was health and science. The specific topic was nutrition. Reading and writing were used as ways to build knowledge and as tools for inquiry.

As part of this inquiry project, the children decided to make peanut butter and jelly sandwiches, a choice that included foods from several food groups. During the two weeks of this project, the class produced several different written texts through interactive writing, including

■ a grocery shopping list
■ a set of directions for making peanut butter and jelly sandwiches
■ a survey question that asked children to choose from among three items which food they liked best.

The survey question was the final activity for the nutrition inquiry project.

Experience: Providing Background and Engaging Children's Interest

Ida knew that the children in her kindergarten class brought to the interactive writing sessions their individual home experiences. On several occasions she invited them to talk about what they liked to eat and other topics related to preparing food. In this classroom, ongoing experiences continually support the emergence of purposeful writing, and food was an important theme. Ida used a variety of children's literature to enhance the learning process. Children were able to participate in the authors' descriptions of foods. How did the authors talk about food? How did they help readers share how food tastes or looks? Building the experiences that underlie interactive writing did not depend on one isolated activity. Rather, it was related to ongoing learning.

Throughout the process, Ida and her students used language as a learning tool, evaluating foods as to their taste and health benefit. They talked about the four food groups, preparing foods to eat, labeling equipment, and planning. This talk not only helped them to establish shared meaning surrounding the topic of nutrition and food but it was specifically used to establish a purpose for the writing.

One of the experiences the children shared was hearing *Peanut Butter and Jelly* read aloud. The children enjoyed this story in verse enormously, joining in over several readings.

They also acted out the story, using hand movements and a great deal of expression.

Talking: Determining a Text's Purpose

Following a rereading of *Peanut Butter and Jelly*, Ida talked with the children to establish a purpose for writing. When the children were assembled, sitting on the classroom rug, she said, "Boys and girls, we've been learning about healthy foods and reading stories, poems, and songs about different kinds of foods, including peanut butter and jelly sandwiches. I thought we would enjoy making these sandwiches ourselves. If we would like to do that, I will need to go to the grocery store to get all the ingredients that we will need."

Composing: Helping Children Decide What to Write

Composing refers to the negotiation of the text, the decision about what will actually be written. Together Ida and the children decided on the items that she would need to buy at the store. In this case, they created a list, as shown in Figure 1-1.

The children decided on the items one at a time and then wrote them down; in this case, composition was limited to individual words. (For most interactive writing, composition consists of a sentence related to an overall plan involving the recounting of an experience or the telling of a story.) Nevertheless, as you can see from the dialogue below, the children's writing was facilitated by negotiation that involved selection and limitation. Children did most of the writing themselves, with Ida's support.

IDA: Now, we said we needed to make a grocery list so that when Miss Patacca goes to the grocery store she will buy all the things we need to make peanut butter and jelly sandwiches. If you have an idea about one thing that Miss Patacca needs to buy, put your hand in the air. Marcus, what should I buy?
MARCUS: You need to buy bread and peanut butter and jelly.

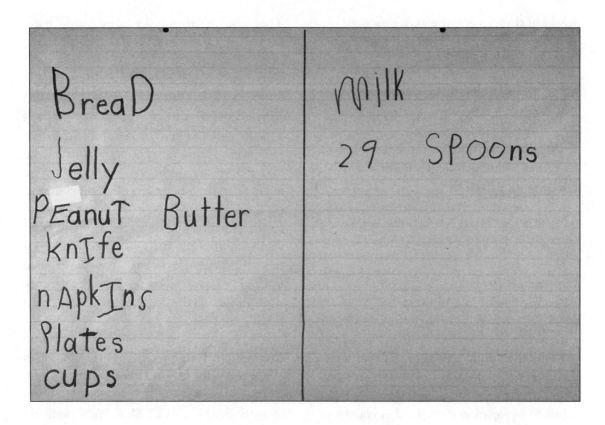

FIGURE 1–1   Grocery List *without* Checks

IDA: Okay, just tell me one of those things though.

MARCUS: You need to buy bread.

Constructing: Engaging Children in Writing the Message

Constructing refers to the "encoding" of the message, that is, actually writing down the message, letter by letter and word by word, organized in the space on the page. Ida asked the children to say the word *bread* slowly, and to think about the sounds that they could hear.

IDA: We're going to write the word *bread*. Say *bread* and listen to how it starts. (Ida enunciates the word slowly.)

CHILDREN: *Bread.* (Children say it slowly with her.)

SEVERAL CHILDREN: *B!*

IDA: B. You're right! Bread starts with a *b*. Buanthearn, come up here and make a *b* for us. (Buanthearn walks to the chart placed on an easel in front of the group.) That *b* is in your name. *Bread* and *Buanthearn* both start with a *b*. (Buanthearn writes a *B* on the chart.) Oh, that's a beautiful *B!* (Buanthearn sits down.)

Ida then helped these beginning writers to relate the construction of the word *bread* to the name of a child in the group. In doing so, Ida helped the children learn how to use a classroom reference—a name chart that she had made in front of them on the first day of the school year. This name chart served as a constant resource for children as they made connections between sounds and letters in the construction of words (see Figure 1-2). You can see that several children had moved in to the class and their names were added. Soon the teacher remade the chart to organize all the names again.

The next portion of the transcript illustrates how children use what they know about the letters and sounds in their names to help them write a new word.

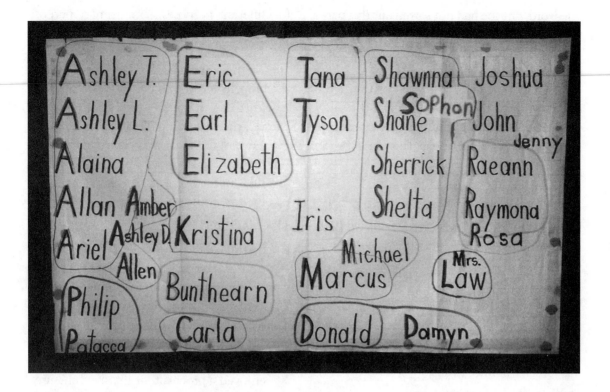

FIGURE 1-2   A Name Chart

IDA: Yes, we'll need to write *jelly* so we are sure to have it for our sandwiches. Say *jelly*.
CHILDREN: *Jelly*.
IDA: Jenny, that starts like your name doesn't it? Bunthearn, point to Jenny's name on the chart. (He does so.) Say *Jenny*.
CHILDREN: *Jenny*.
IDA: Now say *jelly*.
CHILDREN: *Jelly!*
IDA: They are alike at the beginning, aren't they? They both start with…
CHILDREN: *J*.
JOSHUA: My name has a *j*.
IDA: That's right. We have *Joshua, Jenny,* and *jelly*. They all start with *j*. Jenny, come up and make the *j* for us.

Rereading: Teaching Children to Check Their Writing

As a way of checking what they had written and thinking about what they wanted to write next, Ida engaged the children in reading what they had written on the chart. Ida

pointed to the top of the list and helped them read all of the items. That helped the children remember what they had already produced so that they could think of additional ingredients they might need to list.

Some problem solving was evident when the children reread the list. When they got to the entry for peanut butter, Ashley held the pointer on the word *peanut* and all the children read the word. Instead of moving to the next item, Ashley waited, expecting the children to say the word *butter* before she proceeded to the next entry. Ida had previously emphasized crisp pointing with precise word-by-word matching. The class had been taught to say an entire word while the pointer was placed under it and not to say the next word until the child with the pointer moved the pointer to it. Ashley probably thought that *peanut butter* was one word, and she had matched it to the word *peanut*. She was gaining control of space because she knew that several syllables could be matched with just one word, but she had not sorted out this particularly complex construction.

When Ida began to move forward to assist in the pointing process, Ashley quickly recognized that another word was needed. She moved the pointer to *butter* and the subsequent choral reading of her classmates reinforced her learning to read this word.

Summarizing: Focusing on What Was Learned

At the end of the list-producing session, Ida helped the children to focus on what they had learned.

> **IDA:** We made a list that will help us remember what I need to get at the grocery store. You helped write these words today by saying each word slowly and writing letters for some of the sounds you could hear. What helped us think about some of those letters?
> **CHILDREN:** Our names!
> **CHILDREN:** The chart!
> **IDA:** Yes, thinking about the names on the name chart. So when you're working on your writing, you can say words slowly and you can use the chart to help you think about how to start your words.

Revisiting: Noticing the Details of the Text

After rereading the shopping list, Ida revisited the text with the children. She asked them to find something that they knew about the words in the text. As noted above, during the construction of writing, several children had made connections between sounds in words and the letters in their names. She invited them again to find the words that began like Bunthearn's name and two children located *bread* and *butter*. They also found *peanuts* and *plates* and connected them to *Patacca* and *Philip*. Ida made the comment that, "Yes, *Philip* does start with a *p* but in Philip's name the *p* sounds different."

Extending: Helping Children Understand the Uses of Writing

Ida and the children in her class now had a resource in this grocery list that could be used

for different purposes. The primary purpose was to guide the shopping. Later in the day, Ida took the list to the grocery store and purchased the items listed. The next morning, she brought in the grocery bag and unpacked it with the children. As each item was unpacked, the children looked at the list, found the name of the item, and placed a check beside it (see Figure 1-3). The list was reread several times.

By using the grocery list to check off the items that Ida had purchased, the children

- participated in a powerful demonstration that writing has a real purpose, learning that we use written language to help us remember and plan
- searched for specific words, thinking about the letter-sound relationships, using more than just the first letter
- enjoyed a process that involved the use of writing
- felt satisfaction in using, in a functional way, a piece of writing that they created
- were reinforced in creating a text that was meaningful.

The Value of Interactive Writing

Through interactive writing, children become apprentices, working alongside a more expert writer, their teacher. Everyone in the group has the opportunity to see a clear demonstration of the process of producing a piece of writing—from thinking about and composing the message to using the written product. Even children who can read and write very little independently have a chance to see themselves as writers and readers. In a supported situation, they can grapple with some of the problems that writers habitually solve—Is *peanut butter* one word or two? How do I begin to write the word *jelly*? Do I continue on the same line or write each word on a separate line when making a list?

The interactive writing lesson described above allowed children to reach far beyond their present skills so that they could participate in the construction of a text, using words

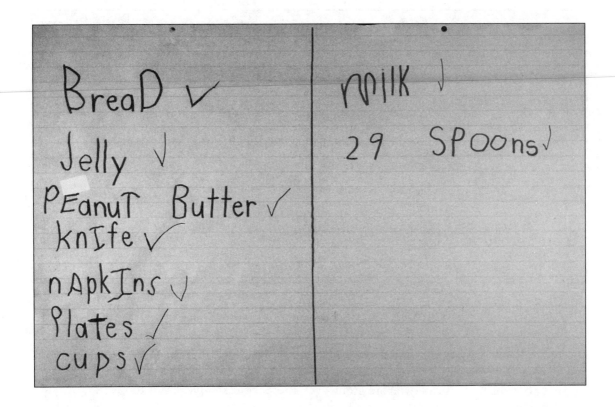

FIGURE 1-3 Grocery List *with* Checks

and conventions that they could not have controlled while working alone. The text that they created and then read was supported by the meaningful conversation in which they had engaged. The children had a sense of control and ownership over the text. As they internalized the characteristics of this text, they gained knowledge that could be used to create other texts. Interactive writing provided a setting within which children could think about the audiences for their writing (in this case, their teacher as she shopped and themselves as they checked to make sure they had all of the necessary ingredients). Finally, and of equal importance, the children had fun. And their list was a significant accomplishment of which they could be proud.

Features of Interactive Writing

Several important features characterize this dynamic literacy event. Interactive writing is not simply a mechanical process to be followed in order to produce a text. While the product is important, the process is what has most value. The key features of interactive writing are listed in Figure 1-4.

Grouping Children for Interactive Writing

You can use interactive writing with a whole class of children or with a small group to whom you want to demonstrate particular concepts. Both situations have advantages. Working with the whole class helps to build a community of learners who can together explore ideas and concepts. You can use interactive writing to record thoughts about a topic of study, or to retell or extend a favorite story that has been read aloud. When you work with the entire group, you can engage children at different levels so that support and challenge is there for all of them.

You can work more closely with the strengths and needs of a small group, focusing on a concept that is important for them at this point in their learning. For example, children who are just gaining control of space

---

Key Features of Interactive Writing

Group children based on learning goals.

Write for authentic purposes.

Share the task of writing.

Use conversation to support the process.

Create a common text.

Use the conventions of written language.

Make letter-sound connections.

Connect reading and writing.

Teach explicitly.

FIGURE 1-4 Key Features of Interactive Writing

in their writing might profit from participating in a small group with instruction focused on that concept. In this case, you are grouping according to the instructional needs of the children. During a whole class session, you might notice that while most of the children are having no difficulty representing consonant sounds with letters, a few are still learning this skill. That same day or the following day, perhaps during writing workshop while most of the children are working independently, you can pull together a smaller group of children and focus more intensively on their common needs.

During the writing of the shopping list discussed above, Ida made the decision to work with the entire class, for the following reasons:

❚ The experience, which involved learning about nutrition and using writing as a tool, was one that she wanted all children to participate in.
❚ It was early in the children's school career and most were just beginning to learn about the craft of writing, so most were at a similar learning level.

Writing for Authentic Purposes

Interactive writing may be used throughout the school day for a range of writing purposes.

Use it at any time that you feel that sharing the writing task will help your students learn more. For example, use it to

❚ write a morning message
❚ summarize or extend a story that has been read aloud
❚ write a survey question that children in the class will answer
❚ add to or summarize a story read in a guided reading session
❚ label art or a classroom item
❚ write a letter to an individual or to another class
❚ record information gained through inquiry (for example, in science or mathematics study).

Authenticity refers to writing for a real purpose. A piece of writing does not have to be a "letter" or note to be authentic in nature. Simply think of all of the ways we employ writing in our society—from note taking to writing stories or diary entries for ourselves. Interactive writing is authentic when it accompanies children's active learning and when it is related to something that they are interested in doing.

The purpose for writing the shopping list emerged from the children's experiences in learning about nutrition and food. They needed a list to support the gathering of ingredients needed to make their peanut butter and jelly sandwiches. Interactive writing provided a way to facilitate their problem solving. The children's purpose was not "practicing writing." Rather, it was making the list and being sure that it included everything they would need.

Sharing the Writing Task

In interactive writing, you will selectively involve individual children in contributing to the composition and construction of the message. The composing of the message is accomplished through ongoing dialogue between you and the children about the words to use to convey their message. Constructing the message involves having the children participate both through continuing the dialogue about what is being written and having the children write selected letters and words.

Decisions to invite individuals to "share the pen" or actually do the writing on the page are based on the instructional needs of the children. The idea is to help children attend to powerful examples that can enable them to learn something about the writing process that they can then incorporate into their own writing. As children gain control of the process, the examples and areas of focus shift. A beginning group might focus on using space, writing left to right, and representing several consonant sounds. A more advanced group might concentrate on the sounds of words and look at different letter patterns that represent the same sound (for example, r*ai*n, pl*ay*).

During the writing of a text, you might invite two or three children to each write in a letter or part of a word to illustrate one of these critical concepts. We caution that the children should not work on completing every single word. That would take too long and make the process tedious. Your teaching decisions must be strategically planned. The idea is not to let every child have a turn every day, to have children write in everything they know, or to work out every single word. Select your teaching points carefully to illustrate principles that can take the children further in their learning. If you focus on too many points, the children's attention will be too widely divided. It's better to concentrate on a few memorable examples so that at the end of the session the children will have in their heads a few clear understandings that they can apply to their own writing.

There will be occasional opportunities to support an individual child's contribution to a text in a way that will help that child gain confidence and use knowledge in a new way. One important individual interaction, within the group setting, may be achievable. But in general, the group writing environment is not designed to teach individuals but to present examples that most children, at any given time, can understand.

In the peanut butter and jelly example, Ida and the children shared the composing of the text, deciding what words to record. They shared the construction of the list format, writing only one item on each line. They shared the construction of each word, with children contributing individual letters based on both what Ida knew about their knowledge base and the teaching points she had decided to make.

Supporting the Process Through Conversation

Interactive writing is based on oral language. The process is infused with meaningful talk. The conversation is ongoing and it involves the skills of both speaking and listening, as the teacher and class:

- ❙ Engage in conversation about the topic.
- ❙ Discuss the purpose of their writing.
- ❙ Talk about composing the message and reach agreement on the particular language to use.
- ❙ Talk about the conventions of written language—how to write what they want to say.
- ❙ Comment on interesting features of words.

- Make connections between the text and other texts.
- Make personal connections between the text and their own experiences.

As children talk with the teacher about the texts they are writing, they expand their oral language capabilities. Moving from talk to written texts creates linguistic demands that help children to consider language in new ways. They learn, for example, that they have to compose a message and then remember it during the writing process. They also learn that the same ideas can be said in different ways and that speakers and writers have choices. Throughout the interactive writing event, children are supported in making connections between their own use of oral language, the oral language of the teacher, the language that they encounter in books and other texts, and the language that they compose for the purpose of writing. The experience is particularly language-enriching for children who are English learners.

The entire interactive writing process is embedded in an ongoing conversation between the teacher and children. The talk between Ida and her class covered a range of topics: deciding what to shop for and use in cooking, the format of a list, the features of words and letters, the connections between this list and other texts. The focus was on language, and on using language to learn.

Creating a Common Text

In interactive writing you and your young students will be sharing the composition and construction of a common text. The position of the text on an easel or chart in full view of the class or small group is significant in this shared experience. You invite children to think of what they want to say and guide their thinking so that they understand that the message must be clear to an audience. Everyone shares in deciding what will be said. A complete message is visible to everyone in the group. Because the purpose for the message has already been decided upon, at-

tending to specific details while writing it is much easier. The children can watch and participate in the features of the printed text as it is produced on the chart in front of them. By the time a text is finished, there is a built-in evaluation: Will our readers understand what we want to say?

Ida and the children decided what the text would be, and the chart was positioned within view of every child so that it could be examined and considered. The text was reread several times and children could continually evaluate whether all the necessary ingredients were present. They had to think about how useful the list would be for their teacher while shopping. And the next day, they used the text together to check to see whether they had everything they needed.

Using the Conventions of Written Language

Ida's final shopping list was produced using conventional spelling and a conventional list format. In creating the list, attention was not paid to proper use of capital and lowercase letters, which reflects the children's continuing development of knowledge of the alphabet. Later in the year there would be discussion about the conventional use of lowercase and capital letters. At this stage the children were simply learning that the letter *E*, for example, is written a certain way and is written that way every time.

Texts created through interactive writing are meant to be read independently later by the children, so these texts must be spelled and punctuated in a standard way. Children are supported as they engage in the thinking processes that they would use if they were working independently. Since you are working closely with them in the interactive writing setting, they collaborate on the task. You are able to support the process by filling in words or word parts that children do not yet know as well as words that children already control. There is no need to bring children up to the chart to write whole words that they already know how to write quickly and easily. These activities should be reserved for supporting what is almost known or promoting new learning.

Making Letter-Sound Connections

Interactive writing supports children in becoming sensitive to sounds (the phonemes) and their position in words so that they can hear component sounds (phonemic awareness) and connect those sounds to the letters and letter clusters (graphemes or symbols) of written language. Especially during the beginning phases of writing, ask children to say words slowly and think about what they hear. Focus on easy-to-hear initial and final sounds with one consonant before addressing consonant clusters and other dominant sounds within words. Use references and examples such as name charts to help children think about how letters look.

For each item they wrote on their shopping list, Ida asked students to say the word slowly and think about the sounds. They were learning that words are made up of sounds in sequence, and becoming more sensitive to individual phonemes (sounds) in oral language. Additionally, they were making connections to the letters that represent sounds. They were learning to search for the visual features that distinguish every letter from every other letter. Making connections to the letters in their names supported the process of visual searching and connecting to the pronunciation of the word.

Connecting the Reading and Writing Processes

Interactive writing engages children in the creation of texts similar to those that they will be reading. They learn that what you say can be written down and that what you write can be read. They learn that forming letters carefully and accurately when they write a message will make it easier later when they become readers of the message. They learn that conventions such as starting on the left and using space helps make a text more readable. They learn that a word is written the same way every time. Later in the year, they learn the value of clustering similar ideas and using precise description so that readers have a better understanding of the message.

In creating the list of grocery items, the children were continually moving from writing to reading and back again. They learned that the items they suggested could be written down and that those items could be recalled through reading and used in a practical way. Rereading helped them think of items that they had forgotten to put on the list. During the writing of a message, you and your students need to reread it many times so that children can learn to

❚ monitor the message they are creating to be sure it says what they want it to say
❚ anticipate what the next words will be
❚ keep the meaning of the whole text in mind.

After children have worked to construct a word by saying it slowly, they often need help in recalling the message as a whole so that they can continue to create it. Rereading from the beginning of the message or the beginning of a sentence supports this process. Children who are just beginning to write will need to reread their text several times during the production of the message. As they gain more control, less rereading will be necessary.

Teaching Explicitly

Through conversation before, during, and after the writing event, point out the specific issues you want the children to learn during that session. This ensures that children will notice and talk about certain aspects of the writing process. Engage children in a summary conversation and restate the key points covered in a lesson so that the children carry over what they have done as a group to what you are expecting each of them to do on their own. You can reinforce this explicit teaching as you confer with the children in journal writing or writing workshop.

Ida made sure that the children knew what she expected of them during the interactive writing process. She talked about where they would start and how they would format the list. Throughout the process, she drew their attention to specific examples (such as the connection between *jelly*, *Jenny*, and *Joshua*).

Keep in mind that the key features of interactive writing are designed to help children do what competent readers and writers do.

Suggestions for Professional Development

1. Begin by analyzing the kinds of writing that you currently support in your classroom literacy curriculum. Look at your schedule and ask yourself:

    ▪ In what kinds of writing do children participate during the course of a week? Do they engage in independent writing, writing workshop, language experience, and other kinds of writing?

    ▪ Where can interactive writing fit into my weekly schedule?

    ▪ Are there any kinds of writing that I now use that would be more powerful as interactive writing?

2. Now look at the content areas you will be studying this year, the instructional themes you plan to investigate, and the children's literature that you will be using. Ask yourself:

    ▪ How can I use interactive writing to extend learning in the content areas?

    ▪ How can interactive writing be part of a theme of study, or used to produce texts like the children's literature that I am reading to the class?

    ▪ What real purposes for writing might emerge from content-area themes or children's literature?

    ▪ How can I use interactive writing to accomplish these purposes?

3. Next, select one piece of children's literature and try out the process.

    ▪ Read the selection several times to be sure that it is a favorite with the children.

    ▪ Talk with the children to develop a purpose for writing. It might be a retelling of the story, their own version of the story, or a list of items to be placed on a story map. Start with a simple task that you can complete in a few days so that you and the children will experience the process from beginning to end.

    ▪ With the children, decide on the kind of artwork that they will do to enhance the piece of writing.

    ▪ Teach the children how to sit quietly, follow directions, and come quickly to the chart or board to contribute a word or letter.

    ▪ Produce a piece of interactive writing, including some supportive art.

4. Reflect on the process. Chances are, not every routine was in place. You may not have had materials perfectly organized. The experience itself may have seemed a little awkward. But you will have made a start. Ask yourself:

    ▪ What letters, words, or word parts did the children write?

    ▪ What sounds did they hear?

    ▪ Where were the sounds located?

    ▪ What whole words did they write from beginning to end without help?

    ▪ Were they able to make a link from something they knew to figure out something new?

    ▪ What did children learn how to do that they will be able to use in their own writing? In future interactive writing sessions?

- What potential does this text have for future use? To read? To locate words that will make good examples?
- How did the process go? Was it too slow? Too fast? Were there too many teaching points? Too few?

5. Having tried out interactive writing, you can work with it again and again as you deepen your understanding of and reflection on the process. The chapters in this book will assist you in doing so.

CHAPTER TWO

Language and Literacy Learning

The Role of Interactive Writing

When we think of a language arts curriculum, we begin with what competent readers and writers actually do. All of the decisions we make about teaching need to focus on helping children learn more about their world, including the literary world, using the processes of reading and writing. Meeting that challenge requires that we help students acquire a wide range of linked language processes. These processes are all directed toward helping the children in the class build on their existing competencies so that they can become more proficient. Interactive writing is only one—albeit powerful—approach among a variety of approaches used to support literacy learning.

In this chapter, we place interactive writing within the perspective of a broader view of language and literacy learning. We talk about its specific purposes and advantages. Our focus here is on writing—but we must always keep in mind that we are writing in connection with talking; we are writing about important content; and we are writing to communicate with ourselves and others. Reading and writing thus are linked through their functional use. Children are learning to write like readers and to read like writers (Smith 1983, Jansen 1987). Through a variety of reading and writing contexts, they are learning how to process text more effectively.

Reading and writing are different—but complementary—processes. In both reading and writing instruction, we teach children how to process continuous text. Each of the instructional approaches places the children in a different context and requires them to process the text with differing levels of teacher support.

Helping Children Build a Reading Process

Children learn to read within a variety of instructional contexts, including

■ interactive read-aloud
■ shared reading
■ literature discussion
■ guided reading
■ buddy reading
■ independent reading.

Although we may examine each of these approaches separately, we must remember that in practice they are interrelated. (See Figure 2-1.)

Interactive Read-Aloud

Reading aloud to children is basic to the teaching of reading and writing in prekinder-

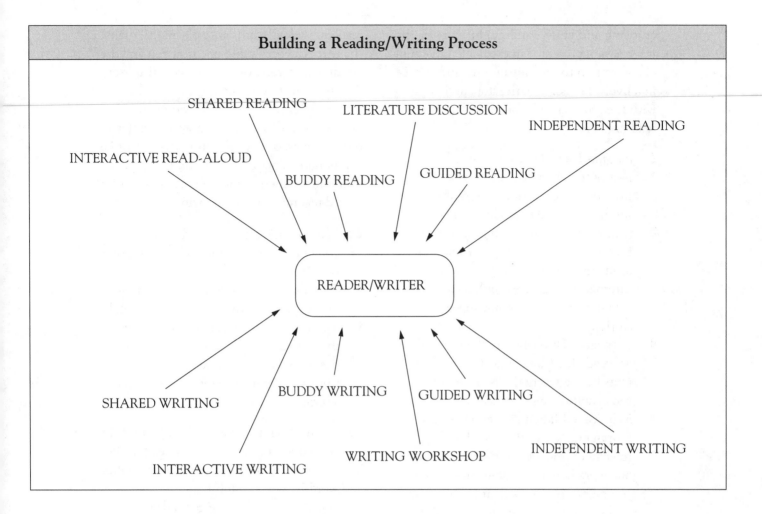

FIGURE 2-1 Building a Reading/Writing Process

garten, kindergarten, and primary classrooms. We call this instructional context *interactive read-aloud* to emphasize the important role that conversation between the children and their teacher plays in this process. Although in read-alouds the teacher is the principal reader of the text, it is important that children make predictions, discuss the story, and that they are encouraged to ask questions and offer opinions. Once they become familiar with texts, children will also join in on the rereading of favorite stories and phrases; for example, they love to shout, "I'll huff and I'll puff and I'll blow your house in!" during readings of "The Three Little Pigs." We recommend rereading books that are rich in language as a basis for helping children internalize both vocabulary words and the structure of sentences.

When you read to children, you build their background knowledge and help them develop important aspects of language usage. This daily nourishment of vocabulary, language sounds, and structure expands the language repository of all children, including those who are learning English as a second language. One way to accomplish this goal is to expose children to a wide selection of children's literature that includes a variety of genres (see Freeman and Person 1998 and Huck, Hepler, and Hickman 1993).

In an interactive read-aloud, you hold the book so that the children can see the illustrations. In most books, the print is too small for them to read or notice details, so it's impractical to call their attention to individual words, letters, spacing, directionality, or other conventions of print. Instead, focus on enjoying and understanding the story or the information presented in the book. Give special attention to the illustrations, and engage in a lively discussion of the story and pictures with the children. The process of interactive read-aloud is

- *integrated.* The books read aloud are a part of the ongoing classroom study of literature or content topics, offering information and extending enjoyment.
- *sustaining.* Children gain power over favorite texts that are read again and again, giving them the opportunity to internalize language structures and vocabulary and also to enjoy repeated stories.
- *connected.* Through talk, the books that are read aloud are connected to other texts by the teacher's discussion of topic, author, and language use.
- *inclusive.* Children are encouraged to join in on parts of the text that they remember from previous readings, to make predictions, to pose questions, to comment, to express their feelings, and to respond to illustrations.

Reading aloud to children not only helps them to appreciate how reading can be enjoyable, it also helps young children begin to think like readers (Cochran-Smith 1984; Holdaway 1979). It can also provide the foundation of experience for interactive and independent writing, supplying children with writing topics as well as introducing them to the ways in which written language works. They learn how good writers express their ideas and can see new possibilities for their own writing.

Shared Reading

In shared reading, you and your students read together from a single, enlarged text (see Holdaway 1979; Hundley and Powell 1999; Button, Johnson, and Furgerson 1996). With your support and that of the group, an individual child can experience the feeling of being a reader even before he or she can read individual words in isolation. Usually, the text is a very simple one that you and the children can read over and over in unison. The text must be appealing so that children will enjoy repeated readings. You can use simple stories with repeating language patterns, poems, songs, or any other text that might be appropriate. The texts that children produce in interactive writing are especially good for shared reading, for the following reasons:

- Children have the ownership that comes from composing and constructing the texts.
- The texts usually relate to some important experience that children have had.
- There are real purposes for rereading these texts (for example, to recall what has been written so that you can continue writing it or to remind yourself of a series of steps).

Shared reading is especially important in helping children develop early reading behaviors such as left-to-right directionality and word-by-word matching.

What follows are some general guidelines to make shared reading successful.

- Be sure that the text is appropriate for this particular group of children—that it is easy enough that the children can follow and join in.
- Arrange the class so that all the children can see the text clearly.
- Be sure that the type is large enough, clearly written, and that there is enough space between words and lines, so that the entire class can see the text clearly.
- Provide a variety of texts that build understanding over time, as children read and enjoy them again and again.
- Once children have become familiar with a text and enjoy reading it in unison, be sure that there are frequent opportunities for talk about the text, including discussion of particular words, text features, how to put expression into the reading, consideration of punctua-

tion, and using what they have learned how to do as readers to process other texts.

Literature Discussion

When children gather as a whole class, in small groups, or with a partner to talk about a text or several texts that they have read or heard read aloud, they learn to converse about books and about all aspects of text. The interactive environment supports them in learning to think like readers. The process expands their language and their knowledge of content. When several people discuss a text, they gain greater understanding of the text. Instead of thinking that there is *one* meaning of a book, for example, they can begin to consider *several* interpretations. Children can explore how the author and illustrator communicated meaning to them as readers. There are important implications here for children as writers, because they are learning how authors and illustrators communicate to readers and how texts work.

Guided Reading

Guided reading is a small-group instructional context in which the teacher supports children's use of strategies in reading novel texts (see Fountas and Pinnell 1996 and Pinnell and Fountas 1998). Group your children according to current ability levels and goals for improvement. To help you get started, consult the following guidelines.

■ Each day, select a book for the children, one that provides just enough challenge to help them use reading strategies effectively.

■ Introduce the book to the children and ask each child to read the whole text or a unified part of it at his or her own pace, either softly (in early stages) or silently.

■ During reading, intervene briefly to support problem solving, but keep in mind that the emphasis is on developing independence and on having children advance to more complex texts and read for increasingly longer periods.

■ After the child reads the text, revisit it with him to focus on examples that help develop a reading process.

Ideally, the texts children encounter in guided reading are "just right"—not too easy and not too hard. Guided reading books, typically, are not connected with ongoing content themes or other classroom activities. They are good books selected to provide the right levels of support and challenge to help children learn an effective reading process through a variety of sources. The books read in guided reading can be extended through group or individual writing.

Using interactive writing in conjunction with guided reading is particularly helpful for beginning readers who are developing a beginning-reading vocabulary, simple letter-sound relationships, and early concepts about print such as left-to-right directionality and spacing between words. Since writing is a "building-up" process, the beginning reader is learning how print works. Writing is very helpful in learning how to read early books.

Buddy Reading

When children work together as "buddies," they assist each other as readers. Buddies are usually assigned to partner with one another for a period of several weeks and have a daily time slot in the language arts block when they are expected to get together to read. They may read the same book—for example, a book they have read in guided reading—or different books. They can read the whole book to each other or take turns reading pages. They can each have different books, or copies of the same book. If you have set up a classroom "browsing box"—a box or basket that contains previously read as well as easily accessible books—children may choose their books from there.

After learning the routines for buddy reading, children engage in it independently. They can be involved in buddy reading while you are working with small groups of children in guided reading or interactive writing.

Independent Reading

Schedule a time every day when each child reads on his or her own. You can provide browsing boxes to help children choose books that they can read successfully. During this time slot, children can use the classroom library for specific purposes—to read books that they have heard read aloud, to find information in science books, or to explore a facet of literature. Allowing children to spend time, on a daily basis, with books that they can read easily will help them become more fluent readers. This rereading of texts is especially important for younger children, since easy reading develops fluency. Young children can also use pieces of text produced through interactive writing for their independent practice.

All of the above reading contexts are valuable in supporting children in the development of a reading process. In participating in these contexts, children encounter texts that they can read fluently, texts that offer opportunities for problem solving, and rich texts that they can hear, learn, and talk about. All of these instructional approaches involve children in talking about aspects of text, including

▌ what writers are trying to say

▌ interesting ways writers use language to please readers

▌ how characters and setting are important in understanding a story

▌ interesting words that are new to them and that they might be able to use in their own writing

▌ how words are connected to other words and are similar in sound or in the way they look.

Phonics and Word Study

In all of the reading contexts described above, you will have many opportunities to bring the structure of words to the attention of children. Phonics and spelling are thus embedded within the larger experience of working with texts.

We recommend that the language arts curriculum also include specific and focused experiences, in which you help children learn specific principles related to the way letters and words work. Sometimes, to help students focus their attention, it is appropriate to study words in isolation. Word study involves a specific minilesson directed at helping children understand a concept or principle; for example, using one word to make another word by substituting the first letter with another (*man, can*). The minilesson is followed by independent application, which might include sorting or building words, making charts with words that sound alike or look alike in some way, and developing a word wall. These word study activities may emerge from any reading or writing activity and, in turn, will contribute to children's growing skill in both writing and reading. (See Pinnell and Fountas 1998 for a comprehensive treatment of word study.)

Connecting Reading and Writing

We know that reading and writing are connected in many ways. The reading contexts discussed above help to form a foundation and provide support for writing. Interactive writing is a powerful tool in helping young children to make the connections between writing and reading. Any story encountered by children may later be linked to a piece of interactive writing that they are working to produce. Books read aloud become a particularly strong foundation for interactive writing.

Approaches to Writing: Helping Children Build a Writing Process

We have found four different approaches to be effective in helping young children begin to build a writing process. They are

▌ language experience

▌ shared writing

▌ interactive writing

▌ independent writing.

Each approach has a different purpose and function, but they are all closely interrelated. We might find all four approaches being employed to produce a single text. You must decide when to use each approach and when to combine them in order to highlight powerful examples for children.

Language Experience

Traditionally, teachers have supported children by acting as scribes to record their ideas in a group setting. By writing for children, you free them to express meanings in oral language without having to concern themselves with the mechanics involved in written language. In language experience, you are demonstrating the writing process, sometimes making comments about the construction of the text. It is important in this approach that all the children can see and hear you as you write legibly on a piece of chart paper or on the board. Typically, you will emphasize using children's exact words to reflect their current oral language abilities as you create texts that are the children's own and that may be read later. In cases in which the resulting texts are too complex for the children to read themselves, the writing process experience is sufficient as a demonstration.

Shared Writing

In shared writing, the teacher again acts as scribe for a group of children, but in this case more emphasis is placed on the composing process and on constructing a text that the children *can* read later. Typically, shared writing is part of an ongoing study of a content area or children's literature. You and the children work together to plan the text. You may use specific repeating structures based on books you have read aloud to the children, or retell a familiar story with events in sequence. Moira McKenzie (1985), who developed this process, said that shared writing is

a collaborative process between teacher and children, and children and children. And although the context and purpose may be similar to other aspects of writing, the teacher assumes more than an equal role. She takes on a teaching role in which she enables children to develop and organize ideas. The emphasis is on the message or story they are creating. She receives their ideas, and through her comments and questions she sustains their interest and production of ideas. She encourages them to think about appropriate language as she helps them to elaborate, or to focus their text. Throughout the process her guidance and the children's discussion contribute to a growing awareness and understanding of what writing is about and what readers can make of their writing. Children begin to "get in on" the craft of writing. (8)

Interactive Writing

Interactive writing grew from teachers' experimentation with shared writing. In interactive writing, as in shared writing, the texts are planned. Shared and interactive writing, both of which are group writing contexts, share the same general purposes and have the same emphasis on composition. The differences arise in the process of constructing the text, because in interactive writing, the teacher and children "share the pen" at strategic points in the construction of the text. Your decisions on when to encourage children to directly participate in the writing process are related to your goals in drawing children's attention to the specific conventions of written language that need to be learned or reinforced. In other words, sharing the pen is not simply a ritual. Each time a child is asked to come up to the easel to contribute a letter, letter cluster, word, or print feature such as punctuation, the action has high instructional value.

Independent Writing

During independent writing, children have the opportunity to work alone and use their current knowledge of the writing process to compose and construct their own texts. Independent writing is often undertaken in the structure of a writers' workshop, but it can also be employed for many purposes, encompassing a variety of genres, throughout the day. Children usually choose their own topics and work with minimal support. You provide explicit teaching in the form of a minilesson to the group, confer with selected children, and reinforce teaching points made during interactive writing or in the minilesson. At the end of the session, writers share their pieces for additional feedback or as a celebration of finished work.

The Four Approaches: An Examination

We hope that a more thorough analysis of the approaches to writing discussed above will be useful in guiding your use of them. Figure 2-2 (on pages 24 and 25) compares the approaches along several important dimensions: purposes, context, roles, text readability, art, spelling and other conventions, and uses of the finished product.

Purposes

The purposes of the three group writing situations (language experience, shared writing, and interactive writing) are similar in that they serve to initiate children into the writing process. All three provide demonstrations of composing and constructing text. Both shared writing and interactive writing involve a detailed planning process that helps to support children's awareness of the features of text and results in a text that is easier for members of the group to read. Interactive writing takes the process further by having children "share the pen" and focus on the details of text construction; for example, writing words, using space, and using punctuation.

In the independent writing setting, children can apply what they have learned in the other three contexts. In the process, they learn more about writing and gain greater control. Through the experience of producing their own texts, they can express their own thoughts, written for their own purposes, for an audience of their own choosing.

Context

Language experience, shared writing, and interactive writing occur in small- or large-group situations, although occasionally a teacher may write for or with an individual child. Shared and interactive writing emphasize group composition to create a shared text. Independent writing involves the child working alone or alongside others in a writing center or at a desk or table. The teacher supports the writers by circulating among the students and having conferences with individual children. The teacher also gives a minilesson before starting an independent writing session to teach an important aspect of writing and help get them started.

Roles

In language experience and independent writing, the children plan and compose the text. In shared writing and interactive writing, the teacher and children are equally involved in planning and composing the text. In language experience and shared writing, the teacher scribes, while in independent writing, the child constructs the text mostly by himself. In interactive writing, the teacher and children work together to construct the text.

Text Readability

Both shared and interactive writing feature the production of a readable text for the children in the class. Notice the careful planning for readability done by Ms. Ramirez, who engaged her kindergarten class in constructing a mural for retelling a favorite folktale, "The Three Billy Goats Gruff" (Figure 2-3 on page 26; see also Appendix 5). The characters are clearly labeled and the story is presented in sequence with repetitive language. The characters make comments that the children have internalized. It is evident that the children have even brought some of their own language to bear as they express the meaning in the story.

Many teachers have worked successfully using interactive writing in Spanish for children whose first language is Spanish and who are learning to read and write in that language. Compared with English, Spanish is more regular in the correspondence between letters and sounds. In addition, the syllable is a very important unit for children to recognize and use in their word solving. Teachers assist children in using all of the sources of information that are helpful to readers and writers—the meaning of a story, sequence of events, letter-sound relationships, syllable awareness, and repetitive language. Figure 2-4 (on page 26 and an enlarged version on page 275) provides another example of children's retelling the story of "The Three Billy Goats Gruff."

The translated text is as follows:

The Three Billy Goats Gruff

(Goat on the left)
Oh no!
Don't eat me.
Wait until my brother comes.
He is bigger than me.

(Middle goat)
Oh no!
Don't eat me.
Wait until my brother comes.
He is bigger than me.

(Troll)
Who's jumping over my bridge?
I am going to eat you.

(Goat on the right)
I am the biggest goat of all.
I have two horns and four hooves
and I am going to knock you over.

This example was completed by Ms. Ramirez's class over a period of about a week. The same goals described for interactive writing in English—learning about how written language works and learning about the writing process—apply in Spanish as well.

Texts produced through interactive writing are readable for several reasons:

- The sessions are planned and shaped by the teacher with the readability of the text in mind.
- The teacher uses a language pattern that the children are already familiar with from previous readings; for example, the repeating sentence structure of a favorite book.
- The children are deeply involved in composing the text and reread it often during the construction.

The texts produced in both shared writing and interactive writing are usually more difficult than those of the books children are expected to read independently. These two approaches provide a way to stretch their reading abilities because of the level of support they received during the writing process.

Ironically, language experience and independent writing both result in texts that most of the children in class cannot read independently. These texts have a complexity similar to that of oral language because the children are composing written text directly from their own talk. In the early reading stages, oral language is much more complex than the language that most beginners can read.

Art

All four approaches to writing provide for the enhancement of text through children's art. In language experience, shared writing, and interactive writing, children contribute drawings or other kinds of art that make the product more readable and attractive and add new meaning. Alternatively, the writing may come after children have created a piece of visual art. In shared and interactive writing, the illustrations are usually more planned and extensive. You can, for example, have a class produce many pages of illustrations for a retelling of a story like "The Little Red Hen."

Spelling and Other Conventions

The written products of language experience, shared writing, and interactive writing are texts that are meant to be read and used by the children. These texts are constructed

Comparison of Writing Approaches

	Language Experience	Shared Writing	Interactive Writing	Independent Writing
PURPOSES	• Create text that documents children's own language and experiences. • Engage children in the composing process. • Demonstrate the process of writing. • Provide a source of reading material. • Help children learn to compose texts in various genres. • Help children learn about the conventions of written language.	• Demonstrate the writing process • Engage children in the composing process. • Create readable text that can be used again. • Help children become aware of the structures and patterns of written language. • Provide demonstrations of how to construct words using letter-sound relationships and other strategies. • Demonstrate the conventions of written language.	• Demonstrate and engage children in the writing process, including composition and construction of text. • Create readable text that can be used again. • Help children become aware of the structures and patterns of written language. • Demonstrate and involve children in constructing words using letter-sound relationships and other strategies. • Help children learn to use the conventions of written language.	• Provide opportunity for individual children to compose and construct written text. • Support children in using their current knowledge to produce readable texts independently. • Encourage children to construct words using current knowledge of letter-sound relationships and other strategies. • Help children experience the publication of their own writing for various audiences. • Provide opportunities for individual children to apply what they have learned in other reading/writing contexts. • Help individual children develop voice in writing.
CONTEXT	Language experience is used in a small or large group setting. It may be used with individual children.	Shared writing is used in a large- or small-group setting. Group composition promotes learning and supports later reading of the text.	Interactive writing is used in a large- or small-group setting. Group composition promotes new learning and supports later reading of the text.	Children use independent writing when working individually. Independent writing may come after a minilesson language experience, shared writing, or interactive writing.
ROLES	• Children compose the text. There are contributions from individuals and some discussion of those contributions. • Teacher acts as scribe. • The teacher often "thinks aloud" to demonstrate processes to children.	• Teacher and children compose the text together. • Teacher acts as scribe. • The teacher often "thinks aloud" to demonstrate processes to children.	• Teacher and children compose the text together. • Teacher and children share in the writing of the text. • The teacher often "thinks aloud" to demonstrate processes to children.	• The individual child composes the text. • The individual child writes the text. • The child engages in the process independently with occasional support from the teacher.

FIGURE 2-2

Comparison of Writing Approaches, *continued*

	Language Experience	Shared Writing	Interactive Writing	Independent Writing
TEXT READABILITY	• The complexity of the text is related to the language used by children. • The layout and complexity may produce a text too difficult for younger children to read independently.	The teacher shapes the children's language and engages them in planning so that the text produced is accessible to the group as readers.	• The teacher shapes the children's language and engages them in planning so that the text produced is accessible to the group as readers. • There is emphasis on creating texts that are easy for children to read.	The text produced is shaped by the individual child, who is usually able to read it.
ART	Children may contribute drawings or other art to enhance the piece of writing.	The teacher helps the children plan illustrations or other artwork that will provide meaning support for the reading of the text.	The teacher helps the children plan illustrations or other artwork that will provide meaning support for the reading of the text.	The individual child may enhance the piece of writing with artwork.
SPELLING AND OTHER CONVENTIONS	• Spelling is conventional. • Teacher and children may discuss aspects of words. • Punctuation, capitalization, and other conventions are standard. • Letter formation and spacing are standard and neat.	• Spelling is conventional. Teacher and children may discuss aspects of words. • Punctuation, capitalization and other conventions are standard. • Letter formation and spacing are standard and neat.	• Spelling is conventional. Children contribute aspects of words they are learning and can control; teacher supports the process by contributing what the children do not yet control. • Punctuation will be conventional. • Capitalization may vary based on children's learning of the alphabet. • Letters have standard features but vary as children are achieving control.	• The text includes some words spelled conventionally and some words that the child attempts based on present knowledge of spelling principles. When the work is published, spelling is conventional; teacher assists in editing. • Use of punctuation, capitalization, and proper letter formation will vary according to children's growing skills.
USE OF TEXT AFTER WRITING	After production, the text is used for reading; it also serves as a record of children's experience and language. Charts provide models of writing that children may use for later reference.	After production, the text is used for reading. The text may also serve as a reference for locating known and new words. Children may use the text as a model or resource for their own writing.	After production, the text is used for reading. The text may also serve as a reference for locating known and new words. Children may use the text as a model or resource for their own writing.	Children's own writing may be used in many ways, for example, displayed, placed on the computer for publication, collected in folders or portfolios.

FIGURE 2-2, *continued*

FIGURE 2–3 *Three Billy Goats Gruff* Mural

with standard letter formation, spelling, capitalization, punctuation, and formatting. The teacher neatly produces the texts in the language experience and shared writing approaches.

In interactive writing, the print varies because different children are contributing letters and words. Make sure that the distinctive features of the letters are clear so that the text is very readable. The emphasis in interactive writing is on the children saying words slowly and engaging in the constructive process of thinking about letter-sound relationships and the parts of words.

FIGURE 2–4 *Tres Chivos Vivos* Mural

Children also use these processes later in independent writing, when they are expected to use the conventions they know. For example, they would be expected to spell the words they know in a standard way. For other words, children make good attempts using what they know about the structure of words in general. The number of conventionally spelled words will grow steadily and the children will also become more skilled at using their knowledge of underlying spelling patterns as they attempt new words. They will also be learning to check themselves as writers by proofreading their own writing. And they will be learning more about conventions such as punctuation, sentence structure, and paragraphing. The products produced in independent writing will reflect children's growing knowledge and will not be completely conventional unless they have been edited by the teacher for publication.

Uses of the Finished Product

The written products of language experience, shared writing, and interactive writing are texts that are meant to be read and used by the children. When they are displayed in the classroom, they provide a permanent demonstration and reminder to the children of how to go about writing. These texts may become the source for particular words or help children think about ways to compose other texts. A favorite activity in kindergarten and

first-grade classrooms is "reading around the room," which involves one child or several children pointing to words on the walls using a dowel rod, chopstick, or other instrument.

In a broad way, the different kinds of reading and writing activities in which children engage are directed toward helping them do what competent readers and writers do. Within that range of approaches, interactive writing is particularly useful in helping young children acquire the beginning understandings that are so important as a foundation for literacy.

Flexible Use of Writing Approaches

We have discussed how each of the four approaches to writing can be used for different purposes across the curriculum. Any time writing is needed, the teacher may select an approach—either group or individual—and involve children in composing and constructing the text. Now we will look at possibilities for combining these approaches in flexible ways.

Ida's Class

Ida, who was working with a group of emergent writers, decided to have the class create a story map (see Figure 2-5). To make the story map, Ida and the children used interactive writing to both create a title for the map and retell the story. Their map title

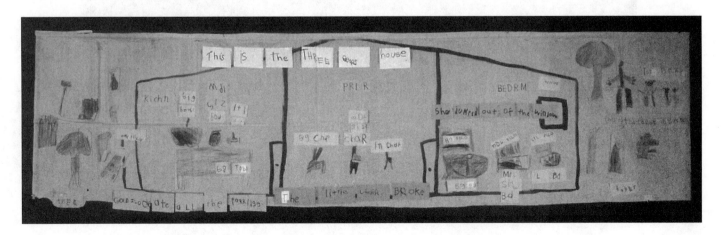

FIGURE 2–5 *Three Bears' House* Mural

reads: "This is the three bears' house." Their story reads: "Goldilocks ate the porridge. The little chair broke. She jumped out the window."

The map was ten feet long and showed three different rooms so that the children could depict and write about what happened in each room. Ida used cards to record the words in both the title and the story. She wanted to emphasize to her young students the concept of words being separate items and the importance of leaving spaces between words.

The children made the artwork for the house and independently wrote labels for many items. These included labeling the bedroom (BEDRM), the middle-sized pillow (mDL PLO), and the big pillow (Big PLO). This example clearly illustrates how children used a strategy they had learned in interactive writing as a way to figure out sound-letter relationships in their independent writing.

In creating the chart about magnets (Figure 2-6), Ida used both interactive writing (the writing on the left) and shared writing (the writing on the right).

This piece of writing provided a record of the results of an experiment the children conducted to determine which everyday objects could be picked up by a magnet. They organized the results of the experiment in a chart with two columns. The children participated actively in composing the headings for both columns. The heading for the first column was constructed during an interactive writing session. The heading for the second column was very similar to the first, so Ida wrote it herself to save time. The class then laid the chart on a table and affixed the tested objects to either of the two sections, based on the results of the magnet test.

Katie's Class
Katie Roth's first graders were further along in the learning process than were Ida's

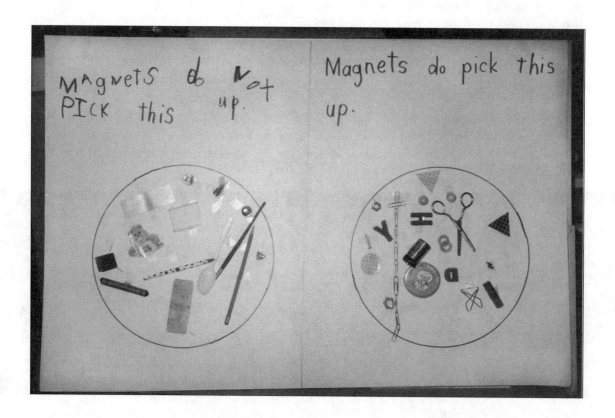

FIGURE 2–6 Things That the Magnet Will Pick Up

FIGURE 2–7 Apples and Seeds Chart

kindergartners. They knew how to spell many words in a standard way, could follow a piece of text with their eyes while writing and reading, and could use space. These children were on their way to controlling the processes of reading and writing, but they were still learning important things about words.

The chart produced by this class (Figure 2-7) summarized an inquiry by the children into the number of seeds in apples. With the teacher's help, they organized the text to report their results clearly. Katie used a combi-

nation of interactive writing (as shown in the line *Do all apples have the same number of seeds?*) and shared writing (the words *question*, *prediction*, and *results*). They created a scientific record—an excellent and useful product—in a short amount of time. In addition, children had an opportunity to participate in the construction of words.

Another example of a scientific record from the same classroom is shown in Figure 2-8 (on page 30). This time, the children were investigating what happens to the inside of an apple when it is exposed to air. The

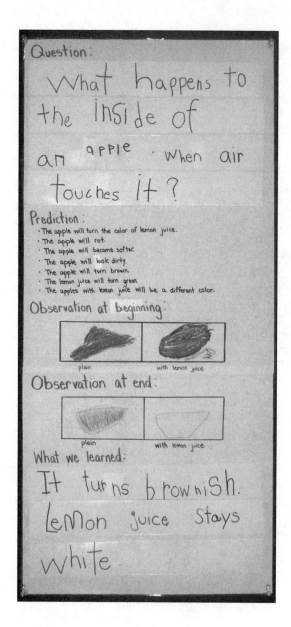

Question: What happens to the inside of an apple when air touches it?

Prediction:
- The apple will turn the color of lemon juice.
- The apple will rot.
- The apple will become softer.
- The apple will look dirty.
- The apple will turn brown.
- The lemon juice will turn green.
- The apples with lemon juice will be a different color.

Observation at beginning:

| plain | with lemon juice |

Observation at end:

| plain | with lemon juice |

What we learned: It turns brownish. Lemon juice stays white.

FIGURE 2–8 What's Inside an Apple?

process required close observation. Katie used a combination of interactive writing (the question and conclusion), shared writing (the labels for the scientific process), and language experience (the children's observations as recorded by their teacher).

The final example in this chapter shows a combination of interactive writing and language experience. The top and bottom pieces of writing in Figure 2-9 (on page 31) were generated through interactive writing by Katie's class of first graders. In this example the children had a chance to explore the construction of difficult words such as *decided* and *happen*. They had to use endings like *ed* and *s*. The text they composed and then constructed was complex. The teacher used language experience to write predictions and record observations. The children were free to think and talk about their experiences and what they were observing and learning while the teacher recorded their ideas. The result was a sophisticated record of learning.

Notice that some of the very easy high-frequency words were written by the teacher (for example, *the, is, and*). Once all of the children have control of an easy word, there is no need to take the time to have a child come up to the chart and write it in. You can save time and move the lesson along by quickly writing in the word yourself. Occasionally, an individual child who is very inexperienced has difficulty finding a way to contribute to a text. Having the child write a high-frequency word that most of the children already know is a way to help him contribute. This strategy fits into having individual goals for every child.

We cannot give you specific guidelines about how much of the text should be written by sharing the pen and how much should be written by the teacher. These decisions depend on

- the needs of particular children, what they know how to do and need to learn
- the nature and complexity of the text being written
- the particular purposes of the interactive writing activity
- the way the text will be used later for reading and other purposes.

Effective use of the writing approaches requires reflecting on the writing process in a continual search to create the most powerful examples for your students.

Levels of Teacher Support

In the examples shown in this chapter, teachers have provided varying levels and

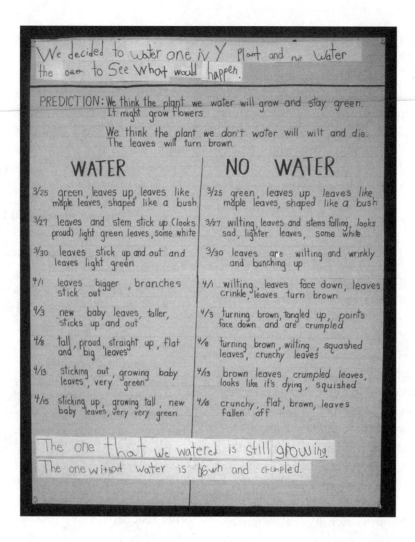

We decided to water one ivy plant and not water the other to see what would happen.

PREDICTION: We think the plant we water will grow and stay green. It might grow flowers.

We think the plant we don't water will wilt and die. The leaves will turn brown.

WATER	NO WATER
3/25 green, leaves up, leaves like maple leaves, shaped like a bush	3/25 green, leaves up, leaves like maple leaves, shaped like a bush
3/27 leaves and stem stick up (looks proud) light green leaves, some white	3/27 wilting, leaves and stems falling, looks sad, lighter leaves, some white
3/30 leaves stick up and out and leaves light green	3/30 leaves are wilting and wrinkly and bunching up
4/1 leaves bigger, branches stick out	4/1 wilting, leaves face down, leaves crinkle, leaves turn brown
4/3 new baby leaves, taller, sticks up and out	4/3 turning brown, tangled up, points face down and are crumpled
4/8 tall, proud, straight up, flat and big leaves	4/8 turning brown, wilting, squashed leaves, crunchy leaves
4/13 sticking out, growing baby leaves, very green	4/13 brown leaves, crumpled leaves, looks like it's dying, squished
4/15 sticking up, growing tall, new baby leaves, very very green	4/15 crunchy, flat, brown, leaves fallen off

The one that we watered is still growing.
The one without water is brown and crumpled.

FIGURE 2–9 Watering Ivy

kinds of support to children in the composition and construction of a text. Language experience involves the highest level of teacher support; the children come up with ideas and the teacher writes them down. Certainly, having a teacher do the writing for the children provides a scaffold for getting their ideas down on paper in a way that they could never do working alone. Independent writing obviously involves the lowest level of teacher support; children are encouraged to do everything they can as writers. That means making attempts at words; for young children, we would not expect standard spelling on every word in their independent writing work.

When we think about creating a readable text, we look at support in a different way. In language experience, the teacher provides high support for writing a text. The written product, however, is not highly supportive as a reading text for beginners because of the complexity of the language. Most children in the group will not be able to read the longer, complex texts produced using this approach.

In interactive writing, the teacher provides support for text construction but provides challenges to the children as part of the process. You and the children negotiate and reach consensus on the text to be written. You guide the children in composing a text, thus demonstrating what a young writer has to do in order to put ideas into written language. This light guidance tends to simplify or shape the language a bit so that it is easier to write and also easier to read later. Making use of literary devices such as repetition contributes to the readability of the text; format and layout are considered as well. Then, children participate actively in the construction of the text, rereading it many times. The final written product is readable for most of the children.

A quality literacy program takes place within a quality learning program, in a classroom in which children are gaining knowledge about interesting things that are connected to their lives. Their focus and their talk might be on finding out how plants grow or how seeds are related to growing different kinds of plants. Children are investigating and learning in the process. As young scientists, the process of learning how to use writing to record one's thinking is important. Language and literacy are tools to be used in a way that is integral to the inquiry processes that children engage in as they read and write about interesting things. Inquiry can also center on literature itself as children explore the content of literature and notice details of the author's craft. Inquiry can even focus on words, as children discover interesting ways that words are connected and constructed.

The classroom is rich in oral language experiences. It is very much a "talking" environment where oral language is demonstrated and valued. Children participate in a variety of oral language contexts. They take part in enjoyable oral language activities such as rhyming and chanting. All of the classroom talk weaves an oral text of shared meanings. When the oral text is rich and varied, the writing will be as well.

Our discussion of the many ways a teacher provides instruction and opportunities for meaningful literacy learning provides a clear picture of primary classrooms. In these kinds of classrooms, children develop competence as well as find pleasure in their literacy journey. They view themselves as readers and writers from the start.

Suggestions for Professional Development

1. Practice flexible use of several different writing approaches. An easy way to get started is to look at an area of curriculum in which you already use writing as part of your study. Ask yourself the following:

   ◾ When and why should I use interactive writing?
   ◾ What kinds of information would best be recorded using language experience and shared writing?
   ◾ What can students write for themselves?
   ◾ When will they need more support and less support?

2. Discuss your choices with a group of colleagues. Look at the examples in this chapter as you talk about your plans for using writing as a way to study in a content area.

3. After working a week or two in the unit of study, share your written products with other teachers. Ask:

   ◾ When did we use interactive writing? Was it effective? In what ways?
   ◾ When did we use other types of writing?
   ◾ Is there anything we would change about our choices of language experience, shared writing, interactive writing, or independent writing? What would extend our students' learning even more?

4. Practice flexible use of several different writing approaches using a piece of children's literature. For example, use several books related to a single theme, such as the life cycle of plants, or compare several versions of the same folktale. (See Appendix 2.)

CHAPTER THREE

Organizing Space and Materials to Support Interactive Writing

We have learned from our work in classrooms that interactive writing is much more effective if it takes place within an orderly, well-managed classroom environment. If you are new to the process, begin by looking around your classroom. Organizing space and equipment will enable your experience with interactive writing to go well right from the beginning.

Organization of Space

The organization of space is a critical factor in the efficiency and order with which interactive writing is conducted.

Space for Group Meeting

Since group meetings are essential for the effective use of interactive writing, we recommend that you organize the classroom to provide a comfortable group meeting space. (You probably already have an area where you routinely gather children for reading storybooks aloud or shared reading.) In the group meeting space, children work together using language to learn literacy. Be sure that the space is large enough so that all of the children in the group can sit comfortably without touching each other. Make sure that there is ample room between the space where children

sit and the easel. If children are crowded up against the easel, it will be hard for them to see and they'll have difficulty getting up quickly and easily when it is their turn to write. (See Figure 3-1, also inside front cover.)

Clearly set off the group meeting area. Many teachers place a carpet on the floor to designate this space. The rug simultaneously defines the physical boundaries of the area and provides comfortable seating for children during group activities. If a large rug is not available or fire regulations prohibit you from using carpet, go to a carpet store and get small sample squares of floor covering, which individual children can sit on. At the appropriate time, the children can take these samples from their storage area and place them in designated spots; after the group activity is over, the mats can be returned to storage. Another way to designate the group meeting area is to place a screen or display board along one side of the space. The board can hold name charts and/or word walls and charts, which are useful in connecting interactive writing to references and resources.

You can also place bookshelves along the edges of the group meeting area. Low bookshelves not only help to define the space more clearly, they also add to the attractiveness of the area. Many of the books displayed

FIGURE 3–1   A Group Meeting Area

are related to the topics children are studying and serve as resources during the interactive writing lesson.

Teachers often meet with children in small groups for interactive writing lessons. These small-group lessons can take place in the large-group meeting area or at tables or small-group areas elsewhere in the room.

Space for Display

As mentioned above, it is helpful to have a display area adjacent to the group meeting area that is easily visible to all the children. For children who are beginning readers and writers, it is important to display the name chart prominently (see McCarrier and Patacca 1999 and the name chart section later in this chapter). The displays in the group meeting area can include

- a name chart
- an alphabet linking chart
- poems or stories for shared reading
- the word wall as well as word charts

- completed or in-progress pieces of interactive writing.

When limited display space is available, you can use a flip chart so that those pieces of writing that are useful to the children can be found easily. You need to analyze your display space carefully. Often the calendar or routine informational pieces such as lunch schedules occupy valuable space that can be better used to accommodate writing resources.

There is a difference between decoration and display. For generations, teachers have "decorated" classrooms, using seasonal materials and other colorful items to make the space look pleasant and inviting. But we have learned that it is more important to fill the walls with work that is created by the children themselves. We also suggest useful displays that engage the children in literacy learning (e.g., word wall or shared reading charts). The classroom thus becomes more functional, engaging the learners. This is not to say that displays should not be attractive to look at, only that their purpose must be more than merely decorative.

During interactive writing lessons, the children's attention should be continually drawn to the print resources on the walls. You might ask children to notice, for example, the similarity between a word that they need to write as part of their message, like *and*, and a name like *Andrew* or *Andrea* on the name chart. Every group of children includes names that are useful for making such connections. Ask children in your class to find a letter on the alphabet-linking chart (discussed later in this chapter) and notice its features when they want to write it in a word. They can find high-frequency words (like *was*) on the word wall.

As you model active "noticing" behaviors, children will readily begin to search for connections. They will remember and find words that they have used in previous pieces of interactive writing. The process mirrors the way that writers actually work:

■ They use their previous knowledge.
■ They link to previously written texts.
■ They are constantly on the alert for meaningful connections between texts.

Having the first simple references and resources available starts children on the road to independence and at the same time reinforces learning.

Displays of interactive writing become important instructional materials during the times that children work on their own writing or read independently. These texts, produced by the children and teacher working together, are usually of high interest to children. The children remember writing them and talking about them. The texts are connected to interesting experiences or to literature that the children love. These texts offer a high degree of support to young readers because of the intimate knowledge that children have as the writers of the texts.

To provide useful resources around the classroom, place a high priority on dedicating all available large spaces to the display of materials that will be used in learning. These include:

■ interactive writing
■ shared reading texts
■ name chart
■ children's artwork
■ children's independent writing
■ word walls and word charts.

Children's artwork and independent writing are important aspects of the print display because they are a way of celebrating individual students' accomplishments. Children benefit from seeing their products on display in the classroom or in the hallway.

Use plain backgrounds for displays of children's interactive writing, word walls, charts, and so on. The best way to help children attend to the print features of displays is to present print without clutter. Fancy figured wrapping paper, for example, may look colorful as a background, but it is highly distracting because it competes with the print.

Place completed pieces of interactive writing on walls or display boards at or slightly above the children's eye level so that the children can have ready access to the print. You can also use the backs and sides of bookshelves and filing cabinets as surfaces for smaller pieces of writing.

We recommend that you minimize the space used for calendars, helpers' charts, birthday charts, and other routine presentations. Such items can be placed on movable cardboard charts to be taken out as needed. Since they are generally used all year and the children become very familiar with them, they do not need to occupy a large amount of space. Instead, reserve the maximum amount of valuable space for literacy materials that change and that contribute in an active way to the children's ongoing literacy learning.

Equipment, Tools, and Materials

You will need a collection of tools and equipment that are easily accessible during interactive writing lessons. Collect these materials before you begin implementing interactive writing in your classroom and arrange them in an orderly way.

The Easel

We recommend using an easel like the one below (Figure 3–2 and Appendix 1) as the writing surface for interactive writing lessons. An easel is useful for several reasons:

■ It has a slanted surface that is easier to write on than a vertical surface.

■ Its height can be adjusted to accommodate the children recording the message.

■ It can be seen easily both from the floor during group time and when students are seated at tables.

■ It allows for a teacher or student to stand to the side of and slightly behind the writing surface to indicate words with a pointer.

■ It is portable, allowing for greater flexibility in designing the group meeting space.

Many teachers have several easels in the room, one or two in the large group meeting area and another next to a table where they work with small groups in interactive writing or guided reading.

Many kinds of easels are available for classroom use. We favor a heavy wooden model because it is stable and will not shift when children lean against it as they write. Most plastic or metal easels are too light and tip over easily. The writing surface must be large enough so that the messages children write have the appearance of continuous text. We strongly recommend a writing surface that is thirty-six inches wide and twenty-four inches high. The width enables young children to have the opportunity to arrange text left to right across a long line.

The model presented in Figure 3-2 has a flat ledge, without a lip, attached to the bottom of the writing surface to hold markers. It is important for the ledge to be flat and at least three inches wide so that both a writing tablet and a big book can be used at the same

FIGURE 3–2   Using An Easel in Interactive Writing

time. This feature allows you to keep the writing tablet on the easel and place a big book on top of it during shared reading. Because the ledge does not have a lip, you can easily turn the pages of the book.

The legs of the easel must be long enough to locate the writing surface at an appropriate height for young children. A flat tray can be added between the legs to hold large pieces of paper and other materials. We have included specific directions for constructing the easel in Appendix 1. High school vocational classes can produce these easels at low cost. Volunteer parents and senior citizens may be able to help as well. Plywood surfaces are adequate for both sides of the easel when paper pads are being used. You may want to have a magnetic board or chart board on one side of the easel so that you can use it for other purposes such as word study or guided reading.

Paper

Selecting paper for interactive writing may seem to be a minor detail; in fact, the color, weight, size, and shape of paper are all important considerations to be made in successful interactive writing.

Color and Type of Paper

We recommend the following types of paper for interactive writing:

■ white or light-colored butcher paper (avoid dark colors such as red, green, or purple)
■ light brown wrapping paper or butcher paper (use a dark black marker)
■ plain newsprint (may be doubled, with pieces of paper fastened together on the edges with masking tape, making a very strong double sheet that will wear well)
■ large-size construction paper in white or light colors.

The type of paper you use will depend on the purpose of the lesson and the availability of the paper. Be sure that markers do not "bleed" through paper you are going to use to make a book, as the print that shows through may distract children as they read.

Size and Shape of Paper

The size and shape of the paper is important because these factors affect the children's learning about how to produce and format text. For interactive writing, you can choose among several sizes and shapes of paper, including

■ unlined chart paper
■ cards (pieces of card stock)
■ strips of paper (these often come in a roll).

Each type of paper is best suited to specific writing purposes. Do not rely solely on any one type of paper because your choice will affect the way the children organize their writing. Having a variety of good paper encourages children to be flexible and creative in the writing process.

Unlined Chart Paper   Large pieces of unlined chart paper or newsprint are ideal for interactive writing. The large sheet of chart paper is similar to the blank piece of paper that a child will encounter in his own writing. Using this wide blank sheet, you can talk with children about where to start and what and where to write next. Remind them that after finishing a line they will need to return to the left side of the page. They will need to think about their text from top to bottom, perhaps leaving space for illustrations. Some of their texts will be organized as lists, whereas others will consist of sentences. Individual letters, too, will be viewed in relation to each other. At first, children will not be consistent in letter size, but you provide a model and guide the size of the production. The idea is to help children know how to organize and place print on a page.

We recommend chart paper that is twenty-four inches long by thirty-six inches wide; in other words, paper that is wider than it is long. We also recommend using pads or tablets of chart paper because they tend to be less expensive than spiral-bound books.

Compare the two pieces of interactive writing presented in Figure 3-3 (on page 39).

Which would be easier for children to read? Which looks more like a text that you might see in a book? When children are just beginning to achieve control over writing, their letters tend to be large and inconsistent in size. Beginners also tend to have difficulty placing more than two or three words in a line unless the paper is very wide. For the earliest writers and readers, a wider paper provides space for more words in each line of print, allowing for more practice of left-to-right movement across text. Additionally, since you want the print to be large enough so that all the children in the group will see it, wider paper is very helpful.

We recommend unlined paper rather than lined paper because it allows young children to organize space with greater flexibility of letter size. Insisting that they write between the lines imposes an unnecessary constraint on their early attempts to write. When children are initially learning to form letters, their attention must be on producing the features of letters that they can control. We expect them to produce the round, straight, slanted, and elongated forms of letters. They are also expected to arrange them from left to right. It increases the demands of the visual/motor task when we also expect beginners to form their letters to fit between two horizontal lines. With this added burden the writing task becomes unnecessarily difficult. The child is asked to attend to too many aspects of print at once. Paying too much attention to horizontal lines may actually interfere with the child's perception of letter forms in the early stages, especially if there is an overemphasis on staying within the lines.

Control will be achieved gradually as children have more and more opportunities to form letters and to attend to them. Soon enough, they will be using lines to guide their writing and they will develop a sense of how written words appear on the same line, even when they are using unlined paper.

If you cannot obtain unlined paper, simply avoid an overemphasis on following the lines during beginning lessons, especially in prekindergarten and kindergarten classes. The children will probably be so busy concentrating on forming letters and moving left to right that the lines will "fade" into the background. They will eventually be able to use lines as a guide, and then even to imagine lines as they organize manuscript and cursive writing.

Cards   If you decide to use another kind or shape of paper, think about the demands that the shape makes on the writing. Some teachers use a card for each word in the sentence instead of using sheets or continuous strips of paper. The children and teacher compose the message orally, repeating it several times. The teacher counts the number of words in the sentence and then either tapes the right number of cards (one for each word) on the paper pad on the easel or adds a card for every new word to be written. The cards are used to demonstrate word boundaries and to help children understand word-by-word matching. Each word that is written through sharing the pen is placed on its own card. If a word is short, the teacher can cut the card to fit the length of the word. Then the teacher glues the cards onto a large piece of paper for rereading. Cards may also be placed as titles on murals or charts and used to label items in a piece of art.

Cards can be effective when children have their first experience working with print on a large piece of paper. We consider cards to be a prop, an external mediator that may be an effective temporary tool for demonstrating the concept of a word to children. When children have a good idea of the use of space to define words, we advise that this prop be abandoned. Not only does it create extra time for the teacher, but it can also "bog down" the lesson. In addition, it removes the opportunity for children to write words in a line, and may lead to a reading of the text that focuses on individual words rather than phrases and sentences, preventing a smooth, meaningful reading.

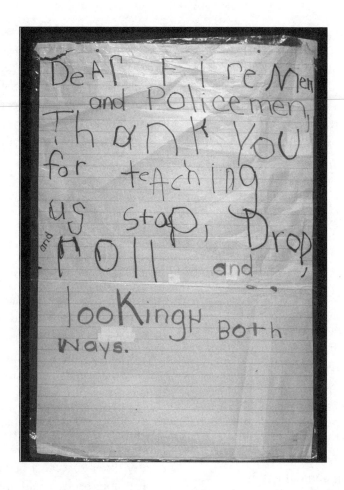

FIGURE 3–3 Two Versions of Interactive Writing

Strips Some teachers use blank strips of paper, approximately three inches tall and two to three feet long, made of either card stock or paper, to facilitate the writing of sentences. They tack the strips onto a cork board and place them on the easel. During the interactive writing lesson, the sentence strips help the children control the size of their letters and produce more standard proportions in their print. The sentence strips can be glued on charts or in big books, producing a neater looking product. Since the print is more uniform in size, it is highly readable. Sentence strips can also be useful if you plan to place the interactive writing in a pocket chart.

One of the challenges that children encounter when using cards or sentence strips is centering their writing vertically on the strip so that "tail" letters such as y do not "fly up" or get cut off because room was not allowed on the bottom of the strip to accommodate the entire letter. The best the children can do is to write within the middle area of the strip to allow for tall and tail letters.

Sentence strips, like cards, are a temporary prop or mediator. Before using them, observe the children's independent writing carefully. There are no precut strips there. Are children able to use space effectively on a blank page as they produce their own writing? Are they gaining control of this aspect of writing on their own? Strips will help you to organize interactive writing and make it readable. Some of the examples included in this book were made using sentence strips. It is important, however, to be sure that children are also learning how to arrange print on a page without the assistance of strips.

Other Paper You can cut many different kinds of paper to required dimensions when you need them for the specific purposes of interactive writing. Light colored construction paper (18" x 24") is useful for making alternative texts or other big books. Light brown or white butcher paper can be folded to make sturdy books.

You need to keep observing children to determine the effects that using a particular kind of paper or type of text layout have on them. Too much reliance on one type of paper or writing format can result in dependence on the paper or format and lack of flexibility in the children's independent writing.

Markers

Because it is so important for children to clearly see print, we will risk repeating, with expansion, some points made earlier. Use broad-tipped thick markers that do not bleed through the paper. We recommend using black, although dark blue or purple may work well for you. Look at the writing from the point of view of the child. It is easier to read print if it is written in clear, dark letters on a white or very light background.

We strongly recommend writing the piece in one uniform color. The final product should look like a unified text, not one that reminds children which letters they wrote and which ones the teacher wrote. Using many different colors breaks up the flow of continuous print. You'll find it convenient to use one marker for both you and the children who contribute letters and words during the construction of text; simply pass the marker back and forth quickly. The idea is to bring children *briefly* into control of part of the process, at a point that helps to draw their attention to an important example. In this way you will be avoiding long, laborious printing by any one child at the easel. The children's attention should be directed toward the print—the letters, words, and sentences that make up the message they helped create. They will read this text many times over the coming weeks. Use of a single color will help them notice visual features of the words rather than the fact that a certain word is written in red. In addition, children will see print in all one color in texts they read.

Correction Tape

One-inch white correction tape, which is available in most office supply stores, is a useful tool for interactive writing. The tape comes in a small, disposable dispenser and can be used as an editing tool, to cover markings on the chart paper that need to be deleted. Using tape to cover mistakes instead of crossing out letters or words or erasing them makes the finished product much more readable and allows for quick error correction. The result is satisfying to children. They are more willing to take risks because they know how easily a letter or word can be altered. Use the tape when

❚ you or a child writes an incorrect letter or word
❚ words are written too close together and one needs to be deleted and rewritten to show the space between
❚ a letter is reversed or a capital is written where a lower-case letter is more appropriate.

There are several alternatives to white correction tape. Some teachers have used white peel-off mailing labels, which they cut as needed. Others use small pieces of paper to which they quickly apply a glue stick. Masking tape has sometimes been used, but presents some problems. When you write with a marker on masking tape, the color is not the same as the rest of the text because the ink is not absorbed into the tape. Children can find it difficult to see a word or letter written on top of masking tape.

When using colored paper, cut up small pieces of the same color paper to use as correction strips, then apply them with a glue stick. That process will make the piece much better looking and more readable than using white tape on a colored background.

Magnetic Letters

We recommend using brightly colored plastic magnetic letters like those shown in Figure 3-4 as a tool for assisting children in writing and also to draw their attention to specific features of letters. We recommend that you store letters on a cookie sheet, arranging

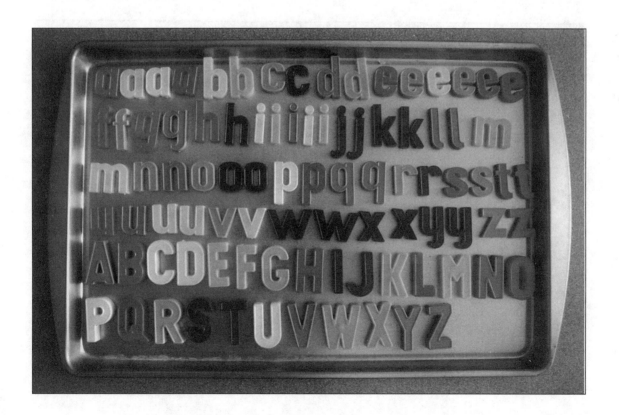

FIGURE 3–4   Cookie Tray with Magnetic Letters

them alphabetically. (Be sure to test the cookie sheet before you buy it. Aluminum cookie sheets will not work with magnets.)

The key to using magnetic letters is having a system that will allow you to find the letter you want quickly. The pace of the interactive writing lesson is important. If there are time periods when children are waiting for you to find a letter, the lesson will drag and lose its effectiveness. You will want to pull out a letter to

▮ provide a child with a form to copy
▮ enable a child to check the shape and direction of a letter against one he or she just wrote.

Magna Doodle

A Magna Doodle, as shown in Figure 3-5, is a plastic board with magnetic filings under the surface that can be used to show children letter forms or words. It can be purchased at most children's toy stores with several magnets of various widths that are used to write

on it. They allow you to make strong black lines of different widths. When working with the whole group, we recommend using the thicker magnets. The image can be erased by simply moving a lever that redistributes the filings. A limitation of this tool is that it is difficult and sometimes impossible to delete only a letter or portion of a word, which is helpful in showing children how to use part of a word they know to figure out a new word.

The Magna Doodle provides a quick way to produce an image for the children—a letter or a word—to help them notice distinctive features.

Whiteboard

A white dry-erase board is still another way to bring children's attention to the features of print. The board should be small enough so that you can easily handle it (about nine inches by twelve inches). You write on the white surface with a dry-erase marker, keeping an eraser or cloth handy to wipe off marks

FIGURE 3-5   Teacher Using Magna Doodle

when they are no longer needed. The whiteboard can be used like a Magna Doodle, to show a child a letter or word in a way that the whole group can see. The whiteboard is a particularly good way to call attention to specific features of print. You can easily write and erase any features of a word, in any location in the word—at the beginning, in the middle, or at the end. You can also underline or circle parts of words.

Pointers

A message written through interactive writing is reread many times during production, so you will need to have a pointing stick available. Your finger as a pointer will not do as your hand and arm will block a clear view of the whole text. You can easily make your own pointing stick by cutting a forty-eight-inch dowel rod in half. Dowels are sold in hardware stores and are very inexpensive. Color the tip of the pointer with a bright or dark color that will draw the children's eyes to the part that is placed under the print.

The pointer should be long and thin enough so that both it and your hand do not block the text. Again, always be mindful of the children's view of the print. One of the best things you can do is actually to sit in the children's position, have someone use the pointer, and get the "real view" of the print. Rereading the text will not be effective unless children's attention is on the print.

Some commercially produced pointers have hands, stars, or other objects represented on the tips. We advise against such embellishments for the same reason cited above: they block the children's view of the print. If your pointer has an apple or some other object on the end of it, use the slim end to point to the print.

When a young child stands to the side of the chart, he or she can easily point to each word with a twenty-four-inch pointing stick. It is very important for all the children in the group to see the text while participating in the rereading of it, so that they are able to remember the message and think of the next word. The children are building the routine of rereading, remembering the message, and thinking of the next word to make them more independent in their own writing. You will need to demonstrate to them the procedure and purpose of pointing.

References and Resources

As mentioned earlier in the discussion of space, some important resources should be available for reference during interactive writing lessons.

Name Chart

A name chart like the one shown in Figure 3-6 (on page 44), listing the names of children in the class, is a key tool for interactive writing (McCarrier and Patacca 1999). Name charts can be made on chart paper or tag board. Names can also be written on cards and placed in a pocket chart.

You should write the names on the chart yourself; the chart then provides the children with a perfect model for writing letters. Name charts can be made in several different ways. They can

- show first names only, grouped alphabetically by the first letter of each name. Each group is circled in a different color, with the first letter of each name printed in a color that contrasts with the rest of the letters (for example, first letter in red and the rest of the name in black).
- show first and last names, with groups in alphabetical order by first or last name.
- show last names only, with groups in alphabetical order.
- show names organized by categories such as boys and girls, same ending letters, same number of syllables, and so on.

For the earliest name charts we recommend simple forms using first names grouped alphabetically.

Simple name charts help children to develop a set of important understandings; for

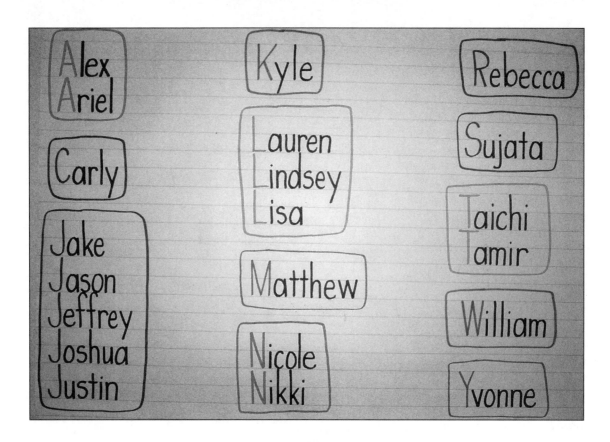

FIGURE 3–6 A First Name Chart

example, that a name is a word. They learn that a word is written the same way each time and that it is made up of a sequence of letters. They learn to define a word by space. The technique of making the first letter of each name in a contrasting color emphasizes the concept of *first* in writing. You can make the first letter of the names beginning with one letter one color, and all those beginning with a different letter a new color, and so forth. (See Figure 3-6.)

The name charts will also help you demonstrate to the children how to use what they know about letters, sounds, and words as they write. For example, if a child does not know how to form a letter, such as the letter *h*, you can refer to that letter in a child's name as a model. If the children are writing the word *cheese*, you can draw their attention to the fact that *cheese* and *Chelsea* sound the same at the beginning. If they know how to write the beginning of Chelsea's name, they will also know how to write the beginning letters of *cheese*.

Alphabet Linking Chart

An alphabet linking chart, shown in Figure 3-7, is a poster that has clearly written alphabet letters in both upper and lower case and a corresponding word, represented by a picture, that helps children associate letters with their respective sounds. (See Fountas and Pinnell 1996 and Pinnell and Fountas 1998 for a reproducible copy.)

Many teachers have enlarged this eight-and-a-half-by-eleven-inch chart to poster size and placed it in the group meeting area for handy reference. You can teach the children to "read" the chart in a shared context, saying each letter name and the word represented by the picture. As you point to each box, the children read, "A, a, apple; B, b, bear," and so on. It can also be read in a variety of other ways—reading all the consonants, reading every other letter, starting at the bottom, and so forth.

After the children are familiar with the chart, you can use it during interactive writing to help them make letter-sound connec-

FIGURE 3–7   Alphabet Linking Chart

tions. For example, the children in one group wanted to write the word *went*, but there was no child in the class with a name that started with a *w*. The teacher told them to say the word *went* slowly and to think about the sound that comes first. Several children ar-

ticulated the sound that they heard but could not name the corresponding letter.

The teacher said, "It's like *window* on our alphabet chart," and pointed to that box on the chart.

The children said, "W."

FIGURE 3–8   Word Wall

The teacher asked them to say, "W, *w*, window," and then called a child up to write a *w* on the piece of interactive writing text.

The chart can also be used to help children find the letter forms that they need to write or to check on a letter form. For example, if they know the uppercase form of a letter and need to find the lowercase form, the chart is a ready reference.

Word Wall

A word wall, as shown in Figure 3-8 is a section of a wall of the classroom that has the letters of the alphabet listed in a row along the top. Under each letter is a list of words beginning with that letter. These words either are high-frequency words or serve as "exemplars" for word solving. Exemplars are words that contain key word features or patterns that the children can use to form other words. The word wall is a powerful tool because it helps the children to write some words quickly and easily as they create a text.

It is also important for them to use words they know as analogies to help them write words that they do not know (Pinnell and Fountas 1998; Hall and Cunningham 1999).

During interactive writing, there are many opportunities to use the word wall as a reference. Having the children use this display is important, since it not only supports the children in writing a particular piece of text but also shows them how to be independent in using references and resources. It is much more powerful with respect to their learning to prompt them to use the word wall than simply to provide them with the letter or the spelling of a word. With teacher encouragement, they learn to habitually look for the word on the wall and use the wall to check on the spelling of words. They may also use the wall to find a word like the one they want to write.

In one class, the children wanted to write the word *knee* and they correctly identified the beginning sound *n*. The teacher wanted them to begin to realize that they have to know something about how a word looks as well as the first sound-letter association. The teacher said, "It does have an *n* sound, but that word starts with a silent letter like a word on our wall—*know*." By using this analogy, children could begin to build an idea of *kn* as a beginning structure for some words. They associated the new word with one they knew as a high-frequency word.

In another class, a group of kindergarten children wanted to write the word *the* during an interactive writing session. *The* is a good example of a high-frequency word that cannot be generated by letter-sound associations. They had worked with the word *the* in several other contexts and it had been placed on the wall, but few of them knew how to write this word at an automatic level. One child came up to the board and wrote the word accurately. Their teacher quickly asked the group to check it using the word wall.

Word Charts

Word charts, which are created during word study minilessons, are valuable resources for children to use during writing. These charts, an example of which is shown in Figure 3-9, are lists of words that you and the children have worked on together. Word charts typically represent the exploration of a spelling principle.

Each chart contains a list of words that have something in common. Some charts contain content words, all related to particular areas of study, that children would not be expected to know how to spell. Other charts contain words that the children have grouped in some way, for example, words that end in *ing* or words that start with *st*. (See Pinnell and Fountas 1998 for a description of the use of interactive word charts.)

During interactive writing, children can use these charts in strategic ways, for example, to check whether or not to double the consonant on a word when adding *ing*. Sometimes children find a word on the chart and then copy it into their own written pieces; however, word charts are not used to list words solely for the purpose of copying. We want children to act on the word in some way—associating letters and sounds where

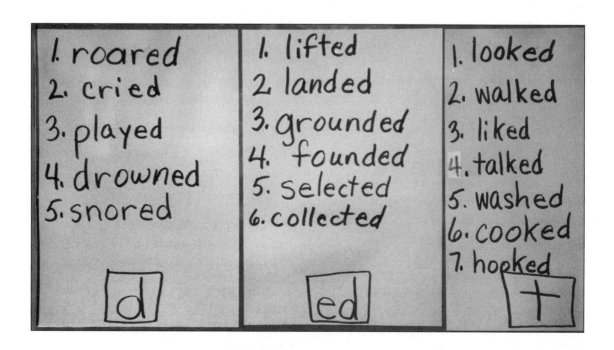

FIGURE 3–9 Word Chart

appropriate, thinking how the word looks, applying some principle, or using the same pattern.

Making Connections to Books

Interactive writing can be related to a wide variety of children's experiences. Many of these experiences are connected to quality children's literature. Literature often is used as a resource in both general and specific ways. (See Appendix 2.)

Children's literature, in general, provides a rich resource for young writers. As they listen to stories read aloud, they begin to internalize how written language sounds. They develop an understanding of story structure and realize that an author's style of writing is related to the genre he or she is writing.

Children's literature can be used in specific ways to support children's writing. Books offer them examples of the types of literature that they can produce themselves. The Children's Bibliography at the end of this book (Appendix 2) presents examples of different genres of literature and books that present a variety of interesting content.

Children's literature can also be used to show children how authors lay out a text, match illustrations and text, and emphasize events. Specific techniques such as the use of "speech bubbles" can be found in many children's books. It is important for children to encounter a variety of books so that they know the wide range of options available to them as writers.

Organization to Support Connections

As you organize the group meeting space, be sure that the books that are currently most popular with the children are most accessible. After all, this is the same space where you will be reading to the children as a group. Of course, you will organize books in different ways in many different places in the classroom. A library corner will hold many different choices. If your supply of books is generous, children may have their own per-sonal book boxes; they may also have browsing boxes, containing books that have been read in guided reading groups or that are "just right" for certain groups of readers. Place the books that are specifically related to an on-going piece of interactive writing on the easel or nearby. You can display books that have stimulated the pieces themselves or those that have the relevant content alongside the piece of completed writing.

Many of the decisions that you make regarding organization, space, and materials will have an impact on the effectiveness of instruction. Proper organization of supplies will help you move your lesson along quickly, without unnecessary pauses. Other decisions, such as to keep resources in view, will help children use tools and supports for writing. Still other actions, such as juxtaposing books with writing, will help students connect writing and reading. In a sense, nothing that we do as primary teachers is "by accident" or merely for convenience. Even seemingly small decisions contribute to the sum total of our ability to have an impact on student learning.

Suggestions for Professional Development

1. Work with a group of colleagues to plan your group meeting space.

2. Make lists of materials you will need.

3. Set up your group meeting space with materials you have collected.

4. Tour colleagues' classrooms and have them tour yours; give each other feedback.

5. Try out interactive writing for two weeks. Try to produce several different forms of writing and display them in the classroom.

6. Meet with colleagues to share name charts and a piece of writing. Share connections your students have made between writing and the name chart, the word wall,

word charts, and previous pieces of interactive writing. Discuss the ease and efficiency with which you were able to work.

7.   Make adjustments and try the process for another two weeks.

8.   At a follow-up meeting, discuss the changes you have noticed in your children as a result of your attention to organization and use of new materials. Talk about the print understandings your students have gained.

CHAPTER FOUR

Getting Started with Interactive Writing

How do you get started with interactive writing? In Chapter 3, we discussed the materials and equipment you will need to support the process and how to organize them. Organization is of critical importance because interactive writing must proceed at a brisk pace in order to engage and hold children's interest. Before you introduce interactive writing in your classroom, consider what is involved in making this process an integral part of the language arts curriculum:

■ planning for the use of instructional time
■ creating an interactive learning community
■ establishing classroom routines
■ communicating with administrators and other teachers
■ communicating with parents.

In this chapter we discuss the practical considerations related to beginning your work in interactive writing. Making a good start is critical to the successful implementation of this powerful way of working with children.

Planning for the Use of Instructional Time

There are several concerns related to the effective use of time in connection with interactive writing. Some common questions are:

■ How can I fit interactive writing into my already crowded school day?
■ How much time should I spend on interactive writing?
■ How long should my interactive writing lessons be?

Scheduling Time for Interactive Writing

If you consider interactive writing to be an "add on" to your language arts curriculum, you will find it difficult to manage time effectively. The best way to incorporate interactive writing into your day is to think about its purposes and then blend those purposes with your curriculum goals. For example, one of your goals is to extend children's understanding of texts and help them interpret events and characters. Oral language is a major vehicle for accomplishing this goal. If you are discussing a story you have read aloud to children, you can accompany your talk with some interactive writing and build understanding of the text while you are helping the children learn about the writing process.

Another curriculum goal is the demonstration of techniques in writing. Many teachers begin writing workshop with an explicit minilesson focusing on some aspect of writing. The purpose may range from helping children compose a title or beginning sentence to using punctuation to matching illustrations and texts. Interactive writing may actually serve the role of the minilesson because you will be reminding children to use the same techniques in their independent writing.

The curriculum also involves social studies, science, and literature. You engage children in various kinds of topic study related to these content areas; they actively investigate questions and ideas and talk about them with each other. Interactive writing is an ideal way to demonstrate to children how they can record facts and ideas in writing to help them in later recall and analysis.

You may have a specific time on your schedule for interactive writing, but be sure that the goal is not just to "do" interactive writing but to show children how to use writing for a variety of purposes. The sample basic schedule in Figure 4-1 shows how interactive writing may be incorporated throughout the day.

This schedule provides for a full day of instruction for preschool through grade two classrooms. The demarcations across grade levels are not rigid but should be thought of more as a continuum. Obviously, the time for more "academic" activities will gradually increase across the grades. Time devoted to reading aloud and interactive writing for preschoolers will increase as these children end kindergarten. For those of you who teach kindergarten, we have provided a sample half-day plan in Figure 4-2.

Adjust the time frames to meet the needs of the children you teach. The role of interactive writing will vary at different times of the day.

❚ Sometimes interactive writing will be the focus of attention, as in the daily morning community meeting. In this session, your main activity is interactive writing. The subject and focus of interactive writing, however, is to extend children's learning experiences. If you take a walk or field trip, for example, use interactive writing to record your observations or tell the story. You can discuss and record active learning in content areas, some of which takes place in the afternoon, during interactive writing the next morning. Also use interactive writing to extend literature study.

❚ Sometimes interactive writing will be an option nested within other instructional approaches. It can be used to extend learning in guided reading or as the minilesson for writing workshop. It can be used as a way of keeping records for science experiences, solving mathematical problems, or making sets of directions for projects. It is wise to keep in mind that interactive writing, like individual writing, is a tool. The advantage to young children is that you can involve them in wide uses of writing before they would be able to engage in such uses independently.

There will also be variations across the week, of course, as you fill in time for special areas such as art or music. On days when you have less instructional time in the classroom, you will need to adjust the schedule. There may be special projects that are served by spending more time on interactive writing for a few days. Extended writing time might be followed by a larger time block devoted to reading or another area during the next few days. With those variations in mind, we encourage you to keep to a standard schedule for most days. Having a predictable schedule that children know helps in the following ways:

❚ You and the children are able to pace your work so that no area is neglected and, in general, instruction moves along at a lively pace.

A Suggested Schedule for Incorporating Interactive Writing

	Classroom Activity	Pre-K to Early K, Full Day	End of K to Early 1st	Middle of 1st to End of 1st	End of 1st to Middle 2nd
COMMUNITY MEETING — WHOLE GROUP	**Reading Aloud to Children and/or Shared Reading** • Relate to literature study • Connect to mathematics/science/social studies projects	20 minutes	20 minutes	15 minutes	20 minutes
LANGUAGE INSTRUCTION	**Interactive Writing and/or Shared Writing** • Relate to literature or content area study • Connect to mathematics/science/social studies projects	20 minutes	20 minutes	15 minutes	Optional use of interactive writing for small groups
	Letter-Word Study • Focused experience appropriate to level • Minilesson and word wall • Relate to interactive writing pieces	not applicable	10 minutes	10 minutes	15 minutes
READING INSTRUCTION — SMALL GROUP	**Guided Reading Groups** • Introduce and read books • Teach after reading • May extend through writing (interactive and individual) *(Teacher with guided reading group while other children engage in independent work)*	60 minutes	60 minutes	60–90 minutes	60–90 minutes
INDEPENDENT WORK	**Managed Independent Learning in Centers or at Tables** *Center Time—Pre-K to Early K: Letters, Blocks, Sand, Water, Art, Drama, Games, Listening Center* *Center Time—K to 2: Browsing Box, ABC, Listening Center, Art, Writing, Reading Around the Room, Independent Reading, Drama, Poem Box, Computer, Overhead Projector, Buddy Reading, Games, Reading Journal, Literature Circle, Pocket Chart*				

FIGURE 4–1

A Suggested Schedule for Incorporating Interactive Writing, *continued*

Classroom Activity	Pre-K to Early K, Full Day	End of K to Early 1st	Middle of 1st to End of 1st	End of 1st to Middle 2nd
WHOLE GROUP AND INDIVIDUAL				
Writing Workshop • Minilesson: may be interactive writing • Individual conferences • Sharing	30 minutes	45 minutes	55 minutes	60 minutes
LUNCH				
WHOLE GROUP				
Reading Aloud Shared Reading	20 minutes	10 minutes	10 minutes	10 minutes
Science/Social Studies	30 minutes	30 minutes	30 minutes	30 minutes
Mathematics	60 minutes	45 minutes	45 minutes	45 minutes
Centers—Pre-K to Early K: *Math, Science, Drama, Social Studies*				
TOTAL	240 minutes	240 minutes	240 minutes	240 minutes

WRITING INSTRUCTION

COMMUNITY MEETING

CONTENT AREA INSTRUCTION

FIGURE 4–1 Suggested Schedule for Incorporating Interactive Writing, *continued*

FIGURE 4–1, *continued*

Sample Daily Plan for Half-Day Kindergarten

Activity	Approximate Time
Opening, Attendance, Pledge, Calendar	5 minutes
Community Meeting • Reading Aloud • Interactive Writing connected to literature study, science, or social studies	25 minutes
Writing • Minilesson • Drawing/Writing • Sharing	20 minutes
Reading Buddies, Book Exploration **Guided Reading Groups** (when appropriate)	30 minutes
Community Meeting: Circle Time • Songs, Charts, Poetry • Story Telling • Shared Reading of Charts and/or Interactive Writing	25 minutes
Integrated Learning Centers • Independent Writing • Math • Art • Dramatic Play/Housekeeping/Class Store • Sand • Water • Extensions Based on Thematic Units	30 minutes
Sharing and Closure	10 minutes
Prepare for Dismissal	5 minutes
TOTAL	**150 minutes**

FIGURE 4-2

- Children develop the daily routines. They feel the security of knowing what is expected of them and what will come next.
- Communication with parents about daily classroom instruction is made easier.

Above all, be sure that the instructional activities you plan are interrelated and meaningful for students, and that effective instruction is being provided within the interactive writing lesson. It is important to plan a time in the school day to accommodate interactive writing; what you do within that time is even more important.

Creating an Interactive Learning Community

The creation of an interactive learning community in the classroom underlies successful interactive writing. You want children to be able to engage in conversation within a fairly large group. That means learning to take turns, respecting one another, listening to each others' responses.

Seating for Interactive Writing

Most of the time that you work with beginners in interactive writing, children will be seated on the floor or carpet, facing an easel. Teach them to sit "on their bottoms." It is worth taking a little time to have children practice sitting correctly on the carpet and to self-evaluate their behavior. Teach them to leave space in front of the easel so that no one is crowded up against it. Leave enough room so that the children in front can see the whole piece of writing on the easel without having to arch their necks.

Some teachers assign seating spaces in the group area; children sit in a designated spot on a patterned rug, for example, or they put their individual mats on X's or lines taped to the floor. This procedure can be helpful at first, when children are just getting the idea of sitting quietly in their own spaces. But move quickly to help children learn how to arrange themselves with consideration for each other. If you have a large group, those at the back can sit in a row of small chairs so that all children can see the easel; the chairs will also provide a visual and physical border for the group area. Avoid having children sit at their desks during interactive writing. Not only is it difficult for children to see—and concentrate on—an easel from their desks, it is difficult for them to come quickly and efficiently to the easel to contribute. Remember, you want to create a shared space that fosters interaction. Look at the seating area in terms of the following:

- Which way are the children facing? It is best not to have them turned in the direction of an open door, where there might be distractions. It is also best that they have easy visual access to the name chart and word wall.
- Is there room for all children in the class to sit in the group area without touching one another?
- Can all children easily see the easel? Being too close or too far away is a problem. Sit on the floor yourself to get an idea of the kids' view.
- Can children see the name chart, ABC chart, and word wall? You will want to make it easy for them to make visual connections among these displays.

Establishing Classroom Routines

Above all, interactive writing must be a meaningful, enjoyable activity. All the organization in the world will amount to nothing if children simply do not become engaged or interested in the process. On the other hand, you need to establish routine procedures in order to successfully carry out each lesson.

A classroom routine is an "operating procedure." It is an explicit description of how something is done in the classroom. Routines are not lists of rules, and they do not imply punishment. Routines are lessons that must be *taught* to enable a group to learn well together. They can govern the simplest of actions, such as the way that children should sit when in the group area. Don't assume that they all know exactly what is meant by the instruction "sit on your bottom." Have one or two children demonstrate the routine and let other children describe what they are doing. Practice having them sit quietly without touching other children. Encourage them to talk about whether they did a good job during an interactive writing lesson.

Make every routine related to interactive writing part of the lesson plan and the lesson evaluation. Soon, routines will become so much a part of the activity that no one will have to think about them. Here are some of the routines related to interactive writing:

- Leave space in front of the easel for the writer or pointer to stand.
- Sit on your bottom and look at the easel and the teacher.
- Keep hands still in your lap, not touching others.
- Take turns during the composition of the text.
- Listen to others during the composition of the text.
- Offer ideas during text composition.
- Move up to the easel quickly when it is your turn.
- Use the pointer in a responsible and safe way.
- Stand to the side of the easel while pointing.
- Write large enough for others to see.
- Sit down quickly when you have finished.
- Say words slowly with the teacher.
- Read with the child or teacher who is pointing.
- Move out of the way when others are going up to the easel.
- Refer to resources such as charts while constructing the text.

All of the above routines require teaching. Some can be established right away; others will require practice. Routines must be part of interactive writing lessons from the very beginning. They make it possible for you and the children to focus on what's really important—the composition, construction, and revisiting of written text.

Introducing Interactive Writing

For your first interactive writing lesson, start with something very simple as a way of introducing classroom routines. In fact, your main goal for the first few interactive writing lessons will be simply to establish the task. Here are some suggestions for your first experience:

1. Spend just enough time so that you engage the children in what interactive writing is without getting "bogged down" in the process.

2. Create a meaningful shared experience that will help children have something to talk and write about. It's a good idea to relate interactive writing to some area of ongoing study so that the subject matter will be familiar and interesting. It might be something related to a favorite story, or it might fulfill some function in the classroom, such as making labels for the gerbil's cage.

3. Set the goal of writing one or two sentences. If you are working with emergent readers/writers, limit your first time to one sentence or to labels.

4. Engage children in discussion and let them know that you are going to decide together on something to write. Make it clear that it's their job to offer suggestions and that the final decision will be made after you have talked about the topic.

5. Don't let the discussion go on too long; begin to bring together some alternatives. For very inexperienced children, select from their responses one that several children have touched on and that they all understand and can articulate.

6. Have them repeat the message several times, saying, "That's what we're going to write."

7. Explain the task clearly, saying, "This is a different kind of writing." Talk about what

writing together means, emphasizing the following points:

- We all decide what we are going to say.
- We say it together.
- We write it down together.
- Sometimes the teacher writes and sometimes children help with the writing.
- Not everyone will get a turn every day but, over time, everyone will get a chance to contribute to the writing.
- It's important for everyone to pay attention and to reread together.

8. Engage children in the construction of the text, word by word.

9. Select a few teaching points.

10. Reread the text while constructing it.

11. After writing the text, revisit it to emphasize the principle involved (for example, using a word you know to write a new word or saying the word slowly to listen for the sounds).

12. Remind children to use what they learned in their own writing.

Don't be afraid to use interactive writing from the very beginning of school. Establishing the routines for interactive writing will facilitate the creation of a whole-group setting within which children can acquire valuable information that will help them in their independent writing and even reading. Interactive writing gives them the tools to get started.

Step-by-Step Plans for Getting Started

In Figures 4-3 and 4-4 (pages 58–61) we have provided day-by-day suggestions for beginning the year with interactive writing. You will want to adjust these plans according to what you know about the children you are teaching. For example, in the kindergarten plan, we recommend teaching children the routine of doing the name puzzle (a child's name cut into individual letters to be put together left to right). You will want to implement some simple assessments to see what

might be appropriate. It is possible that you have a group of kindergarten children who already know how to write their names very well; on the other hand, you may have a group of first graders who need intensive work with the name puzzle.

The plans we present here are suggestions only, but we do want to point out that some general ideas are embodied in them:

- Through reading aloud and shared reading, build a reservoir of familiarity with written text before you ask children to engage in interactive writing related to the text.
- Revisit texts through reading them aloud, inviting children to join in.
- Use pieces of interactive writing for shared reading.
- Introduce tasks in ways that show children what is expected of them.
- Teach routines explicitly and practice them over several days.
- Build routines that will result in children's independent reading and writing so that you can work with both individuals and groups.

Kindergarten

The day-by-day plan for kindergarten suggests a beginning assessment on which to build the first ten days of activity. You can use systematic procedures for observing children during writing (for example, see Clay 1993), and you can closely observe children during shared reading. Another informal technique is to ask them to write their names and draw a self-portrait. This simple assessment activity will tell you a great deal about how you can use the name chart and name puzzle. If you teach preschool, modify this plan to include more play, songs, and simple games. To simplify the name chart, place each child's photograph on a display with his or her name accompanying it. You can ask children to touch the letters in their names; over time, they can work with magnetic letters to make their names.

A Step-by-Step Plan for Starting Interactive Writing in Kindergarten

- Prior to the first week, gather materials and select two or three books to read aloud to the children.
- At least one book should be a nursery rhyme (single edition or anthology).
- Write a nursery rhyme clearly on a piece of chart paper.

WEEK ONE

DAY 1
Read Aloud. Read selected books aloud to the children at several different times during the day.
Shared Reading. Read the nursery rhyme chart to the children and show them how to read it with you. Point while they read the words together with your support. Read several times.
Interactive Writing. Develop a first-name chart with the children.
Independent Writing. Model independent writing for children on the easel. Have children (at their individual seats) draw a picture and write their names. Observe and comment on each child's piece. Share one or two examples.
Teach Routines. Model and practice routines for using writing materials and then putting them away. Develop routines for independent reading by modeling how to
  - choose a book
  - read (look at) every page from front to back, turning pages
  - put the book away when you are finished
Have the children read books. Comment on their performance.

DAY 2
Read Aloud. Reread selected books aloud to the children. Add a new book or rhyme.
Shared Reading. Read the nursery rhyme chart several times. Read the name chart.
Interactive Writing. Make labels for items in the classroom and/or a list of "ways we work together in our room" (Example: "We do our best work. We take good care of materials. We speak with inside voices.")
Independent Writing. Model independent writing for children on the easel. Have the children draw a picture and write a message. Observe and comment on writing. Begin taking photographs of children as they write. Share one or two examples.
Teach Routines. Model again and practice routines for independent reading. Have the children select and read (look at) books.

DAY 3
Read Aloud. Continue to read to children. Reread favorites and add new books. Build a store of books that can be used as a basis for interactive writing.
Shared Reading. Make another rhyme chart. Read charts and the name chart.
Interactive Writing. Add to classroom labels and/or "how we work together in our room."
Independent Writing. Continue independent drawing/writing and finish taking photographs of each child.
Teach Routines. Practice routines for coming to the group area, sitting, and looking at the easel.

DAY 4
Read Aloud. Continue to read to the children and reread favorites. Invite children to join in on refrains. Discuss and retell the nursery rhyme.
Shared Reading. Read charts and the name chart. Show children how to read the ABC chart.
Interactive Writing. Write the first line of your retelling of the nursery rhyme.
Independent Writing. Model independent writing for children on the easel. Have children draw a picture and write a message. Observe and comment on their approximations in writing. Begin taking photographs of the children as they write. Share one or two examples.
Teach Routines. Model again and practice routines for independent reading. Have children select and read (look at) books.

DAY 5
Read Aloud. Reread selected books aloud to the children. Add new books. Keep on display the books you have read so the children can look at them during independent reading time
Shared Reading. Read the nursery rhyme chart several times. Read the name chart and the ABC chart. Read the interactive writing produced yesterday.
Interactive Writing. Complete retelling of the nursery rhyme.
Independent Writing. Continue drawing/writing and conferring. Share examples.
Teach Routines. Model and practice routines related to coming up to the easel, contributing words/letters, and pointing.

FIGURE 4-3

WEEK TWO

DAY 6
Read Aloud. Reread selected favorites to children. Read a folktale (simple, repetitive, like "The Three Billy Goats Gruff"). Talk about a story in preparation for the retelling.
Shared Reading. Read nursery rhymes, the name chart, ABC chart, and the nursery rhyme completed with the interactive writing.
Interactive Writing. Begin a big book about children in the class; use photographs and names. Write the first part (I see _____. [name])
Independent Writing. Draw a self-portrait and write about yourself.
Teach Routines. Show children how to do the name puzzle and do it all together in a circle.

DAY 7
Read Aloud. Reread selected favorites to children. Reread folktale.
Shared Reading. Read nursery rhymes, the name chart, ABC chart, and interactive writing nursery rhyme.
Interactive Writing. Continue work on the big book about the class (another five to eight children).
Independent Writing. Continue drawing/writing and conferring with individuals.
Teach Routines. Do the name puzzle.

DAY 8
Read Aloud. Reread selected favorites to children. Reread folktale.
Shared Reading. Read nursery rhymes, the name chart, ABC chart, and interactive writing nursery rhyme.
Interactive Writing. Finish the big book about the class.
Independent Writing. Continue drawing/writing and conferring.
Teach Routines. Practice making the name puzzle.

DAY 9
Read Aloud. Reread selected favorites to children. Reread the folktale.
Shared Reading. Read nursery rhymes, the name chart, ABC chart, and interactive writing nursery rhyme, and big book about the class.
Interactive Writing. Begin list of illustrations for a story map about the folktale, for example, characters or elements of setting (e.g., the bridge in "The Three Billy Goats Gruff").
Independent Writing. Continue drawing/writing and conferring.
Teach Routines. Practice making the name puzzle.

DAY 10
Read Aloud. Reread selected favorites to children. Reread folktale.
Shared Reading. Read nursery rhymes, the name chart, ABC chart, and interactive writing nursery rhyme.
Interactive Writing. Finish list of illustrations for story map and reread it. Have children "sign up" for what they want to illustrate.
Independent Writing. Continue drawing/writing and conferring.
Teach Routines. Practice making the name puzzle.

WEEKS THREE AND FOUR

DAYS 11–20
Interactive Writing. Continue working on the story map of folktale. Place illustrations on a large piece of paper (four to eight feet long). Arrange it so that the text can be added to the wall story.
Work on labeling the illustration, one sentence about each.
Move into week three and four using as a guide the timeline example for *Peanut Butter and Jelly* (shown in figure 5.5 on page 79).

FIGURE 4-3, *continued*

A Step-by-Step Plan for Starting Interactive Writing in Grade One

- Prior to the first week, gather materials and select two or three books to read aloud to children. Read a predictable pattern book such as *I Went Walking* and related books about "journeys" or "maps" like *Rosie's Walk, Mouse Views, The Gingerbread Boy*.
- Select one book that is a poem or song. Select a predictable pattern book and a story related to a science or social studies topic (for example, "fall" or "families").
- Gather assessment information on children from the kindergarten teacher.

WEEK ONE

DAY 1
Read Aloud. Read selected books aloud to the children at several different times in the day.
Shared Reading. Engage the children in the shared reading of nursery rhyme charts or other songs, rhymes that the children have experienced in kindergarten or that will be very easy for them. Read the ABC chart.
Interactive Writing. Develop a first-name chart with the children. Make labels for the classroom.
Independent Writing. Model independent writing for children on the easel. Have children (at their individual seats) draw a picture and write their names. Observe and comment on each child's piece. Share one or two examples.
Teach Routines. Model and practice routines for using writing materials and then putting them away.
Practice routines for coming to the group area, sitting, and looking at the easel.
Develop routines for independent reading by modeling how to:
- choose a book.
- read (look at) every page from front to back, turning pages.
- put the book away when you are finished.
Have children read books. Comment on their performance.

DAY 2
Read Aloud. Reread selected books aloud to the children. Add a new book or rhyme. Reread a predictable pattern book and add one book like it.
Shared Reading. Read poem charts, the name chart, and the ABC chart.
Interactive Writing. Write class rules—"how we work together" (For example, "We do our best work. We take good care of materials. We speak with inside voices.")
Independent Writing. Model independent writing for children on the easel. Have children draw a picture of themselves. Observe and comment on writing.
Teach Routines. Model and practice routines for using writing materials, putting them away, and placing written products in a designated place. Model and practice routines for sharing written products. Show children how to use the name puzzle.

DAY 3
Read Aloud. Continue to read to children. Reread favorites and add new books. Add one more book like the original predictable pattern books.
Shared Reading. Read class rules, the name chart, and the ABC chart.
Interactive Writing. Start big book about the class ("Here is _____[name].")
Independent Writing. Continue independent drawing/writing.
Teach Routines. Model and practice previously taught routines that are not fully established. Practice the name puzzle with first and last names.

DAY 4
Read Aloud. Continue to read to children and reread favorites. Invite children to join in on refrains. Discuss books that are related (like the "map" books). Add a new book (like *The Gingerbread Boy*).
Shared Reading. Read nursery rhyme charts, class rules, and the name chart.
Interactive Writing. Finish the big book about the class and reread it.
Independent Writing and Reading. Continue independent writing and drawing. Share some examples. Continue independent reading.
Teach Routines. Model and practice routines for using one center or independent activity. Have one group practice while the rest of the children are writing or engaging in independent reading. Model and practice routines for reading print on the walls and the big book about the class. Do the name puzzle—first and last names.

DAY 5
Read Aloud. Reread selected books aloud to the children. Create a display of books you are reading aloud so that children can find them during independent reading time. Add a poem, written on chart paper.
Shared Reading. Read the poem to children several times and invite them to join in. Read the name chart and the big book about the class.
Interactive Writing. Combine art and retelling of a nursery rhyme (for example, make Old Mother Hubbard's Cupboard and label ingredients. Add last names to the name on chart).
Independent Writing. Continue drawing/writing and conferring. Share examples.
Teach Routines. Model and practice routines for using one more center or independent activity.
Do the name puzzle—first and last names.

FIGURE 4-4

A Step-by-Step Plan for Starting Interactive Writing in Grade One

continued

WEEK TWO

DAY 6

Read Aloud. Reread books previously read.

Shared Reading. Read nursery rhymes, the name chart, ABC chart, and the nursery rhyme completed with interactive writing.

Interactive Writing. Tour the school or walk around the block. Decide on the format for interactive writing—a big book or map. Together make a list of what the children saw on the walk. Sign up to illustrate items on the list.

Independent Writing. Have children draw a picture and write about themselves.

Teach Routines. Practice using centers. Do the name puzzle—first and last names. Put the name puzzle together without a model.

DAY 7

Read Aloud. Reread selected favorites to children. Add a new book.

Shared Reading. Read nursery rhymes, the name chart, ABC chart, and a nursery rhyme.

Interactive Writing. Read the list. Work on illustrations and then place them on the map or on pages of the big book. Label the map or write two pages of the big book (for example, "We went walking. We saw _____.")

Independent Writing. Continue drawing/writing and conferring with individuals.

Teach Routines. Practice using centers and put out the name puzzle without a model.

DAY 8

Read Aloud. Reread books.

Shared Reading. Read nursery rhymes, the name chart, and previous interactive writing.

Interactive Writing. Begin writing sentences to place on the wall map—"We saw _____"—or write several more pages of the big book.

Independent Writing. Continue drawing/writing and conferring.

Teach Routines. Complete the name puzzle as needed. Begin to teach routines for using the word study center.

DAY 9

Read Aloud. Reread books.

Shared Reading. Read nursery rhymes, the name chart, ABC chart, big book about the class, and pages of the new book under construction (or wall map).

Interactive Writing. Finish sentences for wall map or big book.

Independent Writing. Continue drawing/writing and conferring.

Teach Routines. Add a minilesson on letter sorting. Model and practice routines for using the ABC or word study center to engage in letter sorting; emphasize putting letters away.

DAY 10

Read Aloud. Reread books.

Shared Reading. Read nursery rhymes, the name chart, ABC chart, big books, and wall map.

Interactive Writing. Select another book (for example, a folktale like "The Gingerbread Man") and discuss it. Together decide on a format for writing an original story related to the tale. For example, children might start with a list of people the Gingerbread Man ran away from and write their own version.

Independent Writing. Continue drawing/writing and conferring.

Teach Routines. Conduct a minilesson on letters; use sorting. Model and practice routines for using the ABC or word study center to engage in letter sorting; emphasize putting letters away. Share what the children have discovered about letters.

WEEKS THREE AND FOUR

DAYS 11–20

Interactive Writing. Continue working on the folktale you have selected. Make illustrations and write sentences about each event.

Move into week three and four using as a guide the timeline example for *Peanut Butter and Jelly* (see Figure 5–5 on page 79).

FIGURE 4–4, *continued*

Over the first ten days, important routines such as independent reading, using writing materials, and interactive writing are explicitly taught and practiced. The first ten days provide a range of experiences for children so that they gain control of letters and sounds in their names. Together the children produce a big book about the class (twenty to twenty-five sentences, all beginning with the phrase "We see . . . "). This book will be a pleasurable experience for the children to reread because it is all about themselves. In addition, most of the children will learn the words *we* and *see*. In this very simple text, they will have the opportunity to practice word-by-word matching and left-to-right directionality. Reading nursery rhymes and folktales provides a literary base for the production of texts in interactive writing that the children can later read. As children grow in their ability to engage in independent reading, they can also use some of the interactive writing that they have produced.

First Grade

As a first-grade teacher, you will have more information about what children already know about literacy when they come into your classroom. Of course, some children will be new to the school and others may have changed over the summer; so you will want to use observation and assessment to get a clearer picture.

During the first ten days of first grade, focus on firmly establishing children's awareness of the letters in their names and connecting those letters to sounds. Classroom routines should be taught and practiced, especially those that allow children to engage in independent work at their desks and in centers or work areas. The routines of independent reading and writing should be firmly in place by the end of the first two weeks. First graders will be able to move faster in their progress than prekindergartners or kindergartners, but they still need explicit teaching and modeling. In interactive writ-

ing, like in kindergarten, we start with building language through reading aloud and some simple experiences; but first graders will make more rapid progress. By the end of the first ten days, children will have produced a big book about the class, class rules, a wall map with labels, and sentences (or a big book) based on a book about a journey and their own experiences. They will have learned the basic procedures and routines of interactive writing.

Communicating with Administrators and Other Teachers

If interactive writing is new to the educators in your school, you will want to have some professional discussion with your colleagues about the process and how it works. You may get questions about the interactive writing work that you display in your classroom or in the hallway. It will be obvious that the writing, while legible, is not perfect. Some of your colleagues may not even realize that the children contributed some of the writing.

Invite grade-level colleagues and your principal to visit your classroom. Show them some of the examples of writing that you and your students have produced. Explain the values of interactive writing. Be sure to specify how interactive writing helps children learn phonics and spelling, and even more important, how it provides a model for learning the purposes and structure of writing. Be sure not to "overdo" your explanation or enthusiasm for the process. It is enough to say that you are learning one new way to help children learn to be better writers. Extend an open invitation to visit your classroom.

If the discussions go further, you can refer administrators to Chapter 15, in which we discuss the rationale and research base for interactive writing. Administrators and teachers may also be interested in reading Chapter 5, in which we discuss essential elements of interactive writing.

Communicating with Parents

It is helpful to have an open house night during which you can talk with parents about interactive writing. During this time, have lots of examples on the walls of the classroom. The more your room looks "full" of children's group and individual writing and artwork, the more positive parents will feel about the atmosphere of the classroom.

One school has a "love of learning night" to inform parents about the total instructional program. Sharon Esswein provides a demonstration of interactive writing with a small group of children. Afterward, she talks with the parents about the process. Parents have a chance to ask questions. In our experience, observers are very pleased and often surprised about how much thought the group of children can generate and how much they can contribute to the written product. They also love to see the children read and reread the piece. This demonstration has multiple values:

■ It helps parents understand an instructional tool that is frequently used in their child's classroom.
■ It establishes the high value placed on children's writing.
■ Parents see the importance of a meaningful text to the children.
■ Important activities, such as pointing to establish word-by-word matching and rereading, are modeled for parents.
■ Parents see and appreciate that their children are learning to read and write.

Letters and Newsletters

You may want to send a letter home to parents explaining interactive writing (see Figure 4-5 on page 64) early in the school year. Many teachers send home regular newsletters to parents reporting on the children's learning activities. Typically, parents respond very positively to these newsletters.

You can easily include several examples of interactive writing in your newsletter. You can take a photograph of one of the pieces of writing your students have produced and then photocopy it or scan it into the computer. Parents will be delighted to see their own children's group product in the newsletter. You can list the values of interactive writing as we discussed them in Chapter 1; you can also provide a brief description of the purpose of the particular examples you present. Make it clear that interactive writing is not an "activity," but it is a way to help children learn what it is like to be writers. And, children are writing about interesting topics—to talk about themselves, to extend literature, and to record ideas in science, math, or social studies investigations.

Assessing Your Own Teaching

We know that any time you begin a new approach, you will develop your own practice with respect to that approach over a period of time. Not everything can be implemented right away and not everything is immediately just as you would like it to be. The idea is to get started and then to continually reflect on and refine your teaching. Collegial discussion will be your best tool for support in this learning process. The Self-Assessment Rubric included at the end of this book (see Appendix 3) is a valuable tool for discussion. The checklist covers a range of factors related to the effective use of interactive writing. You may find that you need to focus on logistics and practical aspects of management. Once those components are in place, you will want to think about and evaluate teaching decisions so that your work is more efficient and effective. This rubric can be the basis for professional development work with colleagues as well as for your own reflection. It underscores the fact that as teachers, we are learners.

Suggestions for Professional Development

1. Identify several routines that you think are critical to your success in implementing interactive writing.

A Sample Letter for Parents

1. Establish the purpose of the letter and the goal of improving writing instruction. ✂

2. Define interactive writing and describe it. ✂

3. Provide and discuss an example. ✂

4. Explicitly establish the values of interactive writing. ✂

5. Communicate that interactive writing helps children learn conventional spelling and other aspects of print. ✂

6. Communicate that children are spending some classroom time on work that they will not be bringing home. ✂

7. Issue an invitation. ✂

Dear Parents,

In our classroom this year, we are going to learn many interesting things. The children will learn to read and write and to use reading and writing to share their learning with each other. All children will write every day. A goal of our school is excellence in writing.

One of the ways that I will help them learn is called interactive writing. Interactive writing is a group writing process. The children and I think of an idea together. We take turns writing the words and parts of words, and supplying the punctuation. Children reread what we have written to check to be sure that the writing can be understood.

Here is an example of interactive writing.

In this example, as you can see, children wrote some of the letters. They were learning how to say the words slowly and think about the first sounds and letters.

Interactive writing has been shown to be a good way to teach children how to write.
- Children learn to express their ideas in writing.
- Children learn letter names, handwriting, and skills.
- Children learn phonics because they see the connections between letters and sounds in words.
- Children learn how to spell many words that they can use for themselves in their own writing.

As you can see in the example, we use correct spelling for interactive writing. Children are learning that words are spelled the same way every time. They are also learning how to use space and punctuation. In their own writing, they will not always spell words correctly, as they are in the early stage of learning. Over time, they will spell many more words correctly in their own writing.

Children will not be bringing home these large pieces of interactive writing because we use them as resources in the classroom. They will bring home their own writing. You will see that they are using what they learn in an independent way!

We invite you to visit our classroom to see more examples of our interactive writing. The children are very proud of their beautiful writing projects.

Sincerely,

FIGURE 4-5

∎ Use the list of routines mentioned in this chapter or generate others.

∎ With a grade-level partner, break down the routine into small steps: What exactly does it mean? How could you explain it to children? What do you need to demonstrate to children?

∎ Make a lesson plan for teaching and practice the routine. Make the plan cover several days or even a week.

2. Discuss the step-by-step plans for kindergarten and/or grade one with grade-level colleagues. Make adjustments in the plan based on

∎ knowledge of the children you teach, their understandings and experience

∎ your teaching schedule

∎ priorities in your curriculum.

3. Share the plan with grade-level colleagues and ask for feedback. Then, implement the plan for five days. Meet again to reflect on the process.

∎ What routines have been established?

∎ What do children already know how to do?

∎ What routines need further teaching?

4. Prepare a parent letter or newsletter about interactive writing. Ask your grade-level colleagues to read the letter and give feedback on its clarity and the appropriateness of the example. If possible ask some members of the community to read the letter as well. Revise the letter or newsletter article.

5. As individuals, read the goals and descriptions in the Self-Assessment Rubric (Appendix 3). Indicate the description that most closely describes your teaching. Discuss your assessment with colleagues.

6. Meet a month later to share your self-assessment again, discussing your growth and problem-solving areas of challenge.

Sharing the Pen with Young Writers

Interactive writing is a dynamic literacy event in which reading and writing come together. Children participate in every element of the writing process—deciding on a topic, thinking about the general scope and form of the writing, determining the specific text to write, and writing it word by word, letter by letter. You and the children work together in an interconnected process that results in a product that you will all prize and use in many ways. Typically, it takes several days to produce a piece of interactive writing, and the product is read many times over the duration of the school year. Through this process, children learn that it is worth the effort to plan and return to a piece of writing several times. They learn to make simple short-term goals and reach them. In Section Two, we use examples to provide an overview of the essential elements of interactive writing.

Essential Elements of Interactive Writing

Interactive writing takes many forms and is used in many ways. Some interactive writing sessions are quick and spontaneous. For example, a group of children might need to write a quick thank-you note to a visiting speaker, label items for classroom use, or create a list of illustrations to be placed on a story board. Interactive writing is a functional tool that can be used at any time during the school day. The advantages of using interactive writing in this spontaneous way are the following:

I Children can see writing as a support for their goals and activities.
I Writing is placed in a functional role, integral to learning.
I The product is very useful, at least in the short term.

At other times, you and the children might be working on a project such as making a class book about a favorite folktale, creating a wall map of a story with labels and an attached description, or keeping records of growing plants. In these cases, interactive writing is a planned part of the ongoing classroom work, with time set aside each day to work on the project. The advantages of planned projects are the following:

I Children have the experience of returning to a piece of work day after day, remembering what they did previously and adding to the piece.
I The product of the writing is something that represents a long-term body of work; children are very proud of the results and can see that sustained effort over time really produces a good product.
I The product is usually a longer piece that has many uses throughout the year.

Both situations offer the potential for children to learn a great deal about composing and constructing text as well as to learn how words work. Sometimes a long-term project that focuses on a theme will include several different kinds of interactive writing. In the example presented in Chapter 1, we saw Ida and her students working within the context of a long-term study of nutrition. They had heard many stories about food and experimented with shopping and preparing foods. Throughout the process there were many learning conversations about how food contributes to health. Let's look at another piece of interactive writing that was part of the same inquiry process.

Ida's Class Revisited

After the children made their peanut butter and jelly sandwiches, the teacher next door said that she would really like to have the directions for making the sandwiches so that she could take them home and share them with her young daughter. The question seemed natural to the children since many in the class really had not known how to make peanut butter and jelly sandwiches before the exercise.

Ida invited the children to compose these directions (Figure 5-1), thinking about each step they had taken when they made the sandwiches. She also asked them to demonstrate the procedure, repeating the actions they engaged in when Ida read aloud Nadine Westcott's *Peanut Butter and Jelly*. Thus, Ida used the children's background knowledge, their experience with books, and a concrete activity to form the foundation for this piece of writing. They also had to think about the audience or readers of their work because they were preparing a set of written directions for others to follow.

In this interactive writing session, Ida asked the children what the directions had to say to do first. Shelta said that the first step was to put the jelly on the bread. Several children agreed that this was the first step. They decided on the first sentence—*Put the jelly on the bread*—and said it aloud together. They repeated the sentence twice more, counting the number of words on their fingers as they said the sentence. (In this instance, the teacher had made the decision to have the children count words as a way of helping them separate their speech flow into word units. Later, counting words would not be necessary.) As they finished saying the sentence the second time, several children contributed the first letter of the writing: *p*.

IDA: *P. P for what?*

DONALD: *Put*

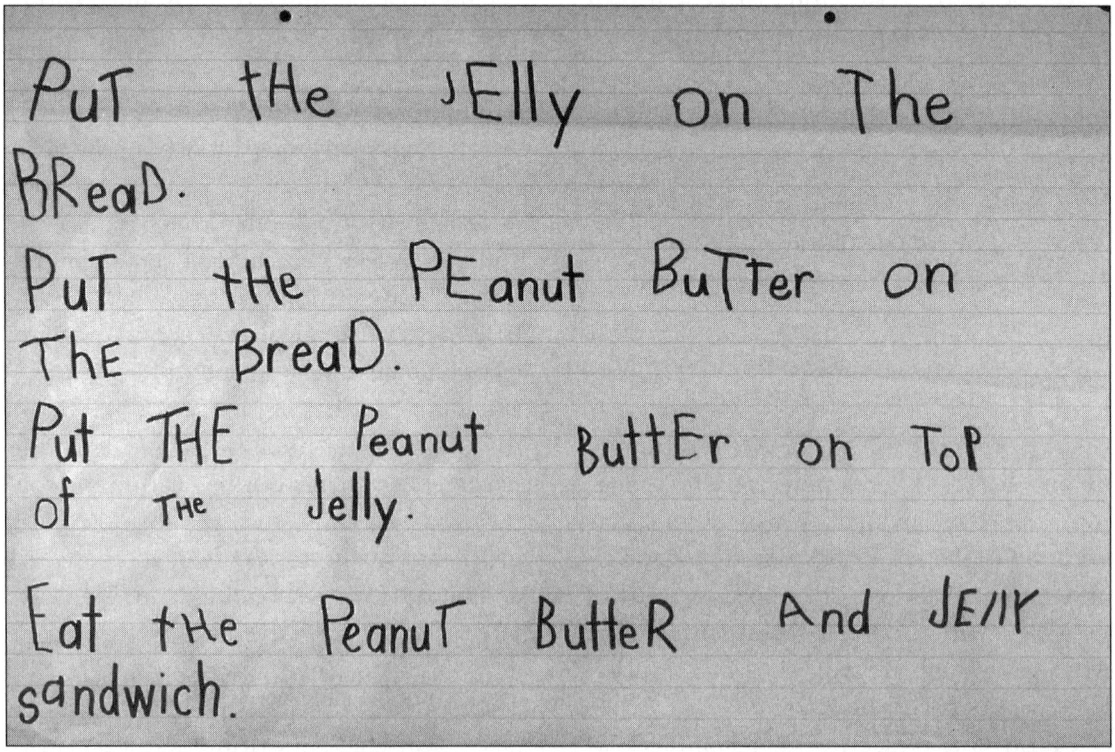

FIGURE 5–1   Directions for Making a Peanut Butter and Jelly Sandwich

IDA: Donald says *p* for *put*. Ashley, is he right?

ASHLEY: (Nods her head in affirmation.)

IDA: What sentence are we writing?

IDA AND CHILDREN: *Put the jelly on the bread.*

IDA: Donald, before you make a *p*, show me where you are going to start writing.

DONALD: (Approaches easel and points to upper-left-hand corner.)

IDA: Now, what are we going to put there?

DONALD: *P*.

IDA: The *p* is for what word?

DONALD: *Put*.

IDA: (Hands Donald the pen.) Can you make a *p*? Do you know how?

DONALD: (Nods his head in affirmation, writes *p*, then returns to his seat.)

IDA: Oh! A beautiful *p*!

IDA: Now watch my mouth and say *put*. Say it slowly with me.

CHILDREN: *Put*. (Children speak the word slowly with the teacher.)

TYSON: *T*!

IDA: Yes, I hear a *t*. Tyson, come up here and write your *t* at the end of *put*. (Ida supplies the *u*.)

TYSON: (Writes in a *t*.)

IDA: Wow! Look at that *t*. Don't go away. I want you to stay right here and point. What does that say?

CHILDREN: (As Tyson points) *Put*.

IDA: What's next?

With Ida's support, one child wrote the word *the* and they read the sentence again from the beginning, generating the word *jelly* as the part to be written next. During the writing of *jelly*, other children connected the word to several names, *John, Joshua,* and *Jenny*. (During the writing of the grocery list, Ida had drawn their attention to this connection; this time, they made the connection themselves.)

IDA: What do we want to write?

CHILDREN: *Jelly*.

IDA: John. Where's John? John, come up here.

CHILDREN: *J, J*.

IDA: (As children say *J*, she speaks to John.) Guess what. The next word is…

JOHN: *Jelly*.

IDA: *Jelly*.

CHILDREN: (Repeating names) John, Joshua, Jenny.

IDA: That's right. John, Joshua, Jenny, jelly. Iris, can you come up here and help us out? There is something else we need to include.

CHILDREN: A space. It's a new word.

IRIS: (Puts her hand on chart to save a space and allow John to start the new word in the right spot.)

IDA: (to John) What letter are you making?

JOHN: *J*.

IDA: *J* for what?

CHILDREN: *Jelly*.

JOHN: (Writes *j* on chart.)

IDA: Very nice *j*. Thank you.

Here is the complete set of directions written by Ida and the children in the exact line arrangement:

Put the jelly on the
bread.
Put the peanut butter on
the bread.
Put the peanut butter on top
of the jelly.
Eat the peanut butter and jelly
sandwich.

The set of directions was written over several days, with children making contributions such as easy-to-hear consonants at the beginning and ending of words, particularly those that linked to their names, as well as some high-frequency words such as *the* and *on*. Ida wrote most of the harder and longer words, such as *peanut*.

Over the three days it took to write the directions, the entire piece, up to the point of new construction, was reread so that the children could recall the text. Each sentence was reread while it was being written. And the piece was reread in entirety after finishing the fourth sentence. Ida called children's attention to the need for spacing between words and between lines. They used periods at the end of each sentence and began each new sentence on the left. Formatting decisions such as these help the children read the piece of writing independently later on. The teacher was constantly making decisions based on

■ what she knew the children knew (for example, sound-letter relationships using the names of children in the class)

■ what they almost knew (for example, some high-frequency words such as *the*)

■ what she wanted to teach them to do (for example, use space to define words and say words slowly).

At the end of each day of writing, Ida briefly summarized learning for the children by calling their attention to some new understandings. Here is a brief segment of their conversation on day one:

IDA: Today when we wanted to write a word, we said the word slowly. That helped us think about what letters we needed to write, didn't it? So what can you do when you want to write a word in your journal today?

CHILD: Say it!

IDA: Yes, but say it very slowly.

CHILD: Think about names.

IDA: That's right. You said the word *jelly* today and then the name chart helped us to write the first letter *j* didn't it? If you were writing a word like *dog*, whose name would help you?

CHILDREN: Donald!

On day two, Ida asked the children to look again at the directions and to evaluate their use of space.

IDA: Look at the directions we wrote. We really did a good job with our space today, didn't we? Can someone come up and show us a place where we left just the right amount of space between words?

JOSH: I know. (He walks to the chart and points.)

On day three, Ida again asked the children to consider details in the piece of interactive writing. This time, she focused on the high-frequency word *the*, a word that she wants the children to be able to use and recognize in their independent writing and reading.

IDA: You know that word *the*? We used that word many times when we wrote our directions. Let's see if we can find *the* every time we wrote it.

Several children pointed to the word *the* at different places in the text. Ida then took a small card and wrote the word *the* on it. She placed the card on the word wall under the *Tt* section and reminded the children that they might want to use the word *the* in their own writing.

On her word wall, Ida had placed library pockets under each letter of the alphabet. The library pocket contained copies of the wall words on index cards. If children found that copying the word from the word wall was too difficult, they could take a word card to the writing table, use it to write the word, and then return the card to the pocket.

The Elements of Interactive Writing

To analyze the structure of interactive writing, we have to see it embedded in learning experiences over days or weeks of time. There is no such thing as a set lesson sequence to be followed every day; yet interactive writing is highly organized and structured. Let's look at the example presented above from a structural point of view, using the eight essential elements included in Figure 5-2.

Providing a Base of Active Learning Experiences

Children's rich store of experiences create the foundation for interactive writing.

■ Some knowledge is *personal*; children bring a pool of experience from their homes and communities, which they

Essential Elements of Interactive Writing
1. Provide a base of active learning experiences.
2. Talk to establish purpose.
3. Compose the text.
4. Construct the text.
5. Reread, revise, and proofread the text.
6. Revisit the text to support word solving.
7. Summarize the learning.
8. Extend the learning.

FIGURE 5–2 **Essential Elements of Interactive Writing**

share through talk. Some experiences are fairly common to the group; others are quite individual.

▮ Some knowledge is gained through *shared experiences* in the classroom. For example, learning conversations take place around the ongoing active learning fostered by the teacher. The context can be taking a field trip, recording an experiment, examining a rock collection, receiving a gift, thanking a visitor, or any other kind of common learning experience. The topics of these learning experiences will vary widely depending on the curriculum of the school and the interests of the children and the teacher. Experience is most powerful for student learning when it includes exploration, discovery, and talk.

▮ Exploration of children's literature is another kind of shared experience. A special kind of language experience is provided when the teacher reads aloud to children from a varied and rich collection. This collection includes poems, rhymes, chants, stories, informational books, and many other kinds of texts. Books can be experienced through shared reading as well. *Literary experiences* are often connected to the active

learning experiences mentioned above, and also have value in themselves as the study of literature.

Experience certainly played a role in Ida's work. The experience was ongoing; it was not simply introduced as a "one-shot" deal so that children would have something to write about. Ida drew from children's personal knowledge as well as their knowledge gained through shared experience and literature.

Talking to Establish Purpose

Classroom discourse supports children's learning. When they engage in discourse about a variety of topics, children use language to communicate with each other, and at the same time learn how to use language in new ways. They expand their language knowledge in important ways because they have new models of language (from peers, from the teacher, and from literature) and because they have new subjects for discussion. Developing oral language through experiences is a primary goal of the language arts curriculum. In a sense, the teacher and children are building an oral text that they continue to expand and share.

Meaningful talk permeates every learning experience that goes on in the classroom. It is obvious that Ida and the children were talking about food and health through ongoing active experiences and while they read books together. When we talk about establishing a purpose in interactive writing, we refer to *specific talk* designed to help the children understand and decide on a function and format for the text. Focused talk helps children to direct their attention to the task at hand. Establishing purpose is an extremely important part of the learning process in interactive writing. This powerful tool helps young children learn that writing serves many different functions. The list served one purpose; the set of directions served another. The two pieces of writing were formatted in different ways depending on what would be most helpful to the readers who would use them.

As a teacher, you understand how writing is used functionally and you see the potential for using writing as it emerges from the learning activities in the classroom. Through specific talk, you suggest to the children that writing can be helpful in some way. In the case of Ida's class, another teacher was involved in asking for the directions for making a sandwich, a request that seemed credible to the children. After establishing a purpose, you and the children decide on the genre or type of writing that will best serve that purpose.

Composing the Text

Having built on a foundation of experience and established a purpose through talk, you and the children are ready to compose an actual text. For this task, children must

▮ think about the message they want to convey

▮ think about the audience who will read the text

▮ form labels, phrases, or sentences (depending on the purpose) that clearly communicate the message

▮ develop an understanding of the constraints that writing places on language; that is, that writing can only occur within certain conventions of space and time

▮ draw on their knowledge of how written language is structured and patterned (for example, the syntax of written language is different from oral language)

▮ draw on their knowledge of how written text is organized and structured (for example, with repeating sentences)

▮ think about the organization of the piece and how best to sequence ideas.

Constructing the Text

Once the text is composed, you and the children together write the text, letter by letter (or letter cluster by letter cluster), word by word, placing graphic symbols in order across the page from left to right, moving back to the left to begin new lines, and leaving appropriate space between words and between lines. Within this process, young children must think about directional movements needed to make specific letters with fine details (such as how many left to right lines make up the capital letter E). They must attend to all of this detail while at the same time keeping in mind the purpose they have set and the message that they have composed.

At the same time that they are actually writing down letters and words, the children are thinking about how they are using language to communicate meaning. There will be diversions as either you or the children direct attention to particular features of words and talk about them. For example, during the list writing, Ida had drawn children's attention to the fact that *jelly* started like *Joshua* and *Jenny*. During writing of the directions, several children noticed and commented that *jelly* started like *Joshua*. One child wrote the *j*; others observed and connected it visually to the names on the name chart that began with *j*. This might seem like a simple connection, but remember that these children are just beginning to weave a web of understanding around the alphabet and words. To make this connection they had to

▮ hear a particular sound at the beginning of the word *jelly*

- remember a particular sound at the beginning of several names
- connect the two sounds as similar even though they appear in different words
- visually notice the letter *j* at the beginning of names
- perceive the form of the *j* with its distinctive features
- remember the curving movement needed to make the *j* on the chart
- locate the *j* at the beginning of a word, with space before it and letters after it

These first connections are complex but children are learning more than the sound of *j* and the form of the letter *j*. They are learning how to learn about print. They are learning how to look, where to look, and what to look at, and they are connecting that knowledge to what they hear and what their fingers do.

Rereading, Revising, and Proofreading the Text

Children learn to reread as a way of remembering the whole text and anticipating the next word in a phrase or sentence. At first, the rereading requires the children to reread the whole piece or sentence. Eventually, children can simply reread the previous phrase or word either out loud or silently. Ultimately, rereading to anticipate the next word may rarely be necessary.

Sometimes during the rereading, children suggest revisions to clarify the meaning. Revision demonstrates to the children that a writer constantly checks the text to be sure it says what he or she wants it to say. Rereading is built into the interactive writing process, which encourages children to routinely reread in their independent writing. This self-monitoring routine helps children to keep the whole message in mind as they work on the details of inscribing, and helps them double-check their writing as they go.

Ida explicitly prompted children to reread several times in the example above because they were just beginning to learn the routines of writing. At this point, she also

asked them to think about how rereading helped them, and encouraged them to use this technique to check their own writing.

Proofreading monitors the text production *during* writing, but it also takes place *after* writing. For instance, you can decide to change a word or a letter or to redo letter formation to improve legibility. Sometimes, as children are rereading a text that has been produced previously, they notice that some improvement is needed (for example, children who are more aware of the role of lower- and uppercase letters might spontaneously notice that there is a capital letter in the middle of a word and ask to change it). The important thing here is not to change the message, but to allow for small edits.

We have linked rereading, revising, and proofreading here because we see them as ongoing, simultaneous processes for these young children as they are producing and using texts in interactive writing. Later in elementary school, proofreading may be more formal and may take place after a piece has been drafted and redrafted. The roots of good proofreading are in these first encounters with text. Children are learning that writers

- constantly check their work as they write
- make sure the text is legible
- recognize the importance of conventions (such as spelling, capitalization, punctuation, and spacing) to assist the reader
- constantly check on the meaning to be sure the text is clear
- check the text against their sense of the structure of language (grammar).

Revisiting the Text to Support Word Solving

Sometimes, after interactive writing, you may wish to take a few minutes to revisit and reinforce particular concepts related to solving words. Word solving means gaining an understanding of the inner workings of words—principles about how words work—so that children can figure out unfamiliar words as they read and spell words as they write (see Pinnell and Fountas 1998 for more information). Becoming a word solver is an inquiry process; children learn how to learn about words. We want them to be able to

∎ notice that some words are like other words in important ways
∎ recognize familiar parts of words
∎ connect words by meaning or by how they look.

A minute or two of quick word study is a powerful minilesson after the interactive writing session. Children have a familiar text with which they have been deeply involved, which they can use as a learning tool. You might, for example, introduce word work after interactive writing by saying something like, "Look at our writing for today. What words start with *b*?"

Summarizing the Learning
Summarizing reinforces what has been learned; children's reflection on what and how they have learned enables them to understand their own learning. Briefly, you call the children's attention to the key understandings that were reinforced and/or those that were new. Do this in a way that helps children use the knowledge in their own learning. Summarizing helps children to consolidate their understanding and think about how they can apply new understandings to their future work. Ida, for example, drew children's attention to the process of saying words slowly, looking for the particular letters or symbols on the name chart, and also evaluating the use of space. She also placed the useful high-frequency word *the* on the word wall, explaining that it would help them in their writing and in their spelling of words such as *then, them,* and *they.* One brief summary will not solidify every child's knowledge, but consistently returning to the text will support the transfer of understanding.

Extend the Learning
Writing is a tool used for a specific purpose. In the process of interactive writing, it is important for children to understand this fun-

damental characteristic of writing. Because the pieces that they produce in interactive writing are most effective when they are part of ongoing learning, it helps to have children use the text in many ways. For example:

∎ The text may be placed on the wall for reading independently.
∎ The text can be used for shared reading.
∎ The text may be reproduced or even typed for children to reread and illustrate.
∎ The children might make illustrations for the text so that it can become a wall book or a smaller book.
∎ The text can be the beginning of a mural onto which labels will be pasted.
∎ The text can be used in a functional way, for example to help children remember a process or an event.
∎ The text can be sent to another audience (for example, another class or the principal) for a response.
∎ The text may be used as part of the documentation of an ongoing experience and may lead to the production of other texts in interactive writing.
∎ Individual children may use the text as a resource for developing their own similarly structured texts or to find a word that they do not know how to spell.

In Ida's classroom, the interactive writing pieces were read many times. Ida and the children extended learning by using the list to check the grocery items and sending the directions to the teacher who requested them, and by recalling other foods and comparing them. They also wrote a survey question using interactive writing. Figure 5-3 shows the tabulation of the results.

Ms. Ramirez's Class
Arising as part of a "farm theme," this example of interactive writing from Carmen Ramirez's class illustrates children using repeated language structures to label farm animals and note something important about each one (Figure 5-4 on page 78, see also Ap-

pendix 5). The class worked on *La Granja* for over a week, generating one or two lines each day. The text, translated, is:

> The Farm *(label)*
> The Stable *(label)*
> I am a sheep and I supply wool.
> I am a cow and I supply milk.
> I am a horse and I am here to ride.
> I am a duck and I can swim.
> I am a hen and I supply eggs.

The resulting text is readable because of its simple organization and simple language, which consists of words that the children had heard and said over and over. The finished text also contains a high level of picture support. Notice that every line of the text begins with the easy words *Yo so un*. In revisiting the text, the teacher has the opportunity to help children link letters in animal names to letters in their own names. The complexity in each sentence comes toward the end of the line, when readers will have built a sense of meaning and structure and can connect the ideas to their background knowledge. This text will provide reading challenge for these children for a long time to come.

We have described eight elements of interactive writing. This list is not meant to be prescriptive or rigidly sequenced; rather, it is a guide for thinking about the many complex aspects of the process that provide learning opportunities. Are the elements meant to be sequential? Yes and no. Certainly there is an underlying sequence suggested here, but it is also evident that elements like "rereading" are present throughout the process. We see this list of elements as a conceptual tool for teachers to use in planning and reflecting on their experiences with interactive writing.

Continuous Learning Through Interactive Writing

We have referred to examples here involving groups of emergent writers. Their learning is continuous and interrelated, with interactive

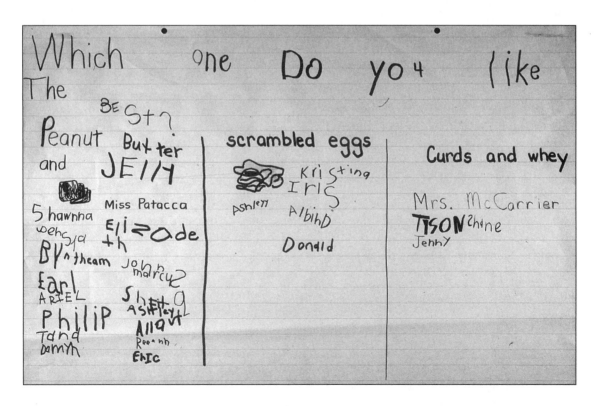

FIGURE 5–3   Results of Survey Question

FIGURE 5–4 *La Granja*

writing being an integral process in that learning. Figure 5-5 (pages 79 and 80) presents a summary of the series of events within which our main example is nested. We have indicated where elements from our list were evident within this sequence.

The timeline in this figure presents a picture of twelve days of instruction. The lessons were not lengthy; they ranged from fifteen to twenty-five minutes, but the experience had a cohesiveness over time. Think, for example, of the range of experiences the children had over the twelve-day period in approximately 150 to 200 total minutes of instruction. They

- engaged in many meaningful conversations that expanded their use of language
- participated in discourse, in the process learning rules such as turn taking, listening, and staying on the topic
- returned to a piece of work day after day, remembering what went before, and, finally, reaching a culminating point for various pieces of writing

- heard two stories read aloud several times and joined in as the texts became familiar
- talked about and responded to the stories, expanding vocabulary and language use in the process
- dramatized the story events, attending to sequence and the structure of text
- recorded the steps of an event to communicate the information to others
- learned that writing has a purpose
- learned about how to compose and arrange text in different genres (e.g. list, directions, survey question)
- learned how to check written work for its clarity in communicating meaning to an audience and for appropriate use of conventions
- engaged in a meaningful experience, learning important content (health)
- learned how to engage in sound analysis and in recording or representing sounds with letters
- learned how to use something they knew (e.g., a name) to work out a new word.

Timeline for Learning Activities Related to Interactive Writing

Day	Learning Activity	Element
DAY 1–5	Talked about and studied nutrition. Sampled scrambled eggs in conjunction with shared reading of *Humpty Dumpty*.	Experience
	Read aloud *Peanut Butter and Jelly*.	Experience
DAY 6	Read aloud *Peanut Butter and Jelly*.	Experience
	Decided to make peanut butter and jelly sandwiches. Talked about the need for a shopping list.	Talk
	Generated items for the shopping list and wrote several on the list.	Compose Construct
	Shared reading of the list to point of construction.	Rereading
DAY 7	Read aloud *Peanut Butter and Jelly*.	Experience
	Finished recording the shopping list.	Compose Construct
	Read the shopping list while writing and after it was finished.	Reread
	Ida took the shopping list to buy food and supplies.	Experience
DAY 8	Read aloud *Peanut Butter and Jelly*.	Experience
	Unpacked groceries; found items on the list and checked them off on the list.	Experience Rereading
	Made peanut butter and jelly sandwiches.	Experience
	Next-door teacher came in to sample sandwiches and asked for directions. Children decided to write directions.	Talk
	Negotiated and composed the message.	Compose
	Children record the first sentence. (*Put the jelly on the bread.*)	Construct Reread
	Ida asked children to find a word that starts like *John*. Then she asked them to find a word that ends like *Donald*. Both words were located by a child.	Revisit
	Ida reminded children to say words slowly and connect them to names when they do their own writing.	Summarize
DAY 9	Read aloud *Peanut Butter and Jelly*.	Experience
	Acted out the steps in making a sandwich.	Experience
	Shared reading of the first step in their directions.	Rereading
	Continued to add to directions for making sandwiches; sentences 2 and 3.	Compose Construct Reread

FIGURE 5-5

Timeline for Learning Activities Related to Interactive Writing, *continued*

Day	Learning Activity	Element
DAY 9	Shared reading of the directions.	Reread
	Ida asked the children to locate the word *the* several times in the text.	Revisit
	Ida asked children to find spaces in the text and reminded them to use spaces in their own writing.	Summarize
DAY 10	Read aloud *Peanut Butter and Jelly.*	Experience
	Acted out making a sandwich.	Experience
	Shared reading of the first three steps in the directions.	Rereading
	Wrote the last step in the directions.	Compose Construct
	Ida asked children to look for words that begin with *p*. They found *put* and *peanut*. (Required distinguishing between beginning and ending of word as well as finding letter in a word.) Ida asked children to locate *the* in the text. She had them trace the word *the* on the carpet in front of them.	Reread Revisit
	Ida placed *the* on a card on the word wall and reminds children that they can find it there if they need it in their writing.	Summarize
DAY 11	Read aloud *Peanut Butter and Jelly.* Reflected on previous experiences with food, including scrambled eggs and curds and whey.	Experience
	Invited children to find out what the favorite for the group was. They decided to write a survey question.	Talk
	Shaped the survey question: *Which one do you like the best?*	Compose
	Wrote the survey question interactively.	Construct
	Teacher wrote the names of the three foods *except* for the contribution of two *t*s in *butter*.	Construct
	After the writing, the children were responsible for reading the survey question individually and voting by writing his/her name in the appropriate column.	Rereading
	Ida asked children to find the question mark and then to locate *the*.	Revisit
	Ida reminded children that they may want to use question marks in their own writing.	Summarize
DAY 12	Shared reading of the survey question.	Rereading
	Discussed the results of the survey.	Experience

FIGURE 5-5, *continued*

■ practiced letter formation
■ developed familiarity with a high-frequency word (*the*).

In this chapter, we have presented a set of elements that capture the complexity and ongoing nature of interactive writing. It is a way of thinking—not a prescription or a set of rigidly defined steps. Our detailed example focused on emergent writers. Later in this book we will explore other examples from writers who are more experienced. We invite you to use all of these elements as you think about your own work in interactive writing.

Suggestions for Professional Development

1. Engage children in interactive writing over a ten-day period. Keep a record of the experiences, day by day. If you wish, use the form we have provided here (Figure 5.6,

page 82) or simply make your own day-by-day record. Record, for example

■ the experience that led to the writing
■ the purposes for the writing
■ the type of text or texts produced—there may be several different kinds or one longer piece
■ details about what children attended to
■ your own teaching points—what you drew to their attention and how you revisited and summarized the text
■ what learning children will be able to use in their independent writing.

2. Meet with a group of colleagues and share your experiences. Then, analyze your notes and records. Specify the elements present on each day, for each notation. Finally, write a summary statement or talk with others about what children were able to take away from this learning experience.

	Record and Analysis of Interactive Writing	
Teacher: _____		
Day	Description of Lesson	Element
1		
2		
3		
4		
5		
6		
7		
8		
9		
10		

FIGURE 5-6   Form for Recording and Analyzing Interactive Writing

CHAPTER SIX

Learning About the Writing Process

Composing a Text

As children compose messages, stories, and other texts in interactive writing, they explore the relationship between reading and writing. As they bring their background knowledge and their language knowledge to the process, they learn to write with the reader in mind. They use reading in important ways to evaluate and reflect on what they have written, learning that reading serves specific and very important functions within the process of writing.

The Process of Composition

Composition is a critical part of instruction in interactive writing. After you and the children have engaged in conversation that brings to mind children's life experiences, and after you have discussed the purpose of their writing, you may then direct talk toward the composition of a specific text.

Composing begins with a consideration of audience. Thinking about the audience influences the "voice" and tone of the writing, perhaps even the layout. The genre, or type, of communication—such as a letter, a folktale, or a report—has profound implications for the planning and structuring of a text.

Thus, the composer engages in a planning process that involves

■ selecting the ideas and concepts that come first
■ organizing concepts into categories for presentation
■ finding ways to address the readers and bring them into the text
■ creating beginnings, middles, and endings for events.

This planning process is not always formal or even conscious. Composing begins when writers start to think about their ideas, the purposes for their writing, and who will read their writing. This process continues as the writer writes, and later may be part of revision or editing.

The Beginning Composer

What does composing mean for young children? As they enter the roles of reader and writer, they are always learning about different types of text. Through hearing stories read aloud, children encounter different demonstrations of how authors put together ideas to communicate meaning. Through shared writing, you are always demonstrating ways to put ideas together into different texts such as letters, stories, and poems. As young children think about their own tentative compositions, they begin to use language to express personal meanings.

In independent writing six-year-old Madeleine, for example, decided to write about a personal experience. She first thought about what she wanted her piece to be about in general—spending time with her dad. She had several ideas in mind but did not put them into words formally. She then decided on a main idea, thought about her message, and composed it in two manageable segments. Her composed message was of a length that she could remember and write:

I went to my Dad's for pizza.

She paused, recalled her second sentence, and wrote it.

We watched TV and had a great time!

Her message indicates that she has some idea of the demands of the writing task and the constraints it places on her composing process. The two sentences comprise a specific, coherent piece of text. Moreover, the author used reference to bring her message together. For example, instead of repeating names, Madeleine used the pronoun *we* to refer to herself and her Dad. In the second sentence, she used *and* to join two ideas. She did not repeat the pronoun *we*, since it is understood from the context. It is obvious that Madeleine was using language in a way that made her message cohesive, with one part referring to other parts so that it would be understandable and sound right. She used the adjective *great* for emphasis.

This beginning composer had become skilled at putting just enough language together to match her writing capability. Later, as she grows more sophisticated, she will structure her writing in different ways based on internalized knowledge of texts that she has encountered in classroom and other experiences.

Interactive writing is a way to make visible to children the inner workings of texts and to raise their awareness of the relationships between genre and text structure. As a teacher, you will use explicit talk about writing different kinds of texts to help children compose text. The idea is for children to have many experiences working with different kinds of writing.

What Children Do When They Compose

As they compose in interactive writing lessons, children make connections between the expression of ideas in oral language and what needs to happen to put those ideas into written form. Specifically, they learn how to

- think of different ways of putting words together to express meaning
- listen to and evaluate what they say and what others say in the process of composing aloud
- generate alternative ways of stating a particular idea, request, or piece of information and then choose from these alternatives
- think of two or more words, both of which would work, and decide between them
- build on a previous idea—their own or another's—so that one idea leads to the next
- reread (or recall) what they have written to determine what will be composed next
- keep their audience in mind as they compose the text
- shape the text and revise it while composing
- limit what they write to the time and space available to them
- keep in mind that the text they have must accomplish the intended purpose
- use punctuation to add to the clarity of a text and make it more interesting and readable
- compose sentences that can stand alone in expressing an idea

- use reference, whereby an element in one sentence or part of a sentence (for example, pronouns) stands for an item in an earlier part of the text
- use adjectives to make the message clearer or more interesting
- select the kind (genre) of text appropriate to the purpose for which you are writing.

The Helping Role of Negotiation

In interactive writing, you and the children negotiate the composition of the text through an active discussion and guided planning. The extent to which the composition is shaped through your interactions requires a delicate balance. Your goals are to ensure that the children

- experience many different kinds of writing
- create a text that will be useful for reading
- understand how their ideas can be turned into written text that they can then read
- learn how to organize ideas in a way that readers can understand
- compose text that is appropriate for the kind of writing they are doing
- communicate the use of social conventions in their writing
- realize that there are different purposes for writing
- keep the audience in mind while composing.

Achieving these goals means that as a teacher, you play an active role in composition. The composing process involves intentional teaching. In the planning process, you are deliberately trying to elicit a particular kind of writing, and you have in mind some of the characteristics of text that you want the children to learn. What they actually compose is the product of negotiation.

Children's ownership of and engagement with the text is of critical importance. They must all be active participants in the negotiation so that they see the text as their own

rather than something dictated by the teacher. Guide them to discuss an overall concept for the piece. Decide when it is appropriate to get suggestions and then select one or take one child's idea and ask if others agree. Sometimes, you may elicit a more formal plan that will allow for the composing of segments that are suitable for the group of children to write. Remember the strengths and skills that they currently have as they enter this process.

If your plan is to write a letter, you will explore with the children the purposes of letter writing and, in the process, guide them to use conventions. Helping children establish their own purposes is part of the negotiation process. Through many experiences, they will internalize these conventions so that when they later are required to use standardized features they will understand the reason for this.

Again, the composed message is reached by consensus rather than being generated by one student or a few students. You and the children will discuss and negotiate the language of the message. Everyone in the group is responsible for thinking about whether the message is clear and what form it should take. Everyone evaluates the precise words that will best convey the intended meaning. You may need to remind the children that the message to be composed will be written rather than spoken. (In written text, they cannot depend on intonation, voice quality, and gestures to support meaning.) Layout and punctuation are important. For example, if we want to sound excited, we have to use an exclamation point. If we're asking a question, we need to use a question mark. The text must convey all information clearly to the readers.

Gently guide the process, suggesting rather than dictating to the children. Help children to hear and consider their message, suggesting ways to shape it so that they learn new aspects of language use. You might say, for example,

- If we start our story with *they*, our readers won't know what we mean. We'll have to tell them exactly who we are talking about in the first part. After that, we can use *they*.

▮ Do you want to say *Goldilocks* again, or do you want to say *she*? Let's say it and see which would sound better.

Getting children to articulate the sentences, not just hear them, will offer them additional opportunity to expand their language. This kind of scaffolding is particularly important for English learners.

A Variety of Composed Texts

One of the reasons that the composing process is such an important part of interactive writing is that it offers children a way to discover the uses and ways of organizing many different kinds of texts. As a writer, you think differently when you are composing for different purposes. We will explore several different examples that illustrate the process.

Composing a Letter

In the following example, Amy Davis and a group of children from Room 3, who have been using interactive writing for most of the school year and also participating in a variety of other literacy and language activities, composed a letter about the "butterfly handshake." These children were able to represent most consonant sounds in different positions in words and could hear and write many easy-to-hear vowels. They had built a small body of high-frequency words that they knew how to write quickly and easily.

The children had been learning and practicing a butterfly handshake (a linked hand movement reminiscent of the flapping wings of a butterfly). The handshake was something that the children enjoyed as a part of their morning greeting. Lately, some children in other classes had mentioned to the group that they wanted to learn the butterfly handshake.

The children decided that they would like to teach the handshake to their friends in Room 5, and that they would write a letter

to the students inviting them to learn the butterfly handshake and setting a time to meet. Once the purpose of the writing was established, the teacher and children decided on the precise message.

AMY: Remember when we wrote the letter to Ms. Meyer (the school principal)? What words did we use to begin our letter?
MATT: *Dear Ms. Meyer.*
AMY: So we could start this letter the same way.
SEVERAL CHILDREN: *Dear Room 5 kids!*
AMY: *Dear Room 5 kids!*

They did not need further attention to this simple greeting because they had engaged in interactive writing daily and had produced several other letters. After writing *Dear Room 5 Kids*, they composed the opening line of the letter: *Can we teach you the butterfly handshake?* This sentence came about in the following way:

AMY: So now what should we say?
MATT: *We want to teach you the butterfly handshake.*
AMY: When you invite someone to do something it's nice to ask them if they want to do it instead of just telling them.
ELIZABETH: *Can we teach you the handshake?*
MARY: *Can we teach you the butterfly handshake?*
AMY: That's good. We want to be sure that they know it's a special handshake. *Can we teach you the butterfly handshake?*
SEVERAL CHILDREN: *Can we teach you the butterfly handshake?*
AMY: Good. Now let's all say what we're going to write. (Repeats question and children join in.)

After writing the question above, the teacher and children went on to compose and construct the rest of the letter, composing another question and ending with the closing *Love, Room 3 Kids*. (See Figure 6-1.)

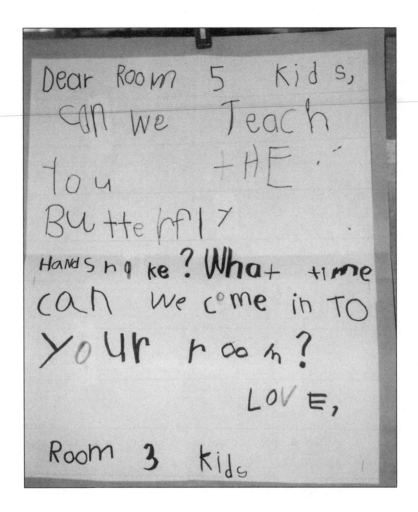

FIGURE 6–1   Butterfly Handshake Letter by Room 3 Kids

The letter from the Room 3 students was sent to Room 5. After talking about the butterfly handshake and how they would like to learn it, the children in Room 5 composed a reply. Beth, their teacher, guided the composition.

BETH: How should we start our letter to the Room 3 kids?

JOE: *Dear Room 3 kids.*

BETH: That's the same way they started their letter. Do you think that would be a good idea?

SEVERAL CHILDREN: Yes!

BETH: Yes, their letter was really nice wasn't it? (They write the salutation.) Now what can we write in our letter to the Room 3 kids?

JORDAN: *Yes we can come.*

MIKELA: *We want to learn the handshake.*

TUHLIZA: *It was nice of you.*

BETH: That's a nice thing to say, Tuhliza. Do you all think it's a good idea to tell them we think that it was nice of them to send the invitation?

CHILDREN: Yes

BETH: Tuhliza said "It was nice of you." Shall we start like that?

SEVERAL CHILDREN: Yes.

BETH: What else shall we say. *It was nice of you to . . .*

TUHLIZA: *It was nice of you to send us the letter.*

BETH: (Repeats message and children join her. They then write the message.)

The Room 5 students went on to compose two more sentences, which specified what the children would like to learn (the butterfly handshake) and the time for the meeting. Their letter is shown in Figure 6-2.

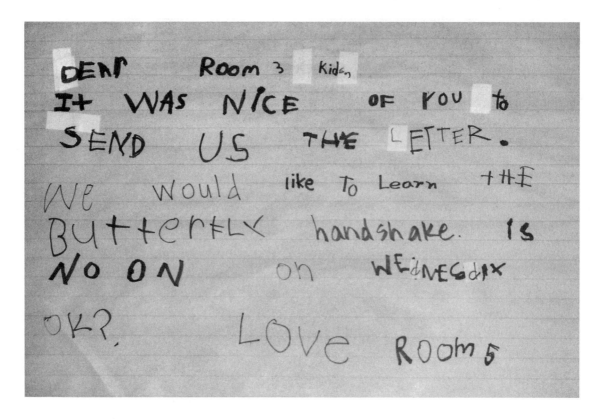

DEAr   Room 3 Kids,
It WAS NICE   Of YOU to
SEND   US   THE   LETTER.
WE   would   like To Learn   tHE
BUTTerFLY   handshake.   IS
NO ON   on   WEdNESdAY
OK?.   LOVe   RooM 5

FIGURE 6–2 Butterfly Handshake Letter by Room 5 Kids

Composing a Story

Most children in the next group we will discuss had acquired a small body of high-frequency words that they controlled in writing; the average score on writing vocabulary assessment was 19[1]. The average score for the group on a measure of phonemic awareness or hearing and recording sounds in words at this point in time was 23[2], so there was a good foundation of knowledge of letters and sounds. They could write endings to words, such as *ing* and *ed*. Many in the group could use known words to get to new words and could add endings to make new words. A few children were still learning the names of the letters and how to make them. Many were still working out the conventional use of capital and lower-case letters.

The group had been working together most of the year and had heard many stories read aloud. Ida, their teacher, had placed particular emphasis on reading folktales to them. The reading of "The Little Red Hen" was part of a larger unit of study on growth; for example, children were growing plants in the classroom and raising butterflies. In response to their reading of the tale, children composed the text shown in Figure 6-3 (on page 90).

Examination of the text reveals that this group of children was participating in the composition of a text that had many of the qualities of a sophisticated literary text, one much more complex than they could have written without assistance.

The story has several repeated episodes and a variety of characters who act in pre-

---

[1] The Writing Vocabulary assessment consists of all of the words a child can write within a ten-minute time limit (see Clay 1993).
[2] The assessment of Hearing and Recording Sounds in Words is a measure of children's ability to represent sounds with letters. It is not a spelling test; rather the goal is to reliably assess children's ability to make phoneme and grapheme connections (see Clay 1993). There is a possible top score of 37 sounds to represent with letters.

dictable ways. It contains dialogue and pronouns used for reference (*and she did!*). All of the qualities of a narrative retelling are there: setting, opening, problem, events, and resolution. Punctuation makes the text meaningful, and the story is laid out in a way that makes it attractive and readable. The story is made up of clearly written language, not just oral expression written down. The children composed it based on their knowledge of literary text.

Only the last line departs from conventional use of language (*You don't get no food*). In this instance, the teacher accepted the children's language as it was given, based on the idea that these children were making a transition to the use of written language but were still relating it to their characteristic way of expressing meaning. In this instance, Ida's decision was to leave the language in their words both for later readability and for the expression of strong meaning. Later, as they became more sophisticated, the children would be able to consider several alternatives and their teacher would help them learn the standard form and why that is important.

Composition of the Little Red Hen piece began when the children and Ida engaged in a discussion after she had read aloud several versions of the story. Ida suggested to the class that they could produce their own Little Red Hen story to put on display in the room, and this idea immediately became popular. They had to decide whether to simply tell the story again so that everyone in the room could read it or to make their story different in some way. They decided that their story would be an alternative version in which the Little Red Hen makes something different from what she makes in the traditional version of the tale. They made a list of what the Little Red Hen might cook and then voted on the possibilities.

The winner was pizza, a favorite food of many children. The negotiations that took place around the nature of their text helped the children think about the story, revisit the language of the original text, and forecast what their own text would say. Ida's suggestions guided the process, but she was sure to accommodate decisions made by the children. They produced a list to help them plan who would create the art for each character (see Figure 6-4 on page 92).

These lists of the foods the Little Red Hen could cook and the art assignments represent another kind of writing that is very important—writing to support planning. The children learned the format of lists and they also learned their function, referring to the lists often in producing the beautiful big book that resulted.

Then the children began to compose the actual text for their story. Ida started by rehearsing the task and ideas, saying, "I asked you before lunch to think of how the story was going to start. Remember, you decided that the Little Red Hen was going to make pizza."

She also reminded them of the characters in the book, referring to the list: snake, dog, and so on. Then, they began the discussion from which their composition emerged. Here is some of their conversation.

ARIEL: *The Little Red Hen did all the work.*

IDA: (Repeats sentence.) That's a good way to start.

MARCUS: *The Little Red Hen did all the work and then she got the idea that she would make a pizza.*

IDA: Oh, that's a really long sentence. I think it might be a bit too long of a sentence. I love all those ideas though.

MARCUS: I can make it shorter.

IDA: How can you make it shorter?

MARCUS: I can do it like this. I can write it and then leave a little space and then do the other part.

IDA: Oh. So you mean just do a part of it. Do *The Little Red Hen made a pizza.* Then stop.

MARCUS: Then stop and rest. And then do more.

IDA: And then do more sentences. So you think we should start with *The Little Red Hen made a pizza.* That's a wonderful idea.

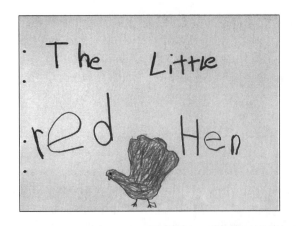

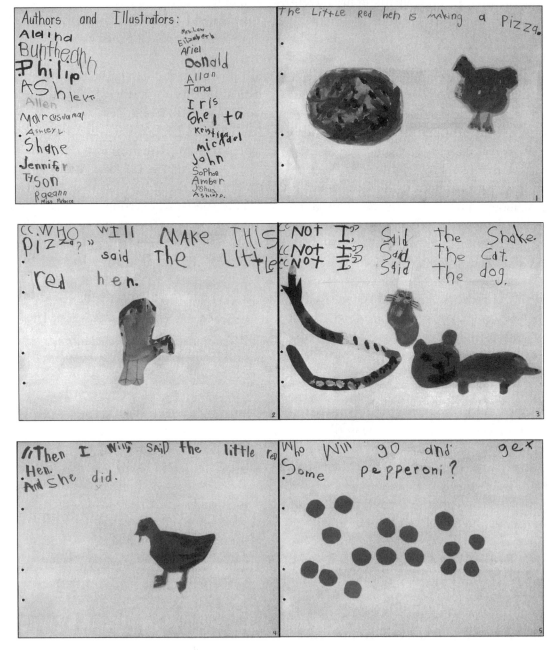

FIGURE 6–3 Little Red Hen

FIGURE 6–3   Little Red Hen, *continued*

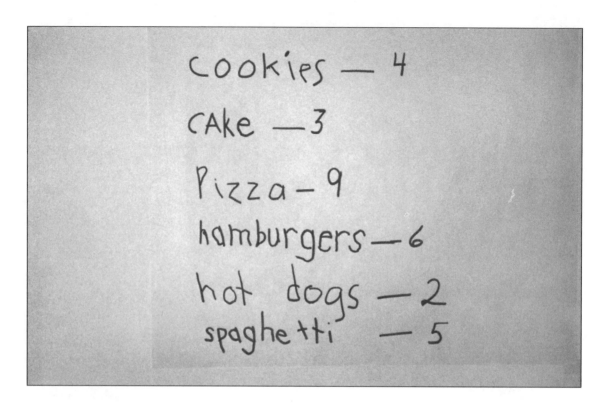

cookies — 4

cake — 3

pizza — 9

hamburgers — 6

hot dogs — 2

spaghetti — 5

FIGURE 6–4   Food List for Little Red Hen

The interchange on page 89 shows how Ida helped children think about composing segments of a larger text that, with her support, they could inscribe. As indicated above in the discussion of Madeleine's independent writing project, part of the problem for any writer is in making the transition from mental composition of specific sentences to the constructing or writing of the sentence itself. At the same time, Ida kept in mind that she wanted this text to be accessible to this group of children as readers. She was controlling the text difficulty so that the links between reading and writing would be clear later on and children could use this text as a resource. The text that they would eventually produce is more complex than that which any of the children could read in a book without support. So, this piece of interactive writing not only demonstrated the composing and writing process but stretched the children's abilities as readers.

IDA: Let's see what other wonderful ideas we have now. Iris.

IRIS: *The Little Red Hen is making a pizza.*

IDA: Oh, Marcus, did you hear that? She thinks we should start with *The Little Red Hen is making a pizza.* That sounds good. Let's get some other ideas and then we'll see. Elizabeth, how do you think we should start?

ELIZABETH: *The Little Red Hen is making a cake for herself and others too.*

TYSON: We are supposed to make pizza!

IDA. So you have a lot of sentences all ready to go. Your first sentence was *The Little Red Hen is making a pizza.* That's a good sentence.

This interchange provides a good example of negotiation in which the teacher works with the children to decide cooperatively exactly what to say. Ida gathered several ideas and then worked to achieve a kind of consensus among the group. She took the children's sentences but shaped the text to create something that would be readable.

IDA: Rayann, what's your idea?

RAYANN: *She ate the pizza.*

IDA: Is that the very first thing we should do in the story? Let's think a minute. Is that how the story is going to start?

RAYANN: (Shakes her head no.)

IDA: No, it can't start like that. Where do you think that sentence should be?

RAYANN: At the end, right? Because that's one of the last things she is going to do.

ALANA: *She ate all the pizza. The Little Red Hen ate all of the pizza.*

IDA: I love that idea. Rayann had that idea, too. But then she said that that idea should go where? Rayann, what did you say?

RAYANN: At the end.

IDA: At the end of the story, Alana, since eating the pizza is probably one of the last things that the Little Red Hen is going to do. First she has to make it, right?

ALANA: *The Little Red Hen is eating the pizza.*

IDA: Okay. Now think a minute. Can she eat the pizza before she makes it?

ALANA: No.

IDA: No. We have to make the pizza first, right? I like the way you figured that out. You know what, the idea that Iris had and Marcus had sounds like the best idea so far. They said, *The Little Red Hen is making a pizza.*

MARCUS: I didn't say that. I said, *The Little Red Hen is making pizza.*

IDA: That's what I said. *The Little Red Hen is making a pizza.* What do you think about using their idea to start our story?

CHILDREN: Yes!

IDA. Let's say the first sentence together. *The Little Red Hen is making a pizza.*

CHILDREN: *The Little Red Hen is making a pizza.*

Further discussion, illustrated above, shows how the conversation supported children's planning of the text. Their ideas were good and they were calling up sentences that could be part of the text as they continued to write. Ida prompted them to think about the order of the text. For example, eating the pizza would come last. Remember that the children knew the story "The Little Red Hen" very well, so they were able to deal with the complexities involved in thinking about the order of events. They could keep those ideas in mind (or the teacher would remind them) to use later in their writing. They had an implicit plan under way and their plan was supported by the knowledge of text that they had gained through hearing that story, and probably others, read aloud. The preceding lists and discussion supported their planning. Later, in their discussion, they would revisit their lists, using written language as a tool to support memory and thinking. Before writing the first sentence of their own version of "The Little Red Hen," Ida prompted the children to articulate the specific message word by word so that they could think about this smaller segment of the larger text that they were now prepared to construct.

The processes of composition and construction interact while children are creating the text. They may also be part of revisiting or revising a text. A few days after they finished writing and putting together their book "The Little Red Hen," children again engaged in the composing process. As they reread the pages of their text, the children decided that they wanted to add another page at the end of the story and that they wanted to add more details to their illustrations. The purpose for the shared reading of the text was to check their work in order to decide if they wanted to make any more changes before the book was laminated and assembled.

After they read *"And I will,"* said the Little Red Hen in the original story, some of the children suggested that they add the words, *"And she did"* to their version. The other children agreed. Just as Kristina began to write the word *And* on the page, Ashley interrupted the process.

ASHLEY: There's a period there. There's a period.

Ida asked Kristina to stop her writing and addressed Ashley's concern.

IDA: There's one thing, though. She is starting a new sentence. So if she leaves space and starts with a capital letter, she can do that. You're allowed to write another sentence after your first sentence even though there's a period there. This is a new idea. That was good thinking, Ashley.

Composition for young children also includes the production of images, in the form of illustrations, that accompany a text. When children are adding details to their pictures, they are thinking about ideas. They may or may not put those ideas into language, but either way, they are part of composition.

Extending Composing Through Informational Texts

In composing expository texts, children need to think about how the words and the organization of language work together so that the reader can understand the information being presented. In Figure 6-5, we present a piece of interactive writing completed during the beginning stage of a unit of study on the planets. Alma Escamilla and her class produced a summary of some facts that students had learned.

The piece shows how students can put together several ideas in one sentence. The text, translated, says:

> Saturn is made up of rock rings, ice and dust.
> Uranus is made up of green gases.
> Neptune has strong winds and is very cold.
> Pluto is made of ice and is always very dark.

They use descriptive words like *verdes* (green), *fuertes* (strong), and *oscuro* (dark). They carefully selected their ideas, and there is an inherent category system evident in the

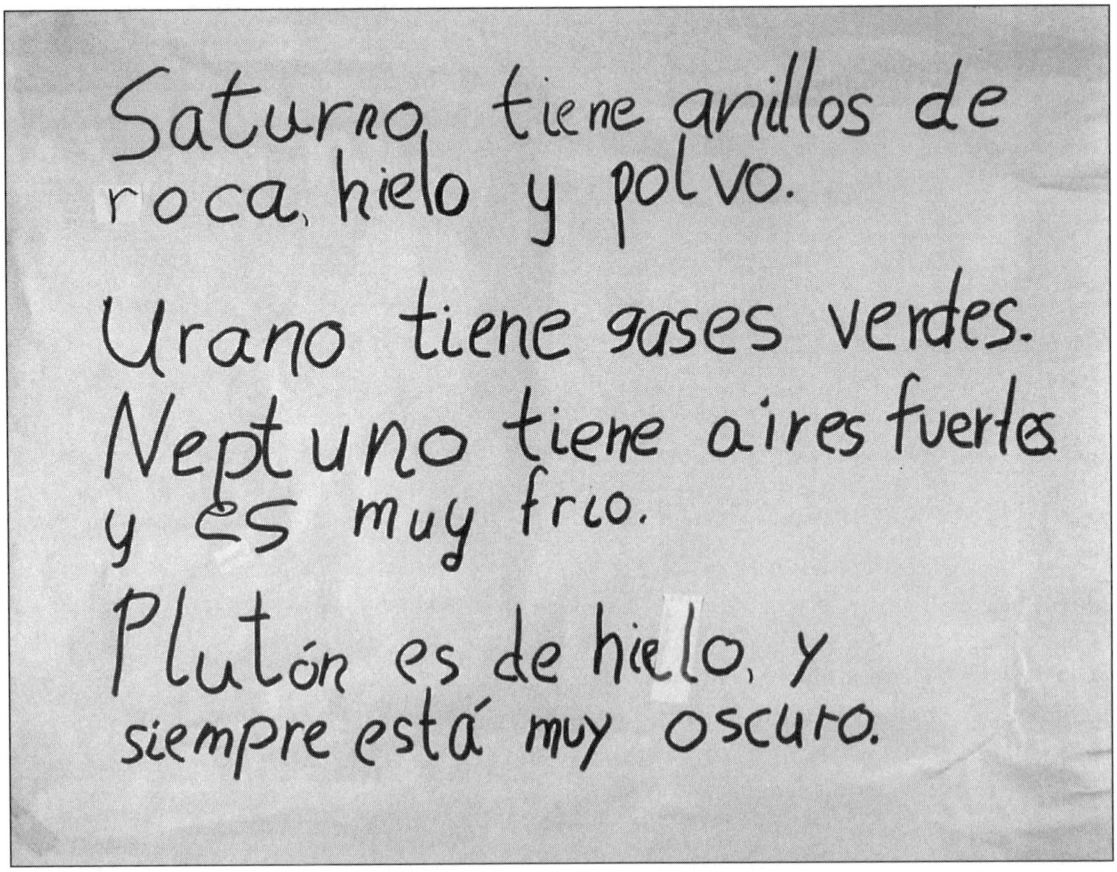

FIGURE 6–5   The Planets (in Spanish)

composition of this piece. Notice that they have commented about the composition of three of the planets and implied something about the weather of Neptune and Pluto. All of the sentences have to do with the atmosphere of the planet. As they selected what was important to say about the planets, students also had to think about how the planets were different. For example, there would be no point in stating that each was round, because roundness is a characteristic of all planets. This piece of writing is carefully

composed to let the reader know more interesting facts about the planets in the form of distinguishable characteristics.

Figure 6-6, showing the work of Katie Roth and her class, is another example of the composition of an informational text. As part of a study of fruits and vegetables, this class visited a market. Following the trip, the children set up their own market, using all of the potential language and literacy activities that could be connected with that experience. This piece of interactive writing provides a

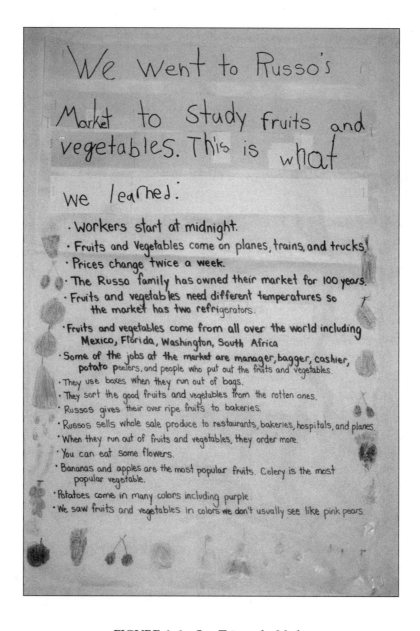

FIGURE 6–6   Our Trip to the Market

summary of everything that this group learned about working in a market.

Notice that the lead sentence was produced through interactive writing. The children had a chance to think about how to introduce and explain the list of information about markets. But the teacher acted as scribe for the rest of the piece. The children wanted to write down all the information about markets that they had gathered so they could read it later. Because the thinking and language of these first graders was so complex, the teacher decided it was better to use shared writing to record their ideas. The use of interactive writing would have limited the amount of text that the children could compose in the given amount of time. Combining interactive and shared writing allowed the children to compose a larger amount of text than interactive writing alone would have allowed.

Learning About Language Through Composition

When children compose a text, they are working on several levels of language at once. They place letters within words, words within phrases, phrases within sentences, and sentences within a longer text. They must first think of meaning in a larger sense and then compose the meaning using precise language. The process requires a shift in attention to the specific words to use and how to combine them for clear meaning. The construction of the text requires further shifts down the language hierarchy, as children attend to specific words, sounds in words, parts of words, and letters. Of course, after using details to write a word, the composer/constructor has to go right back up to the meaning of the larger text in order to think of the next word to write. The composer/constructor of text is always climbing up and down this hierarchy of language, from meaning down to the details and then back up to the meaning.

Relationship Between Composing and Constructing

In texts like those described here, composing and constructing take place alternately throughout the text. The teacher makes a decision about a meaningful unit of text that the children can compose, keep in mind, and construct. Usually this unit is a sentence. This composing and constructing process supports children in gaining a sense of the structure of a sentence. They learn to access the wide-ranging ideas and thoughts of oral language (many of which are not in standard sentences) and transpose them into units that can be expressed in written language. At the same time, they are learning that writers have to somehow think of units that are manageable in terms of remembering them while writing them down. For competent adult writers, composing and constructing are almost simultaneous processes. Nevertheless, they still exist separately and writers have to manage them. Our beginning writers learn the relationship between composing and constructing by experiencing them in a "slowed down" way so that they are visible and learnable.

Suggestions for Professional Development

Think about composing a text.

1. Audiotape or videotape the discussion you have with children while composing a text for interactive writing. Listen to the tape, noting how you and the children are negotiating a message. Select a three- to five-minute segment of the discussion to share with colleagues.

2. Meet with colleagues to share and discuss taped segments. Talk about how teachers are

   ■ making it possible for children to achieve ownership of the text
   ■ negotiating meaning with children

- clarifying the purpose, audience, and genre
- helping children think about text organization
- helping children think about length of sentence and choice of words.

3. Think about the variety of texts. Over several weeks, keep a list of the types of texts that you create with children using interactive writing.

4. Meet with colleagues to share your lists as well as some actual products. Categorize the kinds of texts. Discuss the following questions:

- How does the language of the text change in relation to the purpose and type of text?
- Where is the language simpler and where is it more complex (in different texts, for younger versus older children, and so on)?
- How does the organization and layout of the text change in relation to the type of text?

CHAPTER SEVEN

Constructing a Text

Learning About Letters and How Print Works

Constructing a text refers to the actions that you and the children take to inscribe a composed message or story. Text construction includes writing the actual words, letter by letter; arranging words in space on the page; and using conventions such as space, capitalization, and punctuation to make the text readable. Constructing the text is a cooperative event in which you and the children work together.

During text construction, you and the children will engage in conversation. Children learn a specific vocabulary to talk about writing. They use words like *start, finish, letter, word, first, next, last, period,* and *space.* They learn to talk about the features of letters—for example, *tall, short, uppercase, lowercase, capital, small, tails, sticks.* They discuss issues such as whether to write a word on a line or go to the next line, a decision that requires predicting the length of a word. They discover discrepancies such as the fact that a letter may have more than one sound or that a sound may be represented by more than one letter.

Constructing a text helps young children learn critical skills related to how letters are combined to make words and how

words are put together to create meaning. Composing and constructing are interrelated and interdependent. Throughout the process of construction, children must sustain their sense of meaning and purpose. They must consider the audience for the text, which may be themselves (texts that describe an experience they want to remember or lists that remind them to do certain things) or others (letters to classmates, labels for their art, etc.). The actions taken to use print conventions, leave spaces between words, or construct words with conventional spelling all focus on making the text accessible to readers. When children write with the reader in mind, both meaning and mechanics come into play. Interactive writing provides a setting in which you can support children's "divided attention." This means that you need to help them keep the message in mind while attending to the details of the construction.

In this chapter and the next, we describe opportunities for various kinds of learning during the construction of a text. This chapter focuses on learning about the printer's code and about letters. The next chapter will describe the opportunities to learn about words and how they work.

Learning About the Printer's Code

We think of the printer's code as the sum total of the symbols and conventions used to convey messages and meaning through written language, including

■ letters, their shape and formation
■ upper- and lower-case letters
■ letters in clusters (forming a word)
■ punctuation
■ spacing between words and between lines
■ arrangement of text on a page, for example left to right, top to bottom, continuing over pages, and paragraphs.

We use specific vocabulary to talk about the printer's code, including terms such as *letter*, *word*, *capital* or *uppercase*, *small* or *lowercase*, *period*, *comma*, *question mark*, *sentence*, *left* and *back to the left*, *across*, *indent*, and *paragraph*. We've already mentioned the very specific vocabulary that teachers use to help children notice the features of letters. Learning to talk about written language is part of the task for the young student. It allows the group to discuss writing, and makes teaching more effective because you can direct children's attention to specific items and examples.

Children can take this language to other literacy learning contexts, such as writing workshop or independent reading. Interactive writing is a natural setting for the teacher and group of children to talk about writing in specific ways. In interactive writing, children simultaneously participate in writing, think about letters or words as they need to in order to construct the writing, and use a vocabulary to talk about their work. All of the elements fit together as they focus on what they want to say.

In the following sections, we will explore the printer's code and letter learning by looking at several examples, all produced about the same time of the year—the beginning month of kindergarten. These examples illustrate the importance of having children undertake different kinds of interactive writing for different purposes. Figure 7-1 (on page 100) shows an example from Ida Patacca's classroom.

We especially like this piece of interactive writing because of its clear layout. Ida made sure that there was a consistent amount of space both between words on the line of print and between the lines of print. She also placed illustrations along the line of print in a way that would help children read the text.

Learning How Print Works

A basic understanding for reading and writing is that certain conventions are related to print; that is, print is organized. Interactive writing is a powerful way to help children develop this "big idea" and then notice the details of the conventions of print.

Learning to Differentiate Print and Pictures

In the piece of interactive writing shown in Figure 7-1, children participated in placing the pictures next to the text. They had to find the word *blue*, for example, and place the blue shape right above it. They did the same thing for *yellow*, *green*, *red*, *purple*, *white*, and *pink*. Much discussion focused on the juxtaposition of print and pictures. They contributed such dialogue as "We have the color *red*. Write the word *red* under the color" and "Let's check to be sure we have the word *green* under the color green."

Children were learning that in a coherent text, the words and pictures work together to convey meaning. We *notice* both pictures and print, but we *read* the print.

Directional Movement

In English and many other languages, we write words across the page from left to right. Letters in a word are written left to right. Direction also matters when writing single letters. It is important for young children to develop these concepts related to directional

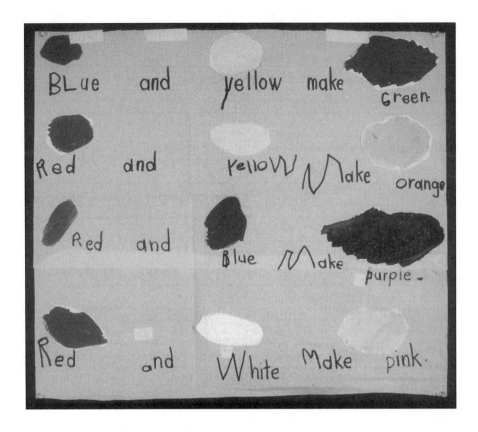

FIGURE 7–1   Colors

movement. Directional understanding is an explicit goal of interactive writing.

In writing the piece about colors, Ida said to the children, "Show me where to start." A child went up to the chart and pointed to the top left part of the page. Ida said, "Right. We always start on the left and point." She demonstrated by moving her hand across the blank piece of paper while saying the words of the text children wanted to write. Pointing to the blank space on a sheet of paper to start the children thinking about laying out the words is a useful technique very early on, but will not be necessary once the children understand the concept.

Children will also learn that the left page of a text is read before the right page. In interactive writing, often several pages of text are produced. In the Little Red Hen example presented in the previous chapter, the children had to organize the text, producing one page after another. It is important to have

many demonstrations of left-to-right directionality so that children can internalize this basic concept related to the way print works.

The Concept of a Word
One of the key understandings that a young writer or reader must develop is the ability to identify individual words in the speech stream. When we talk, we do not indicate word boundaries; in print, however, we use spaces to break up sentences into individual words. Without these spaces, it would be very difficult to make sense of printed words. Young writers must learn to break up the speech stream into the individual words that they want to write and then to construct each word, leaving space between words. Interactive writing provides a context within which breaking up the speech streams can be explicitly demonstrated and practiced. In writing the sentence "Blue and yellow make green," children had to segment the message

into words. Ida asked the children how many words the text contained. This question was related to many previous experiences in this kindergarten class, during which children had practiced segmenting the speech stream into words.

In a different class, in order to write the text "We put the very tiny caterpillars in the cups," the teacher placed words on separate cards (as described in Chapter 3), giving special attention to spaces. Multisyllable words such as *very, tiny,* and *caterpillar* may offer additional challenges to young children. Children may notice syllables, which are easy to hear, and think that each syllable is a separate word (a natural assumption). Children need to learn that longer words may have several sound parts or syllables. During interactive writing, you may have children clap the word to hear its parts, before they are asked to write it.

The Concept of First and Last
In written language, *first* and *last* have particular meanings.

- The first letter of a word is the one on the left. The last letter is the one farthest to the right, just before the white space or end punctuation.
- The first word in a line is the one on the left. The last word is the one farthest to the right.
- The first line is located at the top of the page, or is the first you encounter as your eyes move down from the top. The last line is the one just before the bottom of the page.

Interactive writing lessons are an ideal time to use words such as *first* and *last* and to explicitly demonstrate what they mean on a text that children know because they have composed it. You may ask children to locate the first word or the last word in a line of print.

At first, it will be best to have a child come up and point to the word rather than to simply ask children to look at it. While this concept may seem obvious, it is not so at the beginning. Tools such as the pointer will help.

Using Spaces to Define Words
We have discussed the problem of segmenting the speech stream into individual words. On the page, words are defined by space, which is not at all evident in oral language. Clay (1991a) describes a "space time transformation," referring to the fact that in oral language, words are spoken in time, but in print, they are arranged in space. The young child must learn to "make a match" between this stream of oral language and the groups of letters in a line of print. We call this concept "word-by-word matching" and it is an important early behavior. Interactive writing offers many opportunities to practice word-by-word matching. When words are written, attention is drawn to the use of space to define words. In fact, during the writing of the color example above, several times Ida had one child go up to the easel and place his hand after a word to "hold" the space while another child wrote the first letter of the word. You may call attention to spaces even before children know much about letters and words. They are learning the general layout of print—how it is organized—and this knowledge will help them to focus on words within text.

You should also emphasize word-by-word matching when children reread the text, as they do many times during the construction of a text. In constructing the first line of the example shown in Figure 7-1:

1. Bunthearn wrote the *b* and the *l* for *blue* and Ida finished the word.
2. Another child held the space while Ida wrote *and.*
3. They reread *blue and.*
4. One child held the space after the word *and* while another child wrote the first letter of *yellow.* Ida finished the word.

5. They reread *blue and yellow.*

6. Ida wrote *make.*

7. They reread *blue and yellow make.*

8. One child held the space after *make* while another child wrote the first letter of *green.* Ida finished the word.

9. They reread the entire line: *Blue and yellow make green.*

Each rereading took only a few seconds, but they all provided much needed practice for the children. Writers have to reread what they have previously written. Any given piece of interactive writing will provide many opportunities for rereading and matching word by word; both activities are very important for emergent readers and writers.

Learning the Functions of Punctuation

Punctuation assists the reader in gaining meaning from text. Think about oral language with its intonations, stops, starts, pauses, and inflections. These features do not exist in written language. We use conventions such as question marks to indicate a question, exclamations to indicate emphasis, periods to indicate full stops, commas to indicate brief pauses, and quotation marks to set off direct speech. The writer must learn to use these conventions as part of making meaning.

In interactive writing, you can show children explicitly how to use punctuation, beginning with the simplest forms and moving to more complex use. In our example on colors, Ida made sure that each sentence ended with a period, and she called children's attention to it, saying something like, "We always end with a period" (and then demonstrating this) or, "What do we need at the end of our sentence?" Several times during the construction of this piece of writing, Ida had a child go up to the easel and insert the period.

Learning About Letters

Early experiences in interactive writing offer kindergarten children an opportunity to learn about letters. At the same time, even though they have very limited knowledge of literacy, they are participating in the construction of a meaningful text. Working with letters within a known text is a more powerful learning experience than simply working with a letter in isolation. For one thing, children are highly engaged because they see that letters have a purpose. And, when they read and write, they must recognize letters that are embedded in words that are embedded in sentences. Five-year-old Madeleine, for example, noticed the word *me* in a text that was being read to her. "I have one of those *m*'s in my name," she said. When she located the *m*, she

- remembered the essential features that make *m* different from every other letter
- used her knowledge of *m* to identify the letter within a string of letters
- distinguished the letter from the other letters that surrounded it
- called it by name
- associated the letter with another word.

Madeleine may or may not have connected the letter to a sound, but simply being able to look for and recognize the *m* was a big achievement.

During interactive writing, you can draw children's attention to letters and help them learn how to look at them by using the following teaching directives:

- Have the children say the name of the letter (*m*).
- Talk about the features of the letter (a stick and two humps).
- Demonstrate the motions necessary to make the letter.
- Talk about the motions while making them (pull down, over and down, over and down).
- Have the children trace the letter in the air or on the floor, talking aloud about the motions while making them.
- Show the children how to check the letter against a model (alphabet chart or name chart).

■ Show the children how to make connections between the letter and known words, particularly names.

Figures 7-2 and 7-3 illustrate our second example of interactive writing, which involved labeling the items of food in Old Mother Hubbard's cupboard. This example was produced at about the same time (early fall) by the same group of kindergarten children who wrote the piece on colors.

Most children had little knowledge of the alphabet. Their teacher had read *Old Mother Hubbard* (de Paola) and two versions of *Old Mother Hubbard's Cupboard*, one by Marshall and one by Hawkins. In addition, they had been working on nursery rhymes, which Ida had placed on charts for shared

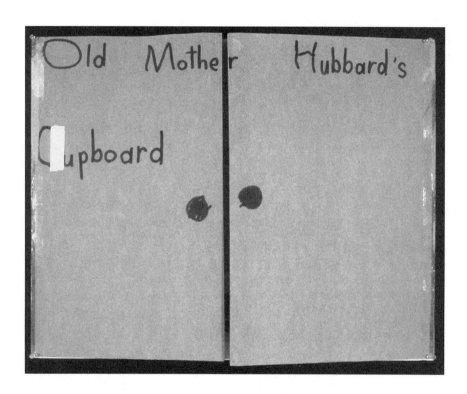

FIGURE 7–2   Old Mother Hubbard's Cupboard (Closed)

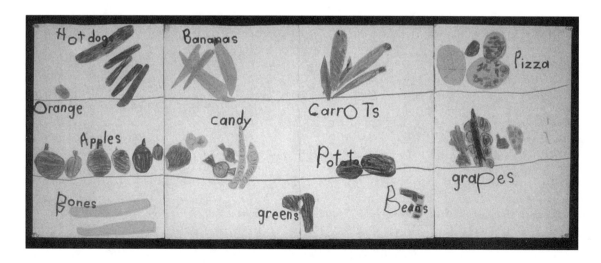

FIGURE 7–3   Old Mother Hubbard's Cupboard (Open)

reading. The children decided to make their own cupboard and decided what kinds of food it would contain. Ida emphasized letter names and letter formation and strongly linked the activity to names. Notice that Ida had written most of the labels on the cupboard. She helped the children connect the *b* in *bananas, bones,* and *beans* with Bunthearn's name. Bunthearn wrote the *b* in *banana* and other children were chosen to make the *b*'s in *beans* and *bones*. Each time, the link with Bunthearn's name was made. For the *c* in *cupboard*, the link was made to Carla's name. Students repeated the word slowly and connected it to Carla's name. Another child was asked to write the *c* but produced an *o* instead, demonstrating that the child was noticing distinctive features but was not using the fine details that distinguish *o* and *c*. In addition, motor control is essential to produce the letter; it is possible that the child had not yet achieved the control necessary to leave the circle open.

Ida said, "That's almost right. Let's look at the *c* in Carla's name. You need to have a space in your circle." She placed white tape over the letter and guided the child's hand to make the *c*. At the same time, Ida said to the group, "All of you make a *c* in front of you on the rug." After the children made the *c*, Ida said, "Let's check our *c* with the one in Carla's name. Is it the same?" The children were guided to look from the *c* on the writing chart to the *c* on the name chart and to evaluate the features.

Ida would not follow this procedure with every letter in the writing of the Old Mother Hubbard's cupboard text. For example, children contributed seventeen of the total of ninety-eight letters in the text. Children wrote fifteen of the ninety-one letters included in the text on colors. Ida likes to keep the writing moving along so that children will not lose interest or meaning.

When Ida asks them to go up to the chart, she is making a decision about instruction. She wants to draw their attention to powerful examples that will focus their attention on just what they need to learn, in this case, learning letters and learning how to write letters. In saying, making, connecting, and checking particular letters, she teaches children more than particular letters and their names. She is teaching them a process for learning letters.

Bringing Early Literacy Learning Together
Joanne Sabik's kindergarten class took a trip to the Tansey Nature Site, and then produced a big book (Figure 7-4) to share and reminisce about their experiences.

This book is a good example of a very early piece of interactive writing. It was designed to be supportive of emergent readers

FIGURE 7–4 Tansey Nature Site Big Book

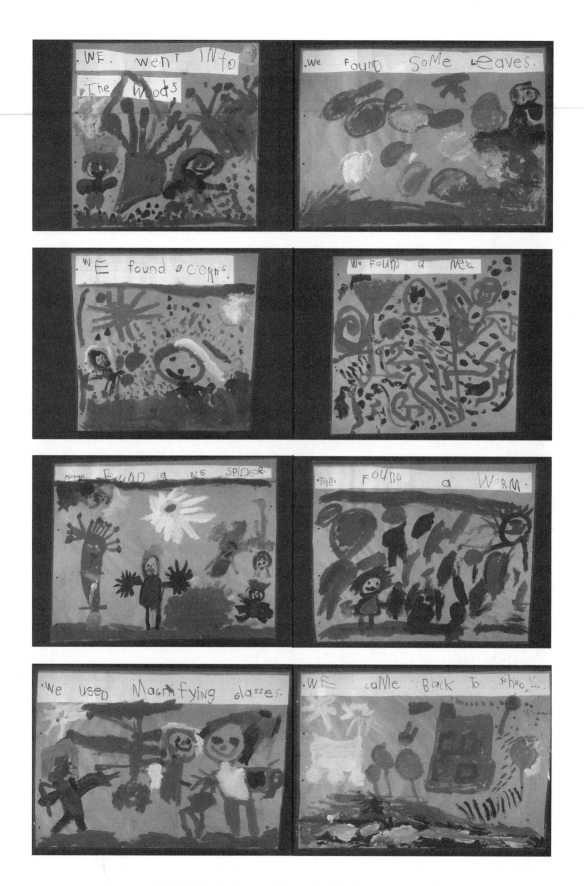

FIGURE 7–4   Tansey Nature Site Big Book, *continued*

and writers. It does this in the following ways:

- The text relates children's experiences from beginning to end in sequential order.
- Each page represents a simple idea.
- Each page begins with a word that all the children know how to read because they have used it in other writing.
- Every page of text begins at the top left starting point and is written on a white background to differentiate it from the drawings that match the text.
- The teacher has assured exaggerated spacing between words to help develop an understanding of word boundaries and one-to-one correspondence in reading.
- The print is large enough for all of the children to see.
- Some upper-case letters have been accepted in the writing, allowing children who are just learning a few letter forms to participate.

The kind of detail described above is exactly what the preschool or kindergarten teacher must consider when guiding children's composition and construction of interactive writing. First-grade teachers will probably agree that some of their students also require this sort of supportive attention to early literacy learning.

Another example of a teacher's understanding of critical aspects of support for early reading and writing strategies is evident in this example from Joanne Sabik's first-grade class (Figures 7-5a and 7-5b).

As part of the children's study of healthy foods, they made a list of the ingredients needed to make a funny face using certain food items. They began by listing the items they would need and gathering the food; they then wrote directions for how they made their funny faces so that they could share them with other classes. Notice how the teacher assured a large amount of space be-

tween words and between lines to make the text very readable. The picture support for every aspect of the text is very strong to help children reread it easily. The teacher has shaped the language of the text so that the first four directions begin with the word *we*, a word well known to the group. Repetition also occurs with *the*, *put*, and *for*. The teacher wrote the difficult parts of the words but enabled children to use some of their letter and letter-sound knowledge in constructing other parts of the words. Notice also that the letter case is appropriate; we expect first graders to use the correct case when writing.

Effective use of interactive writing requires that the teacher decide what to write, what to have the children write, and what to talk about. At first, children may only contribute a few letters and these must be carefully selected. As they learn more, they may contribute more because they can quickly write whole words or parts of words and because it may no longer be necessary to engage in the manual "holding" of a space. In other words, children will recognize spaces by sight. Even though children are producing more of the writing, the lesson can still move along quickly.

As the children become even more competent, you may still want to write some known items, again with the goal of keeping the lesson moving so that children do not lose interest or meaning. Another goal would be to focus attention on what they *need* to learn how to do; for example, choose more complex words that they can construct by parts to provide opportunities that extend learning. These teacher decisions are critical in making interactive writing effective and fun.

Interactive writing is a way to provide minilessons on aspects of writing such as word construction or the use of punctuation. In fact, many teachers use interactive writing as a good minilesson prior to the writing workshop, during which children produce their own writing. The goal is to help chil-

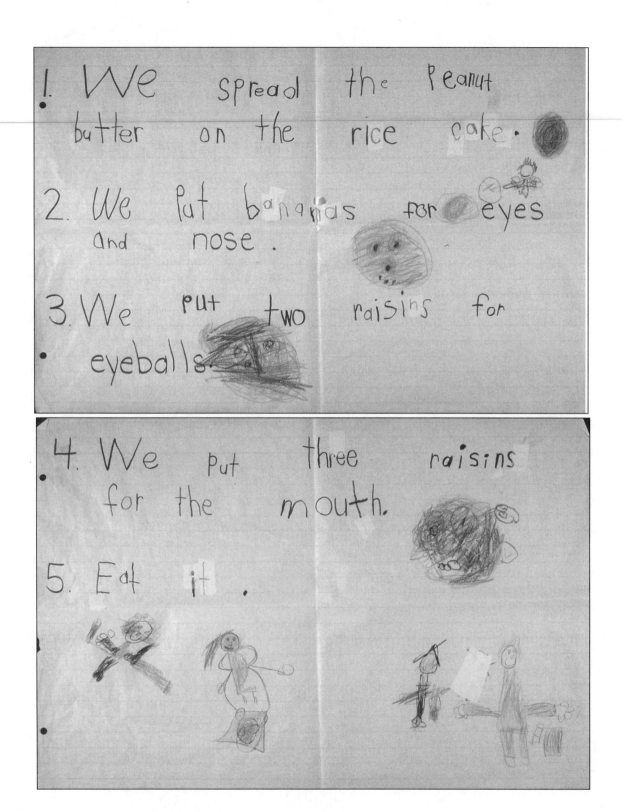

FIGURES 7–5a and 7–5b   How to Make a Funny Face

dren learn the strategies that they will need as independent writers.

Suggestions for Professional Development

Gather several colleagues, and share some pieces of interactive writing from each of your classrooms. Examine the pieces carefully and make a chart addressing questions in several categories, as noted below.

Learning About the Printer's Code

What opportunities were there for children to

■ notice that writing proceeds from left to right and that we return to the left for the second line?

■ distinguish between upper- and lowercase letters?
■ notice and use punctuation?
■ notice and use spacing?

Learning About Letters

1. What opportunities were there for children to

■ notice the features of letters?
■ say the names of letters?
■ practice forming letters?
■ talk about the motions required to form letters?

2. What teaching points were made and when did the teacher simply decide to do the writing?

3. Discuss the reason for the decisions and reflect on their effectiveness.

CHAPTER EIGHT

Constructing a Text

Learning How Words Work

As they work together to produce a meaningful text, children engage in the construction of words. During interactive writing lessons, you will carefully select examples to bring to your students' attention as you consider what all writers must do: first, of course, they must decide on the message they want to compose. As they begin composing—and while keeping their message in mind—writers must begin to write the words that comprise the message, one at a time. Let's consider what a beginning writer has to do to compose a message:

❚ Break up the speech stream into words so that they can be identified and written.

❚ Use space to define words so that the message is easier to read.

❚ Remember a known word (for example, a high-frequency word) and write it rapidly.

❚ Say words slowly and listen for the constituent sounds, in sequence.

❚ Connect new words to known words to help in writing them.

❚ Reread the message to help in remembering what was composed or to revise it in process.

Of course, as experienced writers, our actions are automatic and rapid. We know most of the words that we write or type on the computer and, accordingly, we are not required to think about them. Instead, we can concentrate on our composing and, as a result, we are able to create long and complex texts. Indeed, we are typically unaware of the process of word solving. Only when we approach unfamiliar words such as long names, words from other languages, or those "spelling demons" that inevitably cause us to hesitate do we become aware of word solving.

But our beginning writers and readers are just becoming word solvers. We have defined word solving as "a cognitive process for solving words—recognizing them, taking them apart, putting them together—in the service of meaningful reading and writing" (Pinnell and Fountas 1998, 23). In teaching word solving, we help children learn how to think about words and investigate how words "work"—that is, the principles underlying the construction of words that make up written language. Word solving is related to the child's growing body of known words because words they know can be used as examples and resources in figuring out new words. Word solving is also related to children's acquisition of some of the "building blocks" of language—the letters and the sounds.

Making Words in Interactive Writing—An Example

This example of interactive writing comes from the same group of children described in the previous chapter, but it was produced in May rather than September. This text also arose from the thematic study that produced the Little Red Hen text we presented earlier. Children were studying "growing." They had planted seeds and watched them grow and had also observed pupae hatching into butterflies. Ida, the teacher, used literature throughout the study, with "The Little Red Hen" as one example.

On this particular day, the class decided to bake a cake, an event related to their reading of Margot Zemach's *The Little Red Hen* (1983) and R. Robart and M. Kovalski's *The Cake That Mack Ate* (1986). It is amusing to note that the first item the children mentioned when they started working on a planning sheet for the ingredients they would need was a box. (They were thinking in terms of a cake mix, although ultimately they baked their cake from scratch.)

Part of the planning process involved scheduling a time to bake the cake in the school oven. Ida explained to the children that because many different people used the oven, they would need to reserve it. Marcus suggested that they post a sign on the oven so that it would be available when they got ready to bake the cake. Others agreed and the class composed the message (Figure 8-1).

Ida guided the children as they said the first sentence slowly. Sometimes, Ida indicated words by lifting a finger for each word as it was repeated. This unvoiced "counting" of the words visibly displayed to the children the word separations for the first sentence. This time, Ida simply said the words slowly with accentuation on the spaces between words, ending with the question, "How many words?" Many of the children quickly replied, "Six words."

IDA: What's the first word?
CHILDREN: *Please.*
IDA: Say *please.*
CHILDREN AND IDA: (slowly) *Please.*
SEVERAL CHILDREN: *P, p!*
IDA: That's right. Bunthearn, can you make a *p* for us?
BUNTHEARN: (Walks to the chart and writes the letter *p.*)

Earlier in the year, Ida had made connections to support this learning of consonants

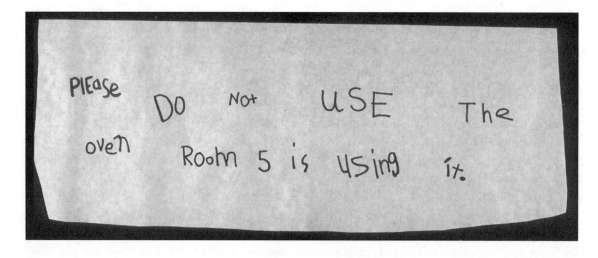

FIGURE 8–1   Oven Door Note

and letters. For example, within many lessons, she pointed out that *p* starts *Patacca*, her last name. At the time of this writing, almost all children in the class had control of connections between consonants and sounds. At this time, Ida had the goal of helping them notice letter clusters within words as well as word endings. In the next few interactions, she took the opportunity to help children notice that the letters *p* and *l* often appear together at the beginnings of words. She wanted to help them notice clusters rather than single letters. In reading and in writing, it is more efficient for children to attend to large parts of words, and it also helps them to begin to internalize the spelling patterns of English, many of which are based on letter clusters. Ida was not specifically teaching the cluster *pl* or the word *please* as items (although many children would learn those specific bits of information). Rather, she was teaching the children to listen to a sequence of sounds and record them.

IDA: Say *please* again.

CHILDREN: *Please.*

SEVERAL CHILDREN: *E!*

IDA: Yes, there's an *e*. But think about the beginning of the word. *Please.* (She accentuates the *pl* at the beginning of the word.) You know how to write *play*. It starts like *play!*

CHILDREN: *Play. Pl . . .*

ONE CHILD: Like on the wall! (Pointing to the word wall.)

IDA: That's right, you hear two consonant letters at the beginning of *please* and *play*. (Bunthearn writes the *p*.)

IDA: That's how *please* starts, *pl*. (She writes the *l*, *e*, *a*, *s*, and *e*.)

IDA: Now what word did we write?

CHILDREN: *Please.*

IDA: What comes next? Please . . .

CHILDREN: *Do.*

IDA: Michael, will you come up and hold your hand here for the space? And Christina, will you write *do*? (Christina and Michael walk up to the chart.)

ASHLEY: It's *don't*.

IDA: Oh, wait a second. Are we writing something wrong here? Which is it—*do not* or *don't*?

SEVERAL CHILDREN: *Do not.*

IDA: Okay, *do not*. Michael's remembering the space. Christina, do the word *do*. (Children laugh at this echo.)

IDA: That's *do*. And (to Michael) what did *you* do?

MICHAEL: Made the space.

The conversation about *don't* and *do not* provided a good opportunity for the children to experience two different ways of expressing meaning—two words or a contraction that combines the words. Ashley might have been prompted to say *don't* because she thought that the word *do* was going to stand alone in the text. She wanted to be sure that the text was communicating the correct message. This complex interaction illustrates the support that a teacher can give children who are just beginning to produce extended text in writing. The task of retaining meaning while thinking about the details of construction is daunting. Group support with a knowledgeable teacher enables beginning learners to deal with greater complexity than they could if working alone.

IDA: (Pointing to the text and leading them to shared reading.) *Please do . . .*

CHILDREN: *Not.*

Ida invites Elizabeth to come up to the board and write *not*, which she writes quickly as a known word.

IDA: (As Elizabeth finishes writing.) How did you know that?

ELIZABETH: The book. (She points to a storybook titled *The Big Fat Worm*.)

IDA: Oh, you remembered that! *Oh, no you're not!* (Quoting from the book.)

SEVERAL CHILDREN: *Oh, yes you are!*

IDA: You're right. It is in there! It's from *The Big Fat Worm!*

Elizabeth reported that her quick recall of the word *not* was related to her seeing it in a book that Ida had read many times to this group of children, *The Big Fat Worm,* by Nancy Van Laan (1987). Perhaps Elizabeth had seen the word *not* in other contexts, and she may even have written it herself, but this interaction reveals the powerful learning that takes place when children have the opportunity to make connections at the word level and the meaning level across elements of the literacy learning contexts. Here, it is clear that Elizabeth was connecting writing to her reading experiences, since *The Big Fat Worm* displays in large, noticeable print the words *Oh, no you're not!* repeatedly throughout the text.

In the next part of the interactive writing session, children engaged in some word construction. They used a word they knew to help write a new word.

IDA: I'm looking for good readers. (The group reads the part of the message that had already been constructed, up to the word *use*.)
SEVERAL CHILDREN: Y-O-U-S.
IDA: Wait a minute! (She takes out a white board and marker.) Oh, that's a different way to put it. *Yous.* Boys and girls, I like how you're thinking. (As she writes on the board.) Some of you are saying Y-O-U because this word sounds like *you* with an *s* on the end. And that really makes a whole lot of sense. And I don't know why they don't have us do it like that, but they don't. Instead, we have to write *use* a different way. So, let's say the word slowly.
CHILDREN: *Use.*
IDA: What sound do you hear first?
CHILDREN: *U.*
IDA: U. (She writes the letter on the white board) Let's say the word slowly again.
CHILDREN: *Use. S!*
IDA: S. (She writes the *s* on the board). Actually, it's *us* and an *e* on the end. That's the word *use.* Isn't that the strangest thing?
ARIEL: If you put an *a* there it is USA.
JENNY: (Comes up to white board and covers the letter E). *Us.*

IDA. Yes, if you cover the *e,* it is the word *us.* (She points to *use* on the white board.) This was a great idea. (Ida then writes the word *use* on the chart.)
PHILLIP: (Points to the text as children read the message up to the word *the.*)
IDA: That's a word everyone knows how to write. Tyson, write it quickly here.

Tyson wrote the word *the* quickly, without spelling it out. The children reread the sentence and Ida wrote the word *oven* as she said it slowly. Prompted by the children, she placed a period at the end, and they reread the entire sentence. The next line was produced in a similar way, with children contributing the *r* for *room,* the number 5, and the *u* in *using.* When they got to the word *using,* some children suggested writing the word *use,* which had been produced earlier, and just adding *ing.* Ida said, "I like the way you are thinking," and she wrote *use* on the white board. "When you add *ing* to this word, you have to get rid of the *e.*" She demonstrated adding the *ing.*

Ida's goal was not to teach these children to recite the rules related to adding *ing,* but to have them internalize the principles related to the rule. At this point, most of the children in the class had noticed words that end with *ing,* such as *making* and *going.* This piece of text brought the word *use* to their attention, followed closely by *using.* The juxtaposition of these two forms of the word prompted Ida to comment on an action taken to meet a convention. Over several years of experience, children will develop a repertoire of examples related to using inflectional endings such as *ing,* and they will be in a good position to derive the rules for usage.

The example above illustrates the kinds of learning opportunities that children may have as they begin to construct a text. They continue to compose during the process, as they recall and reflect on their message. Ashley's comments on *do* and *don't* illustrate the act of consistently checking with the

Twenty-five Easy High-Frequency Words[1]		
a	he	no
at	in	see
an	I	she
and	is	so
am	it	the
can	like	to
do	me	up
go	my	we
		CHILD'S NAME

[1] From Pinnell & Fountas (1998), p. 89.

FIGURE 8–2   Twenty-Five Easy High-Frequency Words

meaning of the message to assure clear communication.

Learning High-Frequency Words

When children are able to write some words quickly as they construct a text, they attend to the message more easily. In writing, they slow down the process to figure out or construct words, but if they have to construct too many words in a given line of print, they may lose the meaning. Having full control of a body of high-frequency words moves the writing along so that attention can be given to the message and to more complex words.

We have identified twenty-five high-frequency words (see Figure 8-2, from Pinnell and Fountas 1998, 89) that all kindergartners can learn through early reading and writing opportunities. These high-frequency words are useful for several reasons:

■ They appear frequently in oral language, so children will need to use them often in their writing.
■ Knowing high-frequency words moves the writing process along because children can write them quickly with little problem solving, leaving more attention for the construction of new words and for composing the text.

■ They serve as examples and resources for writing other words (for example, *is, it, sit, hit, his*).

Children learn these high-frequency words because they write the words often, both in group situations and individually. Sometimes the words are copied and sometimes the teacher writes part of the word, allowing a child to fill in the rest. There is much excitement surrounding children's learning of these types of important words, which appear over and over in the language. We believe that when children gain mastery over words like *to* and *the*, more has been learned than just the words. They have achieved the concept that a word is consistently spelled and that they can identify and produce particular words. The children see themselves as writers who have power over an element of language. They are able to behave as competent writers, writing for themselves or demonstrating the word for others.

Because they are ubiquitous in all forms of oral and written language, high-frequency words naturally occur in interactive writing. There are many opportunities for children to encounter these words daily and teachers need to capitalize on these opportunities, starting with the twenty-five words that we have identified for kindergarten. The language naturally includes many of these high-frequency words, and some of these words may be learned and placed on the word wall. For example, if a child can write the *t* in *to*, you might say, "That's a word that is good to know! Let me show you how to write the rest of that word," and then supply the *o*. You might draw all the children's attention to the word, write it on a whiteboard or card, and place it on a word wall for later reference.

For another word, for example, *hen*, children might attend only to the sound of the first or last letter. Teaching a high-frequency word might even involve children's making the word later in the word study center using magnetic letters or other kinds of materials. The purpose is not simply to learn a word, but to develop a way of learning the features of words, noticing them in different contexts, and using that knowledge as part of a writing or reading process.

Using high-frequency words means engaging children in the construction of extended text. If you focus only on labeling, students will not have the chance to encounter and learn many high-frequency words. In the text "Please do not use the oven. Room 5 is using it," there are four easy high-frequency words: *do, the, is,* and *it.* The children in this class had, by this time, had so much writing experience that they knew these four words. The powerful learning conversations surrounding *use* and *using* were, in part, possible because of the knowledge base.

In the Little Red Hen example given in Chapter 6, a large number of easy high-frequency words helped the children to write a much longer text in a short time. In writing "Our Map," which will be discussed more fully in Chapter 10, a beginning group of kindergarten children gained experience with two useful words, *we* and *a,* by constructing a simple, repetitive, text. They wrote several sentences, beginning with "we made. . . ." In constructing the text, a child named Andrew was able to write *w* for *we* because the letter was in his name. The teacher finished the word, saying, "This is a word we

almost know. Should we put it on our word wall?" She wrote the word on a card and added it to the wall. In several subsequent lessons, the word *we* was used again; children demonstrated several ways of approaching the word. They

- thought of the first sound, connected it with a letter, and checked the word wall
- searched for the word on the word wall and copied it into the text
- wrote the word quickly from memory, then checked the word wall.

Once the word was generally shared knowledge, it would receive little attention in interactive writing; however, individual children who were still gaining control of this word could use the word wall for assistance.

Hearing and Recording Sounds in Words

Interactive writing is an ideal setting for teaching sensitivity to sounds, called "phonemic awareness" by researchers who have identified this area of knowledge as a critical factor in learning to read (see Chapter 14). Once the speech stream has been broken up so that children can identify individual words, they need to think about an individual word and the sequence of sounds within it.

During interactive writing, the teacher first demonstrates and then encourages children to say words slowly. Teaching children to say words slowly and hear the sounds is a critical skill in early writing and reading. We describe an effective instructional process below.

Say Words Slowly

Pronounce a word slowly and have the children watch your mouth as you say it. You want to emphasize sounds but not to artificially segment them within the word. For example, you might say *Please* very slowly with emphasis on the *p*, but would not say *puh* (pause) *uhl* (pause) *e* (pause) *s*, distorting the word so much that children are listening only for individual sounds rather than the smooth sequence of the sounds in the words.

Avoid Hand Gestures or Props

Using hand movements or props like rubber bands to illustrate elongating a word is unnecessary and may unintentionally send the wrong message. You'll want the children to focus on your mouth and to listen for sounds as you say the words. Ask the children to watch your mouth as you say the word; you want them to understand the process as something they do with their own mouths. When they're engaged in their own writing, you'll want them to use their mouths to say a word slowly, not to put their pencils down and start doing something with their hands.

Require Children to Articulate Words

Insist that the children say the words out loud. Through feeling the movement of their tongue, lips, and air flow, children develop a sensitivity to the particular sounds as they articulate them. For example an *m* means that the lips touch each other and air is pushed out through the nose. The vocal cords vibrate. A *p*, on the other hand, produces air that moves out explosively, pushing the lips apart. The *p* is unvoiced, meaning that the vocal cords vibrate but there is simply a puff of air. The *b* uses the same mechanism for articulation, but it is voiced, meaning that there is a definite sound made when the air is pushed past the lips. All of these distinctions seem quite technical when described here, and we would certainly not use this kind of language to talk to children. But, as teachers, our understanding of the importance of articulation helps us to be aware of how necessary it is for children to enunciate words.

Ask Children to Listen for Sounds

As you recite the words and the children repeat them, ask the children to listen for individual sounds. Here, children are detecting phonological patterns that, being speakers of the language, they recognize. Through much language experience, perhaps including hearing rhyming poems and songs, children may

have learned to connect words by how they sound. Now the task is to say words and connect the sounds in these words with the sounds in other words. Here, the name chart is especially helpful. We have illustrated in earlier chapters how you can help children make connections between words and their own names and those of their friends. For example, linking the word *jelly* with the names of *Joshua*, *John*, and *Jenny* helped one class make important phonological connections.

Hearing sounds in words proceeds from simple to more complex tasks. At first, you are simply helping children to make any kind of connection, to identify any sound they can hear at the beginning, middle, or end of a word. In early interactive writing, you might teach a particular word by enunciating it yourself and then asking the class, "Say the word slowly. What do you hear?"

If a child says *t* for *cat*, your response would be "Yes, there is a *t* at the end of *cat*. I'll write the first part." You would then write the *ca* and have a child write in the *t*, followed by having the whole group read the preceding text, including the word *cat*. Later, you can make more demands on children's phonological knowledge. You might ask children to think about the sound at the beginning of the word, at the end, or in the middle. They might listen for endings such as *er*.

Consonant sounds are generally easier to hear than vowels. Children tend to hear final and initial consonants first, especially those that are "easy to hear" like /m/, /b/, /t/, /s/. Most of these easier consonants are strongly connected with letter names, so children who are learning the names of the letters naturally connect that learning with the sounds that they hear. In children's early independent writing, we see examples such as: SL (*school*), MK (*make*), or STR (*sister*). In a multisyllabic word, children may hear the easier consonants as part of syllable breaks.

The easier vowel sounds are those that have the same sound as the letter name, for example *a* as in *make* or *o* as in *no*. Sometimes, children will hear an *e* sound at the end of a word like *baby* and represent the *y* as an *e*. Young children's early attempts at spelling indicate that they are actively searching to make connections between the sounds they hear in words and the letters that are related to those sounds. Children who know how to say words slowly, trying to identify the sounds, have a big advantage in learning about how the written language system works.

Interactive writing is especially designed to foster the ability to hear sounds. The power of this learning is extended as children produce their own writing. The sounds emphasized in interactive writing are deliberately selected by teachers because they know that children will be using them in their individual writing. If children are not saying words slowly while writing, for example, you may advise them explicitly to use this technique when they are writing for themselves.

As children become more knowledgeable about sounds, can record many sounds, and make many connections between words, you can make the task more challenging by asking them what they hear at the beginning of a word, in the middle, or at the end. Asking children to listen for sounds in sequence means that they can think about the word as a whole, know about sequence, and sort what they hear into a sequence. It requires that children know what the teacher means by "first," "next," and "last," terms that have technical meaning when applied to words. If a word contains more than one syllable, always encourage children to listen for the parts (e.g., lem-on, po-ta-to). This procedure will help them hear the sounds within each part more clearly.

Learning About Spelling

Writing involves linking the phonology or sounds of the language to the orthography or symbols of the language. Phonological awareness refers to the individual sounds or clusters of sounds we hear in words; orthographic awareness refers to what we see—the spelling

patterns that are made up of graphic symbols or letters.

One critical area of learning for prekindergarten, kindergarten, and first-grade children is how to look at the letters that make up our alphabet. There are twenty-six letters; each is represented by an upper- and lower-case letter that may appear similar to or quite different from each other. Some letters even have different forms such as the *a* used in printed text and the *a* typically used in handwritten text. Children have to learn to look for the specific features that make one letter different from every other letter. For example, a tall stick distinguishes an *h* from an *n*, while an extra hump makes the *m* different from the *n*. Orientation makes a difference too—between the *u* and the *n*, for example. These small differences make our written language quite efficient to produce. The countless words in our language can all be expressed with just these twenty-six letters. But it is difficult at first for the young learner to perceive them.

The child's task is to discern what makes a letter distinctly itself and then to attach names to each letter and its sounds. In other words, he or she must first perceive the letter and then make connections. The task is complicated by the fact that there is not a one-to-one relationship between sounds and letters. A sound may be related to several letters (/s/ is connected to *c* or *s*, depending on the word it is in). A letter may have several different sounds. The letter *u*, for example, appears in *mule, up, you, could, thought, tune,* and *turn*. It may have no sound connection or several different sounds depending on pronunciation of the word. Letter-sound links may even vary according to regional speech differences.

How Words Look and Sound
One of the goals of interactive writing is to involve children in purposeful writing that requires them to make connections between how words look and how they sound. The overarching concept is that what they say (or compose) can be written down. They are

constructing words, letter by letter, part by part. This "slowed down" learning process might be compared to learning a dance. When you ask children to segment the speech stream, say words slowly, listen to the sounds, and then write some of the sounds, you have, in fact, slowed the writing process so that it is easier to see what is going on.

Ask children to make connections between the sounds and letters. When the children in our example were working to hear and write sounds in the word *use*, they were exploring what they knew about the phonology and orthography of the word, making the connections that made sense to them. Engaging in this process gave the teacher a chance to help them sort out some of these letter-sound-word connections.

Often, the teacher acts as mediator to help children understand the more complex relationships between how words sound and how they look. In our earlier example, Ida

- wrote the *ea* as a vowel pattern in the word *please*
- placed a silent *e* at the end of the words *use* and *please*
- wrote the *o* and the *e* in the word *oven*.

Ida was contributing what the children could not represent. Thus, children were able to feel the power of the sounds they could hear and the links they could make. They also had available to them a visual representation of the word, spelled conventionally. These experiences help them internalize the following important concepts:

- There are letters in words that do not have connected sounds.
- Some letters appear together in a cluster that makes one sound.
- Some letters are more likely to appear together as a cluster than others.
- Hearing sounds in a sequence helps you write more of the letters of a word.
- There are endings that appear over and over in words (like *ing*).

- You can use what you know about words to write new words.
- A word is written the same way, left to right, over and over.

How Words Make Meaning

Spelling is related to the meaning of a word within the context of a particular sentence. In interactive writing, children often have to make decisions such as:

- Which word should we use—*to* as in *to the store* or *two* as in the number? These relatively simply decisions bring children's attention to the selection of words that convey precise meaning.
- Do we need to add *s* to *pigs* (do we have one pig or more than one)?

Thinking about the meaning helps children pay particular attention to the words as they think about the audience for their work. Because writers want their readers to understand their meaning, words and word parts are important. In addition, attention to spelling enables children to learn how to convey a precise meaning. In fact, simply knowing that conventional spelling is important is an outcome of interactive writing.

Using Analogy

When children are constructing words, they benefit by using what they know about a word to figure out new words. We saw an excellent example of this when children tried to construct the word *use* by connecting it to the known word *you*. Readers "constantly search for connections between what they know about words and what they are trying to figure out. The use of analogy is the ability to manipulate and think about words. What is known in one area is used in another area" (Pinnell and Fountas 1998, 80). Here are some ways that teachers have used analogy to help children solve new words:

- When children know the word *the*, it helps them to write *them* and *they*.
- When children know how to write the word *cat*, the teacher shows them how

to change the last letter to write the word *can*.

▮ Teachers help children make a new word by adding letters to a known word, such as adding *b* to *and* to make *band*, or deleting letters, such as taking *c* from *cat* to make *at*.

▮ The name chart is a resource in the process of analogy; for example, since *Mary* and *Bobby* end in *y*, these names will be helpful in writing the ending for the word *very*. *Christopher* will be helpful in writing the ending for the word *worker*. *Roy* can be helpful in constructing the word *boy* or *Stephen* in writing *stop*. *Andrew* certainly can be linked to *and*.

Once you have demonstrated these processes clearly, you can use prompts to remind children to think of words that they already know that can be helpful in constructing new words. A prompt is a call to action; it reminds the child to use a process that he or she understands and has performed in the past.

The idea behind using analogy is not to simply learn specific items or words. Children will inevitably acquire a large body of words that they can write and read. The power of the process, however, is in learning a strategy for solving new words in writing.

Using References and Resources To Aid Spelling

As you work with beginners in interactive writing, you will want to have several references in addition to a name chart mounted on the wall, easy for children to see and touch. This collection would include

▮ a word wall that contains the words that children know and some examples of words that can be used as a reminder of a category of words.

▮ interactive word charts that you and the children have constructed together (see Chapter 5, Pinnell and Fountas 1998). At first these charts may be very simple, for example a chart of words that start with *s* or rhyme with *an*. Later, as children learn more, interactive charts will center on much more sophisticated analyses of words, for example, words that have silent letters at the end or that have irregular spelling patterns.

▮ pieces of interactive writing that the children have previously constructed. Children will refer to these pieces of writing again and again. For one thing, they have read the messages many times. Thus a complex piece of text, one that is usually too difficult for them to read on their own, is available to them. Effective teachers use these pieces of writing as text references; they can find words within them that illustrate spelling principles, even punctuation or ways to lay out a text.

We tend to think of tools such as the computer, dictionary, or encyclopedia as the references that students must learn how to use. But these simple wall charts form the beginning of young learners' use of language tools. It will be helpful to them for you to show them how to refer to charts, word walls, and previously completed writing as they work independently on their own pieces of writing. This kind of instruction may be a minilesson in which you "act out" finding a word like the word you want to write or checking on your spelling of a word when you are not quite sure that it's correct.

Learning About Reading/Writing Relationships

One of the goals of interactive writing is to help children while they are writing a text, to think about what the text communicates to a reader. Because interactive writing emphasizes frequent rereading, children themselves experience being the audience for their written texts. Often, children will notice a detail about a text that should be changed to help the reader—words without enough space between them, a word that should be added to make the meaning clear, or a letter that should be clearer in formation. Frequently, they will point out discrepancies during rereading, and it is not unusual for the teacher and children to make revisions to a text that was written several weeks earlier.

A capital letter mixed into a word or a backward letter might not be noticed or even be important to correct at the very beginning of kindergarten, but as children learn more, this detail becomes more important. Interactive writing thus provides children with their first experiences in revising a text, and the reading-writing connection is often the source of their own self-evaluation.

Discovering More About Words

Through the constant interplay of writing and reading during interactive writing, students learn that

- they can read what they have written
- they can change what they have written to make it clearer or easier to read
- they can remember what words look like, and use that knowledge to help them write other words
- they can remember what words look like as a check on whether they have written a word correctly or not.

Keep in mind that children will learn more than you are actually teaching at any particular time. That's because you have established a context within which they can explore written language for themselves. You will be intentionally teaching children many important things about how written language works. Instruction is not incidental or accidental, because you have a definite plan in mind. But you are dealing here with the richness of language. Leave room for discovery.

We have observed that when children are encouraged to notice features of words, for example, they keep on doing it. You may

be showing children something like an *er* ending, for example, and find that a few children notice that the letter is often doubled when you add an ending. A teacher who says something like, "I like the way you're thinking!" or "I like the way you are noticing words!" will encourage more discovery. The conversations about choice of words, connections between words, punctuation, and sentence structure, and other features of written text will arise naturally during interactive writing. Look for it and encourage it, because discovery will enable children to accelerate their learning.

Suggestions for Professional Development

Gather several pieces of interactive writing. Examine them carefully and make a chart addressing questions in several categories, as noted below.

High-Frequency Words

What opportunities were there for children to

- use high-frequency words (use the chart of high-frequency words and mark those that were used)?
- read high-frequency words?
- place words on the word wall?

Learning to Hear Words in Sentences

What opportunities were there for children to

- identify individual words in shorter sentences? In longer sentences?
- identify words independently?

Learning to Hear the Sounds and Syllables in Words

What opportunities were there for children to

- hear sounds or syllables as you demonstrated?
- say the sounds themselves?
- distinguish sounds?

■ identify where in the word they heard the sounds—beginning, middle, end?

■ identify consonant sounds or vowel sounds?

■ identify easy-to-hear sounds or harder-to-hear sounds?

■ link sounds with names or other words?

Learning About Spelling

What opportunities were there for children to

■ notice how words look and sound?

■ relate spelling to meaning?

■ construct words using analogy?

■ use names and other references as a resource?

Self-Evaluation of Interactive Writing Sessions

To further your own reflection, ask yourself the following:

■ Were there any opportunities for learning that I missed?

■ Was there too much teaching? Was there too little?

■ Were the examples that I emphasized consistent with what children needed to know about constructing written language? For example, did they need to learn how to look at letters? To say words slowly? To connect words by analogy?

Young Writers Engage in Literacy

People use writing for a range of purposes. In classrooms for young children, we are concerned about teaching them *how* to write. But at the same time, we want them to know from the very beginning that writing will play an important role in their lives. They will use writing as a way of expressing their thoughts and ideas, for communicating with others, and as a tool for learning. Literature is a strong foundation for all writing in the primary grades. In Section Three we discuss and provide examples that show how children can use interactive writing as a way to extend their understanding and enjoyment of literature. Reading and writing informational text is a basic skill that young writers will use throughout their school years. Interactive writing gives them a good start toward developing this skill.

CHAPTER NINE

Exploring and Extending the Meaning of Literature

The books that children hear read to them or read themselves are powerful resources for creating their own texts.

Introducing Children to a Variety of Genres

Children who hear or read a variety of literature learn that authors write for various purposes and that they vary the style of their text according to the type, or genre, that they are writing. One of the distinctions children learn to make is between fictional narratives and nonfiction. The language and organizational structures in narrative texts are usually different from those employed in informational texts. For example, a narrative, or story, is usually a continuous text with a beginning, a series of events, and an ending. Informational texts are organized differently. The author of an informational text may highlight the book's layout with headings and a table of contents or an index. The author may also define certain unfamiliar terms, placing them in boldface or italics; narrative fiction normally doesn't contain such information. Children will learn that, when composing a narrative piece, writers will use dialogue to create a livelier, more interesting story. On the other hand, dialogue is not usually used by a writer of an informational piece. The writer of an expository text wants to convey a clear, precise message. Thus, he or she typically seeks to eliminate the need for interpretation or inference on the part of a reader.

Children develop many of these understandings regarding the stylistic and content differences between narrative and informational texts during discussions surrounding the reading of books. If children have the opportunity to hear many books, both fiction and nonfiction, and are encouraged to talk about the differences between the kinds of writing used in them, they are more likely to create pieces that "sound" like expository or narrative texts when they compose. They will internalize the organizational features that other writers employ and will attempt to use these same structures in their own writing.

The composing process itself can lead children back into literature, causing them to attend to texts as writers in ways they might not do as readers. For example, children who are working together to create their own book may adapt a story they have read, use the language of the book, or borrow the organization of the book. They might analyze how the author introduces characters or builds suspense, or observe how the illustrator or photographer includes details that clarify the text or shape the reader's interpretation of the text.

In this chapter we look at some specific examples of ways that knowing literature enriches the writer's pool of resources. We discuss how drawing on these resources sharpens the writer's understanding of some aspect of literature, as well as how interactive writing can be used to help children learn about literature. In other chapters, we have emphasized the composing and constructing aspects of interactive writing, including word construction and letter formation. Here, we emphasize the various ways writing and art are used together to convey literacy meaning and aesthetics.

Exploring Children's Books

Sharon Esswein's students were enjoying reading the books of one of their favorite authors, Eric Carle. As they read Carle's book *Pancakes, Pancakes* (1990), Sharon made a natural link to an ongoing study of food and nutrition. The interactive writing piece they created (Figure 9-1, see also Appendix 5) provided the opportunity for children to

- think about the title of the book and the author/illustrator

- explore the author's/illustrator's craft and the use of media to convey meaning
- say and write some of the words or word parts in the story
- talk and think about concepts like ingredients and utensils
- use oral and written language to assist action
- experience written language in a purposeful way
- construct words by saying them slowly
- become aware of initial and final consonant sounds
- become aware of and write several high-frequency words
- construct a list of directions, in sequence
- put numerals on a list
- use punctuation for a list—periods after numerals and at the end of sentences
- label items in the illustrations.

The teacher and children considered the aesthetic appeal of the piece. Sharon had read the book to the children many times, giving them the opportunity to notice different aspects of the illustrations and text each time. Part of the children's learning was exploring the art in the book as an integral part of the text. Carle, as an author/illustrator, provides a children's book that conveys meaning in many ways. Even the colorful

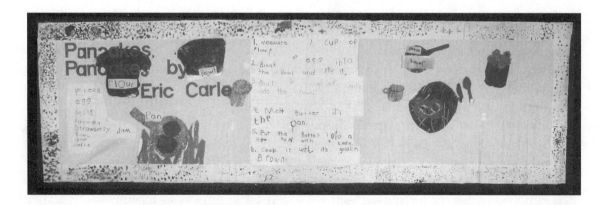

FIGURE 9–1 *Pancakes, Pancakes!* Mural

polka dot pattern on the end papers enhance the feeling and mood of the text. The children loved the end papers in Eric Carle's books. They especially appreciated the art in *Pancakes, Pancakes* and replicated the artist's style in their own illustrations for this recipe. In their own way, they were integrating written text, oral text, and visual images to convey meaning. The colors are the same as those in the books; the style of illustration is reminiscent of Carle, with its spotted borders.

The teacher and children engaged in a good deal of conversation about the layout of the piece and the juxtaposition of text and illustrations. They revisited the text many times to solve different problems. This purposeful "going back into" the text allowed the teacher to bring children's attention to different aspects of reading and writing.

Some of the larger images (bowl, skillet, pancakes) were cut out by Sharon, as she talked with the children, from the larger pieces of paper that they had painted. She provided an explicit model that would help the children see how to use texture, color, and shape. In this way, she was helping them learn about symmetry and form. The ultimate result was a visually pleasing display. When children have explicit examples of how to consider the art that goes with the writing, they can transfer this understanding to their independent writing pieces.

The children shared their understanding in another genre through more interactive writing connected to a related experience. They actually made pancakes and had two choices of what to put on their pancakes. Afterward, they wrote a survey question, "What did you like on your pancakes?" using interactive writing. Figure 9-2 shows the results.

The teacher wrote *strawberry jam* and *syrup* at the top of a sheet. Each child wrote his or her own name under the topping of

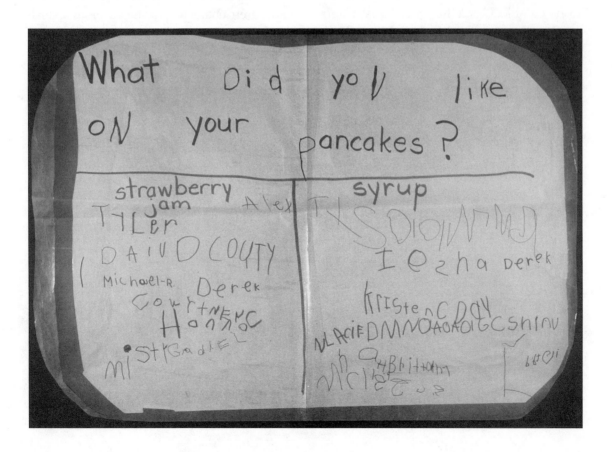

FIGURE 9–2 Pancake Survey Question Results

choice. You can see that the children's signatures reflect the wide diversity in this group. Some children simply string letters together to make their names. Others write their names in accurate detail with upper- and lower-case letters. Whatever their level of expertise, the children all benefited from this writing. Some children simply needed to see that oral language can be recorded using letters on paper. Others were able to increase their knowledge of high-frequency words and of hearing the individual sounds in words.

This piece also shows that interactive writing can be a tool for considering the literary aspects of *Pancakes, Pancakes*. To express their written message, the children had to return to the story many times and had the opportunity to think about the language and events. In this case, the children used the content of the story, including specific vocabulary words in their own piece of writing.

The same group of children compared characters in three different versions of the story "Goldilocks and the Three Bears" (Brett 1987; Galdone 1972; Marshall 1988). They made simple character webs describing Goldilocks as portrayed in each of the three books (Figure 9-3, see also Appendix 5). They used everything that they knew about the character of Goldilocks from looking at pictures and from hearing the stories many times. They gleaned character traits from how the characters looked and behaved. So, they were using two sources of information—details in language and in illustrations. Notice that they used words like "good manners," "spits," and "no self-discipline" to describe behaviors derived from listening to the story. Phrases like "missing a tooth," "3 bows," "striped stockings," "long curls," and "braids" represented details that they had seen in the illustrations. It is important that the children had heard three versions of the story, because there is a subtle comparative element in their work. For example, they might not have described Jan Brett's Goldilocks character as having "good manners" if they had not encountered the horrible Goldilocks in the Marshall book. The Brett character was much more appealing by comparison.

FIGURE 9–3 Goldilocks Character Web

Another example of interactive writing (Figure 9-4, see also Appendix 5) was based on reading Jan Peck's *The Giant Carrot* (1998), an Appalachian version of the "Great Big Enormous Turnip."

Sharon had read the story several times and the children had acted it out. In the story, a little girl "dances around the carrot" and the characters are able to pull up the giant carrot. The children's writing consisted of retelling the story with the innovation of substituting their own names and the teacher's for the original characters' names. We think of this process as "trying on the language of the author." Even simple phrases such as *pulled it*, which were repeated in the story, can be important for children to use and make their own. Their list represented an abstraction of the important points in the text, placed in sequence. Summarizing a story by listing the events in sequence is a basic component of comprehension.

The children made illustrations showing themselves "pulling" the carrot. Then each child wrote a sentence under his or her picture stating, "[Name] pulled it." This activity provided opportunity and motivation for independent writing. Afterward, the children had many chances to read the piece. The point here is not for children to learn the word "pulled," which is not a high-frequency word, but to attend to language and words in specific ways so that they can notice details and use words for themselves.

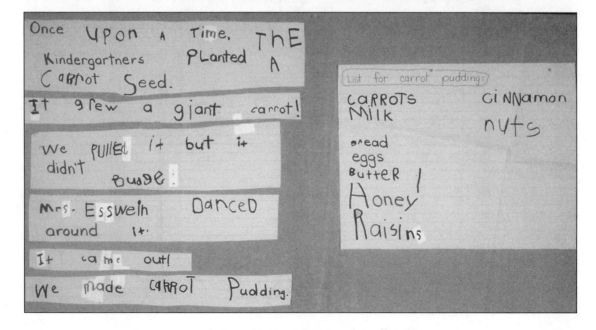

FIGURE 9–4 *Giant Carrot* **Mural**

In this experience the children again used their sense of the aesthetic feature of a book. They had also read Diana Pomeroy's *One Potato* (1996) and made potato prints, which provided an excellent medium for enhancing their version of *The Giant Carrot*. They produced a printed border of carrots that added considerably to the presentation of the whole text.

This learning experience also gave the children a chance to use and learn about another genre of writing. A recipe for carrot pudding is reproduced at the back of *The Giant Carrot*. The children decided to make carrot pudding; so, first they needed to list the ingredients (Figure 9-5).

Making the list required the children to talk about and refer to the recipe. They had the opportunity to use the word *ingredients* and to construct spellings for words like *butter* (with an *er*), *carrots*, and *nuts* (each with an *s* to indicate plurals). The teacher did not stop to make a "lesson" out of these words, but children were building the background experiences that will make later lessons profitable.

Another interesting example of interactive writing was a retelling of *The Hat* by Jan Brett (1997), done by a kindergarten class (Figure 9-6).

In *The Hat*, a girl named Lisa hangs some items of warm clothing out to dry. A strong wind comes along and blows the clothing off the clothesline. A curious hedgehog sees a stocking lying on the snow, crawls headfirst into it, and can't get out. Throughout the story, he keeps trying to shed the stocking until Lisa finally chases him down and takes off the stocking. Wearing the stocking on his head, and feeling quite embarrassed, the hedgehog encounters other animals who question and tease him. Each time, he tells the animal (gander, cat, horse, hen, pig, and dog) that the stocking is a "hat" and gives a

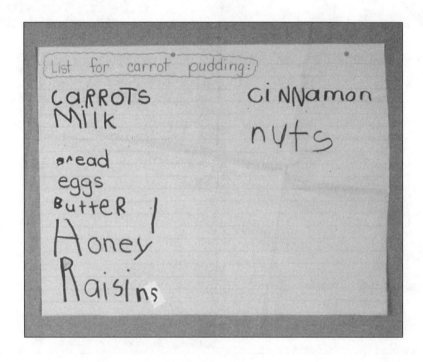

FIGURE 9–5 Ingredients for Carrot Pudding

FIGURE 9–6 *The Hat* Mural

good reason for wearing a hat in winter. At the end of the story, Lisa finds that *all* the animals who initially made fun of the hedgehog are now wearing items of her warm clothing as "hats."

Nowhere in the text does the sentence "I want a hat" appear; but the children's composition of the book sums up the main idea and conclusion of the story. At the end, all the animals do want a hat. The children decided that, in the story, the animals were really jealous because they didn't have hats of their own. They came up with the sentence stating what they thought the animals were really thinking.

The example described above does have to do with writing, but it has even more to do with learning about language. The children were learning to manipulate the ideas they encountered in text, summarize the story, and abstract the main idea. They were beginning to get an idea of the way characters evolve. All of this learning was applied in creating a cohesive and aesthetically pleasing written product.

Brett illustrates her books beautifully with framed pictures and intricate details in the borders. The children reflected their appreciation of this artwork by selecting wrapping paper and pasting on a border for their retelling. The stocking on the line and the one on the hedgehog's head are made of the same piece of wrapping paper. Noticing details like this helps children to

better appreciate the literary quality of books and increases their power of perception. They also enhanced the appeal of their writing by using potatoes to print white "snowflakes" on it. These beginning writers had the experience of planning, writing, and illustrating a coherent and beautiful piece of work.

Connecting Interactive Writing with Nursery Rhymes and Songs

Research indicates that kindergarten children profit from hearing and saying rhymes and songs. Through enjoying familiar poems, children develop more sensitivity to the sounds of the language (phonemic awareness). We can use interactive writing to enhance and extend children's experience with rhymes. A group of kindergarten children illustrated a favorite song, "The Old Lady Who Swallowed a Fly," which can be sung or recited as a poem (Figure 9-7 on page 130).

Ida read several versions of the song aloud to the class. Important activities for the children included reciting the poem over and over and acting it out. They made a big picture of the old lady. The children then talked about the animals the old lady swallowed, drew pictures of them, wrote labels for them, and glued them on to their mural.

Another group of first graders made their own version of "Humpty Dumpty." They wrote a rhyming text for their picture,

FIGURE 9-7   The Old Lady Who Swallowed a Fly

"Humpty Dumpty fell off the hill. Humpty Dumpty had a great spill" (Figure 9-8).

To learn more about the text, another kindergarten class made a wall mural of "Going on a Bear Hunt" (Figure 9-9 on page 131). In addition to playing the traditional hand game, they heard their teacher read aloud *We're Going on a Bear Hunt* by Michael Rosen (1989).

This activity required them to pay attention to a sequence of events in the rhyme. After learning the rhyme, they made illustrations on a mural showing all of the topographical and climatic features mentioned in the poem—grass, river, trees, snow storm— and ended with the bear. Whenever they recited the rhyme on subsequent days, they used puppets to travel across the grass, river and trees, see the bear, and then retreat. It helped them to think about the sequence and then reverse the order. A summary statement, illustrating that even young children

can begin to be aware of the central and most important ideas in a piece of written language, was printed at the top of the mural using interactive writing:

We're going on a bear hunt.
We're not going on a bear hunt again.

The primary goal of using familiar rhymes, poems, and songs is to help children achieve control of enjoyable pieces of language that they can remember and recite, to sensitize them to the sounds of the language, and to help them begin to connect sounds and letters. Rhymes and songs are pleasurable for children to say over and over, and they make language available to children through oral and written retellings.

Using literature to teach brings literary language to children's attention. Their oral language is expanded because there is so

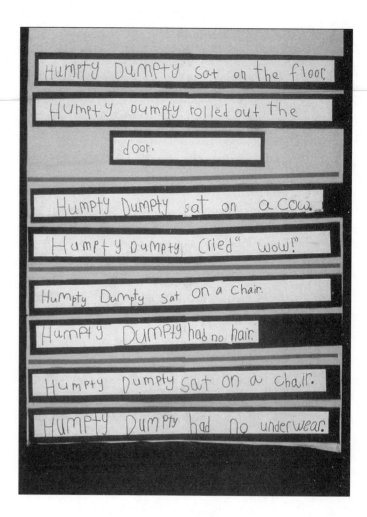

Humpty Dumpty Rhymes

Humpty Dumpty sat on a hill.

Humpty Dumpty had a great

Spill.

All the King's horses.

All the King's men.

Couldn't put Humpty together again.

Humpty Dumpty sat on a cat.

Humpty Dumpty went

Splat!

Humpty Dumpty sat on the floor.

Humpty Dumpty rolled out the

door.

Humpty Dumpty sat on a cow.

Humpty Dumpty cried "wow!"

Humpty Dumpty sat on a chair.

Humpty Dumpty had no hair.

Humpty Dumpty sat on a chair.

Humpty Dumpty had no underwear.

FIGURE 9–8   Humpty Dumpty

FIGURE 9–9   Going on a Bear Hunt

much talk surrounding the text, talk that is employed to

❚ remember the story
❚ plan the text
❚ create the text
❚ judge the results and revise
❚ return to the original text to search for information or language.

When you work on texts like these with your children, you provide them with a rich oral language context to use as they learn how to express meaning through language and art. You broaden the children's literary background in many ways. You provide the opportunity for them to

❚ expand their vocabulary
❚ internalize literary syntax
❚ learn familiar cultural texts such as folk-tales and poems
❚ extend their understanding of particular authors and illustrators and their writing and illustrating styles
❚ increase their ability to notice details in text and illustrations
❚ learn how to talk about text
❚ learn to analyze, criticize, and compare texts
❚ learn to communicate what they understand about texts
❚ respond in different ways to different kinds of texts
❚ attend to particular aspects of comprehending texts, such as sequence, details, character development, authors' choice of language, and ways authors communicate a message or create a mood
❚ learn how stories begin and end
❚ learn the kind of language that is characteristic of different types of stories.

Extending a Story

Let's look at another example that involves not only enjoying and responding to a familiar story but extending the ideas in an imaginative way over several days of instruction. The story of "The Gingerbread Man" was a favorite of Nancy Kelly's class. Several children made a paper gingerbread man, which was "stolen." The children then had a problem to solve: how to retrieve their gingerbread man. They decided to advertise and created a sign (Figure 9-10). A whole sequence of events unfolded from that point.

The sequence of written products shown in Figures 9-10 through 9-14 is evidence of the wide range of interconnected activities that took place over time. The activities included:

❚ hearing the story "The Gingerbread Man" read, then discussing it
❚ making a gingerbread man
❚ writing letters

FIGURE 9-10   Lost

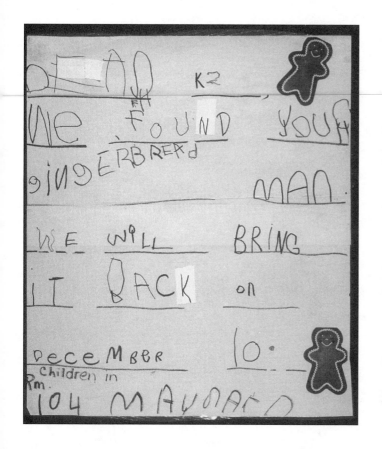

FIGURE 9–11   Letter from Room 104

FIGURE 9–12   Lost with Found Sign

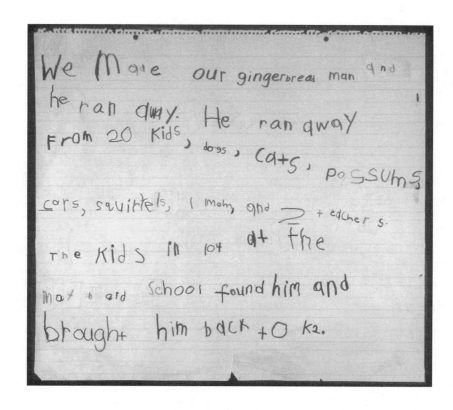

FIGURE 9–13   Story: We Made Our Gingerbread Man

FIGURE 9-14   Typed Book—*Our Gingerbread Man*

FIGURE 9-14   Typed Book—*Our Gingerbread Man,* continued

◾ making signs
◾ reading letters
◾ recalling and recording a series of experiences
◾ making the account into a large book, with separate pages for events and ideas
◾ illustrating the book.

In short, these young children were learning to be literate persons from the very beginning of their school experience as they engaged in using a variety of different texts to communicate and accomplish their goals.

The ability to interpret text and think about the author's craft is basic to all students' later understanding of sophisticated texts. This kind of knowledge and skill is assessed on proficiency tests in third or fourth grade. If we expect students to perform in these sophisticated ways in later grades, we must begin in kindergarten to help them think about and talk about text. Children need years of experience using these ways of comprehending text. Interactive writing is a way to help children explore a piece of children's literature in greater depth. It does extend understanding of children's literature through writing; however, it is the talk that extends the kinds of learning that we value most when it comes to literature. In Appendix 2 we provide a bibliography of high-quality children's literature titles that we have often used, to give you a rich resource for engaging young children in exploring the writer's craft.

Suggestions for Professional Development

1. Look at several pieces of interactive writing from your classroom. Are the pieces connected to children's literature? In what ways? For example, does each piece draw on the language from a book? Did you read an informational text to build or extend the children's knowledge of the topic?

2. Share your analysis of your pieces with several colleagues.

3. Analyze the impact of children's literature on the ways children compose and construct texts in interactive writing.

◾ How did they borrow from the book?
◾ How similar is their piece to the external structure of the book?
◾ Did they replicate the story or innovate on it in some way? How?
◾ Did the children use the same format of the book? Why do you think they made the choice?
◾ Has the language of the book influenced the language they used in composing their text? How?
◾ What impact did the photographer or illustrator have on the way children illustrated their piece of interactive writing?
◾ Did the children use the same media as the illustrator? If so, what did they learn from the experience?

4. Plan a follow-up meeting with your primary-grade colleagues. Bring three picture books that provide opportunities for your children to explore interesting techniques authors and illustrators have used to convey their ideas. Discuss how you can engage children in writing interactively to explore these qualities.

5. Plan to meet a week or two later. Use one of the books and share your pieces with each other. What have the children learned how to do as readers and writers?

CHAPTER TEN

Learning About Expository Text Through Interactive Writing

The best classrooms are places where children learn, talk, read, and write about things that interest them. One way to create exciting classrooms is to help children to read, recognize, learn about, use, and construct informational, or expository, text. Expository text is important for the following reasons:

❚ People use functional writing functionally in their everyday lives. They make lists or notes to support, direct and document their own activities. Documentation ranges from filling out simple forms to preparing legal documents and income tax statements. They also use writing to communicate with others, from the informal notes and messages that we all use on a day-to-day basis to formal business and social letters. Writing is a tool that is deeply interwoven with life in our society and supports social conventions and communication.

❚ People use informational writing as a tool for inquiry. Scientists and historians make notes and use charts and diagrams. They use writing to help them remember important details, to note hypotheses, and to summarize and communicate their results to others.

Through interactive writing, you can help your young students learn how to compose a wide range of informational texts, often engaging them in composing and constructing texts that would be too difficult for them to read or write without adult support. The writing of expository text builds on interesting, enjoyable, common experiences that are surrounded by exciting talk. This experience and conversation builds a foundation for composing well-structured informational texts.

In this chapter we introduce expository text and discuss the role that interactive writing plays in helping students learn how to use writing for planning as well as how to observe social conventions. In the next chapter, we will explore expository writing as a tool for inquiry and describe ways that you can involve students in using written language as part of scientific investigations or in representing areas of content knowledge.

What Is Expository Writing?

Expository text communicates new facts and ideas. Let's think about the kinds of informational texts that any of us might read or write

- planning lists for shopping, things to do, or people to call
- invitations to social and business events
- maps, directions, and travel guides
- recipes and other instructions
- personal and business letters
- airline tickets and itineraries
- forms and directions for filling them out
- signs and advertisements
- timelines and the labels on charts
- biographies and histories
- articles and books describing scientific discoveries
- articles and books on philosophy and healthy living
- newspapers and magazines
- telephone books
- dictionaries, cookbooks, and how-to references.

It is obvious that just living in our society requires reading, writing, and understanding a wide variety of expository texts. Indeed, our engagement with expository text is dramatically on the rise as we spend more and more time on the Internet. Interactive writing is a way to illustrate for children the wide uses of writing in everyday life.

Characteristics of Expository Writing

There are some particular structures that occur with high frequency in expository texts. For example, there might be sequences related to time, descriptions of procedures, lists of directions, embedded definitions or labeling. Background experience is often cited as an important factor in students' comprehending expository text. It is also important for students to learn how these texts are structured and organized. The beginning of understanding expository texts lies in the interactive writing that young children do with your support. Using their firsthand experi-

ences, you can simultaneously build important background knowledge and show children how to organize the information in an expository text.

Values of Reading and Writing Expository Text

According to Freeman and Person (1998, 2–5), informational books can help children

- learn across the curriculum
- see connections between content and concepts
- foster critical thinking and problem solving
- learn about new ideas, people, and places
- extend their learning as they engage in inquiry.

Too often, textbooks make up most of the expository texts that children read and use in school. But textbooks are not sufficient to help children become strong consumers of informational text. These books often lack firsthand accounts, and present material in a condensed and sometimes vague or monotonous manner. A wider variety of informational text is needed.

Freeman and Person (1998) make a strong case for including high-quality informational children's literature books in the elementary curriculum. For example, informational books can help students understand the process of science and learn about scientific exploration (National Research Council 1994). Reading is also important in mathematics, as children learn to apply mathematical skills in reading a bank statement or comparing prices at competing stores. Reading is important as children, learning about the democratic process in history and social studies, glean what they can about political candidates and current events from newspapers.

One note of caution: When working with beginning readers, beware of using too many informational books with difficult words and unfamiliar concepts. A student who is just beginning to build a reading process needs to have the concepts and most of the words available to him in meaningful ways. For prekindergarten, kindergarten, and early first grade, informational books are appropriate for reading aloud to children or for shared reading. As children become readers, you will move into using informational books in guided reading and in the other areas of the curriculum.

Types of Expository Texts

Irwin and Baker (1989) have identified six types of organizational patterns for arranging and connecting ideas in expository text:

1. description
2. temporal sequence
3. explanation
4. comparison/contrast
5. definition
6. problem/solution

We have added a seventh type, social convention, to account for the functional use of writing in everyday life.

Description

Expository text is used to describe places, objects, people, and events. When we read history or biography, the descriptive language helps us "see" places and people in our mind's eye. The writer of descriptive expository text is an expert at selecting details and using words, especially adjectives, to communicate to the reader. Young children participating in interactive writing lessons are asked to think about how something looks or how they felt at a certain time, to come up with details, put them into words, and organize the text so that it communicates to others. In the previous chapter, we presented a "character web" or graphic organizer that children used to note their observations of Goldilocks. The pleasure they took in coming up with descriptive words to paint a picture of Goldilocks would later serve as a stimulus for them to make their own writing more interesting.

In Chapter 2, we discussed the example "What happens to the inside of an apple when air touches it?" (Figure 2-8). In this example, which combined interactive and shared writing, the children posed a question, made predictions, illustrated their observations at the beginning and at the end of the experiment, and wrote one statement about what they learned. Their conclusion was:

It turns brownish.
Lemon juice stays white.

The children who participated in composing and writing this piece had to think carefully about how to describe the apple to others who would read the piece. This piece was produced with the support of conversation and the teachers' expertise at writing words. The text is well beyond what we would expect individual early readers to produce on their own. When it was placed on the wall, this interactive writing provided a strong model that children could refer to when they did their own descriptive writing. Valuable word solving took place during the writing of this piece, involving words like *brownish* and *inside*. The experience, talk, and composing involved in writing the piece were even more important in children's learning.

Figure 10-1 shows a piece of descriptive interactive writing, illustrating the connections that children can make between narrative and expository texts, a skill that is often tested at later grade levels. The children who wrote this piece had heard the teacher read and had talked about "The Gingerbread Man" as part of a study of folktales. They produced this expository piece related to the narrative. Writing this "advertisement" required the children to think about the characteristics of the Gingerbread Man from the point of view of someone who needed to find and recognize him.

Temporal Sequence

We can use expository writing to describe a sequence of events over time. Typically, we

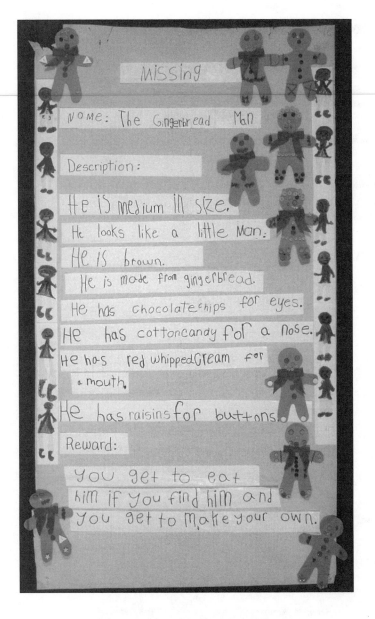

FIGURE 10–1 *Missing* **Poster**

To produce this example, the children had to reflect upon a sequence of events. The process was facilitated by the fact that the children had had the real experience first. This made it easier for this group of emergent readers to work together to describe a sequence of events.

Kristen Thomas and her group of second graders recalled the steps in planting and growing seeds (Figure 10-2 on page 142). These students had watched the seeds carefully, noting details and then producing illustrations. They were then able to put the events in order temporally.

Another group of children followed a similar procedure with growing tadpoles. Before they got their tadpoles, they probed their background knowledge to make some predictions. They recorded their predictions in the text shown in Figure 10-3 (on page 142). Notice that in this piece, the children produced several statements and then considered the order in which events would occur.

Explanation

We use expository writing to predict cause and effect or to explain the reasons for an event. Children in Stephanie Ripley's class documented their search for underlying reasons for an event when they answered the question "Why do you think Humpty Dumpty fell off the wall?" Using interactive writing, they made the following list of possibilities:

- ■ Was he being silly?
- ■ Was he too close to the edge?
- ■ Did he trip?
- ■ Was he dancing?
- ■ Did he not listen to his mother?
- ■ Was he trying to stand up?

Not only does their writing reflect very good thinking, but the text is composed as a series of questions, again providing a language model.

An example shown in Chapter 2 illustrates children's thinking about the relationship between providing water and plant growth. The teacher used shared writing to

use temporal sequence to give driving directions, give step-by-step instructions (such as in a recipe or sewing pattern), and to recount a series of events. In Chapter 5, we discussed children's composing and constructing of directions for making a peanut butter and jelly sandwich. The text read:

> Put the jelly on the bread.
> Put the peanut butter on the bread.
> Put the peanut butter on top of the jelly.
> Eat the peanut butter and jelly sandwich.

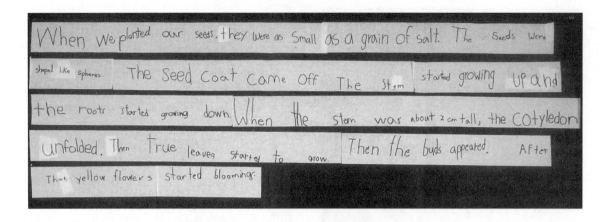

FIGURE 10–2   When We Planted Our Seeds

record the class' observations day by day, providing a comparison upon which to base conclusions about cause and effect. The children concluded the following:

The one that we watered is still growing.
The one without water is brown and crumpled.

Through a combination of shared and interactive writing, Kate Roth and her children

were able to document a rather complex experiment, about which children could later read (Figure 10-4). This piece of shared and interactive writing provided a good model for documenting observations over time and then using the written information as a focus for analysis and conclusion.

The children brought analytic thinking to the consideration of a narrative text and made inferences, another skill that is fre-

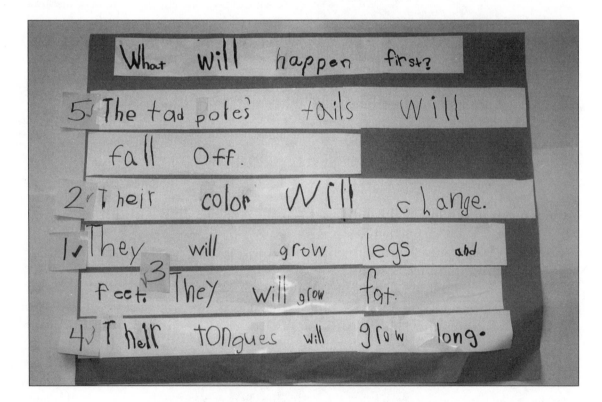

FIGURE 10–3   What Will Happen First?

quently needed by readers and writers in the later grades (Figure 10-5). Using the word *because* over and over, the children were able to organize a clearly written text. The ideas and sentences were more complex than these children would have been able to produce without support.

Comparison/Contrast

We use expository writing to compare and contrast phenomena, characters, events, and texts. Through concrete experiences and the surrounding talk, children are encouraged to notice similarities and differences. The example we described in Chapter 2 (Figure 2-6) was the product of children's exploration with a magnet, finding objects that the magnet will pick up and those that it will not. The text had two statements:

Magnets do not pick this up.
Magnets do pick this up.

The statements comprised the headings for two big circles drawn on a chart. Objects that had been tested were glued onto either circle under the proper heading. The chil-

dren used the circles as graphic organizers for displaying the information they had gathered through investigation. In this text, they were able to create categories, within which they could notice similarities. Notice how Karen King's class was able to use their writing to compare and contrast things that sink and things that float in the same way (Figure 10-6).

Definition

Expository texts can offer definitions and explanations to clarify concepts and ideas. In the example that follows, Toni Newsom and her first graders illustrate that they know how to provide examples to make the meaning of a text clearer.

The writing shown in Figure 10-7 shows elaboration, the use of details, and examples, which is another skill that these children will be expected to use in their own writing.

The task of writing is explained in a longer sequence of text shown in Figure 10-8, which was produced by a group of first graders. Here, they have recorded their knowledge of good writers in "writing workshop." They are explaining a procedure in

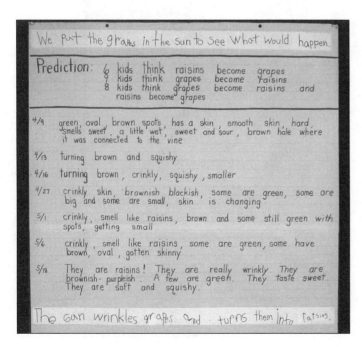

FIGURE 10–4 Science Experiment

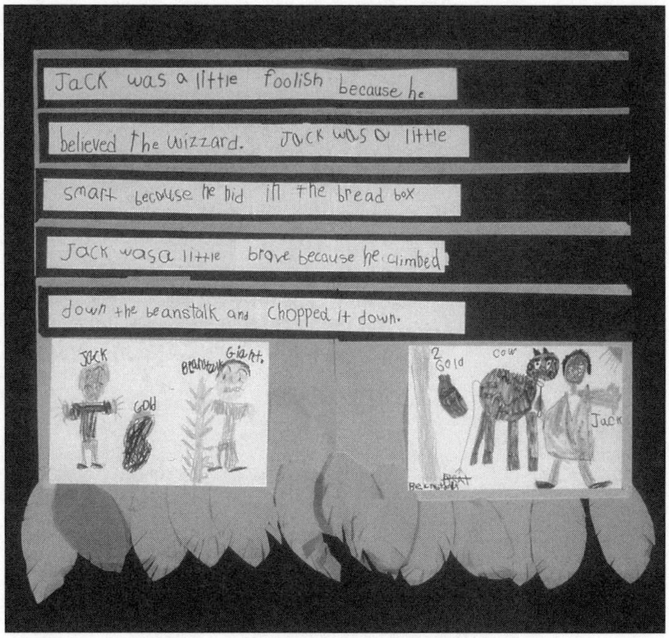

FIGURE 10–5 Jack Was a Little Foolish. . .

which they have engaged and know very well. We find their work to be a great explanation of writer's workshop, especially the part about never being finished!

Problem/Solution

People use expository writing to identify and analyze problems, pose solutions, and document results. Children can write about many problem-solving situations in this group learning process. Chapter 9 presented an example involving the "loss" of a gingerbread man. Children advertised, and through the process, "solved" the problem. While this example was based on fiction, the problem-solving process involved several forms of expository writing. Children can identify problems, documenting them through interactive writing, identify possible solutions, test those solutions, and come to conclusions. They can use writing during the problem-solving process as well as afterward.

Social Convention

We added *social convention* to the six types of organizational patterns identified by Irwin and Baker (1989) because one of the first things children learn about writing is that it is social in nature. Writing is a tool that we use every day, usually without even thinking about it. It weaves our social actions together and supports them. And, as we use writing for a wide range of social purposes, we constantly provide models for children. Writing accompanies almost every human activity. We make lists, write messages, label things, make maps, and so on. It is important for young children to notice written language and use it in their lives. In Chapter 1, we provided an example of children making a grocery list and then checking off items as they unpacked them.

The simple menu shown in Figure 10-9 was interesting for the children to write and also presented a good example of the usefulness of print. They generated the list and made the illustrations. Then children made small order forms in tablets. The list on the order form was exactly the same list as shown on the menu. When "customers" came into the play restaurant to order food, the waiter

FIGURE 10–6 Sink or Float

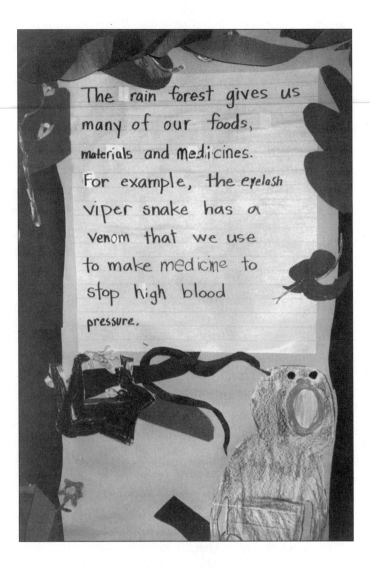

FIGURE 10–7 The Rain Forest Gives Us...

could check off items on the order form. To children, the activity was play, but they were integrating functional literacy as well.

Another example of functional literacy is shown in the letter in Figure 10-10, sent by the little buddies thanking the big buddies for reading to them. In the example shown in Figure 10-11, a class illustrated and labeled the foods that their lizard, Ivan, likes to eat.

Interactive writing can be used for just about any kind of functional writing that would appear in a classroom. Children can label artwork, write rules and directions, label places and materials, write letters, and make lists of things to do. Throughout this book, we have provided examples of children

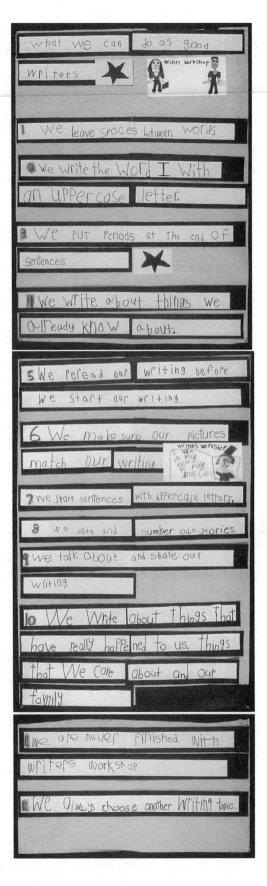

FIGURE 10–8 What We Can Do as Good Writers

FIGURE 10–9   List Menu

learn about print, but they had made good progress in learning letters. The children had taken a walk to the grocery store in their neighborhood.

Figure 10-12 (see also Appendix 5) shows their map, which includes their school, houses, streets, a parking lot, and street signs. In re-creating their neighborhood, the children had to think about how to organize the map spatially, where to place items, and how to label them. The final product turned out to be roughly accurate in the relationship of the school and houses to the grocery store. The detail in the illustrations shows things that the children noticed on their walk. Afterward, the map served as an organizer for thinking spatially about the community. The children took home a Keep Book[1] named *My Map* which extended their learning and conversation into the home. Not surprisingly, many children made their own maps, using their organizing and labeling skills.

Creating a Readable Text

When encountering expository text, a reader may be required to bring background knowledge to the understanding of concepts that are less familiar to them. One of the important advantages of the expository texts created in interactive writing is that they can later serve as reading texts for children. These texts are usually much more difficult than we would expect young children to read independently. They contain technical words and often have longer sentences. The ideas and topics are also complex. These informational texts are accessible to children as readers for the following reasons:

▮ The topics are familiar and well explored.

▮ The written language has been heavily supported by talk.

writing for multiple purposes; the sign on the oven in Chapter 8 and the instructions for the butterfly handshake in Chapter 6 are just two.

Mapmaking is another example of the functional use of written language. At about the end of October, a group of kindergarten children were learning about neighborhoods. All were emergent readers, just beginning to

---

[1] Keep Books are inexpensive (25¢) brief paperback books with colorful covers and interesting stories. The texts of these books are specially designed to support the development of effective reading strategies. Children are introduced to a book at school. They read it several times at school and then take it home to "keep." A structured program of instruction also teaches children to collect, care for, and use the books For more information on Keep Books, contact The Ohio State University, 614-688-3590.

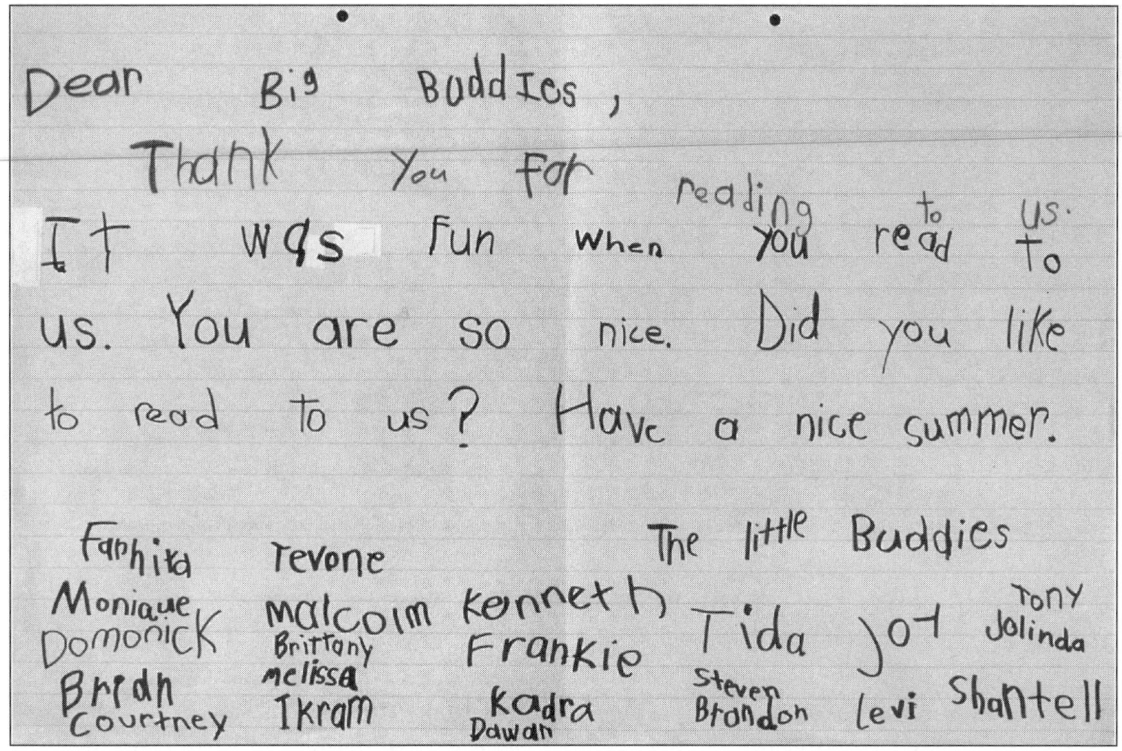

Dear Big Buddies,
Thank You for reading
It was fun when you read to us.
us. You are so nice. Did you like
to read to us? Have a nice summer.

The little Buddies
Farhita   Tevone
Monique   Malcolm   Kenneth   Tida   Joy   Tony
Domonick   Brittany   Frankie   Jolinda
Bredn   Melissa   Steven Levi Shantell
Courtney   Ikram   Kadra   Brandon
                      Dawan

FIGURE 10–10   Thank You

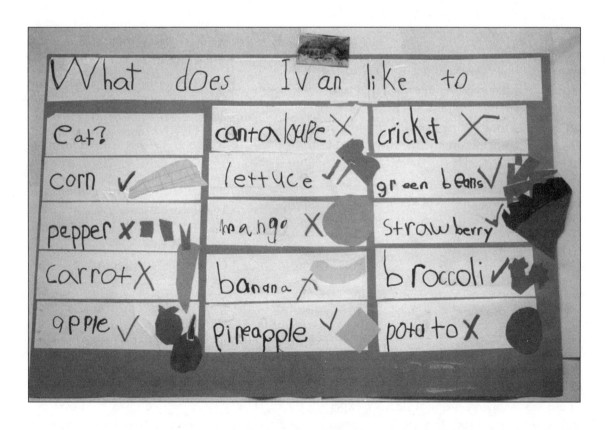

FIGURE 10–11   What Does Ivan Like to Eat?

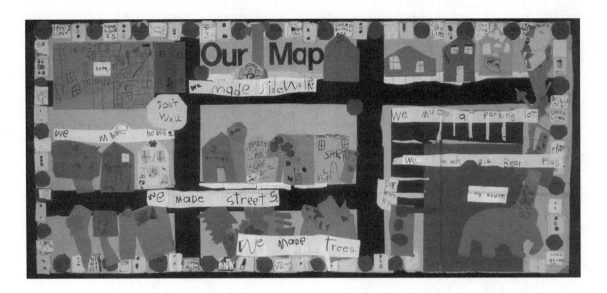

FIGURE 10–12 *Our Map* Mural

∎ The children participated in composing and constructing the piece.

∎ The children have read the piece many times through shared reading.

As children read these pieces of writing posted on the walls of their classrooms, they experience the reading of expository text in the most supported way possible. The primary goal is to get them accustomed to the structure and purpose of informational texts. This goal will be accomplished if you work to create texts that will be readable for the particular group of children with whom you are working.

The purpose of expository text is to communicate information. These pieces of written language may contain specialized vocabulary and they may have a higher "density" of information. Texts may require readers to remember facts and relate them to other information. Many texts require the reader to see similarities and differences.

Interactive writing of expository text provides many text samples that the children can use to practice reading. An important characteristic of interactive writing is that these texts emerge from children's experiences (either content inquiry or literature) and that the texts are used for reading again and again. In the case of expository text, reading may involve extracting various kinds of information, which can be interpreted and used in different ways.

Figure 10-13 is an example of expository interactive writing in the form of a wall book. The text produced is far more complicated than the children could produce or read on their own, but with the support of the teacher, they were able to write and later read it. Sharon Esswein had read *Pumpkin, Pumpkin* by Jeanne Titherington (1986) and *It's Pumpkin Time!* by Zoe Hall (1994) to the children. They made a "wall story" which is a sequence of pages, with illustrations and text, arranged left to right at eye level or a little above for the children. A wall story can consist of the events of a narrative text or, as in this case, it can be a piece of expository text. In this case it is not technically a "story"; however, it helps young children to have labels to designate the names for various formats they use, and "wall story" works very well.

The layout of this text is particularly supportive to beginning readers, for the following reasons:

∎ The spacing between words is good.

∎ There are no more than two lines of text.

FIGURE 10–13   Wall Story of Pumpkin

■ Each line of text starts at the left side of the page.
■ The spacing between lines makes the text easier to read.
■ There is a high level of picture support.
■ The layout is consistent, with the text at the bottom of each picture.

The long, left-to-right arrangement of pictures and text helps readers see the sequence of ideas, an important concept in expository text.

The connections between reading and writing are evident in all of the examples presented in this chapter. As children move into the intermediate grades, their ability to write and read expository texts will have greater and greater value. Through interactive and shared writing in kindergarten and grade one, you can provide a strong foundation.

Suggestions for Professional Development

1. Make an inventory of the kinds of texts that children need to encounter in reading and writing in your classroom.

2. Begin by looking at the range of expository texts that you have exposed children to in your classroom over the past year. Include the texts that you have read aloud. Collect a variety of these texts and examine them, noting:

■ layout of print
■ use of charts and/or diagrams
■ spacing and font size
■ illustrations

◼ format of the text (for example, questions and answers, use of titles, side headings, captions, labels, legends, etc.)

◼ kind of expository text (for example description).

3. Look at the kinds of shared and interactive writing that you have produced. Meet with a group of your colleagues and discuss ways of expanding interactive writing to include many of the characteristics of good expository reading texts.

4. Talk about how shared writing and interactive writing can be combined to make richer examples of texts for children to read.

CHAPTER ELEVEN

Using Expository Writing as a Tool for Inquiry

Interactive writing can be an integral part of inquiry. Scientists need a wide range of writing skills and, conversely, narrative writers need investigative skills.

Integrating Writing Instruction and Content Area Study

When children engage in scientific investigation and learning, they need a flexible repertoire of organizational structures to use in support of inquiry. They use writing as an integral part of inquiry, to

■ take notes
■ draw and label
■ make predictions
■ describe
■ summarize
■ organize information in charts, maps, and diagrams
■ compare and contrast
■ draw conclusions
■ report.

During scientific investigation, children use written language to explore new concepts and ideas. They engage in the process of investigation, not "practicing writing." The teacher acts as a facilitator and guide, helping them see how writing is useful every step of the way.

Content Area Study in the Classroom

Katie Roth's first-grade students were studying pumpkins as part of the autumn curriculum. One of their first activities was to visit a pumpkin patch. Before they went, using their background knowledge they made predictions about what they might see. They recorded their predictions in the list shown in Figure 11-1.

Children wrote the question "What do you think we will see at the pumpkin patch?" in interactive writing. They had to compose the question and think about it. In writing it, they used correct upper- and lowercase letters, wrote high-frequency words, and constructed words using letters, letter clusters, and spelling patterns such as *ill* and *ee*. In order to generate predictions for the chart and probe the children's vocabularies, Katie used shared writing to record their ideas. She wrote each child's name beside a prediction. In this way, each child had a written record of his own hypothesis.

After the class returned from the trip, Katie used a combination of interactive and shared writing to record more ideas. They generated another question—a survey—and used shared writing to label the items that

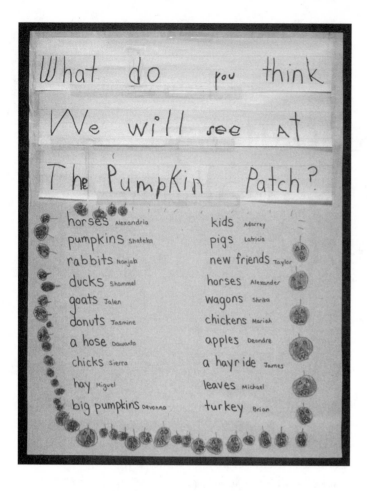

FIGURE 11–1   What Do You Think We Will See at the Pumpkin Patch?

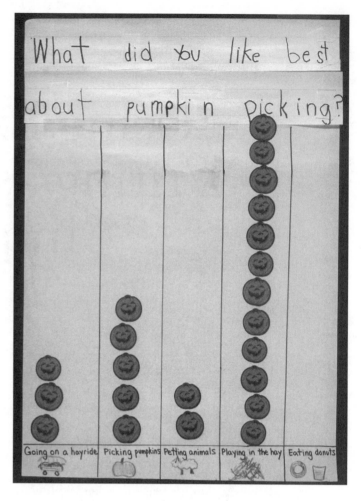

FIGURE 11–2   What Did You Like Best About Pumpkin Picking?

they had enjoyed during their outing. Then children placed pumpkins on the chart (Figure 11-2) to make a simple bar graph totaling and comparing their responses (tallying, synthesizing, and interpreting data).

The class used still another kind of expository text to record estimates of the number of lines on "big orange," their largest pumpkin (Figure 11-3 on page 153). Notice that Katie wrote the children's names and their individual estimates. At this time in the first-grade year, names are important, but there was no need for children to come up to the chart to write them because they were already proficient in writing their names. Interactive writing was used to provide directions for estimating and to summarize the results of counting. Afterward, each child could compare his estimate to the actual count.

The next investigation involved each child's counting the lines on his or her individual pumpkin. Interactive writing was used to write the question (which implied directions). The children wrote their own results on squares, which were pasted on the chart (Figure 11-4 on page 153) in an organized way to make a simple bar graph. Afterward, the children talked about their results and wrote a sentence reporting that most pumpkins had twenty lines.

The next investigation involved measuring the pumpkins' height and circumference. Children knew the routines of investigation well. The two charts they produced (Figures 11–5 and 11–6) showed two more ways of organizing and reporting data. The children wrote the questions using interactive writing. Each child measured his pumpkin, using

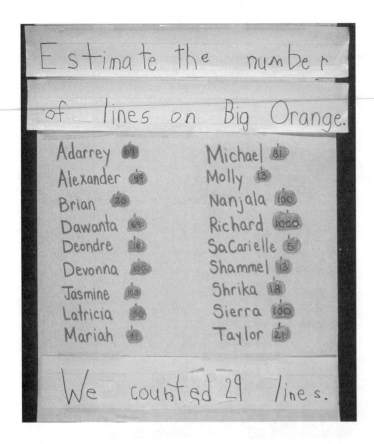

FIGURE 11–3   Estimate of the Number of Lines on Big Orange

strips of paper that were glued on the charts. Over and over, these children were participating in the construction of expository texts that involved visual display and summary statements. They were learning how to look at representational information, a skill that would later be required in test taking and in reading newspapers and other expository texts.

A final investigation involved the children exploring and comparing the weight of pumpkins. Their results are shown in Figure 11-7 (on page 155). Notice the scale at the bottom of the page, with the heavier pumpkins (big orange at twenty-eight pounds) resting on the lower end of the scale and the lightest pumpkins (one pound) on the higher end. This chart shows several ways of communicating information:

■ The numbers represent weight in pounds for each pumpkin.
■ The bar graph shows how many pumpkins fell into each weight category.

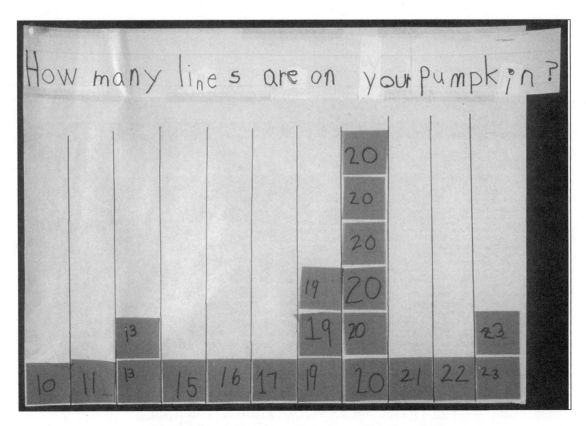

FIGURE 11–4   How Many Lines Are on Your Pumpkin?

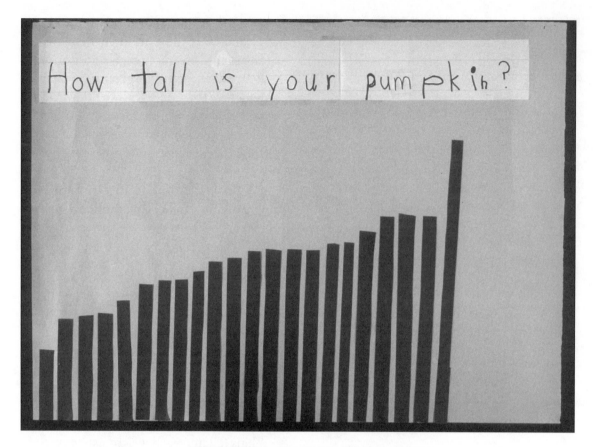

FIGURE 11–5   How Tall Is Your Pumpkin?

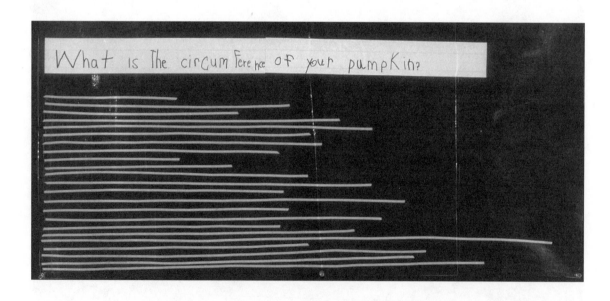

FIGURE 11–6   What Is The Circumference of Your Pumpkin?

- The order arranges pumpkins from lightest to heaviest.
- The pictorial representation of a scale is tipped to the heaviest end.

Just imagine the questions and conclusions that could arise from this chart! For example:

- Do most people pick light pumpkins or heavy pumpkins?
- Thirteen of our pumpkins are only one or two pounds.
- Big Orange is the biggest and the heaviest.
- The pumpkins weighing four pounds are right in the middle of the scale.
- The heavy pumpkins make the scale go down on this side.
- How many little pumpkins would it take to equal big orange?

FIGURE 11–7 How Much Does Your Pumpkin Weigh?

This investigation covered many days. Oral language surrounded the tasks in which children were engaged. Interactive writing served to direct their actions, record their thinking, and organize their information so that they could use it later and others could see the results of their work. Written language became a tool to support learning.

Uses of Expository Writing in the Process of Inquiry

Think of all the ways that scientists use writing. They record observations, take notes, make lists, write tentative hypotheses, sum up their data, write conclusions, make estimates or comparisons, make lists, write reports and share results with others, write abstracts or summaries of those reports. All of these ways of using writing reflect thought and action. The scientists' purpose of writing is not to practice or learn to write, although that might happen in the process of purposeful writing. For them, writing is a tool for thinking and guiding action. Our young children used interactive writing in much the same way.

We can also think about all of the practical ways that people use writing as a tool for inquiry in their everyday lives. Consider planning and preparing a family dinner. You might write a shopping list (and use it to check off items you acquire), write recipes and amounts, read directions, consult the phone book for specialty food shops and write down their addresses.

You use written language to compare and contrast, to persuade, and to get information. The examples we describe elsewhere in this book display a rich variety of the uses of written language. Language was used to communicate information about

- things that a magnet will pick up
- things that sink and things that float
- seeds and apples
- watering ivy
- the life cycle of the butterfly.

All of the examples reflect ongoing inquiry on the part of the children. They were focused on finding out something, comparing something, or observing something interesting. Writing helped them to record and remember their thoughts as well as to communicate their findings to others.

Reporting results of investigations and observations requires thinking, planning, and organization. Expository text presents some challenges to writers and readers that are different from narrative texts.

Labeling an Experiment

In another kindergarten class, children performed an experiment with worms, sand, and dirt (Figure 11-8). The class used drawings to show two stages of the experiment. Indeed, these drawings are reminiscent of the observational sketches made by botanists and zoologists. In the left-hand column, children illustrated their experiment at the beginning,

labeling the position of ingredients in the jar. In the right-hand column, they showed the results of the experiments (worm tunnels). This experiment in animal behavior was summarized in the bottom statement, produced using interactive writing. The entire text, pictures and writing, provide a clear, concise message.

Illustrating Experiments

This next example is a record of an experiment on plants. As part of a larger unit on plants, the same children asked whether plants could grow in the dark and they then performed an experiment. The illustration and organization of the text shown in Figure 11-9 provide a clear record of their experiment.

Reporting a Survey

In answer to the survey question "Do you help at home?" the children generated three categories of chores: folding laundry, setting

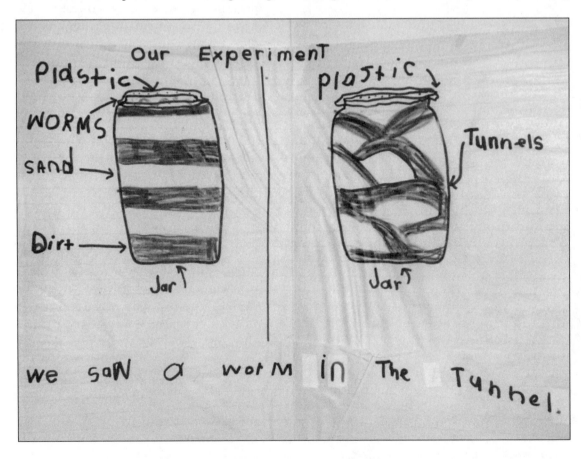

FIGURE 11–8   Our Experiment

FIGURE 11–9   Experiment on Plants

the table, and making beds. Then, as shown in Figure 11-10, each child responded to the items, placing an X in the yes or no column. The result was an organized chart that provided a clear visual picture of what kindergarten children reported that they did at home. They are real workers, aren't they!

Documenting and Illustrating Experiments
A group of children explored the concept of growing and produced some planning documents using interactive writing. They made a list called "What grows?" and used it to guide their next thinking, which involved selecting items from the list and writing sentences about animals that change their names when they grow. This exercise turned out to be both a concept lesson and a vocabulary lesson. They were learning the special names for the young. Finally, they produced *The Growing Book*, with illustrations. (See Figure 11-11.)

Summarizing a Larger Study
A class that was studying habitats as part of the science curriculum produced a book about animals and where they live. They had read a story about the life of a cactus called

FIGURE 11–10   Do You Help at Home?

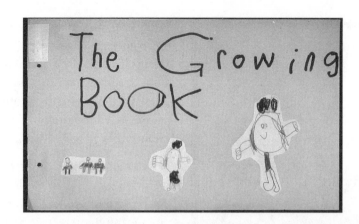

FIGURE 11–11   The Growing Book—Exploring a Concept

FIGURE 11–11   The Growing Book—Exploring a Concept, *continued*

Cactus Hotel (1991) that showed how the cactus becomes the home of many different animals. The children chose this book to help them write their description of animals in the desert. They produced a mural of animals in this habitat and wrote two sentences to describe it (Figure 11-12).

Using subtle tones, browns and purples, they used collage and paint to create the mural. The mural features the same kind of

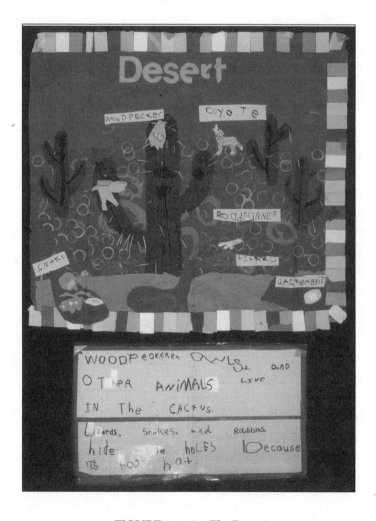

FIGURE 11–12   The Desert

border that they had seen on the end papers of the book *I Am Eyes—Ni Macho* by Leila Ward (1978). The whole effort is pleasing and informative. Notice the labeling of animals. The text the class wrote incorporated the same vocabulary that appears in the animal labels. This text was produced in the spring of their kindergarten year and shows that they had control of many letters and sounds. Their sentences also show a complexity of language, with lists separated by commas and dependent clauses. In all, four animal habitats (desert, grasslands, forest, and jungle) were included in the study, which lasted about three weeks. The wall murals and texts were the result of looking at many different books and pictures, talking about animals, watching films, and learning from a guest speaker from the local zoo.

Connecting Information Through the Study of Symbols

The U.S. flag is an object of daily attention in schools, usually the focus of opening activities. The flag became the center of learning for this kindergarten class.

They began by reading the book *The Flag We Love* (1996). Over several days, the class studied and learned about the flag, connecting it to historical events, such as immigration, national holidays (the Fourth of July), and current events (the Olympics). They examined the icons on the flag and talked about what these represented, with the stripes indicating what "used to be" and the stars representing the current fifty states. This activity promoted deeper understanding of the flag and helped children to create a web of interconnected understanding. In addition, it provided the opportunity to compose, construct, and read the complex sentences shown in Figure 11-13.

The children used past, present, and future perfect tense to combine words and numbers. They had the opportunity to expand their vocabulary and to integrate illustrations and text. They produced the illustrations using drawing and collage for a pleasing aesthetic effect. The children had read *Abuela* by Arthur Dorros (1991) and noticed the illustrator's techniques. In *Abuela*, collage is used to create beautiful and colorful illustrations. Thus, children composed expository text, but used information from another kind of text, narrative picture book, to create their finished product. They read their book about the flag and used it as a reference.

Producing a Descriptive Text

In the example shown in Figure 11-14 (on page 163), a group of children produced a descriptive text. They had to notice the details of how their mynah bird, Moe, looked and behaved.

This book provides details including Moe's color, his tendency to make noise, and what he likes to eat. The text of the book is as follows:

Page 1: Moe is a mynah bird.

Page 2: Moe has an orange and yellow beak.

Page 3: Moe has yellow skin around his neck.

Page 4: He has black feathers and yellow feet.

Page 5: Moe came from India.

Page 6: Moe eats dog food and he drops it sometimes.

Page 7: He eats fruits like watermelon, bananas, and apples. (Illustrations of fruit are labeled.)

Page 8: He makes a lot of noise. (A speech bubble over the bird's mouth contains the text "Oh, look at that!")

Some features of this text provide evidence that children were aware of some important features of expository text:

∎ The text is organized in a logical way, with the first page identifying Moe and the next three pages giving details about how Moe looks. The following page provides information on Moe's origin.

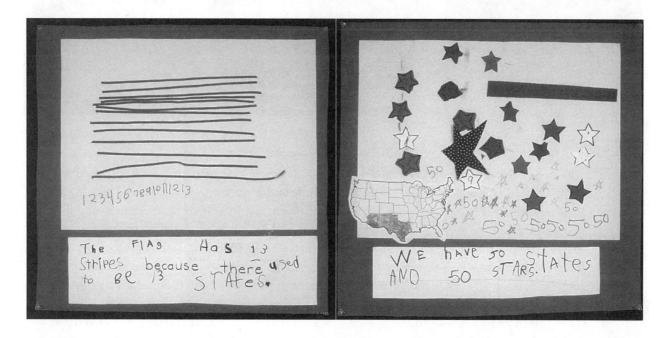

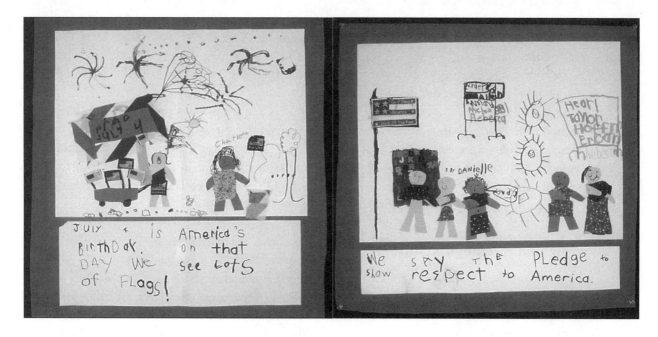

FIGURE 11–13   Our Flag

When people on boats saw the FLAg, they knew they were IN AMERICA.

If we win at the Olympics, they raise our flag.

FIGURE 11–13   Our Flag, *continued*

The next two pages are devoted to describing his eating habits, while the last page describes his behavior. Notice that the pages that go together are in consecutive order.

■ They used present tense on most pages but past tense on the page indicating that Moe came from India.

■ They alternated the use of the word *Moe* and the pronoun *he*, using the referent correctly. *Moe* is used on pages that introduce new categories of description.

■ Colors were tied precisely to the parts of Moe's body rather than just describing him globally.

■ When Moe's eating habits were described, fruits were mentioned as a category, which was further detailed with a list.

■ Illustrations matched the text precisely.

Writing and Reading Expository Text

As Smith has said, "we learn to write from the company we keep" (Smith 1992, 432). By this, Smith meant that we "borrow" structures and techniques from the writers that we

experience. In this chapter we have described how children connect writing and reading as they engage in learning experiences involving inquiry and information gathering and then write a record of their thinking.

The process of connecting texts is evident in the way children organized their texts to include labels and illustrations. As they illustrated expository texts, they revealed their experience with the illustrations in narrative texts. Finally, they experienced reading and rereading a variety of expository texts that were meaningful to them because they had participated in text composition and construction.

In Chapter 9, we described how children use several genres of writing to respond to works of literature. To some extent the same is true in scientific investigations. Chatton and Collins (1999) offer an interesting point of view:

Scientists and writers are investigators. Both are involved in careful consideration of the world around them; both are explorers, observing and formulating ideas about what they see. Too often, though, our curriculum doesn't reflect linkages between subjects like science and writing, and we limit children by assigning cer-

FIGURE 11–14   Description of Moe

FIGURE 11–14 Description of Moe, *continued*

tain types of writing to certain subjects. We ask children to write informatively for science lessons and creatively in language arts. However, if we look at books on science and nature for children, we discover that neither scientists nor writers have such constraints. Poets observe nature through the eyes of scientists, describing what they experience in careful sensory detail. (78)

They go on to say that scientists sometimes write both poetically and humorously.

The young children described in this chapter used many different kinds of writing and symbolism to assist their learning processes and summarize their results. Participating in the construction of simple texts supported the children's internalization of the important characteristics of expository text that they will be required to know and use in schooling and throughout their lives.

Suggestions for Professional Development

Attend to the following items as you meet with grade-level colleagues.

1. Look at the examples of children's interactive writing in this chapter for a beginning list of expository genres. Think about expository language in connection with science, social studies, and communication.

2. Make a list of the kinds of written products that the children in your classes have produced and categorize them by genre.

3. For each genre, discuss the kinds of thinking and investigation that are represented.

4. Now look at the curriculum and talk about some of the social studies and science topics taught at your grade level. Plan for a range of different interactive writing opportunities that will help children see how to use writing to learn more about the topic.

5. Following the study, gather together again to share and discuss the different types of texts.

Young Writers Engage in the Literacy Journey

While interactive writing has a structure and connected routines, it is not a static tool. Interactive writing involves dynamic decision making related to the strengths and needs of the children and kinds of texts selected for writing. Moreover, interactive writing takes different forms; as children grow in their knowledge, teachers are required to adjust the way they implement interactive writing. In Section Four, we explore learning, learners, and changes over time.

We emphasize knowing the learners and provide suggestions for assessing children's literacy knowledge. Further, we relate observations of children and evidence of their progress to the instructional decisions that make interactive writing effective. We also present a continuum of progress and an analysis of the interactive writing texts that are appropriate at various points along the continuum.

Knowing Your Learners

The Foundation for Effective Teaching

You can be an effective teacher using interactive writing if you know your learners well and select the activities that suit them best. Although interactive writing is group instruction, we know that children learn as individuals. Thus, as a teacher, you must recognize the strengths and needs of individuals, and draw out common patterns across small or whole-class groups to guide your lesson planning. In this chapter, we will help you do both, considering both informal and formal procedures for the assessment of writing abilities.

Observation and Assessment: The Foundation of Interactive Writing

Assessment is ongoing for teachers who are good observers. You can gain a great deal of information by observing children's behaviors and examining the writing they produce. Occasionally, you may want to structure your observations by assigning children a standardized writing task.

Using Observational Notes

Teachers use observation and notation as an integral part of their work with children. Many teachers use a simple note-taking system, an adaption of one devised by Mary Ellen Giacobbe, to record behavior. This system employs a form that consists of a class list of names followed by columns headed "knows how," "needs to know how," and "planning for teaching." Over a course of a week, the teacher writes specific observations of the most important behaviors, gathering information from

- individual conferences during writing workshop or journal time
- examination of journals and other written products
- quick notes made right after an interactive writing lesson.

To use this method, in the "knows how" column you would list important behaviors the writer has brought under control, such as writing from left to right, using proper spacing, and recognizing specific letter-sound relationships; you would also record words the student has recently learned. In the "needs to know how" column, you would write notes about behaviors that are just emerging or that the child has potential to learn next. In the "planning for teaching" column, you make specific notes for group minilessons or for individual conferences. (See Figure 12-1 on page 170.) These notes will guide plan-

Child	Knows how to . . .	Needs to know how to . . .	Plan for teaching
Marquella	• Uses mostly capitals. • Left to right but no spacing. • Uses 1 letter to represent a word. • Uses letter forms, mostly from her name.	• Use spaces in writing—understand word boundaries. • Hear sounds in words. • Make more letters.	• Reinforce spacing • Call to be spacer. • Show how to say words slowly. • Extend letter form knowledge.
Taylor	• Uses a cluster of letters for a word. • Understands word concept. • Leaves spaces. • Can write *I* and *a*. • Uses *T* from name—maybe letter/sound—and *h*.	• Hear sounds in words. • Connect more letters/sounds.	• Extend letter forms. • Show how to say words slowly. • Emphasize movements to make letters.

FIGURE 12–1   Analysis of Writing

ning for lessons as well as for the quick, un-planned interactions that are also powerful in pointing out examples to children.

The planning column is especially useful in designing lessons. As this documentation builds, you can glance down the column and take note of emphases that are important for the majority of children. These items will be appropriate for minilessons or for teaching points while you use interactive writing with the entire group.

The documentation will also help you pick out subgroups of children who need in-struction in particular areas or concepts. That information will be the basis for focused small-group instruction. The observational notes can also guide individual teaching. You can keep the list on a clipboard and refer to it quickly during an individual conference with a child. The record evolves as you add to the documentation, with new notes building on previous ones.

It is difficult to take notes during a busy day of teaching, so you will need a system that ensures that you observe all of the chil-dren during the week. Most of the teachers we know find it useful to keep handy a clip-board holding the evaluation form, or indi-vidual cards or Post-it notes that they can later attach to the form. These documenta-tion tools are used to take quick notes while working with children. With all names avail-able on your clipboard, you can be sure that you don't have "gaps" in your observation and you can prioritize your time with chil-dren. Toward the end of an observation pe-riod, you can make sure that you spend some quality time individually with those children who need more support.

Observational note taking is not for the purpose of reporting to others. You need a system that is helpful to you and that you can use daily to inform your own teaching. At grading periods, the notes will make it easier for you to summarize children's progress. The most important thing about ob-servational note taking is that it helps to keep you aware of children's needs so that you can plan powerful teaching. You can make quick notes during teaching, but you can also use planning periods to look at writ-ing. You can look at writing samples informally, for example, browsing through writing folders or journals once a week and using your form for observational notes. Looking at writing samples is an essential means to inform teaching.

Normally, you won't refer to these notes constantly; that would be distracting. You are too busy and involved in what you are doing, and you want to maintain a lively pace. But some quick notes made at the end of the lesson will be helpful. The act of recording and thinking about children's behaviors will serve your memory well. It will help you notice significant individual behaviors and respond to them during the interactive writing lesson and plan for the direction of future teaching decisions. It also will help you keep your "eye on the ball," working toward your priorities for the group as a whole.

Examining Writing Samples Elicited Through Prompts

Children's writing is a rich source of the information you need to make your teaching effective. Periodically, you may want to use a standard writing "prompt," an assigned topic for students to write about, which allows you to look at the strengths and weaknesses of individual writers but also to compare across the group.

A good prompt is a pertinent topic that enables all writers to communicate their ideas in a meaningful way. The prompt should call to mind something that is familiar to the children in your class. A good prompt is not a "story starter" (a beginning sentence that children must finish), nor is it a far-fetched fantasy or science fiction topic that children would not have conceived on their own. The best prompts are those that allow children to draw from their own experiences. Some examples of good prompts are:

- Tell about something special you have done with a friend.
- Write about our trip to the zoo (an experience the class shared together).
- Tell about a birthday that was your favorite.

- Tell about someone who has been very important in your life.
- Tell about something you have had to struggle with in your life.
- Tell about a pet you have or would like to have.

Some of the above prompts would be appropriate for first or second graders and some for older children.

Assessment of writing samples stimulated by prompts is slightly more formal in nature because you are attempting to assess the progress of the group along a continuum and build a profile that will serve as an overarching guide for priorities for the next several weeks.

Using Dictation to Sample Writing Behavior

Dictation is another useful process for assessing children's knowledge of writing. You will want to use dictation periodically, for example, about every month or six weeks. This powerful process takes only about ten minutes, and you will collect a great deal of useful information. Simply dictate one or two sentences to the children as a group. Ask them to write for themselves without conferring with others. Instruct them to attempt words they do not know and to use everything they know about writing. Collect the papers for later examination. When you examine the dictated pieces, you can ask questions such as those illustrated in Figure 12-2 (on page 172).

Using an Observation Survey of Literacy Achievement

We highly recommend using Marie Clay's *An Observation Survey of Early Literacy Achievement* (1993) as a foundational tool for assessment. We know of no other collection of tools that so comprehensively and richly surveys reading and writing behaviors and assists teachers in summarizing and drawing conclusions about children's strengths and needs, as well as planning their teaching. The survey includes the measures explained on the following pages.

Questions to Ask About Writing Samples
1. How do they use spaces?
2. Do they write left to right?
3. What is their knowledge of punctuation?
4. Do they use capitals in appropriate places?
5. Are they using both upper- and lowercase letters?
6. What letter-sound relationships are evident?
7. Are they attending to initial, final, or medial sounds?
8. What words do they spell correctly? Almost correctly?
9. How many high-frequency words can they write?
10. Do they make attempts at spelling words that are new, and how complete are their attempts?
11. Do they represent parts of words like endings? Vowels?
12. How do they organize the sentences on the page?

FIGURE 12–2   Questions to Ask About Writing Samples

Letter Identification (LI)

In an individual assessment situation, children are asked to identify the name, related sound, or a related word for fifty-four characters (the upper- and lowercase letters of the alphabet plus the typeset versions of *a* and *g*). This assessment is critical for kindergarten children and for first graders at the beginning of the year, especially those who have had limited literacy experiences in kindergarten. When you have specific knowledge of the letters children control, you can reinforce and extend children's letter learning within the interactive writing lesson. You can also help children see how their individual letter knowledge can be used in the process of producing text. Letters are not isolated elements; they are embedded in words. Interactive writing helps children feel that the letters are "theirs," because they connect them to something meaningful, as part of writing.

Chances are, prekindergarten and beginning kindergarten children will know some or even all of the letters in their names. Pre-viously, we have talked about the letters in children's names being critical entry points to literacy for many children. When we talk about letter recognition, we are interested in almost anything a child knows about a letter—the sound, the shape, whether it's tall or short, or whether it's connected with the name of a friend or family member. During instruction, you can ask children to locate letters, notice their features, find them in words—at the beginning, end, or middle.

Word Test (WT)

The child is asked to read a list of high-frequency words. Several versions of this assessment are available. This task may not be appropriate for emergent readers; for children who know a few words and some letters and sounds, however, it will provide valuable information. It is helpful for you to know precisely which words children can read and what their attempts at words reveal about knowledge of letter-sound relationships; of course, that does not necessarily mean that the child can write the words. Attempts at words will also help you in knowing what letters and sounds the child can put together to assist him in reading or what visual aspects of words he simply remembers. Children can use those words, visual features, and letter-sound relationships to monitor their rereading of interactive writing texts. And, having that information will help you to make connections between reading and writing in the construction of a text.

Concepts About Print (CAP)

In this assessment the teacher reads a small book and asks the child to "help" by answering twenty-four important questions about print, such as "Where do I begin?" and "Which way do I go?" The child is asked to point to the words on one page while the teacher reads, to match capital and lowercase letters, and to locate words on another page. This assessment is unparalleled in providing information about beginning readers and writers to the teacher.

Interactive writing is a powerful tool to help children learn the critical concepts about how print works. It will help you to know whether children can match word by word on one or two lines of print. If so, interactive writing is a good place to reinforce this early behavior and to make children flexible in moving from line to line. Using terms related to literacy, such as "letter," "word," "space," "period," and "capital," locating words using visual information, talking about the beginning of the sentence and/or the beginning letter of a word—all are important topics of conversation in the construction of a text in interactive writing. Knowing what young writers already control and what they need to learn next (or how they need to make their knowledge extend to longer and more complicated texts) will guide this conversation.

Writing Vocabulary (WV)

In the Writing Vocabulary assessment the child is asked to write all of the words he or she knows how to write in ten minutes, be-

ginning with the child's name. The teacher may use prompts to remind the child of words, but the writing must be independent. The assessment is scored by counting the number of conventionally spelled words, but partially correct attempts are noted because they also provide valuable information. The words the child can write independently provide a good index to what he or she controls in writing. These words are useful for you to know for several reasons.

- If a child completely controls a word (and most of the children in the group do also), that might be a word you would quickly write yourself during independent writing, leaving teaching points for words that children know something about but can't yet write easily.
- A known word might be used as an example for the group to use as an analogy in spelling a word not yet known (e.g., *his, hit* or *the, then*).

The Writing Vocabulary assessment can help you build a beginning picture of the words a child can write; you can add to this list over time. An approach that first-grade teachers have found helpful is to take a list of one hundred high-frequency words and highlight those that the child can spell independently. Periodically, you can highlight more words and use the list as a guide for implementing a spelling and word study system (see Pinnell and Fountas 1998).

Hearing and Recording Sounds in Words (HRSW)

In the assessment called Hearing and Recording Sounds in Words, the children are asked to make their best attempts at listening for sounds and spelling the words in a short message. The teacher reads the whole message aloud and then slowly, word by word. Without evaluative comment, the teacher encourages the children to write as much as they can of the message. This assessment is not a spelling test; rather, it is a test of phonemic awareness, or the children's ability to hear and write the individual sounds of words in sequence. The score is derived from the number of phonemes (sounds) for which each child has provided a corresponding letter. There may be some variations in children's responses (for example, the sound of /s/ in *is* may receive a point if represented by an *s* or a *z*). The information from the test is extremely valuable for informing your teaching in interactive writing. It requires the children to move from the sounds they hear to make a connection with a particular grapheme and then to use the directional movement necessary to make it. When you know the sounds children can hear and record, you can help them use this information in the construction of words. In interactive writing, you will be asking children to say words slowly—those you write for them and those that are produced through sharing the pen.

Running Record of Text Reading (TR)

The running record[1] is a systematic way of coding children's reading behavior of texts so that the teacher can later analyze the behavior and make hypotheses about the strategies children are using and neglecting. The running record yields a score on accuracy of reading as well as the rate of self-correction. You'll find the running record useful in your teaching of reading because it allows you to

■ find the accurate reading "level" for a child, so that you can select books appropriately
■ use analysis to find evidence of children's development of reading strategies, such as using visual information to check on their reading or solving words by taking them apart.

The running record is not useful until children have some reading ability. Later, as children learn more, the running record becomes the most useful tool in analyzing the way they process text. While the running record provides invaluable feedback on the teaching of reading, it also offers additional evidence about the characteristics and level of difficulty of texts that are appropriate for children to read. We have said that in the beginning, the texts that children can compose, construct, and reread for interactive writing are well beyond those that they can read for themselves. We would not, however, want these texts to be so long and complex that they require too much of children. The running record information provides a rough guide to the limits that teachers should place on a text that will be reread. Later on, the running record may help the teacher in deciding to increase the difficulty of text by adding shared writing.

As children learn more about reading, interactive writing texts become too easy to challenge them. When children are reading high levels of text toward the middle and end of first grade, we do not want them to be limited to very simple texts created through interactive writing alone. You will want to expand texts to provide more experience for readers. You can shape the compositions toward experimenting with new genre and ways of organizing texts. Guided by children's conversation and their participation in composition, you can add text yourself (shared writing) to enrich texts as reading material.

---

[1] The running record was developed by Marie M. Clay. For further information about how to take and analyze running records, see

1. *An Observation Survey of Early Literacy Achievement* (Clay 1993), which provides a comprehensive overview of running records, including the research base as well as thorough directions for coding, scoring, and analyzing records of reading behavior.
2. *Knowing Literacy: Constructive Literacy Assessment* (Johnston 1997). The author provides valuable information about the running record, including many examples and directions.
3. *Guided Reading: Good First Teaching for All Children* (Fountas and Pinnell 1996). In this book, the authors provide directions for taking running records and using them in guided reading.

Finally, running records can reveal those children who are self-extending readers—those who can read much more than can be produced in an interactive writing session. This information lets you know when it might be more profitable for children to be working on their independent writing than to engage in group writing. (Writing samples will add significantly to this information.) At this point, you will use interactive writing only for particular purposes with particular children.

Linking Assessment with Instruction

In this section we present four kindergarten students: Lucas, Jason, Marquella, and Taylor. You'll see writing samples from each at the beginning and ending of the year, and you'll learn about their performance on the *Observation Survey of Early Literacy Achievement*.

An Assessment Sampling at the Beginning of Kindergarten

Figure 12-3 (on page 176) shows the writing samples of these four children at the beginning of kindergarten. We selected four very different children to illustrate the ways in which a teacher might examine and analyze individual children and a group as a whole.

Lucas

At the beginning of the year, Lucas was able to identify nine letters, three uppercase and six lowercase. Two of the nine letters were represented by the same form (*Oo, Xx*). Maybe Lucas had played ticktacktoe! He could read from left to right, recognize that print conveys the message, and match some capital and lowercase letters. He did not represent punctuation, nor could he recognize reversals within words. On the Hearing and Recording Sounds in Words (HRSW) task, he could not represent any sounds. His attempts at writing words on the Writing Vocabulary task resulted in scribbles, one representing his name and the other a tornado. He had not yet begun to show letter-like features in his written products.

A classroom writing sample looked very similar, but showed circular lines that represented a face and eyes and horizontal lines that resembled a mouth. Pointing to the circular scribbles next to the drawing, he said, "This says colors on a girl's face," evidence that his drawing represented an idea and an attempt to represent it.

Marquella

Early in the year, Marquella recognized six letter forms, including *X* and *O*. She understood some concepts about print, including reading from left to right, but could not write any words. Her word attempts revealed knowledge of the letters *A, O,* and *R,* and the Hearing and Recording Sounds in Words task showed *Rs, Ms,* and *As* with no spaces; she could represent two sounds, /m/ and /a/. In her writing sample Marquella showed many parallels. Her story was the same letter strings of randomly repeated *Rs, Ms,* and *As.*

Jason

At year start, Jason was not able to identify any letters. He represented *brother* with an *r* and was almost able to write *Jason* (ASON). His other attempts were pictorial, resulting in a score of zero on the Writing Vocabulary test. The early writing sample shows scribbly lines with a picture of goblins swimming in the water. He wrote *JS* at the top.

Taylor

In September, Taylor identified fourteen letters, nine upper case and five lower case. Four of these letters had similar forms in both cases (*Ss, Uu, Zz, Oo*), which means that she recognized a narrower variety of forms. She was not able to write any words, although she attempted some letter forms and understood only a few (seven) of the concepts about print. She recorded two sounds on the Hearing and Recording Sounds in Words task. Her early writing attempt showed spacing between words, correct spelling of *I* and *a*, and possibly two letter-sound correspondences (the /t/ sound in *builded* and the *h* for *house*).

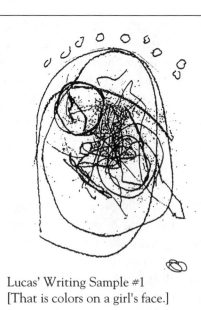

Lucas' Writing Sample #1
[That is colors on a girl's face.]

Marquella's Writing Sample #1
[I am going to the store to get my sister something to drink.]

Jason's Writing Sample #1
[The goblins are swimming in the water.]

Taylor's Writing Sample #1
[I built a house for my mommy.]

FIGURE 12–3 Four Writing Samples—Beginning of Kindergarten

An additional letter-sound correspondence is seen in her squiggled series of peaks (looks like *m*) that represents *my mommy*.

Connecting Observation with Interactive Writing

Suppose you had Lucas, Marquella, Jason, and Taylor in your kindergarten class, and suppose these four children were typical of most of the children in the group. It is obvi-

ous that for most of the children, letter learning would be a big priority. From the beginning, you would want to draw children's attention to the letters that they already know, helping them to see these letters within words and to connect them with sounds. In interactive writing lessons, you would help them attend to the features of letters, write them, name them, and to learn some high-frequency words. It would be especially important for Jason, and children like him, to make those beginning connections with the letters in his name. In addition to interactive writing, you would use the name puzzle (in which the letters of the child's name are written on individual cards to be reassembled by the child and checked against a model) as well as much work with magnetic letters (see Pinnell and Fountas 1998). Taylor, and children like her, also need additional work on letters as well as the opportunity to add to the store of recognized words. For all children, it will be important to learn to say words slowly, listening for sounds and connecting them to letters by using words they know.

As children grow in their knowledge, it will be important to extend their learning producing longer texts in interactive writing and producing more in their independent writing. You may want to "tidy up" letter knowledge by having children make their own ABC books, read the alphabet charts around the classroom, and participate in putting words on the word wall.

An Assessment Sampling at the End of Kindergarten

We reevaluated our four children—Lucas, Marquella, Jason, and Taylor—at the end of a school year in which they engaged in both interactive and independent writing on a daily basis.

Lucas

At the end of kindergarten, Lucas knew all fifty-four letter forms by name and he understood important concepts about print such as directionality. He could recognize many words and knew the difference between a letter and a word. He did not have full control of word-by-word matching, but he could represent thirty-three of the thirty-seven phonemes on the Hearing and Recording Sounds in Words test. He could independently write twenty-three words and was able to communicate several full sentences about a single topic, "The Basketball Game" (see Figure 12-4 on page 178).

Notice that most of the letters are well formed and that he has used space between words. He also controls a high level of letter-sound correspondence. Notice BASGT-BALL and GM, SOM, PONS as strong attempts at sound analysis, and the number of high-frequency words he can spell (*I*, *got*, *a*, *of*, *me*, *and*, *are*, *going*, *to*, *the*, *then*, *was*, *over*). The words are arranged left to right and top to bottom on the page.

Marquella

Year-end results indicate a dramatic difference in Marquella's writing. She knew fifty-two letters and many more concepts about print; she could independently write twenty words on the Writing Vocabulary assessment and could represent twenty-eight of the thirty-seven phonemes on the Hearing and Recording Sounds in Words test.

Her story about getting a perm showed the ability to stay focused on a single topic (see Figure 12-5 on page 179). Her spacing was adequate most of the time, and she arranged her words left to right and top to bottom as she communicated her story. Her attempts at words showed strong phonemic awareness (SLF for *self*, PRN, PM, or PRM for *perm*, PRT for *party*, BI for *buy*), particularly of dominant beginning and ending consonant sounds. She knew some high-frequency words, such as *I*, *a*, *to*, *the*, *me*, and *with*.

Jason

For Jason, year-end assessment reveals a perfect Letter Identification score (54). Jason scored 15 on the Concepts About Print assessment, but still did not have control of word-by-word matching. He was able to represent thirty-three of thirty-seven phonemes in the Hearing and Recording Sounds in Words test, and could write thirty words independently. Jason's dictated sentences showed left to right and return sweep under control, and good word spacing. On the Writing Vocabulary task, Jason wrote thirty words, some as complex as *pizza*, *Garrett*, and *Thompson*.

Jason's end-of-the-year writing sample (Figure 12-6 page 180) was a story about pizza,

FIGURE 12–4   Lucas' Writing Sample #2

FIGURE 12-5   Marquella's Writing Sample #2

I Had
A   I t   PIZZA
L S   hTI
Pe prone   AND   IT   IT Had
wus   gooD.

Then   Sm   d be mf   Dar.
is   At
AND   DAVID   IS   AT
NX   hos.

thenI   wetn   TO

SLP e.

I   will   hp you
GIS   Ken TRash.
uP   The
The   eND

FIGURE 12–6   Jason's Writing Sample #2

showing excellent control of left-to-right directionality and return sweep, word spacing, a mixture of upper- and lowercase letters, and control of numerous high-frequency words (e.g., *had, it, good, and, then, is, will,* and *you*). His strong awareness of phonemes is evident in his attempts including NIT for *night*, PEP-PERONE for *pepperoni*, KLEN for *clean*, and GIS for *guys*. The story showed full sentences in a sequence.

Taylor

End-of-year achievement for Taylor reveals a perfect Letter Identification score of 54; she knew eighteen Concepts About Print and wrote thirty-four words accurately on the Writing Vocabulary test. Her score on Hearing and Recording Sounds in Words was 35, showing a strong understanding of letter-sound relationships.

In her story, "Alexis and Taylor's Fun Day," (see Figure 12-7, on page 182) notice the amount of text written, and the large number of words written correctly (*and, we, on, my, mom, the, for, day, off, she, house*). This demonstrates Taylor's strong knowledge of high-frequency words. Her ability to analyze sounds in words in her stories paralleled her phonemic awareness score, as she made numerous excellent attempts at sound analysis (SDA for *Sunday*, FN for *fun*, OVR for *over*, HOL for *whole*, NIT for *night*, JRAM-PLEN for *trampoline*).

Connecting Assessment and Teacher Decision Making in Interactive Writing

Suppose you received Lucas, Marquella, Jason, and Taylor into your first-grade class in September. You would plan to extend their knowledge of words to encompass a large core of words that they could read and write, contributing to fluency and ease in both processes. For students such as Jason and Lucas, you would want to establish word-by-word matching. Intensive teaching of this concept in interactive writing—perhaps with a small group of students who have particular needs—will help to establish this essential early behavior. Letter names are not an issue;

probably, you will not make use of the name chart for simple connections with initial or final consonants that they already know. However, you may use names as a basis for looking at letter clusters or parts of words such as *ch, en, ar,* or *er*. All students will profit from connecting interactive writing with the word wall and exploring the inner workings of words. Interactive word charts, at first focusing on simple comparisons and principles, will also be helpful.

Documenting the Impact of a Literacy Program That Includes Interactive Writing

For several years, we have been working with interactive writing within a broad framework of literacy learning. As with any instructional approach, interactive writing is intended to be used in combination with other learning approaches. No single "activity" or context is sufficient to help children become competent readers and writers. Interactive writing makes a unique contribution to children's literacy learning during that period when they are beginning to make the first critical connections between oral and written language. Interactive writing plays the important role of demonstrating to young children how written language works and allowing them to participate in writing and reading so that they can develop independent control of a variety of writing strategies over time.

When a teacher is consistently using interactive writing in work with children, one of the goals is for children to develop letter knowledge, letter-sound relationships, and knowledge of words. As mentioned before, the benefits of interactive writing go well beyond that kind of knowledge; however, it is appropriate to assess the general impact of interactive writing on children's understanding related to letters and sounds.

Using Assessment Data to Evaluate Interactive Writing Programs

McCarrier and Patacca (1999) report end-of-year gains in a classroom where the teacher

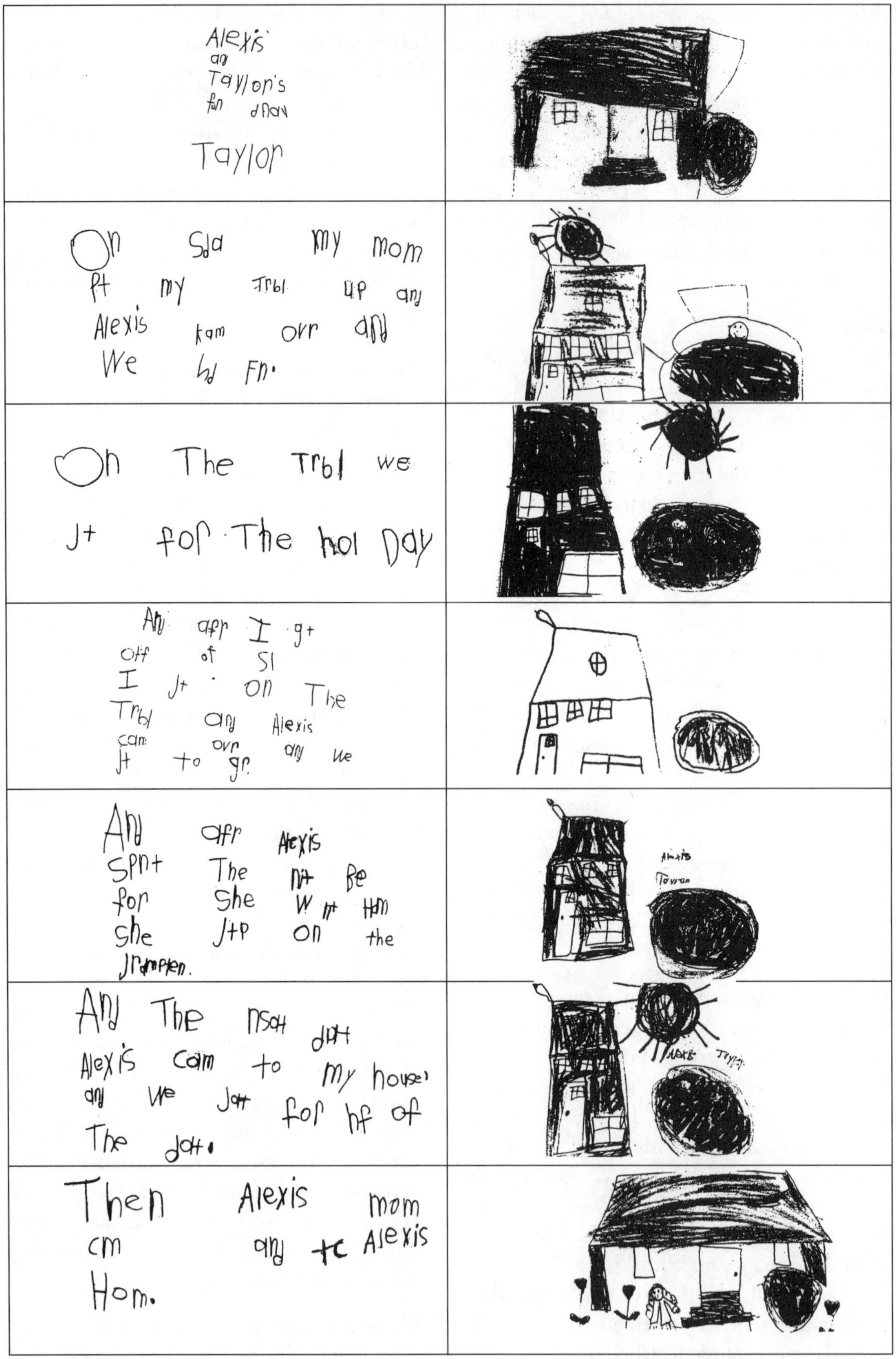
Alexis an Taylor's fn dnav
Taylor
On Sda my mom pt my Trbl up an Alexis kam ovr an We hd Fn.
On The Trbl we Jt for The hol Day
An afr I gt off of Sl I Jt on The Trbl an Alexis cam ovr an we Jt to gr.
An afr Alexis Spnt The nt Be for She W nt Hm She JtP on the Jrmplen.
Alexis
Taylor
An The nSat dat Alexis cam to my house an We Jat for hf of The dat.
Alexis Taylor
Then Alexis mom cm an tc Alexis Hom.

Figure 12-7 Taylor's Writing Sample #2

consistently used interactive writing in combination with the name chart and name puzzle (see Pinnell and Fountas 1999). On the test of letter recognition (Clay 1993) in which children were asked to identify fifty-four characters (including twenty-six upper- and lowercase letters and the print characters for *g* and *a*), children averaged 6.59 on entry to school, with a range of zero to forty-four letters known. By spring, the average score was 49.32, with all but two children knowing almost all of the letters. On a measure of Hearing and Recording Sounds in Words (Clay 1993), the teacher asks children to try to record the sounds (a total of thirty-seven phonemes) in words that are presented in a sentence. The average score for the group in the fall was .81; at the end of the year the average was 24.32, with a range of six to thirty-four sounds. Most of the children demonstrated good understanding of letter-sound relationships.

Ida Patacca, the teacher in this classroom, used no prescribed curriculum for phonics, no commercial programs, no "dittoes," and no worksheets. But she did teach phonics daily in an explicit, consistent, and persistent way. She used the name puzzle until children could easily put together the letters to make their first and last names and those of many of their classmates. She used the name chart dynamically to support interactive writing, and the children engaged in authentic, interesting interactive writing every day. Ida's instruction was highly systematic in that she noticed letter and sound learning and varied her teaching decisions to move children on in their development of knowledge in this critical area. At the same time, the children learned many uses of language. They wrote about their experiences, wrote letters, wrote directions, and used writing to extend their understandings of science and literature. The children in this urban school, more than 90 percent of whom qualified for free or reduced price lunch, became literate. (See Figure 12-8.)

All students (n=24) in the first-grade class taught by Katie Roth were African American children who attended an inner-city school in a large urban area. Upon their entry into school, Katie assessed students on several instruments (Clay 1993), with the following results: Letter Identification (average=42.69), Hearing and Recording Sounds in Words (average=13.12; ten students at or below 10), Writing Vocabulary (average=9.04; fourteen students at or below 10).

Measure	Fall	Spring	Change
Letter Identification Highest score = 54	(n=16)[1] 6.59 Range = 0–44 Middle score = 4	(n = 22)[2] 49.32 Range = 11–54 Middle score = 54	+42.73
Hearing and Recording Sounds in Words Highest score = 37	0.81 Range = 0–8 Middle score = 0	24.32 Range = 6–34 Middle score = 26	+23.51

[1] Class size was 23; however, some children were not enrolled at the beginning of the year but moved into the neighborhood later.
[2] Class size was 23 but one child moved.

FIGURE 12–8   Table 1: Documentation of Achievement on Literacy Measures in a Kindergarten Classroom

The Writing Vocabulary assessment measures all of the words children could write within a limit of ten minutes. Children in this school did not have interactive writing in kindergarten; it was obvious that children had learned the names of letters but needed to learn more about letter-sound relationships and to acquire more words in writing.

Katie consistently used the interrelated group of instructional approaches described in Chapter 2 of this book. Every day, children engaged in interactive writing and guided reading. As the examples in Chapters 10 and 11 show, Katie used interactive writing in an ongoing way as a tool for inquiry. She used a varied combination of shared and interactive writing to produce interesting and readable texts while at the same time focusing children's attention on what they needed to learn about how words work. She also worked with some children in small groups for interactive writing. Her curriculum enabled children to explore complex ideas and work together to write about them. At the end of the year, she again assessed children on measures related to literacy; results were: Letter Identification (average=53.79; one student below 52); Hearing and Recording Sounds in Words (average=35; one student below 30); Writing

Vocabulary (average=47.76; one student below 30). (See Figure 12-9.)

Another first-grade teacher in a different part of the United States implemented a similar program of balanced literacy. Again, interactive writing and guided reading were included every day. Kate Bartley taught in an urban school where most students were eligible for free or reduced-priced lunch; the students made up a rich mix of cultures and languages, although all instruction occurred in English. Toward the end of the year, Kate spent most of her interactive writing time working with small groups of children who needed more support.

At the beginning of the year, her students (n=22 who were present at both beginning and the end of the year) scored as follows: Letter Identification (average=43.1, with seven students below 40); Hearing and Recording Sounds in Words (average=16.2, with nine students below 10); and Writing Vocabulary (average=10, with fifteen students at or below 10). About half of Kate's students came from a strong kindergarten program, but because of high mobility, most of the lower-scoring students were new to the school. She also administered the Concepts About Print assessment (Clay 1993), which

Measure	Fall	Spring	Change
Letter Identification Highest score = 54	(n = 23)[1] 42.69 Range = 17–54 Middle score = 50	(n = 24) 53.79 Range = 50–54 Middle score = 54	+ 11.10
Hearing and Recording Sounds in Words Highest score = 37	13.12 Range = 1–30 Middle score = 10	35.00 Range = 19–37 Middle score = 37	+ 21.88
Writing Vocabulary Limit of 10 minutes	9.04 Range = 1–35 Middle score = 9	47.76 Range = 17–64 Middle score = 57	+38.72

[1] Class size was 24; one child moved.

FIGURE 12–9   Table 2: Documentation of Achievement on Literacy Measures in a First-Grade Classroom

tests children's knowledge of features such as left-to-right directionality and word-by-word matching. Her students averaged 11.80 on this test of twenty-four items. (See Figure 12-10.)

At the end of the year, Kate again assessed her students and the results helped her evaluate the impact of her program. Students scored: Letter Identification (average=52.85, with all students scoring perfect or near perfect); Hearing and Recording Sounds in Words (average=31.55, with seven students scoring below 30); Writing Vocabulary (average=34.55, with eight students scoring below 30).

The three teachers discussed above used assessment data to evaluate their own programs. While they did not make precise use of control groups or random assignment, they documented their work by compiling the data from assessments that are simple to use

and integral to instruction, in order that they could

- acquire (at the beginning of the year) some specific information that they could use to focus their instruction
- identify students who needed further intensive attention as well as intervention
- ensure that all students were acquiring the basic skills as they participated in the balanced literacy program

We invite you to compile results of assessments like these, share them with colleagues, and reflect on program results. We recommend that you administer the entire observation survey (Clay 1993), to first graders, if possible. The particular subtests that will be most helpful for your teaching of interactive writing have been indicated here. You'll have to take a few minutes with each child, but the information you gather will

Measure	Fall	Spring	Change
Letter Identification Highest score = 54	(n = 21)[1] 43.1 Range = 14–54 Middle score = 49	(n = 22)[2] 52.85 Range = 47–54 Middle score = 53	+ 9.75 +9.75
Hearing and Recording Sounds in Words Highest score = 37	16.2 Range = 0–34 Middle score = 33	31.55 Range = 17–37 Middle score = 21	+ 15.35
Writing Vocabulary Limit of 10 minutes	10.00 Range = 0–38 Middle score = 8	34.55 Range = 19–58 Middle score = 33	+24.55
Concepts about Print Highest score = 24	11.80 Range = 3–16 Middle score = 12	19.20 Range = 17–24 Middle score = 19	+7.4

[1] Class size was 24; however, some children were not enrolled and moved to the school later.

FIGURE 12–10   Table 3: Documentation of Achievement on Literacy Measures in a First-Grade Classroom

make your teaching more effective. Administering some subtests midyear will help you check on the progress of children and, if needed, intensify teaching in a particular area. Looking at a summary of information at the end of the year will give you a feeling of accomplishment and also help you set goals for the following year. The bottom line is student learning.

Teacher Networks for Literacy Achievement

The Literacy Collaborative at The Ohio State University methodically collects documentation on children's achievement within schools in the network. Staff members in these schools have made a commitment to long-term professional development and the implementation of a comprehensive approach to literacy development in the primary grades. Williams (1998) reports that schools in which teachers had learned to use

the literacy framework, including interactive writing, and had implemented it for a full year, showed a consistent rise in scores on the Gates-McGinitie Test of Reading Achievement (Figure 12-11).

The University of Chicago (Kerbow, Gwynn, and Jacob 1999), in a report of results in six schools, noted that in classrooms where the framework had high implementation, there was an increase in the level of achievement across measures. These results were especially clear for kindergarten children.

Careful, systematic assessment helps us in four important ways, as illustrated by the work of the teachers reported above. First, and most important, it allows you to know children, as a starting point for making your instruction effective. Second, it provides a way to report to administrators. Third, it provides a foundation for talking to parents. Finally, systematic assessment will allow you and your colleagues to determine the power

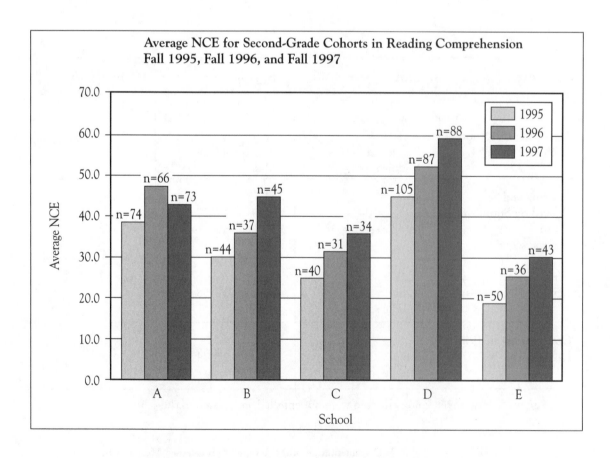

FIGURE 12–11 Comprehension Achievement over Three Years

of your instructional program. Effective use of interactive writing can help children acquire critical concepts about the uses and characteristics of written language. Effective use of assessment can help you focus interactive writing to help your young students in precisely the areas they need.

Suggestions for Professional Development

1. Meet with grade-level colleagues to decide on what specific assessments you will use (e.g., Letter Identification).

2. Administer those assessments and keep observational notes. Meet again.

3. Provide a copy of your data on each of the tasks to each of your group members and discuss your teaching priorities for interactive writing.

4. Bring a piece of interactive writing to a session with colleagues.

5. Share how your decisions were based on what you knew about children.

6. Specifically link your observational notes with examples of teaching points.

7. Critique the whole process, noting how teaching points might have been made more effectively.

CHAPTER THIRTEEN

Making Decisions for Effective Teaching

As a teacher, you make decisions every day to promote learning among your students. When you use interactive writing as a teaching tool, your goals are to

- stimulate and guide the oral language that is the foundation for producing a piece of group writing
- guide children's thinking to shape a text that matches their ability to write, that they can understand, and that will be readable for them not only at the time of writing but afterward
- help children understand the purposes of writing
- help children develop a sense of audience for their writing
- focus children's attention on examples that will help them learn more about written language.

To accomplish these goals, you must connect several different sets of understanding

- knowledge of individual children's strengths and needs as writers, and patterns of strengths and needs across the group of children
- knowledge of the characteristics of text and how text features relate to supporting and challenging readers and writers

- knowledge of the writing process and how it is learned, and its relationship to the acquisition of reading.

In the previous chapter, we focused on knowing the children we teach. The knowledge gained through ongoing observation and other systematic approaches forms one corner of the foundation for teacher decision-making. This chapter focuses on powerful teacher-student interactions, as well as decisions about the construction of text. In Chapter 14, we will address the characteristics of interactive writing at different levels of children's learning.

Teacher Decision Making

Ideally, an interactive writing session ranges from about ten to twenty minutes. Thus, as a teacher, you are constantly making important decisions about what will take place during those minutes. (When we mention time here, we are talking specifically about composing and constructing the text.) Here are some of the aspects of teacher decision making.

Content of Text

Appropriate text content is that which is matched to children's experiences and interests—emotionally, socially, and cognitively. Children should be able to understand the content and purpose of the text. For example, it is much more appropriate for kindergarten children to study their own school and neighborhood than it is for them to write about Harvard University or Tokyo, Japan. Authenticity relates to the appropriateness of the text along all of these dimensions. It is also important for the text to be related to something that the children are learning within the literacy curriculum. So, instead of asking the class, "What shall we write about today?" your lesson will be more effective if you say, "We've been studying the different times of day. Should we write about morning, afternoon, or night?"

Length of Text

Length of text refers to the amount to be written in a single lesson as well as to the length of sentences with which beginners must deal. (In considering length, you may also think in terms of the entire text as it is constructed over several days.) Early on, writing three- or four-word sentences will be sufficient. As children learn more, they can write more (or watch the teacher write) the text they have composed. When interactive writing lessons involve several sentences, you need to make sure that children reread during construction of the sentences.

Pacing and Message Production

Pacing refers both to efficiency in use of time and production of the message. Keeping children engaged and interested requires that the lesson move along at a fast pace. Pacing is also important in helping children keep track of the message that is being produced. If you get bogged down working on every word, or have long interruptions during the production of the message, the excitement and the meaning will be lost. For example, if you work with children for twenty minutes and produce only four or five words, you will want to reexamine your pace and rate of production.

This does not mean that children cannot connect words to other words they know.

During interactive writing, there usually are quick connections and illustrations on the white board that move from one word to the spelling of another. It is best to avoid sandwiching phonics minilessons (such as lists of word families) within the production of a message. If you feel the children need to work on lists of related words, plan to teach a specific minilesson on word study at a later time, not in the middle of trying to communicate an idea.

Choice of Language

Knowing as much as you can about the children's language will help you guide language choice. Children may bring language or dialect differences to the group. This information will help you think about how to shape the language structures used in the composition. If children are using incorrect or incomplete grammatical structures in their own suggestions for composition, or if they are producing structures that will interfere with meaning, you can elaborate on their offerings, demonstrating uses of language that are slightly beyond their oral language capabilities. All of this shaping must be done with great sensitivity, and you may have to ask children to repeat the message several times if it includes unfamiliar syntax. If the sentence is so far removed from their own language that children are unable to say it or later read it, they will not experience ownership of it and the interactive writing lesson will be ineffective. Interactive writing can be used to expand language and model different ways of using language, but it is not intended to be a "grammar lesson."

Often, the structure of children's oral language has more complexity than you want to include in the interactive writing setting. Young children often do not understand the constraints that come with writing something down. Their oral language may produce a message that has many clauses joined by *and*, which may not yield understanding when written down or read. In this case, the teacher must help them shape their oral language into a sentence that makes sense and is accessible to them as readers.

Sometimes you might choose an easier vocabulary word over a harder one because it offers an opportunity to study an aspect of a word that is accessible to children; for example, writing *good* instead of *perfect* or *excellent.* You might also shape the sentence to include more high-frequency words for emergent and early readers. For example, children could be encouraged to extend a sentence like "We saw cows" to "We saw the cows at the farm."

Teaching Points During Message Construction

Perhaps the most difficult teacher decisions converge around which aspects of text or individual words to select for teaching points. As well, you will be making decisions about where in the text to "share the pen" and which children to call up to the easel to perform the task. This also means choosing to write yourself (shared writing) the parts that either are very well known by all the children or that do not yield productive teaching points at this particular time.

Writing Format

You will frequently be making decisions about how the text will be placed as it is constructed. Before working with the children, think about the size of paper, how the print will be arranged on the page, the size of the print, and general ideas about layout. For example, long narrow paper makes it hard to put more than two or three words on a line and increases the difficulty for beginners who may be writing large letters.

Think carefully about the consequences of your decisions. For example, we see no value in having each child write in a different color or the teacher using one color and children using another. The result is a cluttered manuscript in which color interferes with the way children see print. You will want to think about the size of the print (it should be visible to the whole group). A technique like drawing a circle and having children squeeze print into it will present ob-

vious difficulties to children, and the text itself will be hard to read.

Decisions also revolve around whether the text is going to be illustrated in some way, and if so, who will provide the illustrations. If children contribute the artwork, should it be completed before or after the text is written? Where will the illustrations be placed?

Whole or Small Group

Interactive writing is group instruction, not individual tutoring. You can use your knowledge of individual children as you make specific teaching points to the group. This kind of attention to individuals takes place on an incidental level; however, the major thrust in planning for interactive writing comes from assessment of individuals and thinking across the group about common needs.

Incidental learning takes place as children have a chance to share the pen in interactive writing. Teachers are intentional in their choices. For example, in writing workshop, you may have recently taught a child how to add speech marks to indicate dialogue. During interactive writing, this child could be asked to come up to the chart and place quotation marks on the group story. This intentional choice allows you simultaneously to illustrate something important to the group and help an individual child extend learning.

Sometimes teachers erroneously assume that

∎ every child must have a turn every day
∎ there must be a "turn-taking" sequence, such as calling up the children in alphabetical order or drawing names from a can.

These kinds of techniques remove the teacher's opportunity to make the kinds of choices that maximize learning. Having every child take a turn within a certain time period will make interactive writing predictable and tedious. Using a sequential list or drawing names at random interferes with the selective teaching that must occur for interactive writing to be successful. Such approaches result in "hit or miss" teaching. For example, kindergarten children's knowledge is, at the beginning, idiosyncratic. Brandon might know how to write his name as well as a few words and a great many letters and sounds, but Carrie might know only the *a* and may be just beginning to write her name. If the word to be written is *come*, it might be very powerful for Carrie to write the *c*, which she is just beginning to control, and for her and everyone else to notice the connection between *Carrie* and *c*. If Brandon were called to the chart merely because it was "his turn," he may be contributing something that he already has well under control and that would not increase either his learning or the group's.

Many teachers have found it productive to work with children in a small group for interactive writing. As children become fluent writers, they will need less time in interactive writing and some of the simpler concepts may not apply to them. In this case, the teacher may engage the whole group for some aspect of text composition or construction but work with a small "committee" to do some of the detailed work. Convening small groups allows you to work intensively with children who need special opportunities to look at the structure of words.

Principles for Decision Making

Figure 13-1 (on page 192) contains criteria that you can apply to your decision making in interactive writing. These broad decisions are relevant whether you are working with beginners or more advanced writers. One of the most difficult tasks is to select clear examples that are appropriate for most of the group. Interactive writing serves the purpose of helping a good number of the group members move forward in their understandings. The examples must be directed toward a principle that children can apply in their own writing. As in any other instructional

approach, teachers are always faced with a dilemma:

- If the teaching point focuses on something the children already know and can do, time is wasted and instruction is inefficient.
- If the teaching point focuses on something that is far beyond children's basic understandings, time is wasted and instruction is inefficient.
- For any teaching point that is made in a group setting, the idea to be learned will be too easy for some children and too hard for others.

These dilemmas illustrate the difficulties of group instruction; yet, it is impossible and highly inefficient to teach each child, one at a time. Our advice is to make decisions based on a broad profile of the class. You may have a rationale for focusing occasionally on material that will benefit children who are at a more beginning level than the rest of the group. It is possible, for example, to have a child less proficient in writing do the pointing (with teacher guidance), hold the space, or contribute the beginning consonant of a word, when the rest of the class are beyond that level. It would not be wise, however, to move the bulk of instruction to the needs of the children having the most difficulty. Most teachers find that they can send the rest of the children off to work independently and work with a small group of beginners on more elementary concepts for a few minutes. After all, interactive writing involves brief lessons that move at a fast pace. You can accomplish your point in just a few instructional moves.

Teaching for Writing Strategies

Interactive writing involves a combination of demonstrating and prompting techniques. The children are involved in the composition and production of a piece of writing that is purposeful. The production of their writing requires that they perform, step by step, the thinking and motor processes that all writers

Making Teaching Decisions in Interactive Writing

1. Select clear examples to bring to children's attention. If you are going to show a particular principle, show it in a clear example instead of a distorted one.

2. Think about level of difficulty in sequence. Focus on easier concepts before harder concepts. Work on shorter sentences before harder ones. Attend to the regular sound patterns before the irregular sound patterns.

3. Base teaching points on information about children's strengths and needs.

4. Be highly selective in making decisions about children's coming up to the chart to "share the pen."

5. Don't try to teach too much or have children do *all* of the writing on most texts.

6. Decide whether to work with the whole group or a small group.

7. Attend as much to the composition as to the construction. The arrangement of the ideas in language is often a neglected aspect of interactive writing.

8. In general, although some individual teaching will occur, select teaching points in relation to the overall patterns of learning evidenced by most of the group.

9. Select points that have potential for children's application of principles in their own writing.

10. Above all, have several good reasons, related to research or theory about children's learning, for the decisions you make.

FIGURE 13–1   Making Teaching Decisions in Interactive Writing

use. Within this context, you have the opportunity to teach at many levels. Most pieces of interactive writing are rich in possibilities; it is up to us to recognize the opportunities and to choose among them, remembering that

the goal of interactive writing is fluent, independent writing with control of the conventions of text construction (sentences, paragraphs, and whole texts), spelling of words, and punctuation. We want our students to produce writing for many purposes, to be aware of various audiences, and to find their voices as writers, gaining control of conventions as they go along. It is not a matter of either being "creative" *or* producing accurate, conventionally punctuated text. Our job is to help students accomplish both, realizing that learning to write is a process that takes time. (Pinnell and Fountas 1998, 202)

Once you have chosen powerful examples, you must then decide how to draw the point to children's attention. You may choose to provide a demonstration of a process, such as noticing the first letter of a word to locate it or saying it slowly. You may have a child or several children repeat the process, demonstrating it again for others. Once a procedure or technique is learned, you will then need to remind students to use it again and again. We call this kind of teaching "prompting" because you are asking children to use in an active way something that has been previously demonstrated and learned. In the first chapter of this book, we discussed how Ida demonstrated to children the process of saying words slowly and listening for the similarities between *jelly, Jenny,* and *Joshua.* As she engaged the children in interactive writing every day, she provided repeated demonstrations of this technique;

then she prompted them to use it for themselves.

Working with Beginners

When you work with children who are just beginning to learn about written language, you might assume that most of the time you will be using demonstration and direct instruction, and that is true much of the time. But even for beginners, it is important to get children to begin to take action on their own. Once a principle, a concept, an item (a letter or word), or a technique has been demonstrated several times, you can start to prompt children to take action. In the previous chapter, we provided examples of our assessment of Lucas, Marquella, Jason, and Taylor and discussed some priorities for their instruction. In the example below, these four children were involved with other classmates in producing an innovation on the story *Cat on a Mat* by Brian Wildsmith (1982), which had been read to them many times.

As illustrated in Figure 13-2, children were using the language from the text, a repeating pattern in which a new animal is added on each new page. Ida carefully guided the composing process in order to achieve a readable text. First, she read *Cat on a Mat* several times, being sure that children enjoyed the story and inviting them to join in on the reading. The language of the text became part of the group's shared experience and could be accessed during composing. Ida encouraged the children to compose a sentence "like" the book about the cat but to create their own animal characters. It was inevitable that they would use repeating patterns. Ida could have encouraged them to

FIGURE 13–2 The Duck Sat on the Mat

extend the language (for example, to say "the yellow duck" or ". . . sat on the mat and said, 'Quack!'"). With these emergent readers, however, she wanted to make sure that the text was fully accessible.

She also valued the text's repeated use of high-frequency words such as *the*, *sat*, and *on* as well as the opportunity to draw children's attention to beginning consonants and to connect them to their names. Since they would work on the text over several days, Ida could count on children's becoming familiar with the word *the*, perhaps eventually placing it on the word wall. Each sentence was short enough to be inscribed in a brief lesson (about ten minutes).

Ida's priority was to extend children's knowledge of letter names and forms and to help them learn to use letters within words. She also wanted them to learn to connect letters to the names of children in the class and to match word by word while reading. Here are some of the teaching decisions Ida made during the production of this sentence:

▮ She asked Jason to show everyone where to start writing (upper left).

▮ She wrote the word *the*, pointing it out to children as an important word.

▮ She asked children to reread the entire sentence after each word was written.

▮ She demonstrated placement of words on the page by touching the line while saying the sentence.

▮ She invited David to come up to the chart and write the *d* for duck while asking all of the children to say the words *duck* and *David*.

▮ She wrote the rest of the word *duck* quickly.

▮ She asked children to say the word *sat* slowly, listening for the sounds they could hear.

▮ She wrote the *s* herself and asked Ashley to write the *a*.

▮ She asked Taylor to write a lowercase *t* for the end of *sat*.

▮ Lucas was invited to come up and write the *o* (a letter he knew and one that appeared often in his approximated writing).

▮ Ida wrote the *n* for *on* and then the class reread the entire message.

▮ She asked Jason to use his hand to place a space between *on* and *the*.

▮ Taylor came up to the chart and made the *t* for *the*; in doing so she glanced back at the first word of the sentence, making a capital *T*, which Ida accepted.

▮ After asking children to reread, Ida pointed out that there was not enough space left to write *mat* (note that she had previously demonstrated placement of words several times).

▮ She asked children to say the word *mat* slowly, listening for sounds, and asked Marquella to make the *m*, accepting the capital form.

▮ She demonstrated placing a period at the end of the sentence and the whole sentence was read again several times.

▮ She asked several children to come up and locate *the* two times in the sentence.

The piece of language in this example contained many possibilities for helping children learn about words. Here are some of the teaching points that Ida decided *not* to make:

▮ Have children practice writing *the*.
▮ Analyze sounds in the words *duck*, *sat*, and *on*.
▮ Write *sat* on the white board and construct *mat* by substituting the first letter.

The ideas above might have been good teaching decisions for a different group of students; however, that group probably would not have needed to perform some of the actions that Ida emphasized (such as holding a hand for space or writing in a first consonant and connecting it to a name). After most children know high-frequency words such as *the* and *on*, Ida will quickly write them herself (sometimes asking children to "check" them) so that there will be time for more complex word solving. It's all a matter of allocating time to the kind of teaching that is most profitable for children at any given moment.

Extending Writing Abilities

As documented in Chapter 12, Lucas, Marquella, Jason, and Taylor all showed considerable growth in literacy learning by the end of their kindergarten year. Early concepts of print were established, although there was still some concern about a few of the children's control of word-by-word matching. It is reasonable and logical to assume that interactive writing would begin to look quite different by April of the kindergarten year. For one thing, through daily work children had increased their stamina in writing. They could engage in a series of problem-solving events, supported by writing, that would culminate in producing a longer, more complex text. They needed less support from the teacher in the composing of texts; they needed less prompting to reread, to think of the next word, to say words slowly, and to connect with letters and letter clusters. They could hear consonant sounds in words in first, last, and medial positions, and they knew words had vowels. Figures 13-3 and 13-4 show examples from the classroom work in early April.

The children had heard Ida read *The Giant Carrot* by Jan Peck (1998), which includes a recipe for "carrot pudding." They decided to make carrot pudding; and, using the recipe, made their list of ingredients. On the recipe, children were challenged to write words like *carrots, eggs, paper plates, milk, butter, cinnamon, bread, raisins, peeler, grater, baking pan,* and *nuts.* For some items, Ida wrote the entire word; for others, she wrote some of it, helping children to see that they might know a part. For example, for *cinnamon,* she wrote *cinnam* and had a child come up to put in the *on.* Words like *butter* were worked out in entirety, with children contributing all letters. Writing the list of ingredients took up two days of interactive writing sessions.

They introduced the ingredient list with the sentence "This is what you need to make carrot pudding. The Room 5 kids made it."

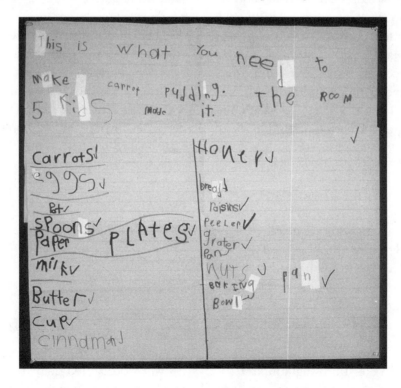

FIGURE 13–3   List of Ingredients for Carrot Pudding

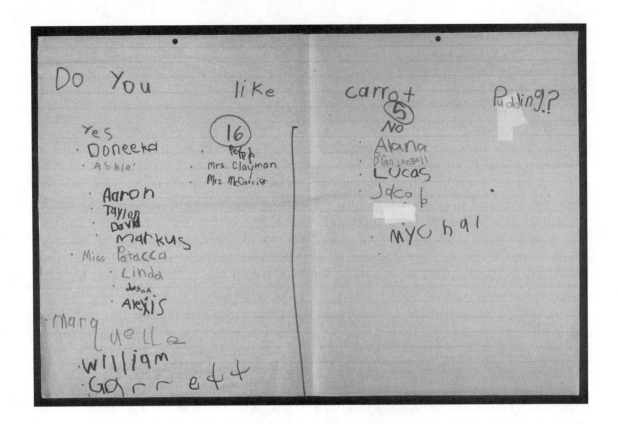

FIGURE 13–4 Survey Results: Do You Like Carrot Pudding?

Ida wrote easy words such as *it, to,* and *is.* There was no need to have a child hold the "space" or for consonant letters to be explicitly connected with names. Children would not be coming up to put in letters from their own names but might notice word parts that were similar to the names of other children in the group. There was still plenty of room in this sentence for word solving; for example:

■ The *ee* in *need* was connected to the *ee* in *Doneeka.*

■ Consonant sounds in the middle of *carrot* and *pudding* and at the end of *room* and *need* were emphasized.

■ Double letters were noticed in *pudding, carrot, Brittany,* and *William.*

■ Children filled in vowel sounds in *make* and *made.*

Some children were still using a mixture of capital and lowercase letters; others were using lowercase letters entirely. Twice, Ida used white correction tape to emphasize the need for lowercase letters.

The survey question offered students a chance to think in a different way about their carrot pudding. They composed a simple question, "Do you like carrot pudding?" which was written quickly. Then, during independent work time, children could write their own names in the correct category "yes" or "no." Notice that all children were fluent in name writing except for Garrett, who was just gaining the motor control needed to represent the letters he knew. Once the survey was completed, the children had to count the responses and calculate a total that could be compared.

Last, the group of children composed and then constructed a thirteen-page book called "The Little Brown Mouse" (see Figure 13-5 on page 198). In composing "The Little Brown Mouse," Ida guided the children to think about an overall plan for the story. They had to create characters and think about what they might say; they had to think of the episodes of the story. In this complex composition, these children put together several sets of information:

- the series of steps needed to make carrot pudding (summarized from their experience)
- the plot and text structure of a familiar story, "The Little Red Hen," which they knew very well
- the idea that characters in the story would all be animals who didn't want to work but wanted to eat, again leaning on their knowledge of "The Little Red Hen"
- memory of the language of "The Little Red Hen."

The resulting text, presented in Figure 13-6 (on page 199), offered many opportunities for word solving. Notice how children have used repeated language in a much more complex way than in "The Duck Sat on the Mat." Alternating composition and construction, these kindergarten children successfully produced a text with 161 words (including title and authors), 27 sentences, 3 characters, 4 episodes, and dialogue. Sentence length ranged from 3 words ("and she did") to 14 words, with an average length of 5.7 words per sentence.

Note that in "The Little Red Hen," all words are one syllable. "The Little Brown Mouse," on the other hand, had many two-syllable words, words ending in *ing* and *ed*, and one compound word. The children used punctuation accurately and with variety, including question marks, exclamation marks, and quotation marks. They even varied dialogue, as characters alternately said, "No!," "Not I!" (a more literary use of language), and "Yes!"

Ida's teaching decisions during the constructing of the text are illustrated by pages 5 and 12, shown in Figure 13-5. On page 5 of "The Little Brown Mouse," Ida made these decisions:

- She had the children say the message several times after composing it; after

the first sentence was composed and constructed, fewer repetitions were needed for the next two sentences.
- She had children say the word *not* and had one child come up to the easel; after the child wrote *no* for *not*, Ida said, "It does start like *no*, add the ending." The children came up with the *t*, which the child wrote. Later, there would be an opportunity to use the white board to compare *no* and *not*.
- She asked a child who was just learning high-frequency words to write the word *I*.
- Children wanted the language to "sound exciting," and Ida prompted them to remember the exclamation mark.
- When a child wrote a backwards *s* for *said*, Ida used white correction tape to enable him to make it again.
- She wrote the *aid* in *said* and prompted the child at the easel to think of and write the beginning.
- She wrote *the* and then helped a child write *duck*, explaining that sometimes the *k* sound is written with a *ck*.
- She wrote almost all of sentence two, leaving the exclamation point and the word *cat* for problem solving; she accepted the capital A in the middle of *cat* from a child who was still working to learn letters.
- She prompted another child to write the words *Not I* quickly and make the exclamation point.
- One child was asked to write *said the dog* quickly, since those were all known words for most of the group.

Ida's decisions helped to move the writing along so that in a short time, children were able to produce and reread this exciting piece of text.

On page 12 of the text, children worked hard to produce four sentences, with the last one being quite long. Ida provided the writing for eleven of the words and also wrote most of words like *cooked* and *myself*. The

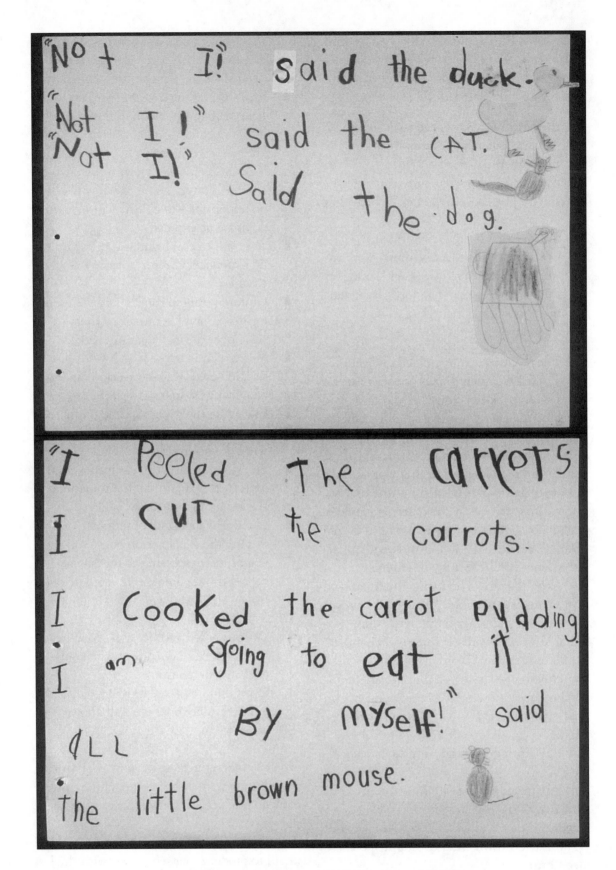

FIGURE 13–5   Two pages of "The Little Brown Mouse"

The Little Brown
Mouse

By Room 6

"Will you help me
MAKE the carrot
pudding?" said the mouse.

1

"No!" said the duck.
"No!" said the cat.
"No!" said the dog.

2

"Then I will," said
the mouse. And she
did.

3

"Who will help me
cut the carrots?" said
the mouse.

4

"Not I!" said the duck.
"Not I!" said the cat.
"Not I!" said the dog.

5

"Then I will!" said the
mouse. And she did.

6

"Who will help
me cook the carrot
pudding?" said the mouse.

7

"Not I!" said the duck.
"Not I!" said the cat.
"Not I!" said the dog.

8

"Then I will!" said
the mouse. And she did.

9

"Will you help me
eat the carrot pudding?"
said the mouse.

10

"Yes!" said the duck.
"Yes!" said the cat.
"Yes!" said the dog.

11

"I peeled the carrots.
I cut the carrots.
I cooked the carrot pudding.
I am going to eat it
all by myself!" said
the little brown mouse.

12

And she did.

13

FIGURE 13–6   Full Text of "The Little Brown Mouse"

word *cook* provided an interesting example to put on the white board because the first and last sounds are the same but the first sound is represented by *c* and the last by *k*. Ida then added the *ed* to the word. Notice that most of the letters in this sample are accurate as to upper or lower case. For one word, *by*, the capital *B* was produced by Garrett, a child with low letter knowledge who needed the chance to contribute what he knew. This piece also provided the opportunity to draw children's attention to double letters, something that happened during the writing and also during rereading.

Using Explicit Language to Prompt Action

The teachers we work with have found that specific language is helpful in prompting children to recall what they know and take action to solve words they want to write. These "prompts" help children because they are the model for instructions that they can begin to give themselves in their own writing. Figure 13-7 offers a list of prompts for word solving in interactive writing. You might want to put a photocopy of this list on your clipboard so you can refer to it and begin to use this explicit language more easily.

Prompting for Word Solving in Interactive Writing: Constructing the Text

During Interactive Writing: Brief Interactions

To teach for sound analysis:

Clap the parts you hear.
   Listen for the parts.
   Listen for the sounds you hear in the first part.
   Say the word slowly. What do you hear first?
   Listen for the consonant sound at the beginning, at the end, in the middle.
   Listen for the vowel sound in the middle, at the beginning, at the end.
   Listen for the ending.
   Say the word slowly. How many sounds do you hear?
   Write the first sound you hear, the next sound, the last sound.

To teach for visual analysis:

   Does it look right?
   What would look right there?
   It's almost right. Add the ending.
   You're nearly right. Add a letter to make it look right.
   It looks like (another word they know).
   Think about how the word looks.
   Think about another word like that.
   Do you know a word like that? Do you know a word that starts (ends) like that?
   It sounds like that, but it looks different.
   There's a silent letter next.
   You need a vowel next.

FIGURE 13–7   Prompting for Word Solving in Interactive Writing

These prompts provide examples of explicit language that can be part of your "repertoire" as you work with children in interactive writing. Remember that prompting is only appropriate if children really know what you mean. You need to teach them the process before calling on them to use it. If you have used the white board, Magna Doodle, or magnetic letters to demonstrate to children how to connect words and notice how they are alike, then it will be appropriate to ask children to "think about another word like that." They will understand the process you are asking them to use. If you have

---

Prompting for Word Solving in Interactive Writing
Revisiting the Text

After interactive writing: a brief period (two minutes at the most) to revisit and reinforce.

Find the letter _____.
Find a word that begins with a capital letter.
Find a word that begins with a lowercase letter.
Find a place where we used good spacing to divide the words.
What word begins with [letter or letter cluster]?
What word begins like [word]?
What word ends like [word]?
What word starts like your name [or someone else's name]?
Which words did we write quickly without stopping to think about them?
What's a word with two sounds [three, four, etc.]?
What word(s) has more letters than sounds?
Which words begin with consonant clusters? A vowel?
What words have one syllable [two, more than two, etc.]?
What word has parts that can be removed?
What words sound exactly like they look?
Which words have a tricky [interesting, hard, new] pattern [spelling]?
What word is tricky [hard, new] for you to write? What will you want to remember about it?
What's a new word you learned to write today?
What words could be spelled another way but sound the same?
What word has a special pattern [spelling] that shows what it means?
How is our story the same as the one we read [if an innovation on the text]?
How is our story different from the one we read [if an innovation on the text]?
Find a color word.
Find a contraction.
Find a compound word.
Find a word that describes [a character or a phenomenon observed].
Find a word that tells what someone did.
Find a word that shows someone was talking. Are there any other words we can use to show someone is talking [for example, variations on "said"]?

FIGURE 13–8 Revisiting the Text

shown children many examples of words with "silent letters" and placed exemplars on the word wall, you can suggest that "there's a silent letter next."

Revisiting a Completed Text for Further Teaching

Following a writing session, you might want to spend a couple of minutes revisiting the text to reinforce or extend learning. Revisiting the Text (Figure 13-8) provides a few examples of the kinds of questions you might use to help children consolidate their understandings and remind them to attend to the word features in their own writing. You might want to put a photocopy of this list on your clipboard so you can refer to it and begin to use this explicit language more easily.

These questions provide guidance for helping children revisit interactive writing to reinforce learning. Think about the revisiting opportunities evidenced on page 12 of "The Little Brown Mouse." You might ask:

- Which words have double letters?
- Which words have endings like *ed* and *ing*?
- Where do the quotation marks go? What is the part that the little brown mouse said?
- Is there a compound word in our story?

Many pieces of interactive writing have ongoing instructional value, either for learning more about reading or learning more about writing. The decisions you make during interactive writing not only result in powerful learning for children during any particular session, but create educational resources on which you and the children can draw for days or weeks to come.

Suggestions for Professional Development

1. If appropriate for your students, try producing a longer piece of interactive writing such as "The Little Brown Mouse." Adjust length and composition to the level of your students.

2. Work at the piece of writing over time. Briefly note teaching points during composition, construction, and revisiting the text.

- When you have finished, print or type out the text and ask a colleague to help you look at it in connection with information from your ongoing observational records of children's writing and reading. You may find it useful to switch pieces of writing for this analysis and then compare notes. In that case, provide either oral or written summaries of what children in your class need to know how to do next as writers. Your typed version of interactive writing will not reveal the decisions you actually made about when in the text children contributed and when you acted as scribe. Ask yourself:
- What do my students know how to do? What do they need to know how to do next?
- What opportunities for teaching exist within the piece of interactive writing (judging from the typed text only)?
- What teaching points would I select for this group of students?

3. Then, compare these analyses with the actual piece of interactive writing and your own memory and records of teaching points.

- Which decisions were powerful and appropriate?
- Which decisions may have wasted some time?
- In your next piece of interactive writing, what will you emphasize in your teaching?

CHAPTER FOURTEEN

Adjusting Interactive Writing as Writers Change Over Time

Learning is a continuous process. Those of us who work with preschoolers, kindergartners, and first and second graders know that these children seem to change almost every day. Because children are continually developing, interactive writing lessons must continually be adjusted. Lessons will be different

▌ for preschool, kindergarten, and first- and second-grade children
▌ for children in any one grade across the year
▌ for different groups of children within the same class.

Making adjustments in instruction to suit learners is a complex process. These adjustments can be made with greater precision if we have knowledge of a continuum of progress that we typically observe in primary age children. We have described interactive writing as a specific technique that is particularly effective for children who are making the transition from the earliest awareness of print to reading beginning "chapter books" and other longer texts, and writing independently for a range of purposes. This transition typically takes place between ages four and eight, although individuals will vary. Based on this, it is possible to outline a framework

for the implementation of interactive writing. We have included an example of such a continuum here. Our categories of readers and writers include:

1. emergent
2. early
3. transitional
4. self-extending

For each category, we consider the following aspects:

▌ characteristics of children as readers and writers
▌ characteristics of texts that support and challenge readers in the early "learning how to read" process
▌ characteristics of texts appropriate for composition and construction in interactive writing
▌ focus of teaching in interactive writing.

No two children follow the same path to learning, but there are some general categories along a continuum that show trends in development.

As we observe children's behavior, we need to keep in mind a continuum of learning. We need to be able to identify characteristics and behaviors as we guide children toward literacy. The goal is to support them in using what they know to get to what they do not yet know. That means knowing our learners and working "on the edge" of learning.

Emergent Readers and Writers

The term *emergent* refers to the idea that children's knowledge of literacy and its purposes gradually emerges throughout their preschool experiences. From birth, children are learning language as they communicate with family and caregivers. In our modern society, children also become acquainted with aspects of literacy at a very early age. Even two- or three-year-olds may notice signs for favorite fast food restaurants or find their favorite cereals in the grocery store. In a broad sense, they are learning that graphic symbols, along with pictures, have meaning. Even very young children (as young as twelve months) recognize their favorite books or stories when they hear them read again and again and their attention is drawn to pictures. Later, if they have a chance to see their names written or to make them with magnetic letters, they begin to recognize that they are seeing the same visual elements again and again. Soon, they learn the name of a letter or two.

On our continuum, the emergent category of readers and writers refers to children as they enter preschool and/or kindergarten settings. Their experience with print and written language will vary widely. Some children already have high expectations of books; they know that when an adult opens a book and looks at the pages, they will be hearing interesting stories and enjoyable language. Others are just beginning to understand that when you hear a story read, it is the same every time. All preschoolers and kindergartners are naturally drawn to hearing stories if there is an enthusiastic adult to read to them; that is one of the goals of preschool education. They will also be interested in print if the environment is rich and there are many opportunities to notice and use it.

In good preschool and kindergarten classrooms, literacy is very much a part of play. In every part of the room, there are chances to play with written language. Play items might include note paper in the drama corner, signs in the classroom store, or pencils and markers in the art center. Books will be available everywhere and children will be encouraged to "write" for themselves.

Characteristics of Emergent Readers and Writers

Emergent readers (Figure 14-1 on pages 205–206) rely on language and meaning as they read simple texts, or texts having only one or two lines of print. They are just beginning to control early behaviors such as matching spoken words one by one with written words, knowledge of how print is arranged on pages, and moving left to right in reading. They are just figuring out what a word really is, how letters go together, and how letters are different from each other. They may know one or two high-frequency words that can be used as anchors.

Emergent writers are learning that what they say and think can be expressed in written language. They are also beginning to understand that writing naturally accompanies human activity and can be used for different purposes. They approximate the "look" of writing and begin to produce both scribbling and letter-like forms, but they are moving toward conventional forms. They are proud of their written products; sometimes they impart meaning to the writing and sometimes they indicate that they simply want to "do writing." Emergent writers are also beginning to realize that writing letters and words is essential for producing a message that someone else can read, and they may learn to represent their names (or parts of names) and a few high-frequency words. As they progress, they acquire more of the simple high-frequency words, perhaps ten to twenty.

Emergent writers are also learning much about letters and sounds. They may know a few letters, perhaps those in their names.

Working with Emergent Readers/Writers in Interactive Writing

Emergent-1	Emergent-2	Emergent-3
Children as readers/writers		
• Is just beginning to notice and find print.	• Read one line of print with clear spaces.	• Reads 2–3 lines of print in previously read texts.
• Recognizes name and a few letters.	• Uses language, repetition to assist reading.	• Points and matches one-to-one.
• Writes a few letters and/or part of name.	• Is beginning to point one-to-one on 1 line of print.	• Knows return sweep.
• Is beginning to hear a few easy-to-hear consonant sounds and connect words with names.	• Notices spaces and uses to monitor on familiar texts.	• Hears almost all easy-to-hear consonants.
• Realizes oral language can be written.	• Hears easy-to-hear consonants in words.	• Hears sounds at beginning and ends of words.
• Joins in during shared reading of familiar rhymes, songs, and stories.	• Recognizes and writes name.	• Is beginning to hear easy-to-hear vowel sounds.
	• Recognizes a few high-frequency words.	• Recognizes and writes 10–20 high-frequency words.
	• Writes a few high-frequency words.	• Knows names of almost all upper- and lowercase letters.
	• Knows names of 10–15 letters.	• Recognizes a few frequently used endings like *ing*.
Examples of Texts children are reading		
• Children are reading nursery rhymes and very simple texts in shared reading.		• Reads level A or B texts independently.
		• "Caption" books with simple sentences, clear illustrations, familiar topics, repetitive language, and 1 or 2 lines of print.

FIGURE 14-1

Working with Emergent Readers/Writers in Interactive Writing, *continued*

Emergent-1	Emergent-2	Emergent-3
Texts created in interactive writing		

Emergent-1	Emergent-2	Emergent-3
• Similar to oral language. • One line of print. • (Messages created and reread over several days to make longer text.) • Clear spaces. • Familiar topics. • Simple words. • Words that link to names. • Labels for art murals.	• Similar to oral language but incorporate some words, phrases from literature. • 1–2 lines of print. • Clear spaces. • Familiar topics. • Simple punctuation. • Mainly simple words with a few words borrowed from literature.	• Similar to oral language but increasing use of written language characteristics. • 2–4 lines of print. • Clear spaces. • Familiar topics, with some content drawn from literature or science.

Focus of interactive writing

• Help children compose and remember simple text by repetition. • Bring children's attention to print. • Talk about where to start and where to go. • Talk about how to make letters (verbal description). • Have children say words slowly. • Link letters, especially consonant sounds, to names. • Have children write in consonants they hear and/or connect to names • Emphasize easy high-frequency words. • Write in capital and lowercase. • Use and bring attention to simple punctuation.	• Assist composition of several lines of print, one at a time. • Use writing to plan activity. • Emphasize rereading and pointing. • Link consonant and vowel sounds to first and last names. • Have children locate and write high-frequency words with fluency. • Use punctuation—periods, questions, exclamation points, and quotation marks. • Make connections with name chart and word wall.

FIGURE 14-1, *continued*

They are discovering that you can hear the sounds in words; they are developing the important idea that there are relationships between the sounds and the letters in words, and they are acquiring important examples of these letter-sound correspondences.

Emergent Readers and Writers and Interactive Writing

When you work with emergent readers and writers in interactive writing lessons, your main goal is to make them aware of the process of writing and its purposes. In interactive writing, they will learn that writing names, words, and sentences can help them revisit and remember enjoyable stories and events. They will develop pride in the written products that are produced cooperatively in the classroom and will go back to them to read them again. Another goal is to help them make beginning connections between their own oral language and the graphic symbols that represent language.

In Figure 14-1, we provide an outline for thinking about emergent readers and writers. Interactive writing is particularly designed to support *beginning literacy learners*. It is important for the preschool and kindergarten teacher to make finely drawn adjustments, raising the level of difficulty by small steps. We have therefore divided this category of learners into three subcategories indicating levels of development.

1. Children are just beginning to know that print exists and to notice it in the environment and in books.
2. Children know about print and have started to use it.
3. Children are beginning to read and write simple texts.

What a transition takes place during these early phases of learning about written language! For some, the "emergence" of literacy understandings may take place over several years, from age one or two to the end of kindergarten. For others, it may happen rapidly during the preschool or kindergarten

year. Interactive writing is a tool for helping children make this transition with ease and enjoyment.

At first, children are participating in shared reading of very simple texts, rhymes, and songs. They are not expected to decode words or recognize isolated words. Instead, the emphasis is on enjoying literacy and beginning to make a match between oral and written language. An important understanding to be developed through hearing stories read by the teacher and participating in shared reading is that a written text is always the same whenever you hear it or read it. That critical concept will later help them "match up" and monitor their own reading of simple texts. As their literacy knowledge emerges from these holistic experiences, children notice more and more about print. Of course, you are constantly drawing their attention to the words during shared reading. They begin to "read for real" simple caption books with one line of print. They learn about left-to-right directionality, matching one spoken word with one cluster of letters on the page, and returning to the left each time you read a line.

In interactive writing, the first texts that children produce are very simple messages, usually labels or one line of print. The topics are familiar. The texts are carefully organized and the layout shows a clear distinction between pictures and print, and the spaces between words are evident. Guide children's composition to be sure that the message is one they can easily remember and repeat. Longer texts can be created over several days, but each part of the longer text must be simple enough for children to read together as a shared reading text.

At first, you will do most of the writing for the children, but they may contribute one or two letters. There is an emphasis on teaching points linked to children's names. Make use of the white board to show aspects of letters and words. Emphasize letter forms and the directional movements necessary to make letters. Talk about the names of the letters. Notice the simple beginning text appropriate for preschoolers' learning about "The Three Little Pigs" (Figure 14-2).

In this example, each pig is making a simple comment, "No!" The comment is captured in a "speech bubble," so it is clear that the pigs are talking. This is an early opportunity for children to learn the differences between pictures and print and to learn that symbols represent oral language. This language refers to the story, of course, in which each pig said, "No!" to the wolf, refusing to let him "come in." The children had heard the story many times and also had acted it out. This lively rendition of "The Three Little Pigs" recalled to their minds the richer language of the original story but also helped them focus on print. Children have the opportunity to search with their eyes, find the print (as opposed to the beautiful art), notice the features of the letters *n* and *o*, and read it three times. This is an exercise in visual perception.

Also emphasize the way space is used to define words. Use language like "first" and "last" to help children talk about print, and have them learn to say words slowly, listening for the sounds. You will find some high-frequency words like *the* occurring in many texts and you can bring these words to children's attention, perhaps placing them on a very simple word wall as they notice them.

Toward the end of the emergent literacy phase, children will recognize quite a few of these useful words and will be making connections between words. Actively foster this kind of thinking by demonstrating with the white board or Magna Doodle (for example, using *no* to figure out *go*). You may want to use interactive writing to make a class alphabet book. Texts will be longer, covering more pages (as in a class book).

Early Readers and Writers

Early readers and writers are well aware of print in the world around them and they seek to use it for many purposes. They have made the basic transition from beginning awareness and have become actual practitioners. For early readers and writers, you can structure texts in interactive writing that help them to greatly expand their knowledge of written texts.

Characteristics of Early Readers and Writers

Early readers have achieved control of early behaviors such as directionality and word-by-word matching. Their eyes are beginning to

FIGURE 14–2   The Three Little Pigs

control the process of reading, and they do some of their reading without pointing. They have acquired a small core of high-frequency words that they can read and write and they use these words to monitor their reading. They can read books with several lines of print, keeping the meaning in mind as they use some strategies to figure out unfamiliar words. They have developed systems for learning words in reading and can use letter-sound relationships in coordination with their own sense of language. They consistently monitor their reading to make sure that it makes sense. They use several sources of information to check on themselves.

Early writers can produce the written forms of almost all letters quickly and easily, and they also have a core of high-frequency words that they can write without much effort. They can write many more words that are not of high frequency. They have learned these words through the numerous occasions on which they've been asked to write them and by their own connecting of groups of words. They have learned "how to learn" words and so their acquisition of words is accelerating. They understand that a word must be written the *same way* every time you use it and that conventional spelling is important if your reader is to be able to understand your message.

Early writers are able to represent many of the sounds in words with the appropriate letters or letter clusters. They write in a left-to-right sequence and are learning key principles for constructing words from parts, for example, adding endings to form plurals. Early writers also notice letter clusters and spelling patterns that appear frequently in the language. They can use the simple words they know to derive new words by association or analogy.

Early Readers and Writers and Interactive Writing

Early readers and writers make some very important transitions as they work with writ-

ten language. Figure 14-3 (on pages 210–211) illustrates the general path of progress for these learners.

Improvements in motor skills in early readers lead to advances in such behaviors as word-by-word matching. They begin by pointing precisely to words while reading so that the hand and finger can help monitor and check their reading. They are careful to be sure that what they say matches what they read; they self-correct using print or visual information. Interactive writing provides powerful support for this learning process. As the teacher, you are writing word by word, emphasizing left-to-right directionality, word boundaries, and rereading, with pointing, during the construction of text. This explicit demonstration will help children to read the text independently, matching word by word. Again, you will find that early readers can handle more complicated and longer texts produced in interactive writing than they could in their independent reading. Shared and independent reading of interactive writing pieces helps them to extend their control to reading lines of print. You will be able to expand their knowledge even more by including dialogue.

Early readers and writers move from knowing a small core of high-frequency words to being able to write and read a core of close to fifty words. At the end of this phase, they will be able to read many more words than they can spell independently. They will begin to connect words by categories, ushering in the time when their reading and writing vocabularies will expand exponentially. Use interactive writing to help children acquire more high-frequency words; you can guide composition to include more words, and you can encourage them to connect writing with the word walls. Interactive writing also provides a context for discussing punctuation and using it in divergent ways.

Help children become more aware of words in several different ways. Teach them how to

Working with Early Readers in Interactive Writing

Early-1	Early-2	Early-3
Children as readers/writers		
• Compose and remember longer sentences. • Write and read 10–20 high-frequency words. • Write words phonetically. • Use some endings, like *er* and *ing*, in reading and writing. • Writes all letters fluently and knows names. • Hear consonant sounds at beginning, end, and middle of words. • Hear most vowel sounds. • Have control of word by word matching on 2–3 lines of text.	• Have control of early behaviors (1–1 matching, etc.) on stories with several lines of print; sometimes reads without pointing. • Read with phrasing. • Notice and use punctuation. • Recognize visual patterns in combination with letter-sound. • Reread to confirm, search, and check. • Use visual information in combination with meaning. • Write and read 20–30 high-frequency words.	• Have full control of early behaviors; read without pointing except at point of difficulty. • Read fluently on easy text; use phrases. • Write known words fluently and solve new words using letter-sound and visual information. • Reread to check, confirm, search for information and self-correct. • Use one source of information to check another; self-correct. • Use known words to get to words they don't know. • Write and read 30–40 words.
Texts children are reading		
• Read levels C/D. • Texts have simple story lines and topics, with 2–6 lines on a page. Some have repeating language patterns; others do not. • Simple syntax.	• Read levels D/E. • Texts have 3–8 lines of text; placement of print varies widely. There is a full range of punctuation; vocabulary words have inflectional endings *ing* and many words require analysis. Some topics are less familiar.	• Read levels E/F. • Texts are longer and print is smaller. Text carries more message than pictures. Texts have literary language; story structure includes more episodes and events that follow chronologically. Punctuation necessary for accurate phrasing; words require analysis.

FIGURE 14–3

Working with Early Readers in Interactive Writing, *continued*

Early-1	Early-2	Early-3
Texts created in interactive writing		
• Involve more literary language. • Use contractions and words with endings. • Extend length of sentences. • Close match between illustrations and text. • Use compound sentences and dialogue.	• Use literary language and vocabulary from literature. • Include dialogue, punctuated with quotation marks and commas. • Have multisyllable words. • Incorporate embedded clauses. Repeat language to extend length of texts. • Include many high-frequency words in text.	• Use literacy language and vocabulary within more extended texts. • Require a plan to structure the writing of texts over several days. • Incorporate dialogue with varied ways to signal speaker. • Use variety of vocabulary to make story interesting. • Use full range of punctuation.
Focus of interactive writing		
• Help children think about the language of the story—what would characters say? • Emphasize match between illustrations and text. • Construct more complex words. • Emphasize word parts: letter clusters, etc. • Connect to word wall and word study.	• Think about literary quality of text: language and illustrators. • Help children remember longer pieces of dialogue or longer sentences. • Emphasize word parts and connections between words. • Connect to word wall and word study.	• Emphasize choice of words for precise meaning and to create interest. • Emphasize connections between words and word construction using parts. • Connect to word wall and word study.

FIGURE 14-3, *continued*

■ select the precise words that make the text accurate or interesting

■ notice the length of words and clap them to notice the syllables

■ notice beginnings and endings of words

■ construct words using letter-sound strategies

■ think about the way words look and make connections between them.

By the end of this early reading/writing phase, children will be tracking print with their eyes and reading and writing many words. The amount and quality of their independent writing will increase dramatically and they will also be reading texts that are much longer than you will be producing in interactive writing.

Transitional Readers and Writers

Transitional readers and writers move from reading texts on familiar topics with repeating patterns to reading texts that are more challenging and have much less repetition. They move from high reliance on pictures to using illustrations only to enhance the text and from simple sentences to complex ones that cover several lines. They are increasing their capacity to read different kinds of texts and to incorporate a flexible range of strategies. They move from producing simple stories to more complex ones that may cover several pages.

Characteristics of Transitional Readers and Writers

Transitional readers have the early behaviors well under control. They can read texts with many lines of print. While they notice pictures and enjoy them, they do not need to rely heavily on them as part of the reading process. They read fluently with some expression, using multiple sources of information while reading for meaning. They have a large core of frequently used words that they can recognize quickly and easily. They are working on how to solve more complex words through a range of word analysis techniques.

Transitional writers produce longer pieces of writing; they have a large body of words that they know and can write quickly. There are many words that they can write with standard spelling; others are worked out with close approximations. They know the words that they are not sure of and can check on them later. They can construct from parts, using known words to write words that they do not yet know. Their stories have more detail and complexity, with beginnings, endings, and episodes.

Transitional writers are able to employ a range of flexible strategies to spell words that they do not know. They can analyze words for parts, using relationships among sounds and letters or letter clusters to spell them. They can also make connections among words, solving new words by analogy or by remembering visual patterns. They can use substitution of letters at the beginning, middle, and ends of words to make new words. They are conscious of the need to learn how to spell more words and have learned strategies for remembering words.

Transitional Readers and Writers and Shared/Interactive Writing

Transitional readers and writers are rapidly expanding their ability to read and write texts (see Figure 14-4). They know a large number of high-frequency words and are acquiring more. They are beginning to move beyond the kinds of texts that can be created effectively in group writing. For example, children will be able to produce longer texts in independent writing and will be able to read much longer texts for themselves.

Interactive writing still has many uses for these students. For example, you can use interactive writing to demonstrate new kinds of writing for children. Many of the chapters in this book illustrate the use of interactive writing in note-taking to record observations during experiments, letter writing, or making comparison charts. You can use interactive writing to help children understand different

Working with Transitional Readers/Writers in Shared/Interactive Writing	Working with Self-Extending Readers/Writers in Shared/Interactive Writing
Children as readers/writers	

Reading:

- Have early behaviors well under control for all texts.

- Read fluently with phrasing and expression; notice punctuation and use it.

- Solve words, usually at point of error.

- Have large core of words that they know.

- Slow down to analyze new words and speed up again while reading.

- Read with phrasing and fluency most of the time.

- Can read about less familiar topics.

- Notice and use punctuation.

Writing:

- Spell many words conventionally and make near accurate attempts at many more.

- Produce longer pieces of writing that include dialogue, beginnings endings, and multiple episodes.

- Employ flexible range of strategies to spell words.

Reading:

- Use all sources of information flexibly to read longer, more complex texts.

- Analyze multisyllable words while reading for meaning.

- Self-correct at point of error and check using multiple sources of information.

- Recognize and use text structure.

- Learn new words and concepts while reading texts.

- Use punctuation and text layout to assist in interpretation while reading.

- Read with phrasing and fluency.

Writing:

- Spell most words conventionally.

- Make near accurate attempts and use references.

- Proofread writing for accuracy and style.

- Produce a wide variety of texts.

- Employ flexible range of strategies to spell words.

Texts children are reading	

- Read levels G/H/I.

- Texts have more challenging ideas and vocabulary with longer sentences and literacy language and structures. Stories have more events; where repetition is used, it is within more complex plots.

- Read levels H/I/J.

- There are a variety of texts, including realism, fantasy, and informational texts. Story structure is complex, with elaborated episodes. Some beginning "chapter" books require sustained reading. Texts are longer with large numbers of words. Characters develop and change as problems are solved in the plot.

FIGURE 14–4

Working with Transitional Readers/Writers in Shared/Interactive Writing	Working with Self-Extending Readers/Writers in Shared/Interactive Writing
Texts in interactive writing	
• Texts are longer and include more dialogue. • Different genres are used, with different forms and ways of organizing texts. • Reference is used to make texts more cohesive and interesting. • Sentences begin in the middle of lines and/or "wrap around." • There is a full range of punctuation.	• Written texts are used for a wide variety of purposes: extending meaning, comparing, expressing points of view. • Use graphic organizers to analyze concepts and ideas. • Emphasize learning how to create new genres. • Compare and contrast texts. • Extend the length of text (through shared writing) to make them more challenging for readers.
Focus of interactive writing	
• Emphasize flexibility in layout and type. • Enrich texts by extending dialogue or adding episodes. • Elaborate texts by using adjectives or dependent clauses. • Emphasize a full range of punctuation. • Make texts more interesting by adding illustrations, diagrams, etc. • Demonstrate revision and editing.	• Demonstrate how to write and read new genres, especially expository texts. • Demonstrate how to reveal characters through dialogue or description. • Demonstrate how to use graphic organizers. • Emphasize creating complex texts for students to use as references and resources. • Engage children in revision and editing of texts.

FIGURE 14–4, *continued*

ways of organizing and interpreting texts, for example:

■ What comes first?

■ What comes next?

■ Which character should speak first?

■ How would this character say that?

■ Where should we place the illustrations on this page?

■ Does everything in the illustration match the text?

■ What kind of punctuation do we need here?

■ Could we say that in a better way? Would another word for *said* be more interesting?

Interactive writing is also very useful for helping children attend to features of words. At this point in time, you would not be having children write the easy high-frequency words on the chart but would be quickly adding those yourself. Attend to new words that appear with high frequency but are not familiar to the children; focus attention on word solving, being very selective about the words that you "call out" from the text.

In any piece of writing, you will want to identify words that have high instructional value. Be careful not to focus on too many words, or children may become confused about the principles you are emphasizing. At this point, begin to coordinate your instructional decisions in interactive writing with the kinds of principles you are exploring in word study. If you are looking at word endings like *ed* or *ing*, those will be the words you select for attention and have children come up to write. If you are looking at words with *ar*, *er*, or double letters, you will want to call attention to those kinds of words in interactive writing lessons. (See Pinnell and Fountas 1998 for a description of a complete word study program.)

Create richer reading texts by adding more shared writing to children's interactive writing pieces. Including shared writing moves the process along and also allows you to illustrate more text features. Children's attention can be focused on punctuation, layout, composition, and particular words that help them learn principles.

Self-Extending Readers and Writers

Self-extending readers and writers have made the "breakthrough" to literacy. They have a basic understanding of the underlying processes related to reading and writing and are continually expanding their abilities simply by engaging in literacy activities. They not only know words, they have *systems* for learning more words and learning more about words—either in reading or in spelling. These readers and writers understand many principles, which they can use automatically and rapidly to take words apart in reading and to spell words in writing. They have moved from "learning to read or write" to "reading and writing" for many purposes.

Characteristics of Self-Extending Readers and Writers

Self-extending readers use all sources of information flexibly while reading texts that are much longer and more complex. They have a large core of high-frequency words and many other words that they can quickly and automatically recognize. Self-extending readers have developed systems for learning more about the process as they read, so they build skills simply by encountering many different kinds of texts with a variety of new words. Self-extending readers can analyze and make excellent attempts at multisyllable words. They are still building background knowledge and learning how to apply what they know to longer and more difficult texts.

Self-extending writers are fluent in composing text and revisiting it "in the head" as needed to revise as they go. They focus on the message, writing most words quickly and easily, although they slow down to think about words of which they are unsure. Their writing vocabulary is large although it is much smaller than their reading vocabulary. Their attempts at words show that they are using knowledge of principles and rules; they connect words in categories so that they are approaching spelling strategically. They can use root words to get to the meaning and/or spelling of new words. They can also effectively use beginning-level resources such as dictionaries and word lists. They can apply early dictionary skills such as alphabetizing. Also, self-extending writers know how to recognize incorrectly spelled words when they check their work. They have become good proofreaders of their own writing.

Self-Extending Readers and Writers and Shared/Interactive Writing

Self-extending readers and writers (see Figure 14-4) are applying their strategies to more difficult texts. The texts that they read and write are much longer than those they create in interactive writing. Interactive writing now emphasizes helping children learn something new about literacy. Explore expository text in many different forms, relating their investigations to written documentation. Through interactive writing, children can learn how to summarize events, state conclusions, make comparisons, and provide supporting details for arguments. Since you will be doing most of the writing through shared writing, longer and richer texts can be completed. Demonstrate the use of different kinds of graphic organizers such as Venn diagrams to emphasize comparison and contrast, character webs to connect descriptive details, and so on. Interactive writing is also an excellent setting for showing children how to reconsider written texts with the goal of revising for clarity. They can, for example, consider two versions of a sentence, asking:

- Which sentence best summarizes what happened?
- Which is the best sentence to tell us about the character?
- Which sentence sounds better?

You can also use a combination of shared and interactive writing to help self-extending readers learn about new genres of text. For example, writing a short biographical summary together will help them think about accuracy of portrayal and supportive details. They can write the biography from several different points of view:

- the person's own words (simulated autobiography)
- a family member
- a neutral third party.

Word work continues as part of interactive writing but is reserved for the analysis of words that will help children become better word solvers. Words emphasized in interactive writing may have features that move children along in their learning.

Varying Text to Support Readers and Writers

One of the issues for teachers is that within any one classroom of students, there will be students with varying levels of experience. It is highly likely that

- a preschool teacher will have mostly emergent readers and writers with one or two early readers and writers
- a kindergarten teacher will likely have a range from emergent to transitional readers and writers
- a first-grade teacher will have a broader range—emergent to self-extending readers and writers and beyond
- a second-grade teacher will most likely have few emergent readers and writers but may have some children who are having difficulty in the early-transitional phase and need more explicit teaching.

With all of these ranges in mind, you need to think about efficient ways to meet the needs of all children in the class. For preschoolers, very simple uses of print are appropriate, with a primary emphasis on their names and print in their environment. The idea is to make them at home in the world of print and to notice some of its features. You want them to see print as part of their lives, their home, their community, and their play areas. If more observant or more experienced children notice more about the print, acknowledge and celebrate their learning. But it is not necessary to have a great deal of direct instruction to bring the others along.

For the emergent and early readers who largely make up kindergarten classes, it is best to keep the texts simple. The text will be one that, in general, children in the group can understand and read with the support of shared reading. More advanced children will enjoy reading the texts and will do so with less support. Additionally, the texts will provide opportunities for these children to notice features of words and use them in their own writing. The learning thus becomes multilevel without having to create many different small groups and without making the text inaccessible to many children. Toward the end of kindergarten, some children who need to learn more about letters may work in a small group so that they have maximum opportunity to add to the writing.

In first grade, children diverge widely in their literacy experiences and in the texts that they can write and read. Interactive writing, pitched in difficulty to the average range of the class, is used to create a common experience and create many written texts that children can read. More advanced children can participate in the activity and, perhaps, take it further in their independent writing. Children who are just beginning to notice print may produce a simpler text as a small group or spend a few minutes with the teacher reading and noticing aspects of the text that the entire group has composed and constructed. Toward the end of first grade, you may want to have more advanced children working on independent projects while you work with the rest of the children in interactive writing.

Usually, you will need to use whole-class interactive writing only occasionally for second graders. Interactive writing will be useful to demonstrate some special kind of text or to show children how to revise and edit written work. You may, though, have a small group of children who can profit from interactive writing frequently. For these children, work intensively on the same kinds of interactive writing that you would use for first graders.

A Comparison of Texts Across Learning Development

We have described a continuum of development from emergent to self-extending readers and writers. Interactive writing is an important instructional tool for each of these groups of writers. It is important to adjust the nature of the task so that children are continually challenged as they grow in their literacy abilities. To underscore the adjustments needed, let's take a focused look at the kinds of texts that we might see across the levels of literacy development. To illustrate our point, we have chosen a single topic, "The Three Bears," as a text that children might find engaging and an appropriate subject for interactive writing. The many variations that could emerge from a study of the text are illustrated in Figure 14-5. Each of these examples would have taken several days for a group of children to produce. As children grow in their writing and reading ability, they can produce more in a single session; however, as you will notice, the texts in general become longer and/or are connected to more complex learning activities.

For beginning emergent readers and writers (see Emergent-1 section, Figure 14-5), the text is simple and repetitive, uses high-frequency words, and is closely tied to the illustrations. Children who know the story of The Three Bears will be able to read this text easily in shared reading sessions. For children who are a little further along (Emergent-2), we present the example of pictures of characters using "speech bubbles." These cartoon-like figures are popular with children; they demonstrate that dialogue can be written. Goldilocks makes the same comment each

Sampling a Gradient of Text in Interactive Writing

Emergent-1

The Three Bears
Here is Papa Bear.
Here is Mama Bear.
Here is Baby Bear.

illustrations

Emergent-2

[Picture of Goldilocks]

The big bowl. — It's too hot!

The middle-sized bowl. — It's too cold!

The little bowl. — It's just right!

[Picture of Goldilocks]

Emergent-3

The Story of Goldilocks
Goldilocks broke in the house.
Goldilocks broke the chair.
Goldilocks ate the porridge.
Goldilocks ran away.

illustrations

Early-1

The Three Bears and Goldilocks

Papa Bear — Someone's been sleeping in my bed!

Mama Bear — Someone's been sleeping in my bed!

Baby Bear — Someone's been sleeping in my bed and there she is!

Early-2

Just Right!

Papa Bear's porridge was too hot.
Mama Bear's porridge was too cold.
Baby Bear's porridge was just right.

Papa Bear's chair was too hard.
Mama Bear's chair was too soft.
Baby Bear's chair was just right.

Papa Bear's bed was too hard.
Mama Bear's bed was too soft.
Baby Bear's bed was just right.

So Goldilocks went to sleep in the bed that was just right.

Early-3

The Three Bears and Goldilocks

1. Once upon a time, there were three bears.
   There was a Papa Bear, a Mama Bear, and a little Baby Bear.

2. The three bears went for a walk.
   Goldilocks came to the house.

3. She tried the chairs.
   "This chair is too hard," said Goldilocks.
   "This chair is too soft," said Goldilocks.
   "This chair is just right!" she said. And she sat in it.

[Pages 4–12 follow the story.]

Transitional Readers/Writers

Dear Three Bears,
I am sorry for breaking your chair, eating your porridge, and sleeping in your bed. I will never do it again.
Sincerely,
Goldilocks

Porridge
Put water in the pan.
Put oatmeal in the pan.
Cook the oatmeal.
Now eat the porridge.

Dear Goldilocks,
Thank you for your letter. We forgive you for breaking our chair, eating our porridge, and sleeping in our bed. Would you like to come for tea next Saturday?
Sincerely,
Father Bear, Mother Bear, and Baby Bear

Missing Person
Please help us find Goldilocks.
She has blonde hair, blue eyes, and freckles.
She is 4 feet tall.
She is rude.
She was last seen going into the woods.

Self-Extending Readers/Writers

The Three Bears and Real Bears

How they are the same:
They live in the woods.
They have black or brown fur.
They have baby bears called "cubs."

How they are different:

Three Bears	Real Bears
Talk	Growl
Wear clothes	Don't wear clothes
Eat porridge	Eat berries and plants
Sit in chairs	
Sleep in beds	

I was just walking through the woods minding my own business when I saw an open door in a little house. I went in the house to see if something was wrong and NO ONE was there. Well, I looked around and saw some porridge just sitting on the table. Something must have happened to the inhabitants! I called 911 right away to report missing persons, and do you know what happened? Three bears came walking in. I tell you what! I ran away as fast as I could. And that is the story of my adventure.
Signed: *Goldilocks*

FIGURE 14-5

time. The labels on the bowls present a bit of challenge in using the relative terms *big, middle-sized,* and *little*; however, children who are familiar with the story will be able to read them after only a little practice. Emergent readers who have had quite a bit of practice in shared reading will be able to follow lines of print with several words in each line. Here (Emergent-3), we present a retelling of the events in the story, specifically everything that Goldilocks did. The text utilizes repetitive language; however, children will be prompted to recall events in order and produce the language as cued by the print.

For beginning early readers and writers (Early-1) we present the prototype of labeled characters who talk in speech bubbles. Notice that Baby Bear's comment varies from the previous two, requiring readers to look closely. In addition, it is a compound sentence of ten words, which will offer a challenge to writers and readers. Also to challenge children, this text requires attention to compound words, to possessives, and to words with *ing* endings. The next two levels of text shown for early readers and writers have many more lines of print. Early-2 is organized around a central theme, "just right"; Early-3 includes literary language and dialogue. The latter example is part of a twelve-page book.

The examples presented as typical of appropriate texts for transitional readers and writers illustrate the value of using text in different ways for different purposes. The teacher and children are using interactive writing as described; however, they are moving from one genre to another and taking different perspectives. Self-extending readers and writers apply thinking and writing skills in even more complex ways. These learners are making connections between the many texts they have encountered. They compare the three bears to information they have gathered on "real bears." You may have noticed that state proficiency tests for third and fourth grades often require students to compare and contrast texts. These first graders are doing so within the supportive context of interactive writing. The second example for self-extending readers and writers, again, displays a skill that is often tested—extending a text by taking a different perspective.

These prototypes are drawn from our experience in working with interactive writing in grades preschool through second. The examples are only a few of the many options open to us as teachers of children in interactive writing. As instruction shifts and changes to meet the needs of learning children, you will be helping them to build language resources. Think of your work as moving along just ahead of children's own independent abilities. You are helping them to learn along the "edges" of their present knowledge and ability so that, tomorrow, more will be possible.

Suggestions for Professional Development

1. Conduct an assessment of text characteristics with cross-grade-level colleagues in your school. From preschool through grade two, have each teacher bring samples from the beginning, middle, and end of the year (or from the current month if you have not been doing interactive writing very long).

2. Keep the original work handy, but ask each teacher to print or type the texts so that the characteristics can be considered without reference to the children's writing.

3. With these typed texts in a manageable form, duplicate them for everyone and then have individual teachers arrange them along a continuum of difficulty.

4. Compare the interactive writing texts with the continuum of development, emergent to self-extending readers and writers, presented in this chapter.

5. Discuss the following:

   ■ What are the characteristics of interactive writing texts along the continuum of development?

- What new vocabulary or language structures are evident across time?
- Have I created texts appropriate for most of my children at the various levels? Consider the language difficulty of the words, complexity of the sentence patterns, and the text meaning.
- What texts might have been too difficult for children? What are the problems involved in creating texts that are too difficult?
- What texts might have been too easy for children? What are the problems involved in creating texts that are too easy?
- How do these texts provide for multiple levels of learning?

- How can I make my choice of text style and layout more effective for children at a given point in development?
- How can I vary text to be sure that transitional and self-extending readers and writers are learning something new?
- How can I incorporate more challenging words and text features?
- Where is it appropriate for me to incorporate more shared writing to increase the reading challenge of texts and help children learn more about text features and words?

The Foundations of Effective Writing Practice

The previous sections of this book have focused extensively on "how" to implement interactive writing. While reasons and rationales have been integrated within these chapters, we focus this section directly on the why interactive writing is an important and effective instructional context for helping young children make the transition to literacy. Our goal in Section Five is to link research and practice. We summarize findings from research over the last several decades, drawing out important areas of learning that we must be concerned about as teachers of young children. We provide a theoretical rationale and related research to support the practices incorporated in interactive writing.

CHAPTER FIFTEEN

Why Interactive Writing Helps Children Learn Literacy

In classrooms where teachers use interactive writing daily, children are invited to use language and literacy as tools for learning. Children develop their competency with oral language, reading, and writing as they participate in interesting experiences, express their ideas, and build a shared set of understandings. The process is carefully guided by a teacher who is aware that these young students are learning in many ways at the same time. Children are developing ideas and expanding their knowledge of the world. At the same time, they are

■ learning to use language in new ways
■ using literacy as a tool for inquiry and expression
■ developing critical and fundamental understanding about letters, sounds, and words
■ learning to work with others and to sustain interest and energy in a project over time.

Throughout this book we have described the process of interactive writing and its many benefits to young readers and writers. In this chapter, we present a series of interactive writing experiences followed by a brief look at the strong underlying rationales that made them so effective. In interactive writing, the complexity of the writing process is maintained. Children learn items of information, such as letters and words, and at the same time learn about the process. The learning is multi-layered and takes place through making connections over time.

Using Interactive Writing as a Tool for Learning

As a context for thinking about learning, let's look at some specific examples of writing experiences that illustrate the range of learning opportunities created through the use of interactive writing in the inquiry process.

A Wall Story Map

The wall story map in Figure 15-1, (page 224, see also Appendix 5) was the result of Ida Patacca's kindergarten class hearing a favorite story read aloud. These children easily connected their own experiences to this story. The text, *Rain*, by Robert Kalan (1978) tells a story through visual experiences as well as words. The story of a weather cycle is told with vivid, bold illustrations that communicate meaning on each page. The story begins with phrases such as "yellow sun." Then we see phrases such as "rain on the red car" printed in red. The colors and words work together to convey meaning. The illustrations grow darker through the text, showing the rain shower as it grows in intensity. Finally, the sun appears again and we see a rainbow, with all of the previously mentioned items shown in the picture. The word *rainbow*, with a different color for each letter, is the final word of the text. Another feature of the text is the use of words as part of the illustration; for example, the word *rain* is written continuously in slanted lines to resemble falling rain.

In their own piece of writing, the teacher and children represented everything that they heard about and talked about in the story. Following the literary pattern of the book, they used painted objects and phrases, being careful to use the correct colors for each item. Notice how they also used the word *rain*. They were learning that print and illustrations work together to convey an idea. This work shows that Ida had guided them to notice detail and to achieve a text that has internal consistency. They had to attend to

■ sequence of events
■ the role of the car in moving through the rainstorm
■ how colors worked as part of the meaning

■ the relationships between visual symbols and printed symbols
■ the placement of text and pictures left to right to convey the development of the weather pattern
■ the construction of words using letter-sound relationships.

The children produced a complex text that individual students would not be expected to produce working alone. This product illustrates the power of interactive writing. The support of the teacher and the interaction of the group made it possible to think of the many facets of this text and to create a product that reflected this complex composition.

Using Shared Experiences as a Basis for Writing Directions

Interactive writing helps beginning writers and readers to go beyond what they can do independently. In the group situation, with teacher support, they experience all aspects of writing and use it for real purposes. As shown in the next example (Figure 15-2), children used interactive writing to record an experience in making applesauce.

Children in a kindergarten classroom were participating in a unit of study focusing on the seasons, particularly fall fruits and

FIGURE 15–1 *Rain* Mural

FIGURE 15–2 Applesauce Recipe

vegetables. The area of exploration incorporated social studies, health, and science. As part of their study, students walked around the neighborhood, where they spotted an apple tree with fruit in one of the yards. They discussed the signs of autumn in their neighborhood. In addition, their teacher brought different types of apples to the classroom. The class discussed the different ways of preparing apples to eat—raw apples, apple pie, dried apples, fried apples, apple cake, and applesauce. In their study, they used interactive writing for several different purposes, and produced the following texts

∎ a graph of their favorite kind of apple
∎ a description of what they saw on their walk through the neighborhood
∎ a list of ingredients for making applesauce.

The recipe shown here was written after the children had actually made and tasted the applesauce. So, they were recording their experiences and at the same time creating a text document that others could use. The format had to conform to a set of step-by-step directions; notice that they numbered the entries, then described the actions in order. To write a set of directions in sequence, children had to reflect back on their activities and remember, in order, the steps to take. This kind of analysis is similar to retelling a story in that it requires sequencing of events. The teacher's support and demonstration made it possible for these young children to analyze their experience and conceptualize it so that it could be put into writing.

At the same time, the teacher helped them to acquire the kind of language they needed to convey meaning. For example, they used imperative case as the approach for giving directions and they had to attend to aspects of the printer's code such as capital letters, periods, and the arrangement of words in lines. For example, each new step had to begin with a numeral on the left. They gave their recipe a title that provided information about the contents. Finally, they had to construct words using letter-sound relationships; this piece also provided the opportunity to use high-frequency words such as *the, and, in* and *it.* These high-frequency words, encountered in the fall of the school year, would appear over and over in interactive writing and shared reading. As children gained experience, they would learn high-frequency words in detail. The teacher might place them on the word wall, and children would use them in their independent writing (see Chapter 8 for information on useful high-frequency words).

The text also had some interesting words like *peel* and *cut* that have easy-to-hear initial consonants as well as easy-to-hear vowels. The teacher placed this text on the classroom wall to serve as an ongoing resource for reading and writing.

Documenting an Investigation

The following spring, this same group of children participated in a scientific study of the life cycle of a butterfly by putting caterpillars in cups and observing their change over time (see Figure 15-3; see also Appendix 5). The children observed the insects every day. Every few days, when significant changes

were noted, they discussed the changes. To keep a scientific record, they created a wall mural recounting the sequence of change. They produced descriptions by writing each word on a short piece of paper.

After composing the message, the teacher put the correct number of cards on the easel, using tape to hold the line of cards in place. This procedure represented a teacher's decision to draw attention to word boundaries. The class repeated the message, for example, "We put the very tiny caterpillars in the cups," pointing to the blank cards while saying it. Then, using interactive writing, the teacher and children constructed a word on each card, trimming off the extra paper after writing the word. The result was a series of cards that communicated the message. Afterward, with children observing, the teacher quickly glued the sentence on each panel of the wall mural. There was opportunity to discuss the placement of the text, to reread it, and to decide on the nature and placement of illustrations. Children produced illustrations as independent work and placed them on the panel later in the day. Following the development of the caterpillars, this wall mural took several weeks to produce.

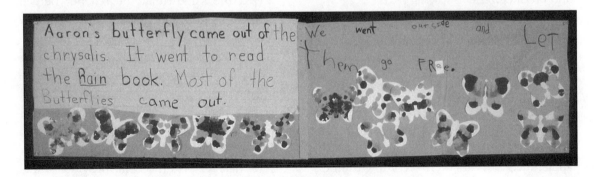

FIGURE 15–3 *Life Cycle of Butterfly Mural*

In producing this piece of work, the teacher supported the children's documentation of their observations, helping them to use written language like a scientist does, to support inquiry. The teacher helped them to bring experiences to conscious attention and use language to talk about their growing understandings. Within the experience, she helped children to make connections with other texts, such as Eric Carle's *The Very Hungry Caterpillar* (1969), which refers to "a tiny and very hungry caterpillar who ate through" leaves. By guiding the children to produce a visible record that could be referred to again, she taught them a beginning form of scientific documentation. The key to children's learning is the teacher's skill in supporting their learning processes. This group of kindergarten children was working at the edge of their understanding, taking on new learning and engaging in complex behaviors that would not have been possible working alone.

We have presented several examples of young children's learning. Each is complex because no single item or type of knowledge was acquired in any of the interactive writing lessons we described. Learning was active; it was supported by oral language; and it resulted in children's engagement in producing print. Thus, many layers of learning took place.

Active, Social, and Constructive Learning

Traditional wisdom suggests that people "learn by doing," and that is certainly true of children. The child is active as a learner and learns through action. Interaction, too, plays a strong role in learning. Some researchers see children's cognitive development as an "apprenticeship" in that the child is supported by an adult or older person who does the part of the task that the child cannot do alone but withdraws, when appropriate, to let the child perform what she can. Cognitive development occurs through this "guided participa-tion" in social activity with companions who support and expand children's understanding of and skill in using the tools of culture. The sociocultural basis of human skills and activi-ties—including children's orientation to participate in and build on the activities around them—is inseparable from the biological and historical basis of humans as a species (Rogoff 1990, vii).

Adult Support in Children's Learning

Supported by an adult, the child is able to do more than she could do alone. The adult's support allows the child to work at the outer limits of his own abilities, so that new learning takes place during the performance of new actions. The child is thus enabled to construct new understanding in a meaningful way so that she can remember them and generalize them to other situations and settings. For example, a young child who is helped by an adult to push the elevator button for the right floor by looking at the numbers is learning more than how to push elevator buttons. The adult's talk, direction, and demonstration assist the child initially; it is the powerful experience of pushing the button, feeling the elevator rise or fall, and stop at the right floor that makes the most dramatic impression. Assisted by the adult, the child can perform what she might otherwise not notice or do. The child is learning to look for numbers and notice that the features of numbers have meaning. With many different experiences, in which the adult brings the child's attention to the features of numbers, the child will begin to be mindful of them and use them independently. The result is the "construction" of a set of understandings. Wood (1988) believes that this constructive experience is essential for learning: "Only when the child constructs his own understanding would we expect him to remember and generalize what he has been taught" (83). Wood goes on to explain the theories of Vygotsky, a Russian psychologist whose studies of children's learning and the role of "more expert others" has influenced learning theory today.

For Vygotsky, then, *co-operatively achieved success* lies at the foundations of learning and development. Instruction—both formal and informal, in many social contexts, performed by more knowledgeable peers or siblings, parents, grandparents, friends, acquaintances and teachers—is the main vehicle for the cultural transmission of knowledge. Knowledge is embodied in the actions, work, play, technology, literature, art and talk of members of a society. Only through interaction with the living representatives of culture, what Bruner terms the "vicars of culture," can a child come to acquire, embody and further develop that knowledge. Children's development thus reflects their *cultural* experiences and their opportunities for access to the more mature who already *practice* specific areas of knowledge. (25)

In the interactive writing experiences connected to *Rain*, the teacher's support, in addition to good group interaction, helped these kindergarten children notice details in illustrations and features of text that might not otherwise have been accessible to them. As Clay (1991) states:

The teacher's role is critical in helping children learn accurately. If she works alongside of a child letting him do all that he can but supporting the activity when he reaches some limit by sharing the task she is more likely to uncover the cutting edges of his learning. He, on the other hand, will not be bored by doing ten times over something he already knows how to do, but is likely to be challenged to risk attempting the novel, knowing that help will be offered for shared completion of the task if he cannot do it alone. (65–66)

Language Learning

From their first experiences as infants, children search to make sense of their world. Family members and caregivers provide new and stimulating experiences from which children learn more every day. Children connect familiar noises and faces with food, comfort, and amusement. They gradually notice patterns, which might include recurring noises, touches, and tastes, and their responses reveal a growing awareness of these patterns. They are surrounded by talk, from which they begin to construct meaning. Their first utterances, no matter how primitive, are greeted with delight and suffused with meaning, which is interpreted by caregivers.

Even infants begin to learn to interact. Research on children's language acquisition provides strong evidence that children respond very early to familiar voices and even begin to engage in "turn taking" and other language communication before they can actually say words (Cazden 1988). Research on caregivers and language learning reveals that, while adults talk differently to children than to other adults, they do not limit language to one- or two-word utterances. Sentences addressed to children are complex, with no limit on vocabulary; in fact, adults seem to chatter on and on to babies, often repeating phrases over and over. Children seem to abstract meaningful words from the language they hear and begin to use them. The result is very rewarding; for example, a young child who says "up" is picked up by a caregiver. They move from holistic utterances (one word) to "telegraphic" speech in which they have put together two or three words that convey meaning, for example, "go bye bye" or "more cookie."

The interesting thing about the young child's language is that, with a few exceptions, the child is producing language structures that he or she has never or rarely heard. It appears that the child is putting words together to construct statements that have a "grammar" of their own. The child is working to communicate within the limits of words he or she can say. Studies of language learning from all over the world indicate very similar stages in the acquisition of language, with children moving from one- or two-word language structures to the complex structures that kindergarten and first-grade children use (Lindfors 1987). The similarities are so strong that linguists have determined a genetic basis for language; that is, they believe that human brains are somehow "programmed" to develop language. Of course, they must have rich interactions with others in the environment, but, given that, all healthy children develop language.

Researchers suggest that children "construct" language in a way that is predictable and is related to the function of language in their lives (Halliday 1975). Children use language for real purposes, for example, to get what they need or want, and, as they do so, they develop the forms they need. They use language for social purposes, to establish relations with others, to inform others, and to ask questions about their world. Young children use language for the joy of it; they love the sound of it, as exemplified by their delight at the rhyme and rhythm of songs and nursery rhymes.

When children learn language, they are learning more than a collection of words. They are learning a system of underlying rules that they can use to generate an unlimited number of sentences and longer texts to communicate meaning. These "rules" are not rules in the sense of "correct grammar." They are the principles for mapping meanings onto the speech that others will understand; words follow each other in patterned ways. There are "rules" for how the voice rises and falls as sentences are spoken. Every speaker of every language puts words together in certain ways that communicate meaning to others.

Clay (1991) has described language as an example of a "self-extending system." Literacy, Clay says, should be a natural "follow on from what they have already learned to do well" (26). This does not mean that, having learned language, children will automatically learn literacy without teaching. It does mean that children learn best if the teacher is helping them to make links between new language and literacy learning and what they already know.

A critical feature of interactive writing is talking with children. In that way, it is quite similar to individual writing development (Calkins 1983, 1986). Interactive writing works best within a broader learning context, one in which children have experiences surrounded by meaningful talk. In the "planning" or "background" element of interactive writing, the teacher is really working on oral language rather than on specific skills related to literature. The discussion and negotiation that precedes composing a text is rich in opportunity for children to extend their language. The teacher's conversation provides a scaffold; she may use sentences, phrases, or words, and invite children to repeat them or use them in new ways. This oral language process helps children expand listening and speaking vocabularies and develop new syntactic patterns. When they approach the task of composing a specific text, then, they have more to bring to it. In planning and composing, talk

- lets children know that you value what they say
- helps to establish common goals
- helps children think and talk about genre and/or format of the piece
- activates prior knowledge and leads children to vocalize it
- exposes children to examples of written language through the teacher's reading books aloud
- allows children to use new words and linguistic structures while engaged in concrete experiences and while discussing them afterward
- helps children think about and discuss the structure of text
- enables children to think about and discuss the audience for their written language
- prompts children to consider necessary constraints, such as length, space, sentence structure, etc., when turning an oral text into a written one.

Talk surrounds the constructing process in the interactive writing lesson. The experience of writing about applesauce prompted children to talk about text as well as about features of written language. This "language about language" raises awareness and focuses children's attention on important "items" of information (such as individual letters, letter clusters, or words) that they need to learn. But, more important, talking about written language helps children notice and internalize the "rules" that will allow them to produce many words using the alphabet system and to put words together in meaningful texts.

In the talk and writing that surrounded the experiences with applesauce and the life cycle of a butterfly, children had a chance to use language in new ways while simultaneously talking about text and learning new words. As Clay (1998) has said, "The act of writing provides one with the means of making one's own language somewhat opaque, revealing things about oral language to young writers" (137). In this way, the learning was multidimensional. As in early language development, they were learning language through use.

Literacy Learning

Literacy learning is highly related to language learning; however, some important new understandings are important to consider as we work with kindergarten and first-grade children. It appears that development of oral language and knowledge of the purposes of reading are important *in combination with* specific learning about literacy. The findings of the National Committee on the Prevention of Reading Difficulties in Young Children indicate that "there is abundant empirical and observational evidence that the children who are particularly likely to have difficulty with learning to read in the primary grades are those who begin school with less prior knowledge and skill in certain domains, most notably, general verbal abilities, phonological sensitivity, familiarity with the basic purposes and mechanisms of read-

ing, and letter knowledge" (Snow, Burns, and Griffin 1998, 117).

Here, we list several important early understandings about written language and note how interactive writing can contribute to learning in this area.

Phonological and Orthographic Awareness
The concepts of phonological and orthographic awareness have received much attention in recent years. Here are established definitions from *The Literacy Dictionary* (Harris and Hodges 1995):

■ Phonological awareness is awareness of the constituent sounds [phonemes] of words in learning to read and spell.
■ Orthographic awareness is awareness of the symbols [graphemes] that represent sounds in a writing system.

So, phoneme awareness refers to what you *hear* and grapheme awareness refers to what you *see*. Phoneme awareness means that children are sensitive to the sounds in words. They can consciously examine language; they can tell when words start alike or end alike; eventually they are able to break up words by sounds, syllables, or onsets (the first part of the word—*s*ay, *tr*ay, *pr*ay) and rimes (the rest of the word—s*ay*, tr*ay*, pr*ay*). Children become sensitive to sounds through oral language that incorporates games, rhymes, and poems. They connect sounds to graphemes (or written symbols) when they both say and see the print.

The whole system seems to work together. There is some evidence that when letters and sounds are taught together, the learning is accelerated (Bradley and Bryant 1983). For students who have begun noting sounds in words and also recognize written letters, associating sound cues with visual cues results in greater growth in phonemic awareness (Hohn and Ehri 1983).

Research indicates that phonemic awareness (that spoken words consist of a sequence of sounds) is an important understanding that is basic to grasping the alphabetic principle (Ball and Blachman 1991; Bradley and Bryant 1983; Bryant, MacLean, Bradley, and Crossland 1990; Bryant, Bradley, Camlean, and Crossland 1989). This means understanding that written words are made up of letters and that these letters are approximately matched to the sounds of language.

The construction element of interactive writing is especially effective in helping children attend to the sounds in words and connect those sounds with graphic symbols. Within a piece of language that children have composed, have enunciated several times, and can fully understand, the support for learning sounds and letters together is very high. In the construction of the text, there are ample opportunities for the teacher to ask children to say words slowly and to think about the sounds. When the teacher particularly wants to emphasize a word or part of a word, she has a child come up to the easel and fill in a letter, letter cluster, or other word part, or (sometimes) the entire word, emphasizing the relationships between letters and sounds. Linking the name chart to words being written provides further examples for children in connecting sounds and letters, learning more about both in the process.

Concepts About Print

Learning to write means learning more than letters and words. Children learn that written texts are constructed in certain ways (Clay 1991a). After all, oral speech comes out in time (rather than "left to right") and there are no "spaces." Written language is arranged visually on a page, from left to right and top to bottom. Words are separated by space and follow each other on a line that is usually invisible but assumed. When you write, you need to think of the message and then represent it, letter by letter in space. When you read, you must match one spoken word with one cluster of letters representing a word. "First" in writing means the top word on the left or the left letter in a sequence of letters that make up a word. All of these concepts are critical to the child's early literacy learning and cannot be taken for granted.

Interactive writing provides a way to talk about the conventions of the printer's code. The teacher models how to think about where to start and which way to go. For example, if there is not enough room at the end of the line, the teacher will explicitly show the children to go back to the left again and start a new line. Then, children apply these concepts themselves with the support of the teacher in the group setting.

Letter Learning

Letter learning is necessary, although not sufficient, for becoming literate. Letter learning is given significant attention in the first year of school, and for good reason. The names of letters represent important information for preschool, kindergarten, and first-grade children (Pressley 1998; Venezky 1970; Walsh, Price, and Gillingham 1988). Adams (1990) has said that "knowledge of letter names is the single best predictor of success in first-grade reading" (21). Snow et al. (1998) report that "the strongest predictor on its own is letter identification." Through early experiences with letters, children learn that a letter has features that distinguish it from every other letter, that letters have names, that directional movements are required to make letters, that letters come in a certain order in the alphabet, that there is a limited set of letters (twenty-six upper and lower case), and that letters are related to sounds you can hear.

Interactive writing alone is not sufficient to assure that children learn about letters; we recommend its use in combination with a great deal of direct study. Children enjoy work with magnetic letters, name puzzles, alphabet books, posters and rhymes, and so on, and these experiences have high instructional value (see Pinnell and Fountas 1998). Interactive writing is, however, a powerful context within which children can notice, make, and use letters. For children who are still learning letters, during construction of a text, teachers emphasize letter names and features. Children connect them to letters in their names, noticing features that are alike, and practice the directional movements needed to write them.

Word Learning

It is useful for young children to acquire some high-frequency words that they know in detail and can write and recognize. These first words provide good examples from which they can derive the following understandings:

▌ Words are made up of letters and space is used to separate words.

▌ You can hear the sounds in words when you say them and connect them to letters in the words.

▌ Words are written from left to right.

▌ Words can be connected to each other in the way they look or sound; that is, they have some of the same parts.

▌ Some letters often go together in words (like *st*, *oo*, *sh*) and some letters never go together in words (like *xb*, *sb*).

As children are beginning to learn to read, they will not have in place the skills needed for decoding, so they must often learn words by sight (Ehri 1991). Knowing some high-frequency words helps emergent readers to begin to monitor their reading by recognizing words and to produce more coherent pieces of writing. These early sight words help readers move more easily to the application of letter-sound relationships to reading words (Ehri and Wilce 1985). The more words children know, the easier it is for them to learn more. They can connect these known words to words that they do not yet know, making word learning occur more rapidly. In a longitudinal study, Juel (1988) found that first graders who had good word recognition read twice as many words in books than do those with low knowledge. Juel, Griffith, and

Gough (1986) found that children not only could read more rapidly when they knew words but they also understood more.

Interactive writing is a powerful context for early word learning. The redundancy of language (plus the teacher's careful shaping of the text) ensures that high-frequency words are written over and over again and subsequently read. Over time, children learn to recognize many words. These words become a shared resource for the whole group and are transferred to the children's own writing.

Spelling Strategies

Expert writers can accurately write many words independently and they can also use a range of strategies to spell them. Children who have been immersed in literacy experiences have learned that print is something unique. It is not like pictures but instead contains letters that are connected to speech sounds and thus to meaning in complex ways. Interactive writing provides a context in which children learn how "words work." They can become word solvers who not only recognize known words but have strategies for figuring out unknown words. Good spellers

▌ write the sounds they hear in words

▌ write words left to right, letter by letter, using what they know to check on accuracy

▌ use letter-sound relationships in flexible ways to spell words

▌ know aspects of words, such as the presence of a vowel in every word and in every syllable of a longer word

▌ connect unknown words to known words and use that connection to attempt spellings

▌ know how to check on words they write to see whether they are spelled correctly

▌ know how to use resources (such as a word wall for younger children or a dictionary for older children) in connection with partially known information about a word. (Pinnell and Fountas 1998)

Evidence of children's using the strategies listed above can be seen when you observe an interactive writing lesson. As children learn more about words, the teacher will make appropriate learning explicit. In the beginning, the name chart may be the reference that children use to connect words or to check on words; as they learn more, word walls and word charts can be used. Even when you are doing most of the writing because children can already write many words, you can still select one or two complex words to extend their word-solving skills or to demonstrate using references and resources.

Working with a Language Hierarchy

In the writing process, children construct a text by organizing symbols and space to communicate meaning. They must keep the meaning of the larger text in mind while at the same time focusing on words, letters within words, the order of letters, the use of space, the arrangement of lines of print, and punctuation. We describe this process as shifting from a "bigger view," or the meaning, down to the smallest symbol (letter or letter feature), and then back to the meaning level. Writing requires using the smallest details of language without losing sight of the meaning and sequences of words that make up the whole text. Known words assist in the process because they can be written quickly and automatically, leaving attention for the more complex words.

Beginning writers often have difficulty with this complex process because every word represents a challenge. When you have to work excessively on the smallest details of words, it's hard to stick with an overall idea or plan. Interactive writing presents the opportunity for writers to be freed from some of the challenges involved in producing a text. They participate in composition with the language support of the teacher. Their written contributions are carefully organized so that they are working on the edge of their learning. To save time, the teacher writes words that children already know automati-

cally, as well as words that are much too difficult for children. But, words that present powerful examples because children are attending to the very features represented and need to learn more about them may be highlighted through sharing the pen. In this "apprentice-like" fashion, the teacher keeps the process moving quickly, allowing children to engage in quick problem-solving without losing meaning. According to Clay (1993), "When the eye, ear and hand are jointly involved in the management of a task, each may be regarded as offering a check on the other. Writing activities can make the learner aware of new ways to check upon the language he has been saying and using. He can examine his speech in another form. He gains a new means of exploring and comparing segments of language" (109). Interactive writing thus gives children access to the ways of using text that parallel what writers actually do. The process is visible to children in important ways.

Connections Between Writing and Reading

Strong reading/writing connections are inherent in the elements of interactive writing. Letter learning and phonological and orthographic awareness have been shown to be factors in children's learning to read. The more they know in these important areas, the more likely they are to be successful in early reading (Snow, Burns, and Griffin 1998).

Word recognition, too, is important learning for early reading. Pieces of interactive writing are read and reread many times both during construction and afterward. As Adams (1990) has said, "repeated readings and repetitive texts set the stage for the acquisition of a broad sight vocabulary" (69). As children have more experience, they develop *ways of learning words* and learning accelerates. For fluent reading with understanding, readers need instant recognition of about 95 percent of words in the text (Adams 1990).

The spelling strategies children use in interactive writing are highly related (although they are not the same) to the decoding/phonics strategies children use while reading. Writing "slows down" the process of looking at and thinking about words so that children can learn more about the principles. Interactive writing clearly demonstrates the processes related to constructing words and helps students develop the kind of knowledge they need to take words apart while reading. Readers use letter-sound relationships in combination with attention to larger word parts and spelling analysis. The ability to analyze words efficiently and rapidly in reading is a major element in skilled reading (Nagy et al. 1989). Readers who are fully aware of the orthographic features of words begin to see common sequences and spelling patterns, which, in turn, help them read more words (Ehri and McCormick 1998). For skilled readers, word identification is based on rapid use of both visual and phonemic information with words. This information is checked with meaning and context (Adams 1990; Daneman 1991; Ehri 1991; Juel 1991; Stanovich 1991). When children independently reread texts created in interactive writing, it is easy for them to coordinate meaning with visual and phonetic information. The meaning and context are available and children can give their full attention to processing the print. As the process of recognizing words becomes more and more automatic, word learning is rapid.

Interactive writing helps children on the way to reading and accelerates their learning in writing. Over the first three years of school, children's reading skill begins to exceed their writing skill. They will become fluent in both writing and reading. Interactive writing foreshadows the kind of reading students will do by opening up the structure of the text for them to think about. The support of the teacher in writing and the opportunity to read a more complicated text than they could on their own facilitates the process of becoming fluent.

Speed and fluency are highly related to reading comprehension (Pinnell, Pikulski,

Wixson, Campbell, Gough, and Beatty 1995). Becoming a fluent reader has to do with rapid, automatic word recognition in combination with meaning and language use. Good readers do not simply read quickly; they seem to process larger idea units and phrases. Their understanding goes beyond individual words; it allows them to interpret text (Reutzel, Hollingsworth, and Eldredge 1994). In interactive writing, children know the structure of the text and the unique way sentences are put together to express the desired meanings. The process also offers children a chance to read a broader range of texts (informational as well as narrative) than would be possible with their present reading skills. The National Research Council Committee on the Prevention of Reading Difficulties in Young Children (Snow, Burns, and Griffin 1998) recommends that students have "sufficient practice in reading to achieve fluency with different kinds of texts written for different purposes" (223).

Working with the language hierarchy in writing (from meaning to details) also has implications for supporting learning in writing. The information gained as children work through a text in interactive writing and later in their own writing becomes part of the foundation of understandings that can be used in beginning reading. Clay (1991) describes writing as a "building up" process. In order for a message to be communicated, you need to construct it letter by letter, from letters to words to phrases to sentences to stories and other texts. All of those symbols must be organized in space in a way that communicates the features of the genre. For example, space is used differently in lists, invitations, letters, and stories.

Reading, on the other hand, involves a "breaking down" process. A text exists, which the reader has to read as a whole, constructing meaning while doing so and dropping down to take words apart when needed.

The building-up processes complement the visual analysis of text which is a breaking-down process, and although both building-up and breaking-down processes occur in reading, the constructive nature of the task in writing is probably more obvious to the young child. It is probably by these two processes that the child comes to understand the hierarchical relationships of letters, words, and utterances. (Clay 1991, 109)

Interactive writing, in connection with other literacy experiences, helps children learn about the building up and breaking down processes within a familiar, purposeful, and interesting language experience.

Dimensions of Learning Through Interactive Writing

We have drawn from a number of areas of research to provide a theoretical rationale for engaging children in interactive writing. When interactive writing is implemented successfully, learning takes place along many dimensions (see Figure 15-4.)

Because interactive writing is patterned on the thinking and behaviors in which writers (and also readers) engage, the learning is multilevel in nature. Children are learning how to write; at the same time, they are be-coming writers who make language a tool for learning, for communication, and for enjoyment. In the process, they also begin to become readers who consume, use, enjoy, learn from, and even evaluate written texts.

Suggestions for Professional Development

1. Gather a group of grade-level colleagues and request that a volunteer videotape one interactive writing session. Be sure to discuss the fact that there is no such thing as a perfect lesson, but that a shared experience will help everyone become more analytic about her teaching decisions.

2. Meet to view the videotape and interactive writing piece. Discuss the following questions:

Learning Theory

- How actively engaged were the children? At what particular points did you see evidence of specific individuals' learning something new?
- What did the teacher help the children attend to?

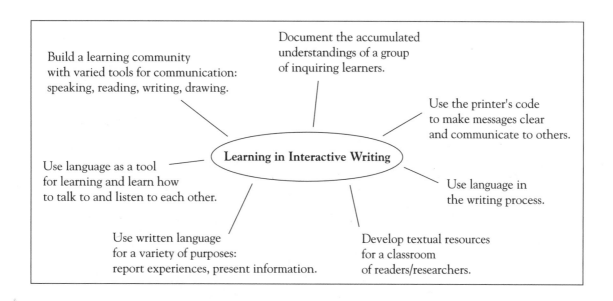

FIGURE 15–4   Dimensions of Learning through Interactive Writing

Language Learning

- How much language surrounded the teaching and learning?
- Were there examples of the teacher's expansion of children's language?
- What examples showed language about language? (e.g., "words")

Literacy Learning

- Were there examples of the children's listening for word boundaries or word parts (syllables)?
- List all the examples of the teacher's demonstrating saying words slowly, the children and teacher saying words slowly together, and the children's independently saying words slowly.
- What concepts of print were reinforced or taught? Which ones were assumed?

- What attention to letter formation, letter names, or letter-sound relationships were evident in the lesson?
- Was there any reference to the words on the word wall?
- How many high-frequency words did the children or teacher write into the text quickly?
- Were there opportunities to learn new high-frequency words?

Reading-Writing Relationships

- What did you notice about how the children were able to read what was written?
- Were there challenges?
- Did they learn how to read something new?

Language and Literacy: How It All Comes Together

Interactive writing has opened a new conversation for us—one that crosses classrooms, schools, and grade levels. With the current focus on literacy education, the search for ways to bring children into the world of literacy is intense. National standards call for a broad base of knowledge even for entering first graders. The quest is especially strong for children who may be disadvantaged in the school setting because their preschool experiences did not especially focus on literacy. Children's own language and knowledge are the key.

How can we achieve a vision of joyful, competent literacy for every child by grade three? It is obvious that every moment of the first years is important. Our best chance is to capture children's attention and direct it toward purposeful and enjoyable uses of literacy from the very beginning. Through interactive writing, children learn to see themselves as writers. Interactive writing provides a way to show them what writing is all about, that it can be used to express themselves and tell about their life experiences. At the same time, children have a window on the mysterious processes related to literacy. Through interactive writing, their language and literacy come together. The talk, writing, and reading described in this book provide a supportive framework from which children can grow in independence.

Not a minute of early education can be wasted. Those years are short, and there are only a few hours in each school day. We have selected interactive writing as an essential component of kindergarten and first-grade literacy curriculum because it makes possible so many levels and kinds of learning. When we work with children in interactive writing, we can involve them in an experience that expands their language competence while at the same time focusing their attention on the details of print and how it works. The process so closely parallels independent writing that children learn what it feels like to be writers of many varieties of texts long before they can create such texts on their own. Interactive writing is true apprenticeship. Children work alongside a supportive teacher who engages them at the point of beneficial learning. Interactive writing is an effective way of stretching children's knowledge and making their first writing experiences productive, as well as instilling in them pride and a sense of accomplishment.

We see interactive writing as a bridge between oral and written language. In this book, we have shared our own learning and development of the process. We have described how excellent teachers are finding ways to involve children in real writing and reading through interactive writing. We invite the readers of this book to participate in that conversation through sharing the writing task with children. It is easy to start interactive writing and we hope that this book has intrigued you enough to make you want to do so; but more important, we hope that you will continue to explore this powerful instructional medium through refining your decision making and helping children extend and expand their knowledge of text and of how written language works.

As children enter their literacy apprenticeship, they learn that every piece of writing must have an ending. We close this book with a commonly used and valued ending, provided here by one young writer.

Madeleine Gifford
1999

Appendices

Appendix 1
Easel Specifications

**The Ohio State University Literacy Collaborative® Basic Directions
for Easel Construction.**

Supply List

2	1" x 24" x 36" veneer plywood (table)
4	1" x 3" x 48" oak (legs)
2	1" x 3" x 36" pine or poplar (ledge)
2	3" hinges
2	12" x $^1/_8$" chain
46	1 $^1/_4$" wood screws (approximately)
4	$^1/_4$" wood screws (approximately)
	wood glue

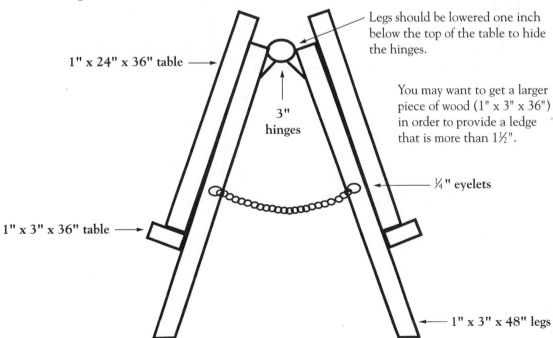

1" x 24" x 36" table →

Legs should be lowered one inch below the top of the table to hide the hinges.

3" hinges

You may want to get a larger piece of wood (1" x 3" x 36") in order to provide a ledge that is more than 1½".

$^1/_4$" eyelets

1" x 3" x 36" table →

1" x 3" x 48" legs

Directions

1. Attach 1 x 3 x 36" ledge to the bottom edge of each table with glue and screws.
2. Attach legs to the back of each table with 6 wood screws and glue.
    Use glue first and clamp leg to table. Drill pilot holes and screw together before removing clamps.
    Legs should be lowered one inch below the top of the table to hide the hinges.
3. Attach 3" hinge to the top of each leg. Insert eyelets approximately 3" above the ledge and attach the chain.
4. Stain or finish as you wish. We suggest using three coats of polyurethane semi-gloss.

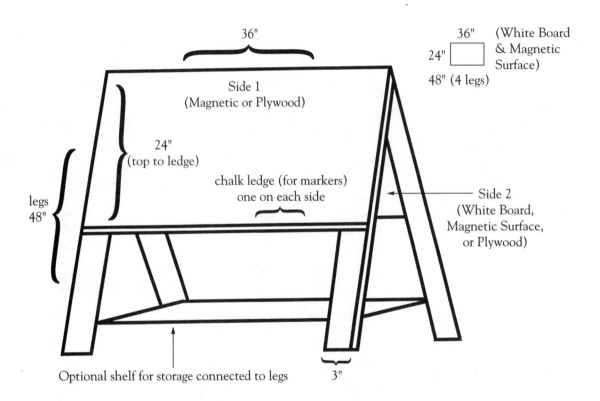

© The Ohio State University Literacy Collaborative

Appendix 2:
Children's Literature

In this section, we have gathered together children's literature titles that are integral to interactive writing and grouped them in four main categories: Concept Books, the Rhythm of Language, Folk Tales, and Theme Collections. The books in each category are listed in alphabetical order by author.

For your convenience, at the end of this section we have also provided ordering information for the majority of these books in the form of a table listing each book by title, author, publisher, and ISBN.

Concept Books

ABC Books

Anno, Mitsumasa. 1974. *Anno's Alphabet*. New York: Thomas Y. Crowell.

Aylesworth, Jim. 1992. *Old Black Fly*. New York: Henry Holt.

Bayer, Jane. 1984. *A My Name Is Alice*. New York: Dial.

Bowen, Betsy. 1991. *Antler, Bear, Canoe*. Boston, MA: Little, Brown.

Garten, Jan. 1994. *The Alphabet Tale*. New York: Greenwillow.

Grundy, Lynn. 1980. *A Is for Apple*. Lewiston, ME: Ladybird.

Hoban, Tana. 1987. *26 Letters and 99 Cents*. New York: Greenwillow.

Isadora, Rachel. 1999. *ABC Pop!* New York: Viking/Penguin.

Kightley, Rosalinda. 1986. *ABC*. Boston, MA: Little, Brown.

Lobel, Anita. 1990. *Alison's Zinnia*. New York: Greenwillow.

Martin, Bill Jr., and John Archambault. 1989. *Chicka Chicka Boom Boom*. New York: Simon & Schuster.

Onyefulu, Ifeoma. 1993. *A Is for Africa*. New York: Cobblehill.

Powell, Richard. 1993. *I Spy in the Garden*. New York: Puffin/Penguin.

Sandvd, Kjell B. 1996. *The Butterfly Alphabet*. New York: Scholastic.

Schnur, Steven. 1997. *Autumn: An Alphabet Acrostic*. New York: Clarion/Houghton Mifflin.

Schories, Pat. 1996. *Over Under in the Garden*. New York: Farrar Straus Giroux.

Color

Charles, N. N., L. Dillon, and D. Dillon. 1994. *What Am I?* New York: The Blue Sky Press/Scholastic.

Chocolate, Debbi. 1996. *Kente Colors*. New York: Walker.

De Bourgoing, Pascale, and Gallimard Jeunesse. 1989. *Vegetables in the Garden*. New York: Scholastic.

Ehlert, Lois. 1989. *Color Zoo*. New York: J. B. Lippincott.

Fleming, Denise. 1992. *Lunch*. New York: Henry Holt.

Hamanaka, Sheila. 1994. *All the Colors of the Earth*. New York: William Morrow.

Heller, Ruth. 1995. *Color*. New York: Putnam and Grosset.

Hoban, Tana. 1989. *Of Colors and Things*. New York: Scholastic.

Jeunesse, Gallimard, and Pascale de Bourgoing. 1991. *Colors*. New York: Scholastic.

Jeunesse, Gallimard, Claude Delafosse, and Perols. 1994. *Atlas of Plants*. New York: Scholastic.

Jonas, Ann. 1989. *Color Dance*. New York: Greenwillow.

Kalan, Robert. 1978. *Rain*. New York: Greenwillow.

Martin, Bill. 1983. *Brown Bear, Brown Bear, What Do You See?* New York: Holt, Rinehart and Winston.

McMillan, Bruce. 1988. *Growing Colors*. New York: Lothrop, Lee and Shepard.

Peek, Merle. 1985. *Mary Wore Her Red Dress and Henry Wore His Green Sneakers*. New York: Clarion.

Pinkwater, Daniel M. 1977. *The Big Orange Splot*. Mamaroneck, New York: Hastings House.

Rotner, Shelley, and Anne Woodhull. 1996. *Colors Around Us*. New York: Simon & Schuster.

Sis, Peter. 1989. *Going Up!* New York: Greenwillow.

Stinson, Kathy. 1982. *Red Is Best*. Toronto, Canada: Annick Press.

Walsh, Ellen S. 1989. *Mouse Paint*. New York: Harcourt Brace Jovanovich.

Williams, Sue. 1989. *I Went Walking*. New York: Harcourt Brace Jovanovich.

Young, Ed. 1992. *Seven Blind Mice*. New York: Philomel/Putnam and Grosset.

Counting Books

Bowen, Betsy. 1995. *Gathering*. New York: Little, Brown.

Carter, David A. 1988. *How Many Bugs in a Box?* New York: Little Simon/Simon & Schuster.

Crews, Donald. 1986. *Ten Black Dots*. New York: Greenwillow.

Ehlert, Lois. 1990. *Fish Eyes: A Book You Can Count On*. New York: Harcourt Brace Jovanovich.

Evans, Lezlie. 1999. *Can You Count Ten Toes? Count to 10 in 10 Different Languages*. New York: Houghton Mifflin.

Falwell, Cathryn. 1993. *Feast for 10*. New York: Clarion.

Grover, Max. 1995. *Amazing and Incredible Counting Stories*. New York: Browndeer/Harcourt Brace.

Harshman, Marc. 1993. *Only One*. New York: Cobblehill.

Hutchins, Pat. 1982. *1 Hunter*. New York: Greenwillow.

Inkpen, Mick. 1987. *One Bear at Bedtime*. Boston, MA: Little, Brown.

Kitchen, Bert. 1987. *Animal Numbers*. New York: Dial/Penguin.

Koch, Michelle. 1989. *Just One More*. New York: Greenwillow.

Koller, Jackie F. 1999. *One Monkey Too Many*. New York: Harcourt Brace.

Long, Lynette. 1996. *Domino Addition*. Watertown, MA: Charlesbridge.

McCarthy, Bobette. 1992. *Ten Little Hippos*. New York: Bradbury/Macmillan.

McMillan, Bruce. 1986. *Counting Wildflowers*. New York: Lothrop, Lee and Shepard.

Merriam, Eve. 1999. *Ten Rosy Roses*. New York: HarperCollins.

Micklethwait, Lucy. 1992. *I Spy Two Eyes: Numbers in Art*. New York: Greenwillow.

Peek, Merle. 1981. *Roll Over!* New York: Clarion/Houghton Mifflin.

Pomeroy, Diana. 1996. *One Potato*. New York: Harcourt Brace.

Rees, Mary. 1988. *Ten in a Bed*. Boston, MA: Joy Street Books/Little, Brown.

Samton, Sheila W. 1991. *Moon to Sun: An Adding Book*. Honesville, PA: Carolyn House/Boyds Mills Press.

Saul, Carol. 1998. *Barn Cat*. Boston, MA: Little, Brown.

Schlein, Miriam. 1996. *More Than One*. New York: Greenwillow.

Serfozo, Mary. 1989. *Who Wants One?* New York: Macmillan.

Wood, Jakki. 1992. *Moo Moo, Brown Cow*. New York: Harcourt Brace Jovanovich.

Miscellaneous Concept Books

Baker, Keith. 1991. *Hide and Snake*. New York: Harcourt Brace Jovanovich.

Burton, Robert. 1994. *Egg*. New York: Dorling Kindersley.

Cohen, Caron Lee. 1996. *Where's the Fly?* New York: Greenwillow.

Davis, Katie. 1998. *Who Hops?* New York: Harcourt Brace.

Dodds, Dayle A. 1994. *The Shape of Things*. Cambridge, MA: Candlewick.

Evans, Katie. 1992. *Hunky Dory Ate It*. New York: Dutton.

Merriam, Eve. 1995. *The Hole Story*. New York: Simon & Schuster.

Miller, Margaret. 1988. *Whose Hat?* New York: Greenwillow.

Miller, Margaret. 1990. *Who Uses This?* New York: Greenwillow.

Miller, Margaret. 1991. *Whose Shoe?* New York: Greenwillow.

Miller, Margaret. 1994. *My Five Senses*. New York: Simon & Schuster.

Miller, Margaret. 1998. *Big and Little*. New York: Greenwillow.

Murphy, Mary. 1997. *I Like It When…* New York: Harcourt Brace.

Roddie, Shen, and Frances Cony. 1991. *Hatch, Egg, Hatch!* New York: Little, Brown.

Royston, Angela. 1991. *Duck: See How They Grow*. New York: Lodestar Books/Dutton.

Wagner, Karen. 1990. *Chocolate Chip Cookies*. New York: Henry Holt.

Weiss, Nicki. 1990. *An Egg Is an Egg*. New York: G. P. Putnam's Sons.

Wheeler, Cindy. 1995. *Simple Signs*. New York: Penguin.

The Rhythm of Language

Songs and Rhymes

Baker, Keith. 1994. *Big Fat Hen*. New York: Harcourt Brace.

Brown, Marc. 1980. *Finger Rhymes*. New York: E. P. Dutton.

Christelow, Eileen. 1989. *Five Little Monkeys Jumping on the Bed*. New York: Clarion.

Cousins, Lucy. 1989. *The Little Dog Laughed and Other Nursery Rhymes*. New York: E. P. Dutton.

Craig, Helen. 1992. *I See the Moon, and the Moon Sees Me*. New York: Willa Perlman/HarperCollins.

De Paola, Tomie. 1986. *Tomie de Paola's Favorite Nursery Tales*. New York: G.P. Putnam's Sons.

De Regniers, Bernice S. 1988. *Sing a Song of Popcorn*. New York: Scholastic.

English, Tracey. 1993. *Old MacDonald Had a Farm*. New York: Golden Books/Western Publishing.

Hale, Sarah J. 1990. *Mary Had a Little Lamb*. Illustrated by Bruce McMillan. New York: Scholastic.

Halpern, Shari. 1994. *Little Robin Redbreast*. New York: North-South.

Hawkins, Colin, and Jacqui Hawkins. 1984. *Old Mother Hubbard*. New York: G. P. Putnam's Sons.

Hawkins, Colin, and Jacqui Hawkins. 1991. *Old MacDonald Had a Farm*. Los Angeles, CA: Price Stern Sloan.

Hayes, Sarah. 1988. *Clap Your Hands*. New York: Lothrop, Lee and Shepard.

Hennessy, B. G. 1989. *The Missing Tarts*. New York: Viking/Penguin.

Karas, Brian G. 1964. *I Know an Old Lady*. New York: Scholastic.

Kelley, True. 1993. *Spider on the Floor*. New York: Crown/Random House.

Koller, Jackie F. 1999. *One Monkey Too Many*. New York: Harcourt Brace.

Kovalski, Maryann. 1987. *The Wheels on the Bus*. Boston, MA: Little, Brown.

Little, Jean, and Maggie De Vries. 1991. *Once Upon a Golden Apple*. New York: Viking/Penguin.

Marshall, James. 1991. *Old Mother Hubbard and Her Wonderful Dog*. New York: Farrar Straus Giroux.

Miranda, Anne. 1997. *To Market, to Market*. New York: Harcourt Brace.

O'Malley, Kevin. 1992. *Froggy Went a-Courtin*. New York: Stewart, Tabori and Chang.

Opie. 1996. *My Very First Mother Goose*. Candlewick, MA.

Paparone, Pamela. 1995. *Five Little Ducks*. New York: North-South.

Parkinson, Kathy. 1988. *The Farmer in the Dell*. Niles, IL: Albert Whitman.

Peek, Merle. 1985. *Mary Wore Her Red Dress and Henry Wore His Green Sneakers*. New York: Clarion.

Prater, John. 1993. *Once Upon a Time*. Cambridge, MA: Candlewick.

Prelutsky, Jack. 1986. *Read-Aloud Rhymes*. New York: Alfred A. Knopf.

Raffi, Jose Aruego, and Ariane Dewey. 1989. *Five Little Ducks*. New York: Crown.

Rojankovsky, Feodor. 1970. *The Tall Book of Mother Goose*. New York: HarperCollins.

Rounds, Glen. 1989. *Old MacDonald Had a Farm*. New York: Holiday House.

Sloat, Teri. 1998. *There Was an Old Lady Who Swallowed a Trout!* New York: Henry Holt.

Taback, Simms. 1997. *There Was an Old Lady Who Swallowed a Fly*. New York: Penguin.

Trapani, Iza. 1993. *The Itsy Bitsy Spider*. Boston, MA: Whispering Coyote Press.

Wegman, William. 1996. *Mother Goose*. New York: Hyperion.

Westcott, Nadine B. 1987. *Peanut Butter and Jelly*. New York: E. P. Dutton.

Westcott, Nadine B. 1988. *The Lady with the Alligator Purse*. Boston, MA: Little, Brown.

Westcott, Nadine B. 1989. *Skip to My Lou*. Boston, MA: Little, Brown.

Wickstrom, Sylvie K. 1988. *Wheels on the Bus*. New York: Crown.

Wood, Jakki. 1992. *Moo Moo, Brown Cow*. New York: Gulliver/Harcourt Brace.

Wyndham, Robert. 1968. *Chinese Mother Goose Rhymes*. New York: Philomel/Putnam and Grosset.

Yolen, Jane. 1992. *Street Rhymes Around the World*. Honesdale, PA: Wordsong/Boyds Mills Press.

Poetry

Alba, Juanita. 1995. *Calor*. Waco, TX: WRS Publishing.

Cassedy, Sylvia, and Kunihiro Suetake. 1992. *Red Dragonfly on My Shoulder*. New York: HarperCollins.

Cole, William. 1981. *Poem Stew*. New York: HarperTrophy/J. B. Lippincott.

Demi. 1993. *Demi's Secret Garden*. New York: Henry Holt.

De Paola, Tomie. 1988. *Book of Poems*. New York: G. P. Putnam's Sons.

Esbensen, Barbara J. 1996. *Echoes for the Eye*. New York: HarperCollins.

Florian, Douglas. 1994. *Beast Feast*. New York: Harcourt Brace.

Frost, Robert. 1969. *Stopping by Woods on a Snowy Evening*. New York: Dutton.

Giovanni, Nikki. 1996. *The Sun Is So Quiet*. New York: Henry Holt.

Greenfield, Eloise. 1978. *Honey, I Love*. New York: Reading Rainbow/HarperCollins.

Greenfield, Eloise. 1988. *Nathaniel Talking*. New York: Black Butterfly Children's Books/Writers and Readers.

Greenfield, Eloise. 1991. *Night on Neighborhood Street*. New York: Dial.

Grimes, Nikki. 1994. *Meet Danitra Brown*. New York: Lothrop, Lee and Shepard.

Halpern, Shari. 1994. *Little Robin Redbreast*. New York: North-South.

Hoberman, Mary Ann. 1991. *A Fine Fat Pig*. New York: HarperCollins.

Hoberman, Mary Ann. 1994. *My Song Is Beautiful*. New York: Little, Brown.

Huck, Charlotte. 1993. *Secret Places*. New York: Greenwillow.

Lewis, J. Patrick. 1998. *Doodle Dandies*. New York: Atheneum/Simon & Schuster.

Lewis, J. Patrick. 1998. *The Little Buggers: Insect and Spider Poems*. New York: Dial.

Lewis, J. Patrick. 1999. *The Bookworm's Feast*. New York: Dial/Penguin.

Moore, Lilian. 1992. *Adam Mouse's Book of Poems*. New York: Atheneum/Macmillan.

Prelutsky, Jack. 1984. *It's Snowing! It's Snowing!* New York: Greenwillow.

Rogasky, Barbara. 1994. *Winter Poems*. New York: Scholastic.

Thomas, Joyce C. 1993. *Brown Honey in Broomwheat Tea*. New York: HarperCollins.

Yolen, Jane. 1997. *Once Upon Ice*. New York: Wordsong/Boyd Mills Press.

Predictable Pattern

Butterworth, Nick, and Mick Inkpen. 1993. *Jasper's Beanstalk*. New York: Bradbury.

Campbell, Rod. 1982. *Dear Zoo*. New York: Four Winds.

Carle, Eric. 1984. *The Very Busy Spider*. New York: Philomel.

Carter, David. 1991. *In a Dark, Dark Wood: An Old Tale with a New Twist*. New York: Simon & Schuster.

Carter, David A. 1988. *How Many Bugs in a Box?* New York: Little Simon/Simon & Schuster.

Evans, Katie. 1992. *Hunky Dory Ate It*. New York: Dutton.

Fox, Mem. 1992. *Hattie and the Fox*. New York: Bradbury/Macmillan.

Ginsburg, Mirra. 1972. *The Chick and the Duckling*. New York: Macmillan.

Martin, Bill Jr. 1967. *Brown Bear, Brown Bear, What Do You See?* New York: Henry Holt.

Miller, Margaret. 1990. *Who Uses This?* New York: Greenwillow.

Miller, Margaret. 1991. *Whose Shoe?* New York: Greenwillow.

Tafuri, Nancy. 1984. *Have You Seen My Duckling?* New York: Greenwillow.

Tafuri, Nancy. 1988. *Spots, Feathers and Curly Tails*. New York: Greenwillow.

Ward, Cindy. 1988. *Cookie's Week*. New York: Putnam.

Wildsmith, Brian. 1982. *Cat on a Mat*. Oxford, England: Oxford University Press.

Williams, Sue. 1998. *I Went Walking*. New York: Harcourt Brace.

Williams, Sue. 1998. *Let's Go Visiting*. New York: Gulliver/Harcourt Brace.

Cumulative Tales

Bolam, Emily. 1992. *The House That Jack Built*. New York: Dutton.

Brown, Ruth. 1981. *A Dark Dark Tale*. New York: Dial.

Brown, Ruth. 1985. *The Big Sneeze*. New York: Lothrop, Lee and Shepard.

Carter, David. 1991. *In a Dark, Dark Wood*. New York: Simon & Schuster.

Cole, Henry. 1995. *Jack's Garden*. New York: Greenwillow.

Fox, Mem. 1989. *Shoes from Grandpa*. New York: Orchard.

MacDonald, Amy. 1990. *Rachel Fister's Blister*. Boston, MA: Houghton Mifflin.

Robart, Rose, and Maryann Kovalski. 1986. *The Cake That Mack Ate*. Boston, MA: Joy Street Books/Little, Brown.

Wood, Audrey. 1984. *The Napping House*. Orlando, FL: Harcourt Brace Jovanovich.

Folk Tales

Cinderella

Climo, Shirley. 1989. *The Egyptian Cinderella*. New York: HarperCollins.

Huck, Charlotte. 1989. *Princess Furball*. New York: Mulberry/Greenwillow.

Louie, Ai-Ling. 1982. *Yeh-Shen*. New York: Philomel.

Martin, Rafe. 1992. *The Rough-Face Girl*. New York: G. P. Putnam's Sons.

Onyefulu, Obi. 1994. *Chinye: A West African Folk Tale*. New York: Penguin.

San Souci, Robert. 1989. *The Talking Eggs*. New York: Dial/Penguin.

San Souci, Robert. 1994. *Sootface*. New York: Bantam Doubleday Dell.

Gingerbread Boy

Aylesworth, Jim. 1998. *The Gingerbread Man*. New York: Scholastic.

Galdone, Paul. 1975. *The Gingerbread Boy*. New York: Clarion/Houghton Mifflin.

Little Red Hen

Barton, Byron. 1993. *The Little Red Hen*. New York: HarperCollins.

Galdone, Paul. 1973. *The Little Red Hen*. New York: Clarion/Houghton Mifflin.

Zemach, Margot. 1983. *The Little Red Hen*. New York: Farrar Straus Giroux.

Some Other Books to Read with the Little Red Hen

Hutchins, Pat. 1968. *Rosie's Walk*. New York: Macmillan.

Kasza, Keiko. 1987. *The Wolf's Chicken Stew*. New York: G. P. Putnam's Sons.

Percy, Graham. 1992. *The Cock, the Mouse, and the Little Red Hen*. Cambridge, MA: Candlewick.

Wallace, Karen. 1993. *My Hen Is Dancing*. Cambridge, MA: Candlewick.

Wallace, Karen. 1994. *Red Fox*. Cambridge, MA: Candlewick.

Little Red Riding Hood

Coady, Christopher. 1991. *Red Riding Hood*. New York: Dutton.

Ernst, Lisa Campbell. 1995. *Little Red Riding Hood*. New York: Simon & Schuster.

Hyman, Trina Schart. 1983. *Little Red Riding Hood*. New York: Holiday House.

Young, Ed. 1989. *Lon Po Po*. New York: Scholastic.

The Three Bears

Barton, Byron. 1991. *The Three Bears*. New York: HarperCollins.

Brett, Jan. 1987. *Goldilocks and the Three Bears*. New York: Dodd, Mead.

Cauley, Lorinda B. 1981. *Goldilocks and the Three Bears*. New York: G. P. Putnam's Sons.

De Luise, Dom. 1992. *Goldilocks*. New York: Simon & Schuster.

Galdone, Paul. 1972. *The Three Bears*. New York: Clarion/Houghton Mifflin.

Marshall, James. 1988. *Goldilocks and the Three Bears*. New York: Dial/Penguin.

Roberts, Tom. 1990. *Goldilocks*. Westport, CT: Rabbit Ear.

Stevens, Janet. 1986. *Goldilocks and the Three Bears*. New York: Holiday House.

Watts, Bernadette. 1984. *Goldilocks and the Three Bears*. New York: Henry Holt.

Some Other Books to Read with the Three Bears

Alborough, Jez. 1994. *It's the Bear!* Cambridge, MA: Candlewick.

Bowen, Betsy. 1991. *Antler, Bear, Canoe.* Boston, MA: Little, Brown.

Fleming, Denise. 1997. *Time To Sleep.* New York: Henry Holt.

Glen, Maggie. 1990. *Ruby.* New York: G. P. Putnam's Sons.

Rosen, Michael. 1989. *We're Going on a Bear Hunt.* Macmillan.

Schindler, Regine. 1990. *The Bear's Cave.* New York: Dutton.

Schoenherr, John. 1991. *Bear.* New York: Philomel/Putnam and Grosset.

Stevens, Janet. 1995. *Tops and Bottoms.* New York: Harcourt Brace.

Tollhurst, Marilyn. 1990. *Somebody and the Three Blairs.* New York: Orchard.

Witmark, M., and Sons. 1951. *The Teddy Bears' Picnic.* New York: Aladdin/Macmillan.

The Three Billy Goats Gruff

Galdone, Paul. 1973. *The Three Billy Goats Gruff.* New York: Clarion/Houghton Mifflin.

Kimmel, Eric. 1990. *Nanny Goat and the Seven Little Kids.* New York: Holiday House.

Rounds, Glen. 1993. *Three Billy Goats Gruff.* New York: Holiday House.

Stevens, Janet. 1987. *The Three Billy Goats Gruff.* New York: Harcourt Brace Jovanovich.

The Three Little Pigs

Bishop, Gavin. 1989. *The Three Little Pigs.* New York: Scholastic.

Galdone, Paul. 1970. *The Three Little Pigs.* New York: Clarion.

Hooks, William H. 1989. *The Three Little Pigs and the Fox.* New York: Macmillan.

Kellogg, Steven. 1997. *The Three Little Pigs.* New York: Morrow.

Marshall, James. 1989. *The Three Little Pigs.* New York: Dial/Penguin.

Ross, Tony. 1983. *The Three Pigs.* New York: Pantheon/Random House.

Rounds, Glen. 1992. *Three Little Pigs and the Big Bad Wolf.* New York: Holiday House.

Trivizas, Eugene. 1993. *The Three Little Wolves and the Big Bad Pig.* New York: Macmillan.

Some Other Books to Read with the Three Little Pigs

Geisert, Arthur. 1993. *Oink Oink.* Boston, MA: Houghton Mifflin.

Ling, Mary. 1993. *Pig, See How They Grow.* New York: Dorling Kindersley.

Lowell, Susan. 1992. *The Three Little Javelinas.* Flagstaff, AZ: Northland.

Scieszka, Jon. 1989. *The True Story of the 3 Little Pigs!* New York: Penguin.

Waddell, Martin. 1992. *The Pig in the Pond.* Cambridge, MA: Candlewick.

Town Mouse and Country Mouse

Brett, Jan. 1994. *Town Mouse Country Mouse.* New York: G. P. Putnam's Sons.

Cauley, Lorinda Bryan. 1984. *The Town Mouse and the Country Mouse.* New York: G. P. Putnam's Sons.

Craig, Helen. 1992. *The Town Mouse and the Country Mouse.* Cambridge, MA: Candlewick.

Stevens, Janet. 1987. *The Town Mouse and the Country Mouse.* New York: Holiday House.

Modern Folktale Style

Campbell, Ann. 1993. *Once Upon a Princess and a Pea.* New York: Stewart, Tabori and Chang.

Cole, Babette. 1987. *Prince Cinders.* New York: G. P. Putnam's Sons.

Emberley, Michael. 1990. *Ruby.* Boston, MA: Little, Brown.

Forest, Heather. 1998. *Stone Soup.* Little Rock, AR: August House/Little Folks.

Hunter, C. W. 1992. *The Green Gourd.* New York: Whitebird/G. P. Putnam Sons.

Kimmel, Eric. 1990. *Nanny Goat and the Seven Little Kids.* New York: Holiday House.

Lewis, J. Patrick. 1994. *The Frog Princess.* New York: Dial/Penguin.

Lowell, Susan. 1992. *The Three Little Javelinas.* Flagstaff, AZ: Northland.

Minters, Frances. 1994. *Cinder-Elly.* New York: Viking/Penguin.

Morgan, Pierr. 1990. *The Turnip.* New York: Philomel, Putnam and Grosset.

Parkinson, Kathy. 1986. *The Enormous Turnip.* Niles, IL: Albert Whitman.

Patron, Susan. 1991. *Burgoo Stew.* New York: Orchard.

Peck, Jan. 1998. *The Giant Carrot.* New York: Dial/Penguin Putnam.

Percy, Graham. 1992. *The Cock, the Mouse, and the Little Red Hen.* Cambridge, MA: Candlewick.

Rounds, Glen. 1992. *Three Little Pigs and the Big Bad Wolf.* New York: Holiday House.

Scieszka, Jon. 1989. *The True Story of the 3 Little Pigs!* New York: Penguin.

Scieszka, Jon. 1991. *The Frog Prince Continued.* New York: Viking/Penguin.

Tollhurst, Marilyn. 1990. *Somebody and the Three Blairs.* New York: Orchard.

Trivizas, Eugene. 1993. *The Three Little Wolves and the Big Bad Pig.* New York: Macmillan.

Vozar, David. 1993. *Yo, Hungry Wolf!* New York: Bantam Doubleday Dell.

Other Tales Too Good to Miss

Brett, Jan. 1989. *The Mitten.* New York: G. P. Putnam's Sons.

Brett, Jan. 1997. *The Hat.* New York: G. P. Putnam's Sons.

Brown, Marcia. 1975. *Stone Soup.* New York: Aladdin/Macmillan.

Demi. 1990. *The Empty Pot.* New York: Henry Holt.

Demi. 1997. *One Grain of Rice.* New York: Scholastic.

Diakite, Baba Wague. 1999. *The Hatseller and the Monkeys.* New York: Scholastic.

Galdone, Paul. 1968. *Henny Penny.* New York: Clarion/Houghton Mifflin.

Ginsburg, Mirra. 1997. *Clay Boy.* New York: Greenwillow.

Hobson, Sally. 1994. *Chicken Little.* New York: Simon & Schuster.

Huck, Charlotte. 1996. *Toads and Diamonds.* New York: Greenwillow.

Kellogg, Steven. 1985. *Chicken Little.* New York: Mulberry/William Morrow.

Kimmel, Eric A. 1988. *Anansi and the Moss-Covered Rock.* New York: Holiday House.

Ormerod, Jan. 1985. *The Story of Chicken Licken.* New York: Lothrop, Lee and Shepard.

Stevens, Janet. 1995. *Tops and Bottoms.* New York: Harcourt Brace.

Tresselt, Alvin. 1964. *The Mitten.* New York: Lothrop, Lee and Shepard/Mulberry.

Young, Ed. 1992. *Seven Blind Mice.* New York: Philomel/Putnam and Grosset.

Theme Collections

Alaska: Learning About Alaska

Carlstrom, Nancy White. 1992. *Northern Lullaby.* New York: Philomel.

Carlstrom, Nancy White. 1997. *Raven and River.* Boston, MA: Little, Brown.

Cobb, Vicki. 1989. *This Place Is Cold.* New York: Walker.

Dixon, Ann. 1994. *The Sleeping Lady.* Seattle, WA: Alaska Northwest Books.

Ekoomiak, Normee. 1988. *Arctic Memories.* New York: Henry Holt.

George, Jean C. 1997. *Arctic Son.* New York: Hyperion.

Hoyt-Goldsmith, Diane. 1991. *Arctic Hunter.* New York: Holiday House.

Joose, Barbara M. 1991. *Mama, Do You Love Me?* San Francisco, CA: Chronicle.

Kalman, Bobbie D., and William Belsey. 1988. *An Arctic Community.* New York: Crabtree.

Kalman, Bobbie D., and Ken Faris. 1988. *Arctic Whales and Whaling.* New York: Crabtree.

Kendall, Russ. 1992. *Eskimo Boy.* New York: Scholastic.

Kreeger, Charlene. 1978. *Alaska ABC Book.* Homer, Alaska: Paws IV Publishing.

Lester, Helen. 1994. *Three Cheers for Tacky.* Boston, MA: Houghton Mifflin.

McMillan, Bruce. 1998. *Salmon Summer.* Boston, MA: Houghton Mifflin.

Miller, Debbie. 1997. *Disappearing Lake.* New York: Walker.

Miller, Debbie. 1994. *A Caribou Journey.* New York: Little, Brown.

Murphy, Claire R. 1994. *A Child's Alaska.* Seattle, WA: Alaska Northwest Books.

Pandell, Karen. 1993. *Land of Dark, Land of Light.* New York: Dutton.

Reynolds, Jan. 1992. *Far North.* New York: Harcourt Brace Jovanovich.

Scott, Ann H. 1972. *On Mother's Lap.* New York: Clarion.

Sis, Peter. 1993. *A Small Tall Tale from the Far Far North.* New York: Alfred A. Knopf.

Butterflies

Carle, Eric. 1969. *The Very Hungry Caterpillar.* New York: Philomel.

Faulkner, Keith. 1993. *Butterfly. My First Wildlife Book.* Basingstoke, Hampshire, England: HarperFestival/HarperCollins.

Florian, Douglas. 1986. *Discovering Butterflies.* New York: Aladdin/Macmillan.

French, Vivian. 1993. *Caterpillar Caterpillar.* Cambridge, MA: Candlewick.

Gibbons, Gail. 1989. *Monarch Butterfly.* New York: Holiday House.

Goor, Ron, and Nancy Goor. 1990. *Insect Metamorphosis.* New York: Atheneum/Macmillan.

Haas, Irene. 1997. *A Summertime Song.* New York: Simon & Schuster.

Herberman, Ethan. 1990. *The Great Butterfly Hunt.* New York: Simon & Schuster.

Ling, Mary. 1992. *Butterfly. See How They Grow.* New York: Dorling Kindersley.

Watts, Barrie. 1985. *Butterfly and Caterpillar.* Morristown, NJ: Silver Burdett Company.

Change

Ehlert, Lois. 1995. *Snowballs*. San Diego, CA and New York: Harcourt Brace.

Ford, Miela, and Sally Noll. 1995. *Sunflower*. New York: Greenwillow.

Gibbons, Gail. 1991. *From Seed to Plant*. New York: Holiday House.

Hall, Zoe. 1994. *It's Pumpkin Time!* New York: Scholastic.

Hall, Zoe. 1996. *The Apple Pie Tree*. New York: The Blue Sky Press/Scholastic.

King, Elizabeth. 1990. *The Pumpkin Patch*. New York: Dutton.

Lucht, Irmgard. 1994. *The Red Poppy*. New York: Hyperion.

Maass, Robert. 1990. *When Autumn Comes*. New York: Henry Holt.

Miller, Margaret. 1996. *Now I'm Big*. New York: Greenwillow.

Peterson, Cris. 1996. *Harvest Year*. Honesdale, PA: Boyds Mills Press.

Pfeffer, Wendy. 1997. *A Log's Life*. New York: Simon & Schuster.

Robbins, Ken. 1990. *A Flower Grows*. New York: Dial.

Rockwell, Anne. 1998. *One Bean*. New York: Walker.

Samton, Sheila W. 1991. *Moon to Sun: An Adding Book*. Honesville, PA: Carolyn House/Boyds Mills Press.

Slawson, Michele B. 1994. *Apple Picking Time*. New York: Crown.

Titherington, Jeanne. 1986. *Pumpkin Pumpkin*. New York: Greenwillow.

Seasons

Winter

Brett, Jan. 1989. *The Mitten*. New York: G. P. Putnam's Sons.

Brett, Jan. 1997. *The Hat*. New York: G. P. Putnam's Sons.

Briggs, Raymond. 1978. *The Snowman*. New York: Random House.

Carlstrom, Nancy W. 1991. *Goodbye Geese*. New York: Philomel.

Carlstrom, Nancy W. 1992. *Northern Lullaby*. New York: Philomel.

Chapman, Cheryl. 1994. *Snow on Snow on Snow*. New York: Dial.

Cuyler, Margery. 1998. *The Biggest, Best Snowman*. New York: Scholastic.

Ehlert, Lois. 1995. *Snowballs*. San Diego, CA and New York: Harcourt Brace.

Frost, Robert. 1969. *Stopping by Woods on a Snowy Evening*. New York: Dutton.

George, Jean C. 1993. *Dear Rebecca, Winter Is Here*. New York: HarperCollins.

Jeunesse, Gallimard, and Rene Mettler. 1995. *Penguins*. New York: Scholastic.

Johnson, Angela. 1990. *Do Like Kyla*. New York: Orchard.

Maass, Robert. 1993. *When Winter Comes*. New York: Henry Holt.

Martin, Jacqueline B. 1998. *Snowflake Bentley*. Boston, MA: Houghton Mifflin.

McCully, Emily A. 1985. *First Snow*. New York: Harper and Row.

Nielsen, Laura L. 1995. *Jeremy's Muffler*. New York: Atheneum/Simon & Schuster.

Rogasky, Barbara. 1994. *Winter Poems*. New York: Scholastic.

San Souci, Daniel. 1990. *North Country Night*. New York: Doubleday.

Shulevitz, Uri. 1998. *Snow*. New York: Farrar Straus Giroux.

Tresselt, Alvin. 1964. *The Mitten*. New York: Lothrop, Lee and Shepard/Mulberry Books.

Tresselt, Alvin. 1988. *White Snow Bright Snow*. New York: Lothrop, Lee and Shepard.

Yolen, Jane. 1987. *Owl Moon*. New York: Philomel.

Spring

Carlstrom, Nancy W. 1997. *Raven and River*. Boston, MA: Little, Brown.

De Coteau Orie, Sandra. 1995. *Did You Hear the Wind Sing Your Name? An Oneida Song of Spring*. New York: Walker.

Autumn

Ehlert, Lois. 1991. *Red Leaf, Yellow Leaf*. New York: Scholastic.

Fleming, Denise. 1997. *Time to Sleep*. New York: Henry Holt.

Maass, Robert. 1990. *When Autumn Comes*. New York: Henry Holt.

Robbins, Ken. 1998. *Autumn Leaves*. New York: Scholastic.

Schnur, Steven. 1997. *Autumn: An Alphabet Acrostic*. New York: Clarion/Houghton Mifflin.

Zolotow, Charlotte. 1980. *Say It!* New York: Greenwillow.

All Seasons

Allen, Marjorie, and Shelley Rotner. 1991. *Changes*. New York: Macmillan.

Esbensen, Barbara J. 1996. *Echoes for the Eye*. New York: HarperCollins.

Changes: Rural to Urban

Baker, Jeannie. 1991. *Window*. New York: Greenwillow.

Bolam, Emily. 1992. *The House That Jack Built*. New York: Dutton.

Brett, Jan. 1994. *Town Mouse Country Mouse*. New York: G. P. Putnam's Sons.

Bunting, Eve. 1996. *Secret Place*. New York: Clarion/Houghton Mifflin.

Burmingham, John. 1989. *Hey! Get off Our Train*. New York: Crown.

Cauley, Lorinda Bryan. 1984. *The Town Mouse and the Country Mouse*. New York: G. P. Putnam's Sons.

Craig, Helen. 1992. *The Town Mouse and the Country Mouse*. Cambridge, MA: Candlewick.

Fleming, Denise. 1996. *Where Once There Was a Wood*. New York: Henry Holt.

George, Lindsay B. 1995. *In the Woods: Who's Been Here?* New York: Greenwillow.

Gibbons, Gail. 1990. *How a House Is Built*. New York: Holiday House.

Grifalconi, Ann. 1986. *The Village of Round and Square Houses*. Boston, MA: Little, Brown.

Johnson, Steven P. 1995. *Alphabet City*. New York: Viking/Penguin.

Lyon, George E. 1992. *Who Came Down That Road?* New York: Orchard.

Morris, Ann. 1992. *Houses and Homes*. New York: Lothrop, Lee and Shaperd.

Robbins, Ken. 1984. *Building a House*. New York: Four Winds/Macmillan.

Grow, Grow, Grow! Eat, Eat, Eat!

Appelbaum, Diana. 1997. *Cocoa Ice*. New York: Orchard.

Aylesworth, Jim. 1998. *The Gingerbread Man*. New York: Scholastic.

Barton, Byron. 1993. *The Little Red Hen*. New York: HarperCollins.

Brown, Marcia. 1975. *Stone Soup*. New York: Aladdin/Macmillan.

Bunting, Eve. 1994. *Flower Garden*. New York: Harcourt Brace.

Bunting, Eve. 1996. *Market Day*. New York: Joanna Cotler Books/HarperCollins.

Bunting, Eve. 1996. *Sunflower House*. New York: Harcourt Brace.

Butterworth, Nick, and Mick Inkpen. 1993. *Jasper's Beanstalk*. New York: Bradbury.

Carle, Eric. 1969. *The Very Hungry Caterpillar*. New York: Philomel.

Carle, Eric. 1987. *The Tiny Seed*. New York: Scholastic.

Carle, Eric. 1990. *Pancakes, Pancakes!* New York: Simon & Schuster.

Charles, N. N., L. Dillon, and D. Dillon. 1994. *What Am I?* New York: The Blue Sky Press/Scholastic.

Cole, Henry. 1995. *Jack's Garden*. New York: Greenwillow.

Cooney, Barbara. 1982. *Miss Rumphius*. New York: Viking.

Delafosse, Claude, and Rene Mettler. 1991. *Flowers*. New York: Scholastic.

Delafosse, Claude, and Perols. 1994. *Atlas of Plants*. New York: Scholastic.

Demi. 1990. *The Empty Pot*. New York: Henry Holt.

Demi. 1997. *One Grain of Rice*. New York: Scholastic.

DK Direct Limited. 1992. *What's Inside? Plants*. New York: Dorling Kindersley.

Ehlert, Lois. 1987. *Growing Vegetable Soup*. New York: Harcourt Brace Jovanovich.

Ehlert, Lois. 1988. *Planting a Rainbow*. New York: Harcourt Brace Jovanovich.

Ehlert, Lois. 1989. *Eating the Alphabet: Fruits and Vegetables from A to Z*. New York: Harcourt Brace Jovanovich.

Ehlert, Lois. 1991. *Red Leaf, Yellow Leaf*. New York: Scholastic.

Ehlert, Lois. 1997. *Hands*. Orlando, FL: Harcourt Brace.

Esbensen, Barbara J. 1996. *Echoes for the Eye*. New York: HarperCollins.

Falwell, Cathryn. 1993. *Feast for 10*. New York: Clarion/Houghton Mifflin.

Florian, Douglas. 1991. *Vegetable Garden*. New York: Voyager/Harcourt Brace.

Ford, Miela, and Sally Noll. 1995. *Sunflower*. New York: Greenwillow.

Galdone, Paul. 1973. *The Little Red Hen*. New York: Clarion/Houghton Mifflin.

Galdone, Paul. 1976. *The Magic Porridge Pot*. New York: Clarion/Houghton Mifflin.

Gibbons, Gail. 1991. *From Seed to Plant*. New York: Holiday House.

Gibbons, Gail. 1997. *The Honey Makers*. New York: Morrow.

Hall, Zoe. 1994. *It's Pumpkin Time!* New York: Scholastic.

Hall, Zoe. 1996. *The Apple Pie Tree*. New York: The Blue Sky Press/Scholastic.

Hausherr, Rosmarie. 1994. *What Food Is This?* New York: Scholastic.

Hunter, C. W. 1992. *The Green Gourd*. New York: G. P. Putnam's Sons.

Hutchins, Pat. 1983. *You'll Soon Grow into Them, Titch*. New York: Greenwillow.

Kellogg, Steven. 1988. *Johnny Appleseed*. New York: William Morrow.

King, Elizabeth. 1990. *The Pumpkin Patch*. New York: Dutton.

King, Elizabeth. 1993. *Backyard Sunflower*. New York: Dutton.

Lember, Barbara H. 1994. *A Book of Fruit*. New York: Ticknor and Fields/Houghton Mifflin.

Lerner, Harriet, and Susan Goldhor. 1996. *What's So Terrible About Swallowing an Apple Seed?* New York: HarperCollins.

Lucht, Irmgard. 1994. *The Red Poppy*. New York: Hyperion.

Maass, Robert. 1998. *Garden*. New York: Henry Holt.

Marshall, James. 1991. *Old Mother Hubbard and Her Wonderful Dog*. New York: Farrar Straus Giroux.

McMillan, Bruce. 1986. *Counting Wildflowers*. New York: Lothrop, Lee and Shepard.

Micucci, Charles. 1992. *The Life and Times of the Apple*. New York: Orchard.

Micucci, Charles. 1995. *The Life and Times of the Honeybee*. New York: Ticknor and Fields.

Miranda, Anne. 1997. *To Market, to Market*. New York: Harcourt Brace.

Moore, Lilian. 1992. *Adam Mouse's Book of Poems*. New York: Atheneum/Macmillan.

Morgan, Pierr. 1990. *The Turnip*. New York: Philomel/Putnam and Grosset.

Parkinson, Kathy. 1986. *The Enormous Turnip*. Niles, IL: Albert Whitman.

Patron, Susan. 1991. *Burgoo Stew*. New York: Orchard.

Peck, Jan. 1998. *The Giant Carrot*. New York: Dial.

Peterson, Cris. 1996. *Harvest Year*. Honesville, PA: Boyds Mills Press.

Pomeroy, Diana. 1996. *One Potato*. New York: Harcourt Brace.

Pomeroy, Diana. 1997. *Wildflower ABC*. New York: Harcourt Brace.

Powell, Richard. 1993. *I Spy in the Garden*. New York: Puffin/Penguin.

Robart, Rose, and Maryann Kovalski. 1986. *The Cake That Mack Ate*. Boston, MA: Joy Street Books/Little, Brown.

Robbins, Ken. 1990. *A Flower Grows*. New York: Dial.

Rockwell, Anne. 1998. *One Bean*. New York: Walker.

Roddie, Shen. 1991. *Animal Stew*. Boston, MA: Houghton Mifflin.

Rotner, Shelley, and Julia Pemberton Hellums. 1996. *Hold the Anchovies!* New York: Orchard.

Schories, Pat. 1996. *Over Under in the Garden*. New York: Farrar Straus Giroux.

Slawson, Michele B. 1994. *Apple Picking Time*. New York: Crown.

Stern, Maggie. 1997. *The Missing Sunflowers*. New York: Greenwillow.

Stevens, Janet. 1995. *Tops and Bottoms*. New York: Harcourt Brace.

Vagin, Vladimir. 1998. *The Enormous Carrot*. New York: Scholastic.

Wagner, Karen. 1990. *Chocolate Chip Cookies*. New York: Henry Holt.

Walter, Virginia. 1995. *"Hi, Pizza Man!"* New York: Orchard.

Watts, Barrie. 1987. *Dandelion*. Englewood Cliffs, NJ: Stopwatch Books/Silver Burdett Press.

Westcott, Nadine B. 1987. *Peanut Butter and Jelly*. New York: E. P. Dutton.

Zemach, Margot. 1983. *The Little Red Hen*. New York: Farrar Straus Giroux.

Habitats

Bowen, Betsy. 1991. *Antler, Bear, Canoe*. Boston, MA: Little, Brown.

Bunting, Eve. 1996. *Secret Place*. New York: Clarion/Houghton Mifflin.

Burmingham, John. 1989. *Hey! Get Off Our Train*. New York: Crown.

Cherry, Lynne. 1990. *The Great Kapok Tree*. New York: Harcourt Brace Jovanovich.

Dorros, Arthur. 1997. *A Tree Is Growing*. New York: Scholastic.

Gibbons, Gail. 1994. *Nature's Green Umbrella*. New York: Morrow.

Guiberson, Brenda. 1991. *Cactus Hotel*. New York: Henry Holt.

Hirschi, Ron. 1987. *Who Lives in... the Forest?* New York: Dodd, Mead.

Hirschi, Ron. 1992. *Discover My World: Desert*. New York: Bantam.

Miller, Debbie. 1994. *A Caribou Journey*. New York: Little, Brown.

Miller, Debbie. 1997. *Disappearing Lake*. New York: Walker.

Pfeffer, Wendy. 1997. *A Log's Life*. New York: Simon & Schuster.

Pringle, Laurence. 1995. *Fire in the Forest*. New York: Atheneum/Simon & Schuster.

Reed-Jones, Carol. 1995. *The Tree in the Ancient Forest*. Nevada City, CA: Dawn Publications.

Rosen, Michael. 1994. *All Eyes on the Pond*. New York: Hyperion.

Royston, Angela. 1991. *Jungle Animals*. New York: Simon & Schuster.

Vieira, Linda. 1994. *The Ever-Living Tree*. New York: Walker.

Relationships and Family

Alba, Juanita. 1995. *Calor*. Waco, TX: WRS Publishing.

Beil, Karen M. 1992. *Grandma According to Me*. New York: Bantam Doubleday Dell.

Best, Cari. 1995. *Red Light, Green Light, Mama and Me*. New York: Orchard.

Blume, Judy. 1974. *The Pain and the Great One*. New York: Bradbury.

Bunting, Eve. 1994. *Flower Garden*. New York: Harcourt Brace.

Bunting, Eve. 1996. *Going Home*. New York: Joanna Cotler Books/HarperCollins.

Burningham, John. 1984. *Granpa*. London, England: Jonathan Cape Ltd.

Caines, Jeannette. 1982. *Just Us Women*. New York: HarperCollins.

Cannon, Janell. 1993. *Stellaluna*. New York: Harcourt Brace.

Castaneda, Omar S. 1993. *Abuela's Weave*. New York: Lee and Low.

Chocolate, Debbi. 1995. *On the Day I Was Born*. New York: Cartwheel/Scholastic.

Collard III, Sneed B. 1997. *Animal Dads*. Boston, MA: Houghton Mifflin.

Cooney, Barbara. 1994. *Only Opal, the Diary of a Young Girl*. New York: Philomel/Putnam and Grosset.

Cooper, Melrose. 1995. *I Got Community*. New York: Henry Holt.

Cousins, Lucy. 1995. *Za-ZA's Baby Brother*. Cambridge, MA: Candlewick.

Cowen-Fletcher, Jane. 1993. *Mama Zooms*. New York: Scholastic.

Cowen-Fletcher, Jane. 1994. *It Takes a Village*. New York: Scholastic.

Curtis, Munzee. 1997. *When the Big Dog Barks*. New York: Greenwillow.

Cutler, Jane. 1993. *Darcy and Gran Don't Like Babies*. New York: Scholastic.

Danis, Naomi. 1995. *Walk with Me*. New York: Cartwheel/Scholastic.

Duncan, Alice F. 1995. *Willie Jerome*. New York: Simon & Schuster/Macmillan.

Falwell, Cathryn. 1993. *We Have a Baby*. New York: Clarion.

Fox, Mem. 1984. *Wilfrid Gordon McDonald Partridge*. Brooklyn, NY: Kane/Miller.

Fox, Mem. 1988. *Koala Lou*. New York: Gulliver/Harcourt Brace Jovanovich.

Fox, Mem. 1989. *Shoes from Grandpa*. New York: Orchard.

Franklin, Jonathan. 1991. *Don't Wake the Baby*. New York: Farrar Straus Giroux.

Frasier, Debra. 1991. *On the Day You Were Born*. New York: Harcourt Brace.

Greenfield, Eloise. 1978. *Honey, I Love*. New York: Reading Rainbow/HarperCollins.

Greenfield, Eloise. 1988. *Grandpa's Face*. New York: Philomel.

Greenfield, Eloise. 1988. *Nathaniel Talking*. New York: Black Butterfly Children's Books/Writers and Readers.

Hamanaka, Sheila. 1994. *All the Colors of the Earth*. New York: William Morrow.

Henkes, Kevin. 1986. *A Weekend with Wendell*. New York: Greenwillow.

Henkes, Kevin. 1990. *Julius, the Baby of the World*. New York: Greenwillow.

Henkes, Kevin. 1991. *Chrysanthemum*. New York: Greenwillow.

Henkes, Kevin. 1993. *Owen*. New York: Greenwillow.

Hoffman, Mary. 1991. *Amazing Grace*. New York: Dial/Penguin.

Hopkins, Lee Bennett. 1992. *Through Our Eyes: Poems and Pictures About Growing Up*. Boston, MA: Little, Brown.

Hutchins, Pat. 1983. *You'll Soon Grow into Them, Titch*. New York: Greenwillow.

Hutchins, Pat. 1991. *Tidy Titch*. New York: Greenwillow.

Hutchins, Pat. 1993. *My Best Friend*. New York: Greenwillow.

Johnson, Angela. 1990. *Do Like Kyla*. New York: Orchard.

Johnson, Angela. 1995. *Shoes Like Miss Alice's*. New York: Orchard.

Johnson, Angela. 1997. *Daddy Calls Me Man*. New York: Orchard.

Kasza, Keiko. 1992. *A Mother for Choco*. New York: G. P. Putnam's Sons.

MacLachlan, Patricia. 1982. *Mama One, Mama Two*. New York: Harper and Row.

Maestro, Betsy. 1989. *Snow Day*. New York: Scholastic.

McKissack, Patricia C. 1988. *Mirandy and Brother Wind*. New York: Alfred A. Knopf.

McKissack, Patricia C. 1997. *Ma Dear's Apron*. New York: Atheneum/Simon & Schuster.

McLerran, Alice. 1992. *I Want to Go Home*. New York: Tambourine.

Mitchell, Margaree K. 1993. *Uncle Jed's Barbershop*. New York: Simon & Schuster.

Mollel, Tololwa. 1995. *Big Boy*. New York: Clarion/Houghton Mifflin.

Moore, Elaine. 1995. *Grandma's Smile*. New York: Lothrop, Lee and Shepard.

Moore, Julia. 1996. *While You Sleep*. New York: Dutton Books/Penguin.

Morris, Ann. 1990. *Loving*. New York: Lothrop, Lee and Shepard.

Noll, Sally. 1991. *That Bothered Kate*. New York: Greenwillow.

Parkinson, Kathy. 1988. *The Farmer in the Dell*. Niles, IL: Albert Whitman.

Patrick, Denise L. 1993. *Red Dancing Shoes*. New York: Tambourine/William Morrow.

Pellegrini, Nina. 1991. *Families Are Different*. New York: Scholastic.

Polacco, Patricia. 1990. *Thunder Cake*. New York: Philomel/Putnam and Grosset.

Polacco, Patricia. 1992. *Chicken Sunday*. New York: Philomel.

Rochelle, Belinda. 1994. *When Jo Louis Won the Title*. Boston, MA: Houghton Mifflin.

Rotner, Shelley. 1996. *Lots of Moms*. New York: Dial/Penguin.

Rotner, Shelley, and Sheila M. Kelly. 1997. *Lots of Dads*. New York: Dial/Penguin.

Smalls, Irene. 1991. *Irene and the Big, Fine Nickel*. New York: Little, Brown.

Soto, Gary. 1993. *Too Many Tamales*. New York: G. P. Putnam's Sons.

Soto, Gary. 1997. *Snapshots from the Wedding*. New York: G. P. Putnam's Sons.

Tafuri, Nancy. 1984. *Have You Seen My Duckling?* New York: Greenwillow.

Thomas, Joyce C. 1993. *Brown Honey in Broomwheat Tea*. New York: HarperCollins.

Titherington, Jeanne. 1988. *Where Are You Going, Emma?* New York: Greenwillow.

Van Laan, Nancy. 1996. *La Boda. A Mexican Wedding Celebration*. New York: Little, Brown.

Waddell, Martin. 1992. *Owl Babies*. Cambridge, MA: Candlewick.

Watts, Jeri Hanel. 1997. *Keepers*. New York: Lee and Low.

Williams, Sherley A. 1992. *Working Cotton*. New York: Harcourt Brace Jovanovich.

Williams, Vera B. 1982. *A Chair for My Mother*. New York: Greenwillow.

Williams, Vera B. 1990. *"More More More" Said the Baby*. New York: Scholastic.

Wyeh, Sharon D. 1995. *Always My Dad*. New York: Alfred A. Knopf.

Zolotow, Charlotte. 1980. *Say It!* New York: Greenwillow.

Spiders, Bugs, and Other Things That Creep and Crawl

Brenner, Barbara. 1997. *Thinking About Ants*. Greenvale, NY: Mondo.

Carle, Eric. 1984. *The Very Busy Spider*. New York: Philomel.

Carle, Eric. 1990. *The Very Quiet Cricket*. New York: Philomel.

Carter, David A. 1988. *How Many Bugs in a Box?* New York: Little Simon/Simon & Schuster.

Chinery, Michael. 1991. *Life Story: Spider*. Mahwah, NJ: Troll.

Demi. 1993. *Demi's Secret Garden*. New York: Henry Holt.

Demuth, Patricia B. 1994. *Those Amazing Ants*. New York: Macmillan.

Facklam, Margery. 1994. *The Big Bug Book*. New York: Little, Brown.

Fleming, Denise. 1991. *In the Tall, Tall Grass*. New York: Henry Holt.

Gibbons, Gail. 1993. *Spiders*. New York: Holiday House.

Glaser, Linda. 1992. *Wonderful Worms*. Brookfield, CT: Millbrook.

Godkin, Celia. 1995. *What About Ladybugs?* San Francisco, CA: Sierra Club.

Hepworth, Cathi. 1992. *Antics!* New York: G. P. Putnam's Sons.

Joyce, William. 1996. *The Leaf Men and the Brave Good Bugs*. New York: HarperCollins.

Karas, Brian G. 1964. *I Know an Old Lady*. New York: Scholastic.

Kelley, True. 1993. *Spider on the Floor*. New York: Crown/Random House.

Kirk, David. 1994. *Miss Spider's Tea Party*. New York: Scholastic.

Lewis, J. Patrick. 1998. *The Little Buggers: Insect and Spider Poems*. New York: Dial.

Maxner, Joyce. 1989. *Nicholas Cricket*. New York: Harper and Row.

Mound, Laurence. 1993. *Amazing Insects*. New York: Alfred A. Knopf.

Parker, Nancy W., and Joan R. Wright. 1987. *Bugs*. New York: Greenwillow.

Royston, Angela. 1992. *Insects and Crawly Creatures*. New York: Aladdin/Macmillan.

Royston, Angela. 1992. *What's Inside? Insects*. New York: Dorling Kindersley.

Schnieper, Claudia. 1989. *Amazing Spiders*. Minneapolis, MN: Carolrhoda.

Selsam, M. E., and R. Goor. 1981. *Backyard Insects*. New York: Scholastic.

Sloat, Teri. 1998. *There Was an Old Lady Who Swallowed a Trout!* New York: Henry Holt.

Smith, Trevor. 1990. *Amazing Lizards*. New York: Alfred A. Knopf.

Taback, Simms. 1997. *There Was an Old Lady Who Swallowed a Fly*. New York: Penguin.

Trapani, Iza. 1993. *The Itsy Bitsy Spider*. Boston, MA: Whispering Coyote.

Van Allsburg, Chris. 1988. *Two Bad Ants*. New York: Houghton Mifflin.

Van Laan, Nancy. 1987. *The Big Fat Worm*. New York: Alfred A. Knopf.

Trips and Journeys

Appelbaum, Diana. 1997. *Cocoa Ice*. New York: Orchard.

Aylesworth, Jim. 1998. *The Gingerbread Man*. New York: Scholastic.

Bunting, Eve. 1996. *Going Home*. New York: Joanna Cotler/HarperCollins.

Caines, Jeannette. 1982. *Just Us Women*. New York: HarperCollins.

Carlstrom, Nancy W. 1991. *Goodbye Geese*. New York: Philomel.

Carlstrom, Nancy W. 1997. *Raven and River*. Boston, MA: Little, Brown.

Coady, Christopher. 1991. *Red Riding Hood*. New York: Dutton.

Cooney, Barbara. 1982. *Miss Rumphius*. New York: Viking Press.

Crews, Donald. 1991. *Big Mama's*. New York: Greenwillow.

Dorros, Arthur. 1991. *Abuela*. New York: Dutton.

Ernst, Lisa Campbell. 1995. *Little Red Riding Hood*. New York: Simon & Schuster.

Frost, Robert. 1969. *Stopping by Woods on a Snowy Evening*. New York: Dutton.

Galdone, Paul. 1975. *The Gingerbread Boy*. New York: Clarion/Houghton Mifflin.

Hines, Anna Grossnickle. 1993. *Gramma's Walk*. New York: Greenwillow.

Hutchins, Pat. 1968. *Rosie's Walk*. New York: Macmillan.

Hyman, Trina Schart. 1983. *Little Red Riding Hood*. New York: Holiday House.

Johnson, Angela. 1992. *The Leaving Morning*. New York: Orchard.

Kovalski, Maryann. 1987. *The Wheels on the Bus*. Boston, MA: Little, Brown.

Lacome, Julie. 1993. *Walking Through the Jungle*. Cambridge, MA: Candlewick.

McKissack, Particia. 1986. *Flossie and the Fox*. New York: Dial.

Miller, Debbie. 1994. *A Caribou Journey*. New York: Little, Brown.

Paulsen, Gary. 1993. *Dogteam*. New York: Delacorte.

Rylant, Cynthia. 1985. *The Relatives Came*. New York: Bradley.

Stevens, Janet. 1987. *The Town Mouse and the Country Mouse*. New York: Holiday House.

Titherington, Jeanne. 1988. *Where Are You Going, Emma?* New York: Greenwillow.

Wickstrom, Sylvie K. 1988. *Wheels on the Bus*. New York: Crown.

Williams, Sue. 1989. *I Went Walking*. New York: Harcourt Brace Jovanovich.

Williams, Sue. 1998. *Let's Go Visiting*. New York: Gulliver Books/Harcourt Brace.

Turtles, Frogs, Toads and Where They Live

Arnold, Tedd. 1993. *Green Wilma*. New York: Dial/Penguin.

Cherry, Lynne. 1992. *A River Ran Wild*. New York: Gulliver Green/Harcourt Brace Jovanovich.

Demi. 1991. *Find Demi's Sea Creatures*. New York: Putnam and Grosset.

Faulkner, Keith. 1993. *Frog: My First Wildlife Book*. Hampshire, England: HarperCollins.

Fleming, Denise. 1993. *In the Small, Small Pond*. New York: Henry Holt.

Gibbons, Gail. 1995. *Sea Turtles*. New York: Holiday House.

Gibbons, Gail. 1998. *Marshes and Swamps*. New York: Holiday House.

Hirschi, Ron. 1994. *Turtle's Day*. New York: Cobblehill/Penguin.

Huck, Charlotte. 1996. *Toads and Diamonds*. New York: Greenwillow.

Kasza, Keiko. 1995. *Grandpa Toad's Secrets*. New York: G. P. Putnam's Sons.

Kilborne, Sarah. 1994. *Peach and Blue*. New York: Alfred A. Knopf.

Lember, Barbara H. 1997. *The Shell Book*. Boston, MA: Houghton Mifflin.

Lewis, J. Patrick. 1994. *The Frog Princess*. New York: Dial/Penguin.

London, Jonathan. 1992. *Froggy Gets Dressed*. New York: Viking/Penguin.

London, Jonathan. 1995. *Froggy Learns to Swim*. New York: Viking/Penguin.

O'Malley, Kevin. 1992. *Froggy Went a-Courtin*. New York: Stewart, Tabori and Chang.

Oxford Scientific Films. 1976. *The Stickleback Cycle*. New York: G. P. Putnam's Sons.

Parker, Nancy W., and Joan R. Wright. 1990. *Frogs, Toads, Lizards, and Salamanders*. New York: Greenwillow.

Parker, Steve. 1992. *Frogs and Toads*. London, England: Quarto.

Pfeffer, Wendy. 1994. *From Tadpole to Frog*. New York: HarperCollins.

Pirotta, Saviour. 1997. *Turtle Bay*. New York: Farrar Straus Giroux.

Rosen, Michael. 1994. *All Eyes on the Pond*. New York: Hyperion.

Royston, Angela. 1991. *Frog: See How They Grow*. New York: Lodestar Books/Dutton.

Scieszka, Jon. 1991. *The Frog Prince Continued*. New York: Viking/Penguin.

Miscellaneous

Jenkins, Steve. 1995. *Biggest, Strongest, Fastest*. New York: Scholastic.

Jenkins, Steve. 1995. *Looking Down*. Boston, MA: Houghton Mifflin.

Lankford, Mary D. 1992. *Hopscotch Around the World*. New York: Morrow/William Morrow.

Lankford, Mary D. 1998. *Dominoes Around the World*. New York: Morrow/William Morrow.

Ryan, Pam M. 1996. *The Flag We Love*. Watertown, MA: Charlesbridge.

Shields, Carol Diggory. 1993. *I Am Really a Princess*. New York: Dutton.

Ward, Leila. 1978. *I Am Eyes: Ni Macho*. New York: Greenwillow.

Title	Author	Publisher	ISBN Number
1 Hunter	Hutchins, Pat	Greenwillow	0-688-06522-8
26 Letters and 99 Cents	Hoban, Tana	Greenwillow	0-688-06361-6
A Is for Africa	Onyefulu, Ifeoma	Cobblehill	0-525-65147-0
A Is for Apple	Grundy, Lynn	Ladybird	0-7214-5052-0
A My Name Is Alice	Bayer, Jane	Dial	0-8037-0123-3
ABC	Kightley, Rosalinda	Little, Brown	0-316-49930-7
ABC Pop!	Isadora, Rachel	Viking/Penguin	0-670-88329-8
Abuela	Dorros, Arthur	Dutton	0-515-44750-4
Abuela's Weave	Castaneda, Omar S.	Lee and Low	1-880000-00-8
Adam Mouse's Book of Poems	Moore, Lilian	Atheneum/Macmillan	0-689-31765-4
Alaska ABC Book	Kreeger, Charlene	Paws IV	0-933914-01-6
Alison's Zinnia	Lobel, Anita	Greenwillow	0-688-08865-1
All Eyes on the Pond	Rosen, Michael	Hyperion	1-56282-475-9
All the Colors of the Earth	Hamanaka, Sheila	William Morrow	0-688-11131-9
Alphabet City	Johnson, Stephen T.	Viking/Penguin	0-670-85631-2
Alphabet Tale, The	Garten, Jan	Greenwillow	0-688-12702-9
Always My Dad	Wyeh, Sharon D.	Alfred A. Knopf	0-679-83447-8
Amazing and Incredible Counting Stories	Grover, Max	Browndeer/Harcourt Brace	0-15-200090-9
Amazing Grace	Hoffman, Mary	Dial/Penguin	0-8037-1040-2
Amazing Insects	Laurence, Mound	Alfred A. Knopf	0-679-83925-9
Amazing Lizards	Smith, Trevor	Alfred A. Knopf	0-679-80819-1
Amazing Spiders	Schnieper, Claudia	Carolrhoda	0-87614-518-7
Anansi and the Moss-Covered Rock	Kimmel, Eric A.	Holiday House	0-8234-0689-X
Animal Dads	Collard III, Sneed B.	Houghton Mifflin	0-395-83621-2
Animal Numbers	Kitchen, Bert	Dial/Penguin	0-8037-0459-3
Anno's Alphabet	Anno, Mitsumasa	Thomas Y. Crowell	0-690-00540-7
Antics!	Hepworth, Cathi	G. P. Putnam's Sons	0-399-21862-9
Antler, Bear, Canoe	Bowen, Betsy	Little, Brown	0-316-10376-4
Apple Picking Time	Slawson, Michele B.	Crown	0-517-58971-0
Apple Pie Tree, The	Hall, Zoe	The Blue Sky Press/Scholastic	0-590-62382-6
Arctic Community, An	Kalman, Bobbie D., and William Belsey	Crabtree	0-86505-157-7
Arctic Hunter	Hoyt-Goldsmith, Diane	Holiday House	0-8234-0972-4
Arctic Memories	Ekoomiak, Normee	Henry Holt	0-8050-2347-X
Arctic Son	George, Jean C.	Hyperion	0-7868-0315-0
Arctic Whales and Whaling	Kalman, Bobbie D., and Ken Faris	Crabtree	0-86505-156-9
Asbjornsen and Moe	Brown, Marcia	Harcourt Brace Jovanovich	0-15-690150-1
Atlas of Plants	Jeunesse, Gallimard, Claude Delafosse, and Perols	Scholastic	0-590-58113-9
Autumn: An Alphabet Acrostic	Schnur, Steven	Clarion	0-395-77043-2
Autumn Leaves	Robbins, Ken	Scholastic	0-590-29879-8
Backyard Insects	Selsam, M. and Goor, R.	Scholastic	0-590-42256-1
Backyard Sunflower	King, Elizabeth	Dutton	0-525-45082-3
Barn Cat	Saul, Carol	Little, Brown	0-316-76113-3
Bear	Schoenherr, John	Philomel/Putnam and Grosset	0-399-22177-8
Bear's Cave, The	Schindler, Regine	Dutton	0-525-44553-6
Beast Feast	Florian, Douglas	Harcourt Brace	0-15-295178-4
Big and Little	Miller, Margaret	Greenwillow	0-688-14748-8

© 1999 by A. McCarrier, G. S. Pinnell, & I. C. Fountas from *Interactive Writing*. Portsmouth, NH: May not be reproduced without written permission of the publisher.

Title	Author	Publisher	ISBN Number
Big Boy	Mollel, Tololwa	Clarion/Houghton Mifflin	0-395-67403-4
Big Bug Book, The	Facklam, Margery	Little, Brown	0-316-27389-9
Big Fat Hen	Baker, Keith	Harcourt Brace	0-15-292869-3
Big Fat Worm, The	Van Laan, Nancy	Alfred A. Knopf	0-394-88763-8
Big Mama's	Crews, Donald	Greenwillow	0-688-09950-5
Big Orange Splot, The	Pinkwater, Daniel	Hastings House	0-8038-0777-5
Big Sneeze, The	Brown, Ruth	Lothrop, Lee and Shepard	0-688-04665-7
Biggest, Best Snowman, The	Cuyler, Margery	Scholastic	0-590-13922-3
Biggest, Strongest, Fastest	Jenkins, Steve	Scholastic	0-590-95922-0
Book of Fruit, A	Lember, Barbara H.	Ticknor and Fields/Houghton Mifflin	0-395-66989-8
Bookworm's Feast, The	Lewis, J. Patrick	Dial/Penguin	0-8037-1692-3
Brown Bear, Brown Bear, What Do You See?	Martin, Bill	Holt, Rinehart and Winston	0-8050-0201-4
Brown Honey in Broomwheat Tea	Thomas, Joyce	HarperCollins	0-06-021087-7
Bugs	Parker, Nancy W., and Joan R. Wright	Greenwillow	0-688-06623-2
Building a House	Robbins, Ken	Four Winds/Collier Macmillan	0-02-777400-7
Burgoo Stew	Patron, Susan	Orchard	0-531-05916-2
Butterfly: My First Wildlife Book	Faulkner, Keith	HarperFestival/HarperCollins	0-694-00463-4
Butterfly: See How They Grow	Ling, Mary	Dorling Kindersley	1-56458-112-8
Butterfly Alphabet, The	Sandvd, Kjell	Scholastic	0-590-48003-0
Butterfly and Caterpillar	Watts, Barrie	Silver Burdett	0-382-09958-3
Cactus Hotel	Guiberson, Brenda	Henry Holt	0-8050-1333-4
Cake That Mack Ate, The	Robart, Rose, and Maryann Kovalski	Little, Brown	0-316-74890-0
Calor	Alba, Juanita	WRS	1-56796-069-3
Can You Count Ten Toes?	Evans, Lezlie	Houghton Mifflin	0-395-90499-4
Caribou Journey, A	Miller, Debbie	Little, Brown	0-316-57380-9
Cat on the Mat	Wildsmith, Brian	Oxford University Press	0-19-272123-2
Caterpillar Caterpillar	French, Vivian	Candlewick	1-56402-206-4
Chair for My Mother, A	Williams, Vera B.	Greenwillow	0-688-00914-X
Changes	Allen, Marjorie, and Shelley Rotner	Macmillan	0-02-700252-7
Chick and the Duckling, The	Ginsburg, Mirra	Macmillan	0-02-735940-9
Chicka Chicka Boom Boom	Martin, Bill Jr., and John Archambault	Simon & Schuster	0-671-67949-X
Chicken Little	Hobson, Sally	Simon & Schuster	0-671-89548-6
Chicken Little	Kellogg, Steven	Mulberry/William Morrow	0-688-07045-0
Chicken Sunday	Polacco, Patricia	Philomel	0-399-22133-6
Child's Alaska, A	Murphy, Claire R.	Alaska Northwest	0-88240-457-1
Chinese Mother Goose Rhymes	Wyndham, Robert	Philomel/Putnam and Grosset	0-399-21740-1
Chinye: A West African Folk Tale	Onyefulu, Obi	Penguin	0-670-85115-9
Chocolate Chip Cookies	Wagner, Karen	Henry Holt	0-8050-1268-0
Chrysanthemum	Henkes, Kevin	Greenwillow	0-688-09699-9
Cinder-Elly	Minters, Frances	Viking/Penguin	0-670-84417-9
Clap Your Hands	Hayes, Sarah	Lothrop, Lee and Shepard	0-688-07692-0
Clay Boy	Ginsburg, Mirra	Greenwillow	0-688-14409-8
Cock, the Mouse, and the Little Red Hen, The	Percy, Graham	Candlewick	1-56402-008-8

© 1999 by A. McCarrier, G. S. Pinnell, & I. C. Fountas from *Interactive Writing.* Portsmouth, NH: May not be reproduced without written permission of the publisher.

Title	Author	Publisher	ISBN Number
Cocoa Ice	Appelbaum, Diana	Orchard	0-531-30040-4
Color	Heller, Ruth	Putnam and Grosset	0-399-22815-2
Color Dance	Jonas, Ann	Greenwillow	0-688-05990-2
Color Zoo	Ehlert, Lois	J. B. Lippincott	0-397-32259-3
Colors	de Bourgoing, Pascale, and Gallimard Jeunesse	Scholastic	0-590-45236-3
Colors Around Us	Rotner, Shelley, and Anne Woodhull	Simon & Schuster	0-689-80980-8
Cookies Week	Ward, Cindy	G. P. Putnam's Sons	0-399-21498-4
Counting Wildflowers	McMillan, Bruce	Lothrop, Lee and Shepard	0-688-02859-4
Daddy Calls Me Man	Johnson, Angela	Orchards	0-531-30042-0
Dandelion	Watts, Barrie	Stopwatch/Silver Burdett	0-382-24016-2
Darcy and Gran Don't Like Babies.	Cutler, Jane	Scholastic	0-590-44587-1
Dark Dark Tale, A	Brown, Ruth	Dial	0-8037-1672-9
Dear Rebecca, Winter Is Here	George, Jean C.	HarperCollins	0-02-021140-7
Demi's Secret Garden	Demi	Henry Holt	0-8050-2553-7
Did You Hear Wind Sing Your Name? An Oneida Song of Spring	De Coteau Orie, Sandra	Walker	0-8027-8350-3
Disappearing Lake	Miller, Debbie	Walker	0-8027-8474-7
Discover My World: Desert	Hirschi, Ron	Bantam	0-553-08012-1
Discovering Butterflies	Florian, Douglas	Aladdin/Macmillan	0-689-71376-2
Do Like Kyla	Johnson, Angela	Orchard	0-531-05852-2
Dogteam	Paulsen, Gary	Delacorte	0-385-30550-8
Domino Addition	Long, Lynette	Charlesbridge	0-88106-877-2
Dominoes Around the World	Lankford, Mary	Morrow/William Morrow	0-688-14051-3
Don't Wake the Baby	Franklin, Jonathan	Farrar Straus Giroux	0-374-31826-3
Doodle Danies	Lewis, J. Patrick	Atheneum/Simon & Schuster	0-689-81075-X
Duck: See How They Grow	Royston, Angela	Lodestar/Dutton	0-525-67346-6
Eating the Alphabet	Ehlert, Lois	Harcourt Brace Jovanovich	0-15-224435-2
Echoes for the Eyes	Esbensen, Barbara	HarperCollins	0-06-024398-8
Egg	Burton, Robert	Dorling Kindersley	1-56458-460-7
Egg Is an Egg, An	Weiss, Nicki	G. P. Putnam's Sons	0-399-22182-4
Egyptian Cinderella, The	Climo, Shirley	HarperCollins	0-690-4822-X
Empty Pot, The	Demi	Henry Holt	0-8050-1217-6
Enormous Carrot, The	Vagin, Vladimir	Scholastic	0-590-45491-9
Eskimo Boy	Kendall, Russ	Scholastic	0-590-43695-3
Families Are Different	Pellegrini, Nina	Scholastic	0-590-46317-9
Far North	Reynolds, Jan	Harcourt Brace Jovanovich	0-15-227179-1
Farmer in the Dell, The	Parkinson, Kathy	Albert Whitman	0-8075-2271-6
Feast for 10	Falwell, Cathryn	Clarion	0-395-62037-6
Find Demi's Sea Creatures	Demi	Putnam and Grosset	0-399-22112-3
Fine Fat Pig, A	Hoberman	HarperCollins	0-06-022425-8
Finger Rhymes	Brown, Marc	E. P. Dutton	0-525-29732-4
First Snow	McCully, Emily A.	Harper and Row	0-06-0241128-4
Fish and Flamingo	Carlstom, Nancy	Little, Brown	0-316-12859-7
Fish Eyes: A Book You Can Count On	Ehlert, Lois	Harcourt Brace Jovanovich	0-15-228050-2
Five Little Ducks	Raffi, Jose Aruego, and Ariane Dewey	Crown	0-517-56945-0

© 1999 by A. McCarrier, G. S. Pinnell, & I. C. Fountas from *Interactive Writing*. Portsmouth, NH: May not be reproduced without written permission of the publisher.

Title	Author	Publisher	ISBN Number
Five Little Ducks	Paparone, Pamela	North-South	1-55858-473-0
Five Little Monkeys Jumping on the Bed	Christelow, Eileen	Clarion	0-89919-769-8
Flag We Love, The	Ryan, Pam Munoz	Charlesbridge	0-88106-845-4
			0-88106-844-6
Flossie and the Fox	McKissack, Particia	Dial	0-8037-0250-7
Flower Garden	Bunting, Eve	Harcourt Brace	0-15-228776-0
Flower Grows, A	Robbins, Ken	Dial	0-8037-0764-9
Flowers	Delafosse, Claude, and Rene Mettler	Scholastic/Cartwheel	0-590-46383-7
Frog: My First Wildlife Book	Faulkner, Keith	HarperCollins	0-694-00464-2
Frog: See How They Grow	Royston, Angela	Lodestar/Dutton	0-525-67345-8
Frog Prince Continued, The	Scieszka, Jon	Viking/Penguin	0-670-83421-1
Frog Princess, The	Lewis, J. Patrick	Dial/Penguin	0-8037-1623-0
Froggy Gets Dressed	London, Jonathan	Viking/Penguin	0-670-84249-4
Froggy Learns to Swim	London, Jonathan	Viking/Penguin	0-670-85551-0
Froggy Went a-Courtin	O'Malley, Kevin	Stewart, Tabori and Chang	1-55670-260-4
Frogs and Toads	Parker, Steve	Quarto	0-87156-466-1
Frogs, Toads, Lizards, and Salamanders	Parker, Nancy W., and Joan R. Wright	Greenwillow	0-688-08680-2
From Seed to Plant	Gibbons, Gail	Holiday House	0-8234-0872-8
From Tadpole to Frog	Pfeffer, Wendy	HarperCollins	0-06-445123-2
Garden	Maass, Robert	Henry Holt	0-8050-5477-4
Gathering	Bowen, Betsy	Little, Brown	0-316-10371-3
Giant Carrot, The	Peck, Jan	Dial	0-8037-1823-3
Gingerbread Boy, The	Galdone, Paul	Clarion/Houghton Mifflin	0-395-28799-5
Gingerbread Man, The	Aylesworth, Jim	Scholastic	0-590-97219-7
Going Home	Bunting, Eve	Joanna Cotler/HarperCollins	0-06-026296-6
Going on a Whale Watch	McMillan, Bruce	Scholastic	0-590-45768-3
Going Up!	Sis, Peter	Greenwillow	0-688-08125-8
Goldilocks	DeLuise, Dom	Simon & Schuster	0-671-74690-1
Goldilocks and the Three Bears	Marshall, James	Dial/Penguin	0-8037-0542-5
Goldilocks and the Three Bears	Stevens, Janet	Holiday House	0-8234-0608-3
Goldilocks and the Three Bears	Watts, Bernadette	Henry Holt	0-8050-0172-7
Goldilocks and the Three Bears	Brett, Jan	Dodd, Mead	0-396-08925-9
Goldilocks and the Three Bears	Cauley, Lorinda B.	G. P. Putnam's Sons	0-399-20794-5
Goldilocks	Roberts, Tom	Rabbit Ear	0-88708-146-0
Goodbye Geese	Carlstrom, Nancy W.	Philomel	0-399-21832-7
Gramma's Walk	Hines, Anna G.	Greenwillow	0-688-11480-6
Grandma According to Me	Beil, Karen M.	Bantam Doubleday Dell	0-440-40995-0
Grandma's Smile	Moore, Elaine	Lothrop, Lee and Shepard	0-688-11075-4
Grandpa	Burningham, John	Jonathan Cape	0-224-02279-2
Grandpa Toad's Secrets	Kasza, Keiko	G. P. Putnam's Sons	0-399-22610-9
Grandpa's Face	Greenfield, Eloise	Philomel	0-399-22106-9
Great Butterfly Hunt, The	Herberman, Ethan	Simon & Schuster	0-671-69428-6
Green Gourd, The	Hunter, C. W.	G. P. Putnam's Sons	0-399-22278-2
Green Wilma	Arnold, Tedd	Dial/Penguin	0-8037-1313-4
Growing Colors	McMillan, Bruce	Lothrop, Lee and Shepard	0-688-07844-3
Growing Vegetable Soup	Ehlert, Lois	Harcourt Brace Jovanovich	0-15-232575-1
Hands	Ehlert, Lois	Harcourt Brace	0-15-201506-X

© 1999 by A. McCarrier, G. S. Pinnell, & I. C. Fountas from Interactive Writing. Portsmouth, NH: May not be reproduced without written permission of the publisher.

Title	Author	Publisher	ISBN Number
Harvest Year	Peterson, Cris	Boyds Mills	1-56397-571-8
Hat, The	Brett, Jan	G. P. Putnam's Sons	0-399-23101-3
Hatch, Egg, Hatch!	Roddie, Shen, and Frances Cony	Little, Brown	0-316-75345-9
Hatseller and the Monkeys, The	Diakite, Baba Wague	Scholastic	0-590-96069-5
Hattie and the Fox	Fox, Mem	Bradbury/Macmillan	0-02-735470-9
Have You Seen My Duckling?	Tafuri, Nancy	Greenwillow	0-688-02797-0
Henny Penny	Galdone, Paul	Clarion/Houghton Mifflin	0-395-28800-2
"Hi, Pizza Man!"	Walter, Virginia	Orchard	0-531-06885-4
Hide and Snake	Baker, Keith	Harcourt Brace Jovanovich	0-440-84980-2
Hold the Anchovies!	Rotner, Shelley, and Julia Pemberton Hellums	Orchard	0-531-09507-X
Hole Story, The	Merriam, Eve	Simon & Schuster	0-671-88353-4
Honey, I Love	Greenfield, Eloise	Reading Rainbow/ HarperCollins	0-690-01334-5
Honey Makers, The	Gibbons, Gail	Morrow	0-688-11386-9
Hopscotch Around the World	Lankford, Mary	Morrow/William Morrow	0-688-08419-2
House that Jack Built, The	Bolam, Emily	Dutton	0-525-44972-8
Houses and Homes	Morris, Ann	Lothrop, Lee and Shepard	0-688-10168-2
How a House Is Built	Gibbons, Gail	Holiday House	0-8234-0841-8
How Many Bugs in a Box?	Carter, David A.	Simon & Schuster	0-671-64965-5
Hunky Dory Ate It	Evans, Katie	Dutton	0-525-44847-0
I Am Eyes: Ni Macho	Ward, Leila	Scholastic	0-590-44854-4
I Am Really a Princess	Shields, Carol D.	Dutton	0-525-451-38-2
I Got Community	Cooper, Melrose	Henry Holt	0-8050-3179-0
I Know an Old Lady	Karas, G. Brian	Scholastic	0-590-46575-9
I Like It When . . .	Murphy, Mary	Harcourt Brace	0-15-200039-9
I See the Moon, and the Moon Sees Me	Craig, Helen	Willa Perlman/HarperCollins	0-06-021453-8
I Spy in the Garden	Powell, Richard	Puffin/Penguin	0-14-055979-5
I Spy Two Eyes	Micklethwait, Lucy	Greenwillow	0-688-12640-5
I Want to Go Home	McLerran, Alice	Tambourine	0-688-10144-5
I Went Walking	Williams, Sue	Harcourt Brace Jovanovich	0-15-200471-8
In a Dark, Dark Wood	Carter, David	Simon & Schuster	0-671-74134-9
In the Small, Small Pond	Fleming, Denise	Henry Holt	0-8050-2264-3
In the Tall, Tall Grass	Fleming, Denise	Henry Holt	0-8050-1635-X
In the Woods: Who's Been Here?	George, Lindsay B.	Greenwillow	0-688-12318-X
Insect Metamorphosis	Goor, Ron	Atheneum/Macmillan	0-689-31445-0
Insects and Crawly Creatures	Royston, Angela	Aladdin/Macmillan	0-689-71645-1
Irene and the Big, Fine Nickel	Smalls, Irene	Little, Brown	0-316-79898-3
It Takes a Village	Cowen-Fletcher, Jane	Scholastic	0-590-46573-2
It's Pumpkin Time!	Hall, Zoe	Scholastic/The Blue Sky Press	0-590-47833-8
It's Snowing! It's Snowing!	Prelutsky, Jack	Greenwillow	0-688-01512-3
It's the Bear!	Alborough, Jez	Candlewick	1-56402-486-5
Itsy Bitsy Spider, The	Trapani, Iza	Whispering Coyote	1-879085-77-1
Jack's Garden	Cole, Henry	Greenwillow	0-688-13501-3
Jasper's Beanstalk	Butterworth, Nick, and Mick Inkpen	Bradbury	0-02-716231-1
Jeremy's Muffler	Nielsen, Laura L.	Atheneum/Simon & Schuster	0-689-80319-2
Johnny Appleseed	Kellogg, Steven	Morrow	0-688-06417-5

© 1999 by A. McCarrier, G. S. Pinnell, & I. C. Fountas from *Interactive Writing*. Portsmouth, NH: May not be reproduced without written permission of the publisher.

Title	Author	Publisher	ISBN Number
Julius, the Baby of the World	Henkes, Kevin	Greenwillow	0-688-08943-7
Jungle Animals	Royston, Angela	Simon & Schuster	0-689-71519-6
Just One More	Koch, Michelle	Greenwillow	0-688-08127-4
Just Us Women	Caines, Jeannette	HarperCollins	0-06-443056-1
Keepers	Watts, Jeri Hanel	Lee and Low	1-880000-58-X
Kente Colors	Chocolate, Debbi	Walker	0-8027-8388-0
Koala Lou	Fox, Mem	Gulliver/Harcourt Brace Jovanovich	0-15-200502-1
La Boda, A Mexican Wedding Celebration	Van Laan, Nancy	Little, Brown	0-316-89626-8
Lady with the Alligator Purse, The	Westcott, Nadine B.	Little, Brown	0-316-93135-7
Land of Dark, Land of Light	Pandell, Karen	Dutton	0-525-45094-7
Leaf Men and the Brave Good Bugs, The	Joyce, William	HarperCollins	0-06-027237-6
Leaving Morning, The	Johnson, Angela	Orchard	0-531-05992-8
Let's Go Visiting	Williams, Sue	Gulliver/Harcourt Brace	0-15-201823-9
Life and Times of the Honeybee, The	Micucci, Charles	Ticknor and Fields	0-395-65968-X
Life and Times of the Apple, The	Micucci, Charles	Orchard	0-531-05939-1
Little Buggers, The	Lewis, J. Patrick	Dial	0-8037-1769-5
Little Dog Laughed and Other Nursery Rhymes, The	Cousins, Lucy	E. P. Dutton	0-525-44573-0
Little Red Hen, The	Galdone, Paul	Clarion/Ticknor Fields/ Houghton Mifflin	0-395-28803-7
Little Red Hen, The	Barton, Bryon	HarperCollins	0-06-021675-1
Little Red Hen, The	Zemach, Margot	Farrar Straus Giroux	0-374-34621-6
Little Red Riding Hood	Ernst, Lisa Campbell	Simon & Schuster	0-689-80145-9
Little Red Riding Hood	Hyman, Trina Schart	Holiday House	0-8234-0470-6
Little Robin Redbreast	Halpern, Shari	North-South	1-55858-247-9
Lon Po Po	Young, Ed	Scholastic	0-590-44069-1
Looking at Penguins	Patent, Dorothy H.	Holiday House	0-8234-1037-4
Lots of Dads	Rotner, Shelley, and Sheila Kelly	Dial/Penguin	0-8037-2086-6
Lots of Moms	Rotner, Shelley	Dial/Penguin	0-8037-1891-8
Loving	Morris, Ann	Lothrop, Lee and Shepard	0-688-06341-3
Lunch	Fleming, Denise	Henry Holt	0-8050-1636-8
Ma Dear's Apron	McKissack, Patricia C.	Atheneum/Simon & Schuster	0-689-81051-2
Magic Porridge Pot, The	Galdone, Paul	Clarion/Houghton Mifflin	0-395-28805-3
Mama, Do You Love Me?	Joose, Barbara M.	Chronicle	0-87701-759-X
Mama One, Mama Two	MacLachlan, Patricia	Harper and Row	0-06-024081-4
Mama Zooms	Cowen-Fletcher, Jane	Scholastic	0-590-457748
Market Day	Bunting, Eve	Joanna Cotler	0-06-025364-9
Marshes and Swamps	Gibbons, Gail	Holiday House	0-8234-1347-0
Mary Had a Little Lamb	Hale, Sarah J.	Scholastic	0-590-43773-9
Mary Wore Her Red Dress and Henry Wore His Green Sneakers	Peek, Merle	Clarion	0-89919-324-2
Meet Danitra Brown	Grimes, Nikki	Lothrop, Lee and Shepard	0-688-12073-3
Mirandy and Brother Wind	McKissack, Patricia C.	Alfred A. Knopf	0-394-88765-4
Miss Rumphius	Cooney, Barbara	Viking	0-670-47958-6
Miss Spider's Tea Party	Kirk, David	Scholastic	0-590-47724-2
Missing Sunflowers, The	Stern, Maggie	Greenwillow	0-688-14873-5
Missing Tarts, The	Hennessy, B. G.	Viking/Penguin	0-670-82039-3

© 1999 by A. McCarrier, G. S. Pinnell, & I. C. Fountas from *Interactive Writing*. Portsmouth, NH: May not be reproduced without written permission of the publisher.

Title	Author	Publisher	ISBN Number
Mitten, The	Brett, Jan	G. P. Putnam's Sons	0-399-21920-X
Monarch Butterfly	Gibbons, Gail	Holiday House	0-8234-0773-X
Moo Moo, Brown Cow	Wood, Jakki	Harcourt Brace	0-15-200533-1
Moon to Sun: An Adding Book	Samton, Sheila W.	Carolyn House/Boyd Mills	1-878093-13-4
More More More, Said the Baby	Williams, Vera B.	Scholastic	0-590-45198-7
More Than One	Schlein, Miriam	Greenwillow	0-688-14102-1
Mother for Choco, A	Kasza, Keiko	G. P. Putnam's Sons	0-399-21841-6
Mother Goose	Wegman, William	Hyperion	0-7868-0218-9
Mouse Paint	Walsh, Ellen S.	Harcourt Brace Jovanovich	0-15-256025-4
My Best Friend	Hutchins, Pat	Greenwillow	0-688-11485-7
My Five Senses	Miller, Margaret	Simon & Schuster	0-671-79168-0
My Hen Is Dancing	Wallace, Karen	Candlewick	1-56402-303-6
My Song Is Beautiful	Hoberman, Mary Ann	Little, Brown	0-316-36738-9
My Very First Mother Goose	Opie, Iona Archibald	Candlewick	1-564-02620-5
Nanny Goat and the Seven Little Kids	Kimmel, Eric	Holiday House	0-8234-0789-6
Napping House, The	Wood, Audrey	Harcourt Brace Jovanovich	0-15-256708-9
Nathaniel Talking	Greenfield, Eloise	Black Butterfly/Writers and Readers	0-86316-200-2
Near the Sea	Arnosky, Jim	Lothrop, Lee and Shepard	0-688-08164-9
Nicholas Cricket	Maxner, Joyce	Harper and Row	0-06-024216-7
Night on Neighborhood Street	Greenfield, Eloise	Dial	0-8037-0777-0
Nights of the Pufflings	McMillan, Bruce	Houghton Mifflin	0-395-70810-9
North Country Night	San Souci, Daniel	Doubleday	0-385-41319-X
Northern Lullaby	Carlstrom, Nancy W.	Philomel	0-399-21806-8
Now I'm Big	Miller, Margaret	Greenwillow	0-688-14077-7
Of Colors and Things	Hoban, Tana	Scholastic	0-590-44060-8
Oink Oink	Geisert, Arthur	Houghton Mifflin	0-395-64048-2
Old Black Fly	Aylesworth, Jim	Henry Holt	0-8050-1401-2
Old MacDonald Had a Farm	Rounds, Glen	Holiday House	0-8234-0739-X
Old MacDonald Had a Farm	Hawkins, Colin, and Jacqui Hawkins	Price Stern Sloan	0-8431-2884-4
Old MacDonald Had a Farm	English, Tracey	Golden Western Publishing	0-307-17601-0
Old Mother Hubbard	Hawkins, Colin, and Jacqui Hawkins	G. P. Putnam's Sons	Out of Print
Old Mother Hubbard and Her Wonderful Dog	Marshall, James	Farrar Straus Giroux	0-374-35621-1
On Mother's Lap	Scott, Ann H.	Clarion	0-395-58920-7
On the Day I Was Born	Chocolate, Debbi	Cartwheel/Scholastic	0-590-47609-2
On the Day You Were Born	Frasier, Debra	Harcourt Brace	0-15-257995-8
Once Upon a Golden Apple	Little, Jean, and Maggie De Vries	Viking/Penguin	0-670-82963-3
Once Upon a Princess and a Pea	Campbell, Ann	Stewart, Tabori and Chang	1-55670-289-2
Once Upon a Time	Prater, John	Candlewick Press	1-56402-177-7
Once Upon Ice	Yolen, Jane	Wordsong/Boyds Mills	1-56397-408-8
One Bean	Rockwell, Anne	Walker	0-8027-8648-0
One Bear at Bedtime	Inkpen, Mick	Little, Brown	0-316-41889-7
One Grain of Rice	Demi	Scholastic	0-590-93998-X
One Monkey Too Many	Koller, Jackie F.	Harcourt Brace	0-15-200006-2
One Potato	Pomeroy, Diana	Harcourt Brace	0-15-200-3000-2
Only One	Harshman, Marc	Cobblehill	0-525-65116-0

© 1999 by A. McCarrier, G. S. Pinnell, & I. C. Fountas from Interactive Writing. Portsmouth, NH: May not be reproduced without written permission of the publisher.

Title	Author	Publisher	ISBN Number
Only Opal: The Diary of a Young Girl	Cooney, Barbara	Philomel/Putnam and Grosset	0-399-21990-0
Over Under in the Garden	Schories, Pat	Farrar Straus Giroux	0-374-35677-7
Owen	Henkes, Kevin	Greenwillow	0-688-11449-0
Owl Babies	Waddell, Martin	Candlewick	1-56402-101-7
Owl Moon	Yolen, Jane	Philomel	0-399-21457-7
Pain and the Great One, The	Blume, Judy	Bradbury	0-02-711100-8
Pancakes, Pancakes!	Carle, Eric	Simon & Schuster	0-88708-120-7
Peach and Blue	Kilborne, Sarah	Alfred A. Knopf	0-679-83929-1
Peanut Butter and Jelly	Westcott, Nadine B.	E. P. Dutton	0-525-44317-7
Penguins	Jeunesse, Gallimard, and Rene Mettler	Scholastic	0-590-73877-1
Pig in the Pond, The	Waddell, Martin	Candlewick	1-56402-050-9
Place Is Cold, The	Cobb, Vicki	Walker	0-8027-6852-0
Planting a Rainbow	Ehlert, Lois	Harcourt Brace Jovanovich	0-15-262609-3
Poem Stew	Cole, William	HarperTrophy/J. B. Lippincott	0-06-440136-7
Prince Cinders	Cole, Babette	G. P. Putnam's Sons	0-399-21502-6
Princess Furball	Huck, Charlotte	Mullberry/Greenwillow	0-688-13107-7
Puffins Are Back!, The	Gibbons, Gail	HarperCollins	0-06-021603-4
Pumpkin Patch, The	King, Elizabeth	Dutton	0-525-44640-0
Pumpkin Pumpkin	Titherington, Jeanne	Greenwillow	0-688-05695-4
Rachel Fister's Blister	MacDonald, Amy	Houghton Mifflin	0-395-52152-1
Rain	Kalan, Robert	Greenwillow	0-688-80139-0
Raven and River	Carlstrom, Nancy W.	Little, Brown	0-316-12894-5
Read-Aloud Rhymes	Prelutsky, Jack	Alfred A. Knopf	0-394-87218-5
Red Dancing Shoes	Patrick, Denise L.	Tambourine/William Morrow	0-688-10392-8
Red Dragonfly on My Shoulder	Cassedy, Sylvia, Kunihiro Suetake, and Molly Band	HarperCollins	0-06-022624-2
Red Fox	Wallace, Karen	Candlewick	1-56402-422-9
Red Is Best	Stinson, Kathy	Annick Press	0-920236-24-3
Red Leaf, Yellow Leaf	Ehlert, Lois	Scholastic	0-590-46516-3
Red Light, Green Light, Mama and Me	Best, Cari	Orchard	0-531-09452-9
Red Poppy, The	Lucht, Irmgard	Hyperion	0-7868-0055-0
Red Riding Hood	Coady, Christopher	Dutton	0-525-44896-9
Relatives Came, The	Rylant, Cynthia	Bradbury	0-02-777220-9
River Ran Wild, A	Cherry, Lynne	Gulliver Green/Harcourt Brace Jovanovich	0-15-200542-0
Roll Over!	Peek, Merle	Clarion/Houghton Mifflin	0-395-29438-X
Rosie's Walk	Hutchins, Pat	Macmillan	0-02-745850-4
Rough-Face Girl, The	Martin, Rafe	G. P. Putnam's Sons	0-399-21859-9
Ruby	Glen, Maggie	G. P. Putnam's Sons	0-399-22281-2
Ruby	Emberley, Michael	Little, Brown	0-316-23643-8
Salamanders	Bernhard, Emery	Holliday House	0-8234-1148-6
Salmon Summer	McMillan, Bruce	Houghton Mifflin	0-395-84544-0
Say It!	Zolotow, Charlotte	Greenwillow	0-688-80276-1
Sea Turtles	Gibbons, Gail	Holiday House	0-8234-1191-5
Secret Place	Bunting, Eve	Clarion	0-395-64367-8
Secret Places	Huck, Charlotte	Greenwillow	0-688-11669-8
See How They Grow: Pig	Ling, Bill, and Mary Ling	Dorling Kindersley	1-56458-2043
Seven Blind Mice	Young, Ed	Philomel/Putnam and Grosset	0-399-22261-8

© 1999 by A. McCarrier, G. S. Pinnell, & I. C. Fountas from *Interactive Writing*. Portsmouth, NH: May not be reproduced without written permission of the publisher.

Title	Author	Publisher	ISBN Number
Shape of Things, The	Dodds, Dayle A.	Candlewick	1-56402-224-2
Shell Book, The	Lember, Barbara H.	Houghton Mifflin	0-395-72030-3
Shoes from Grandpa	Fox, Mem	Orchard	0-531-05848-4
Shoes Like Miss Alice's	Johnson, Angela	Orchard	0-531-06814-5
Simple Signs	Wheeler, Cindy	Penguin	0-670-86282-7
Sing a Song of Popcorn	De Regniers, Beatrice S.	Scholastic	0-590-40645-0
Skip to My Lou	Westcott, Nadine B.	Little, Brown	0-316-93137-3
Sleep Rhymes Around the World	Yolen, Jane	Wordsong/Boyds Mills	1-56397243-3
Sleeping Lady, The	Dixon, Ann	Alaska Northwest	0-88240444-X
Small Tall Tale from the Far Far North, A	Sis, Peter	Alfred A. Knopf	0-679-84345-0
Snapshots from the Wedding	Soto, Gary	G. P. Putnam's Sons	0-399-22808-X
Snow	Shulevitz, Uri	Farrar Straus Giroux	0-374-37092-3
Snow Day	Maestro, Betsy	Scholastic	0-590-41283-3
Snow on Snow on Snow	Chapman, Cheryl	Dial	0-8037-1456-4
Snowballs	Ehlert, Lois	Harcourt Brace	0-15-200074-7
Snowflake Bentley	Martin, Jacqueline B.	Houghton Mifflin	0-395-86162-4
Snowman, The	Briggs, Raymond	Random House	0-394-83973-0
Somebody and the Three Blairs	Tolhurst, Marilyn	Orchard	0-531-05878-6
Sootface	San Souci, Robert	Bantam Doubleday Dell	0-385-31202-4
Spider: Life Story	Chinery, Michael	Troll	0-8167-2109-2
Spider on the Floor	Kelley, True	Crown	0-517-59381-5
Spiders	Gibbons, Gail	Holiday House	0-8234-1006-4
Stellaluna	Cannon, Janell	Harcourt Brace	0-15-280217-7
Stickleback Cycle, The	Oxford Scientific Films	G. P. Putnam's Sons	0-399-20638-8
Stone Soup	Brown, Marcia	Alladin/Macmillan	0-689-71103-4
Stopping by Woods on a Snowy Evening	Frost, Robert	Dutton	0-525-40115-6
Story of Chicken Licken, The	Ormerod, Jan	Lothrop, Lee and Shepard	0-688-06058-7
Street Rhymes Around the World	Yolen, Jane	Wordsong/Boyds Mills	1-878093-53-3
Summertime Song, A	Haas, Irene	Simon & Schuster	0-689-50549-3
Sun Is So Quiet, The	Giovanni, Nikki	Henry Holt	0-8050-4119-2
Sunflower	Ford, Miela, and Sally Noll	Greenwillow	0-688-13301-0
Sunflower House	Bunting, Eve	Harcourt Brace	0-15-200483-1
Talking Eggs, The	San Souci, Robert	Dial/Penguin	0-8037-0619-7
Tall Book of Mother Goose, The	Rojankovsky, Feodor	HarperCollins	0-06-025055-0
Teddy Bears' Picnic, The	Witmark, M. and Sons	Aladdin/Macmillan	0-689-71362-2
Ten Black Dots	Crews, Donald	Greenwillow	0-688-06067-6
Ten in a Bed	Rees, Mary	Joy Street Books/Little, Brown	0-316-73708-9
Ten Little Hippos	McCarthy, Bobette	Bradbury/Macmillan	0-02-765445-1
Ten Rosy Rosies	Merriam, Eve	HarperCollins	0-06-027887-0
That Bothered Kate	Noll, Sally	Greenwillow	0-688-10095-3
There Was an Old Lady Who Swallowed a Fly	Taback, Simms	Viking/Penguin	0-670-86939-2
There Was an Old Lady Who Swallowed a Trout!	Sloat, Teri	Henry Holt	0-8050-4294-6
Thinking About Ants	Brenner, Barbara	Mondo	1-57255-210-7
Those Amazing Ants	Demuth, Patricia B.	Macmillan	0-02-728467-0
Three Bears, The	Barton, Byron	HarperCollins	0-06-020423-0
Three Bears, The	Galdone, Paul	Clarion/Houghton Mifflin	0-89919-401-X
Three Billy Goats Gruff, The	Galdone, Paul	Clarion/Houghton Mifflin	0-395-28812-6
Three Billy Goats Gruff, The	Stevens, Janet	Harcourt Brace Jovanovich	0-15-286396-6
Three Little Javelinas, The	Lowell, Susan	Northland	0-87358-542-9

© 1999 by A. McCarrier, G. S. Pinnell, & I. C. Fountas from Interactive Writing. Portsmouth, NH: May not be reproduced without written permission of the publisher.

Title	Author	Publisher	ISBN Number
Three Little Pigs, The	Bishop, Gavin	Scholastic	0-590-43358-X
Three Little Pigs, The	Galdone, Paul	Clarion	0-89919-275-0
Three Little Pigs, The	Kellogg, Steven	Morrow	0-688-08731-0
Three Little Pigs, The	Marshall, James	Dial/Penguin	0-8037-0594-8
Three Little Pigs and the Fox, The	Hooks, William H.	Macmillan	0-02-744431-7
Three Little Wolves and the Big Bad Pig, The	Trivizas, Eugene	Macmillan	0-689-50569-8
Three Pigs, The	Ross, Tony	Pantheon/Random House	0-394-96143-9
Three Billy Goats Gruff	Rounds, Glen	Holiday House	0-8234-1015-3
Three Cheers for Tacky	Lester, Helen	Houghton Mifflin	0-395-66841-7
Three Little Pigs and the Big Bad Wolf	Rounds, Glen	Holiday House	0-8234-0923-6
Through Our Eyes	Hopkins, Lee Bennett	Little, Brown	0-316-19654-1
Thunder Cake	Polacco, Patricia	Philomel/Putnam and Grosset	0-399-22231-6
Tidy Titch	Hutchins, Pat	Greenwillow	0-688-09963-7
Time to Sleep	Fleming, Denise	Henry Holt	0-8050-3762-4
Tiny Seed, The	Carle, Eric	Scholastic	0-590-42566-8
To Market to Market	Miranda, Anne	Harcourt Brace	0-15-200035-6
Toads and Diamonds	Huck, Charlotte	Greenwillow	0-688-13680-X
Tomie de Paola's Book of Poems	De Paola, Tomie	G. P. Putnam's Sons	0-399-21540-9
Tomie de Paola's Favorite Nursery Tales	De Paola, Tomie	G. P. Putnam's Sons	0-399-21319-8
Too Many Tamales	Soto, Gary	G. P. Putnam's Sons	0-399-22146-8
Tops and Bottoms	Stevens, Janet	Harcourt Brace	0-15-292851-0
Town Mouse Country Mouse	Brett, Jan	G. P. Putnam's Sons	0-399-22622-2
Town Mouse and the Country Mouse, The	Stevens, Janet	Holiday House	0-8234-0633-4
Town Mouse and the Country Mouse, The	Craig, Helen	Candlewick	1-56402-102-5
Town Mouse and the Country Mouse, The	Cauley, Lorinda B.	G. P. Putnam's Sons	0-399-21123-3
True Story of the 3 Little Pigs!, The	Scieszka, Jon	Penguin	0-670-82759-2
Turtle Bay	Pirotta, Saviour	Farrar Straus Giroux	0-374-37888-6
Turtle's Day	Hirsch, Ron	Cobblehill/Penguin	0-525-65172-1
Two Bad Ants	Van Allsburg, Chris	Houghton Mifflin	0-395-48668-8
Uncle Jed's Barbershop	Mitchell, Margaree K.	Simon & Schuster	0-671-769693
Vegetable Garden	Florian, Douglas	Harcourt Brace/Voyager	0-15-201018-1
Vegetables in the Garden	De Bourgoing, Pascale, and Gallimard Jeunesse	Scholastic	0-590-33946-X
Very Quiet Cricket, The	Carle, Eric	Philomel	0-399-21885-8
Village of Round and Square Houses, The	Grifalconi, Ann	Little, Brown	0-316-32862-6
Walk with Me	Danis, Naomi	Cartwheel Story Corner/ Scholastic	0-590-45855-8
Walking Through the Jungle	Lacome, Julie	Candlewick	1-56402-137-8
Watching Water Birds	Arnosky, Jim	National Geographic Society	0-7922-7073-8
We Have a Baby	Falwell, Cathryn	Clarion	0-395-62038-4
We're Going on a Bear Hunt	Rosen, Michael	Macmillan	0-689-50476-4
Weekend with Wendell, A	Henkes, Kevin	Greenwillow	0-688-06325-X
Whales	Simon, Seymour	HarperTrophy/HarperCollins	0-06-446095-9
What About Ladybugs?	Godkin, Celia	The Sierra Club	0-87156-549-8
What Am I?	Charles, N. N., L. Dillon, and D. Dillon	The Blue Sky Press/Scholastic	0-590-47891-5
What Food Is This?	Hausherr, Rosmarie	Scholastic	0-590-46583-X
What's Inside Plants	DK Direct Limited	Dorling Kindersley	1-56458-005-9

© 1999 by A. McCarrier, G. S. Pinnell, & I. C. Fountas from *Interactive Writing*. Portsmouth, NH: May not be reproduced without written permission of the publisher.

Title	Author	Publisher	ISBN Number
What's Inside? Insects	Royston, Angela	Dorling Kindersley	1-56458-003-2
What's So Terrible About Swallowing an Apple Seed?	Lerner, Harriet, and Susan Goldhor	HarperCollins	0-06-024523-9
Wheels on the Bus	Wickstrom, Sylvie K.	Crown	0-517-56784-9
Wheels on the Bus, The	Kovalski, Maryann	Little, Brown	0-316-50259-6
When Autumn Comes	Maass, Robert	Henry Holt	0-8050-1259-1
When Jo Louis Won the Title	Rochelle, Belinda	Houghton Mifflin	0-395-66614-7
When the Big Dog Barks	Curtis, Munzee	Greenwillow	0-688-09539-9
When Winter Comes	Maass, Robert	Henry Holt	0-8050-2086-1
Where Are You Going, Emma?	Titherington, Jeanne	Greenwillow	0-688-07081-7
Where Once There Was a Wood	Fleming, Denise	Henry Holt	0-8050-3761-6
Where's the Fly?	Cohen, Caron Lee	Greenwillow	0-688-14044-0
While You Sleep	Moore, Julia	Dutton/Penguin	0-525-45462-4
White Snow Bright Snow	Tresselt, Alvin	Lothrop, Lee and Shepard	0-688-41161-4
Who Came Down That Road?	Lyon, George E.	Orchard	0-531-05987-1
Who Hops?	Davis, Katie	Harcourt Brace	0-15-201839-5
Who Lives in…the Forest?	Hirschi, Ron	Dodd, Mead	0-396-09121-0
Who Uses This?	Miller, Margaret	Greenwillow	0-688-08278-5
Who Wants One?	Serfozo, Mary	Macmillan	0-689-50474-8
Whose Hat?	Miller, Margaret	Greenwillow	0-688-06906-1
Whose Shoe?	Miller, Margaret	Greenwillow	0-688-10008-2
Wildflower ABC	Pomeroy, Diana	Harcourt Brace	0-15-201041-6
Wilfrid Gordon McDonald Partridge	Fox, Mem	Kane/Miller	0-916291-26-X
Willie Jerome	Duncan, Alice F.	Simon & Schuster/Macmillan	0-02-733208-X
Window	Baker, Jeannie	Greenwillow	0-688-08917-8
Winter Poems	Rogasky, Barbara	Scholastic	0-590-42872-1
Wolf's Chicken Stew, The	Kasza, Keiko	G. P. Putnam's Sons	0-399-21400-3
Wolves	Wolpert, Tom	Northwood	1-55971-087-X
Wonderful Worms	Glaser, Linda	Millbrook	1-56294-703-6
Working Cotton	Williams, Sherley A.	Harcourt Brace Jovanovich	0-15-299624-9
Yeh-Shen	Louie, Ai-Ling	Philomel	0-399-20900-X
Yo, Hungry Wolf!	Vozar, David	Bantam Doubleday Dell	0-385-30452-8
You'll Soon Grow into Them, Titch	Hutchins, Pat	Greenwillow	0-688-01770-3
Za-Za's Baby Brother	Cousins, Lucy	Candlewick	1-56402-582-9

© 1999 by A. McCarrier, G. S. Pinnell, & I. C. Fountas from *Interactive Writing*. Portsmouth, NH: May not be reproduced without written permission of the publisher.

Appendix 3
Self-Assessment Rubric for
Interactive Writing

Teacher_____ **Grade level**_____

Assessment: General_____   **OR**   **1 lesson (length of time):**_____

Directions   Mark the characteristic that most clearly describes your teaching at this time.

Materials   **My goal is to have all necessary materials present, organized, and accessible for use during the lesson.**

☐ I do not have the materials I need for interactive writing.	☐ I have some materials but I am at a beginning point in my organization.	☐ I have all necessary materials but am just beginning to organize them and make full use of them.	☐ I have all the materials I need, including easel, white tape, paper, markers, white board, Magna-doodle, pointer, etc.; they are organized and accessible.

Lesson Management   **My goal is to manage the lesson well with children demonstrating that they know the routines and to have all teaching procedures in place, in appropriate order.**

☐ My management of the lesson is uneven; children do not understand the routines and need a great deal of direction.	☐ I have the general procedures of interactive writing in place but there are times when children do not attend and the lesson "bogs down."	☐ All procedures are in place for interactive writing; children know the routines; I am working on a better-managed pace.	☐ My lesson is well managed with all procedures in place; children know what is expected of them and initiate action.

Self-assessment Rubric for Interactive Writing from McCarrier, Pinnell, & Fountas (1999). *Interactive Writing: How Language and Literacy Come Together, K-2*. Portsmouth, NH: Heinemann.

Engagement   My goal is to engage children's attention throughout the lesson.

☐ The lesson is often interrupted by attention to behavior or by materials not being accessible; children's attention is inconsistent across time and group.

☐ My materials are accessible and I can engage children for periods of time but engagement is not consistent; some groups are more difficult than others.

☐ Children are generally engaged (all groups) and the lesson goes smoothly.

☐ Engagement is high; children are attentive and eager to participate and this is consistent across groups.

Pace   My goal is to produce the interactive writing message fluently and to keep the lesson moving at an appropriate pace.

☐ Lessons are slow and consistently take too long and this disrupts the rest of my schedule.

☐ The time of the lesson is about right but we do not accomplish much because "sharing the pen" takes a long time; the pace is slow.

☐ My lessons are about the right length of time and are moderately fast -paced; we are able to produce (with children's sharing the pen) print and read it.

☐ For the most part, my lessons are fast-paced and exciting; we produce a large amount of print in a short time.

Composition   My goal is to elicit individual ideas, get children to agree on a group composition and to guide the composition skillfully so that the material has contains a range of language and vocabulary.

☐ I have not yet begun to involve children in composing the message for interactive writing; generally I make up the message.

☐ I invite children to participate in composing but have difficulty in generating what I think is a good message; either I direct too much or there are so many ideas I can't bring them together.

☐ I invite children to participate in composing and we usually have a successful collaboration; I would like to work more on generating messages with more potential for language and word learning.

☐ I guide the composition to demonstrate the composing process and to assure that children understand how to produce a text; the message constructed has opportunities for expanding language and studying words.

Self-assessment Rubric for Interactive Writing from McCarrier, Pinnell, & Fountas (1999). *Interactive Writing: How Language and Literacy Come Together, K-2*. Portsmouth, NH: Heinemann.

Construction   My goal is to involve children in producing the message, word by word, keeping in mind the meaning and giving attention to words, letters, and punctuation.

☐ I usually write the message myself or have children participate a little; they have trouble attending to word construction; I am just beginning to learn how to link writing to what they know; there is little rereading.

☐ I involve children in writing the message as much as possible but the process is uneven; I have some trouble with management; the process is slow; I do not consistently have them reread when needed in order to anticipate the next word or phrase.

☐ I have established "sharing the pen," and we consistently reread the message when needed during writing. I need to work on teaching for strategies that writers will be able to use independently.

☐ The message is collaboratively produced, smoothly managed, and reread many times; I draw attention to word construction through hearing and writing the sounds and through linking known words to writing new ones.

Teaching Decisions   My goal is to select powerful teaching examples that are based on what the children need to learn how to do as writers and that illustrate how written language works.

☐ I am not sure how I make my teaching decisions but I have difficulty connecting with what children know; I am not observing shifts in learning. I tend to have too many teaching points and the lesson drags.

☐ I am implementing the mechanics of the situation but am not yet involving children in a way that lets me focus on my teaching decisions and get more power. I still have either too many teaching points or two few.

☐ I am comfortable with the procedures and consistently reflect on my teaching decisions. I generally make an appropriate number of teaching points but am still working to select the most powerful for learning.

☐ My decisions are well timed and powerful in illustrating processes and allowing children to use what they know in a strategic way.

Self-assessment Rubric for Interactive Writing from McCarrier, Pinnell, & Fountas (1999). *Interactive Writing: How Language and Literacy Come Together, K-2.* Portsmouth, NH: Heinemann.

Text **My goal is to use interactive writing as a tool for helping children understand, read, and write a variety of texts.**

☐ I have used inter-active writing in a limited way, tending to produce only 1 or 2 kinds of texts. I have not yet found ways to link interactive writing to literature or content area study and to combine shared and interactive writing effectively.

☐ I have experimented with several different kinds of texts, including narrative, functional, and informational, but tend to use only 1 or 2 kinds of texts on a daily basis. I still need to link texts more to children's own writing, to literature, and to areas of content study. I am incorporating shared writing at times.

☐ With the children in my class, I regularly compose and con-struct several different kinds of texts, in-cluding functional, narrative, and expos-itory. I still need to link texts more to children's own writing, to literature, and to areas of content study. I incorporate shared and interactive writing to make texts more informative and readable.

☐ I consistently link interactive writing texts with content area study, literature, ongoing classroom events, word study, and children's own writing Children in my class compose and write a wide variety of narrative, functional, and expository texts on a daily basis. I incorporate shared writing in a skillful way to make texts richer.

Self-assessment Rubric for Interactive Writing from McCarrier, Pinnell, & Fountas (1999). *Interactive Writing: How Language and Literacy Come Together, K-2*. Portsmouth, NH: Heinemann.

Appendix 4
Analysis of Writing

Child	Knows how to . . .	Needs to know how to . . .	Plan for Teaching

Appendix 5
Murals

Three Billy Goats Gruff

La Granja

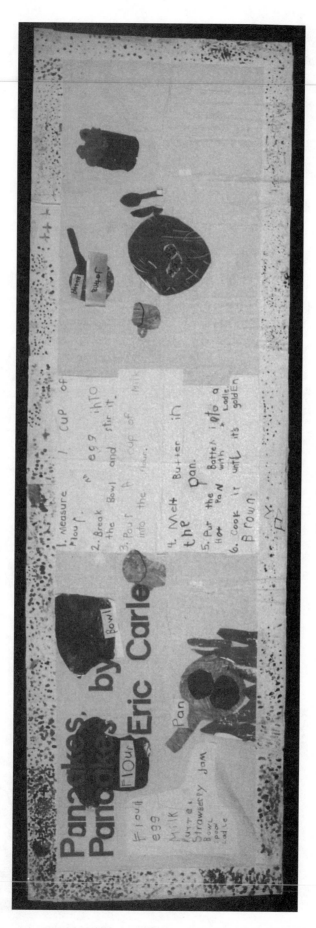

Pancakes! Pancakes!

Character Web from Goldilocks

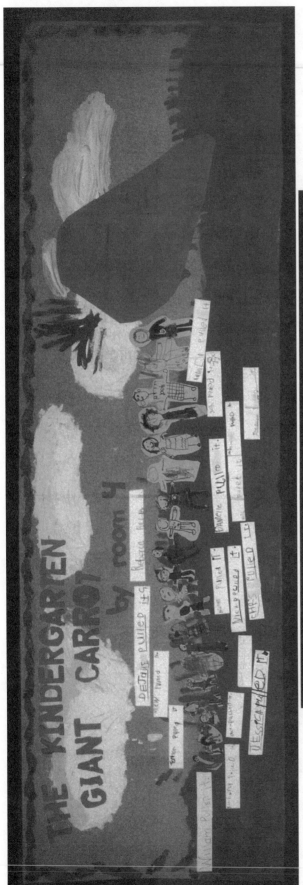

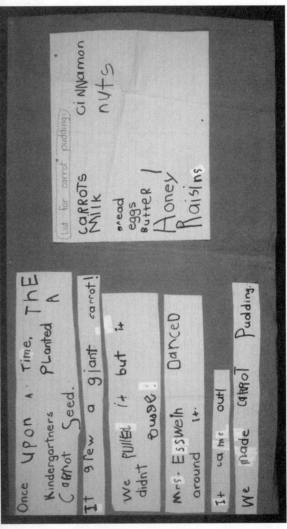

Giant Carrot

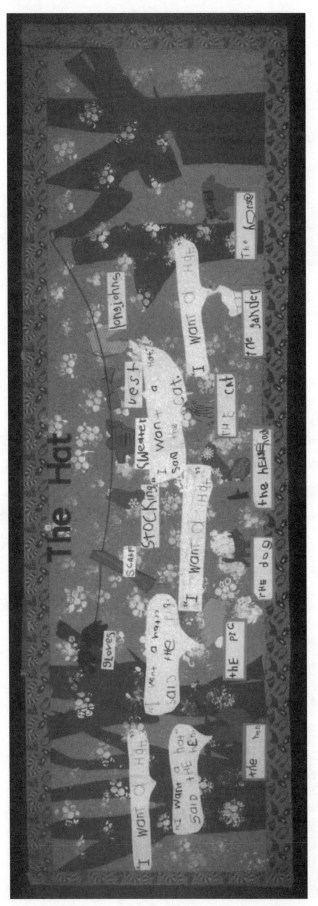

The Hat

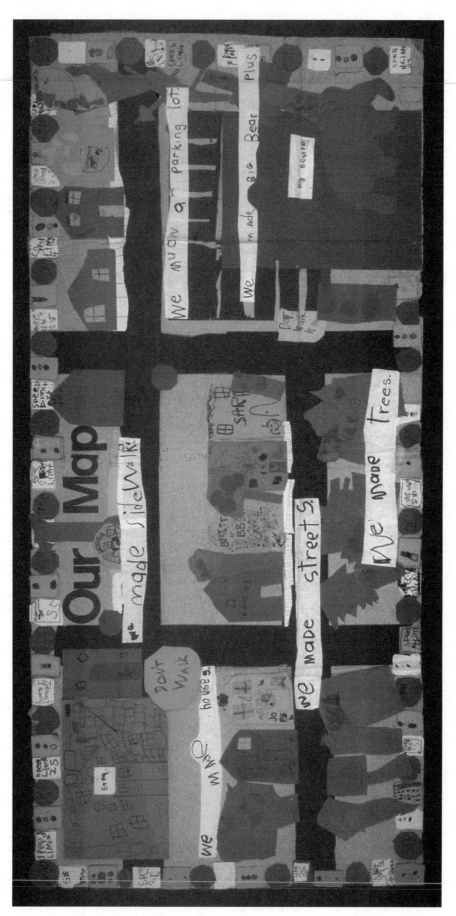

Our Map

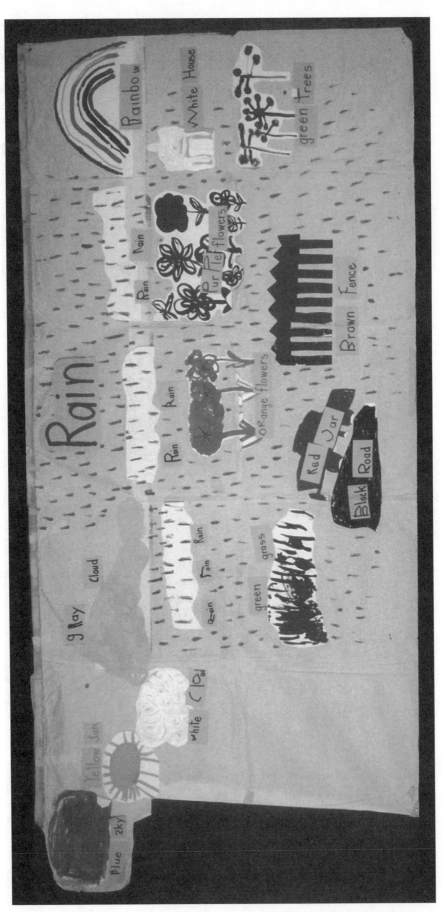

Rain

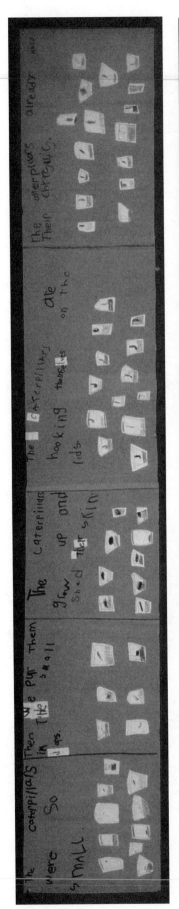

Butterfly Cycle

Bibliography

Adams, M. J. 1990. *Beginning to Read: Thinking and Learning About Print*. Cambridge, MA: MIT Press.

Ball, E. W., and B. A. Blachman. 1991. "Does Phoneme Awareness Training in Kindergarten Make a Difference in Early Word Recognition and Developmental Spelling?" *Reading Research Quarterly* 26 (1): 49–66.

Bear, D. R., M. Invernizzi, S. Templeton, and F. Johnston. 1996. *Words Their Way*. Saddle River, NJ: Prentice Hall.

Bissex, G. 1980. *GNYS AT WRK: A Child Learns to Write and Read*. Cambridge, MA: Harvard University Press.

Bodrova, E., and D. L. Leong. 1996. *Tools of the Mind: The Vygotskian Approach to Early Childhood Education*. Columbus, OH: Merrill.

Bradley, L., and P. E. Bryant. 1983. "Categorizing Sounds and Learning to Read: A Causal Connection." *Nature* 301: 419–421.

Bredekamp, S., and C. Copple, eds. 1997. *Developmentally Appropriate Practice in Early Childhood Programs*. Washington, DC: National Association for the Education of Young Children.

Bruck, M., and R. Treiman. 1992. "Learning to Pronounce Words: The Limitations of Analogies." *Reading Research Quarterly* 27: 374–388.

Bryant, P. E., L. Bradley, M. Camlean, and J. Crossland. 1989. "Nursery Rhymes, Phonological Skills and Reading." *Journal of Child Language* 16: 407–428.

Bryant, P. E., M. MacLean, L. L. Bradley, and J. Crossland. 1990. "Rhyme and Alliteration, Phoneme Detection, and Learning to Read." *Developmental Psychology* 26 (3): 429–438.

Button, K., M. Johnson, and P. Furgerson. 1996. "Interactive Writing in a Primary Classroom." *The Reading Teacher* 49 (6): 446–454.

Calkins, L. M. 1983. *Lessons from a Child: On the Teaching and Learning of Writing*. Portsmouth, NH: Heinemann.

———. 1986. *The Art of Teaching Writing*. Portsmouth, NH: Heinemann.

Cazden, C. B. 1988. *Classroom Discourse: The Language of Teaching and Learning*. Portsmouth, NH: Heinemann.

Chatton, B., and N. Lynne Decker Collins. 1999. *Blurring the Edges: Integrated Curriculum Through Writing and Children's Literature*. Portsmouth, NH: Heinemann.

Chomsky, C. 1971. "Write First, Read Later." *Childhood Education* 47: 296–299.

Clay, M. M. 1975. *What Did I Write?* Portsmouth, NH: Heinemann.

———. 1991a. *Becoming Literate: The Construction of Inner Control.* Portsmouth, NH: Heinemann.

———. 1991b. "Developmental Learning Puzzles Me." *Australian Journal of Reading* 14 (4): 263–275.

———. 1993. *An Observation Survey of Early Literacy Achievement.* Portsmouth, NH: Heinemann.

———. 1998. *By Different Paths to Common Outcomes.* York, ME: Stenhouse.

Cochran-Smith, M. 1984. *The Making of a Reader.* Norwood, NJ: Ablex.

Daneman, M. 1991. "Individual Difference in Reading Skills." In *Handbook of Reading Research*, Vol. II, edited by R. Barr, M. L. Kamil, P. Mosenthal, and P. D. Pearson. New York: Longman.

De Paola, Tomie. 1985. *Tomie de Paola's Mother Goose.* New York: Putnam.

Ehri, L. C. 1991. "Development of the Ability to Read Words." In *Handbook of Reading Research*, Vol. II, edited by R. Barr, M. L. Kamil, P. Mosenthal, and P. D. Pearson. New York: Longman.

———. 1998. "Grapheme-Phoneme Knowledge Is Necessary for Learning to Read Words in English." In *Word Recognition in Beginning Literacy*, edited by J. Metsala and L. C. Ehri. Mahwah, NJ: Lawrence Erlbaum.

Ehri, L. C., and S. McCormick. 1998. "Phases of Word Learning: Implications for Instruction with Delayed and Disabled Readers." *Reading and Writing Quarterly* 20: 163–179.

Ehri, L. C., and L. S. Wilce. 1985. "Does Learning to Spell Help Beginners Learn to Read Words?" *Reading Research Quarterly* 22: 47–65.

Fountas, I. C., and G. S. Pinnell. 1996. *Guided Reading: Good First Teaching for All Children.* Portsmouth, NH: Heinemann.

———, eds. 1999. *Voices on Word Matters: Learning About Phonics and Spelling in the Literacy Classroom.* Portsmouth, NH: Heinemann.

Freeman, E. B., and D. G. Person. 1998. *Connecting Informational Children's Books with Content Area Learning.* Needham Heights, MA: Allyn and Bacon.

Gentry, J. R. and J. W. Gillet. 1993. *Teaching Kids to Spell.* Portsmouth, NH: Heinemann.

Gettinger, M. 1993. "Effects of Invented Spelling and Direct Instruction on Spelling Performance of Second-Grade Boys." *Journal of Applied Behavior Analysis* 26: 281–291.

Goswami, U., and P. Bryant. 1990. *Phonological Skills and Learning to Read.* East Sussex, U.K: Erlbaum Associates.

Graves, D. H. 1983. *Writing: Teachers and Children at Work.* Portsmouth, NH: Heinemann.

Halliday, M. A. K. 1975. *Learning How to Mean: Explorations in the Development of Language.* London: Edward Arnold.

Harris, T. L., and Richard E. Hodges. 1995. *Literacy Dictionary.* Newark, DE: International Reading Association.

Henderson, E. H. 1981. *Learning to Read and Spell: The Child's Knowledge of Words.* DeKalb: Northern Illinois University Press.

———. 1990. *Teaching Spelling.* 2d ed. Boston: Houghton Mifflin.

Henderson, E., T. Estes, and S. Stonecash. 1972. "An Exploratory Study of Word Acquisition Among First Graders at Midyear in a Language Experience Approach." *Journal of Reading Behavior* 4: 21–30.

Hohn, W., and L. C. Ehri. 1983. "Do Alphabet Letters Help Prereaders Acquire Phonemic Segmentation Skill?" *Journal of Educational Psychology* 75: 752–762.

Holdaway, D. 1979. *The Foundations of Literacy.* Sydney: Aston Scholastic

Huck, C., S. Hepler, and J. Hickman. 1993. *Children's Literature in the Elementary School.* Madison, WI: Brown and Benchmark.

Hundley, S., and D. Powell. 1999. "Investigating Letter and Words Through Shared Reading." In *Voices on Word Matters: Learning about Phonics and Spelling in the Literacy Classroom*, edited by I. C. Fountas and G. S. Pinnell. Portsmouth, NH: Heinemann.

International Reading Association and National Association for the Education of Young Children. 1998. Learning to Reading and Write: Developmentally Appropriate Practices for Young Children. A Joint Position Statement. Newark, DE: IRA; Washington, DC: NAEYC.

Irwin, J. W., and I. Baker. 1989. *Promoting Active Reading Comprehension Strategies.* Englewood Cliffs, NJ: Prentice-Hall.

Johnston, P. H. 1997. *Knowing Literacy: Constructive Literacy Assessment.* York, ME: Stenhouse.

Juel, C. 1988. "Learning to Read and Write: A Longitudinal Study of 54 Children from First Through Fourth Grades." *Journal of Educational Psychology* 80: 437–447.

———. 1991. "Beginning Reading." In *Handbook of Reading Research*, Vol. 32, edited by

R. Barr, M. L. Kamil, P. B. Mosenthal, and P. D. Pearson. New York: Longman.

Juel, C., P. L. Griffith, and P. B. Gough. 1986. "Acquisition of Literacy: A Longitudinal Study of Children in First and Second Grade." *Journal of Educational Psychology* 78: 243–255.

Kerbow, D., J. Gwynn, and B. Jacob. 1999. Evaluation of Achievement Gains at the Primary level. Paper presented at the National Conference of the American Educational Research Association, Montreal, CA.

Liberman, I. Y., D. Shankweiler, F. W. Fischer, and B. Carter. 1974. "Explicit Syllable and Phoneme Segmentation in the Young Child." *Journal of Experimental Child Psychology* 18: 201–212.

Liberman, I., D. Shankweiler, and A. Liberman. 1985. The Alphabetic Principle and Learning to Read. U.S. Department of Health and Human Services. [Reprinted with permission from The University of Michigan Press by the National Institute of Child Health and Human Development. Adapted from "Phonology and the Problems of Learning to Read and Write." *Remedial and Special Education* 6: 8–17. 1985.]

Lindfors, J. W. 1987. *Children's Language and Learning.* 2d ed. Englewood Cliffs, NJ: Prentice-Hall.

Lomax, R. G., and L. M. McGee. 1987. "Young Children's Concepts About Print and Meaning: Toward a Model of Word Reading Acquisition." *Reading Research Quarterly* 22: 237–256.

Lundberg, I., J. Frost, and O. P. Petersen. 1988. "Effects of an Extensive Program for Stimulating Phonological Awareness in Preschool Children." *Reading Research Quarterly* 23: 264–284.

Marshall, James. 1991. *Old Mother Hubbard and Her Dog.* New York: Farrar Straus Giroux.

McCarrier, A., and I. Patacca. 1994. "Children's Literature: The Focal Point of an Early Literacy Learning Program." In *Extending Charlotte's Web*, edited by B. Cullinan and J. Hickman. Norwood, MA: Christopher-Gordon.

———. 1999. "Kindergarten Explorations of Letters, Sounds, and Words." In *Voices on Word Matters: Learning About Phonics and Spelling in the Literacy Classroom*, edited by I. C. Fountas and G. S. Pinnell. Portsmouth, NH: Heinemann.

McKenzie, M. G. (1985) Shared Writing: Apprenticeship in Writing in Language Matters, London: Centre for Language in Primary Education.

McKenzie, M. G. 1986. *Journeys into Literacy.* Huddersfield, England: Schofield and Sims.

Nagy, W. E., R. C. Anderson, M. Schommer, J. Scott, and A. Stallman. 1989. "Morphological Families in the Internal Lexicon." *Reading Research Quarterly* 24: 262–282.

Pappas, C. C. 1991. "Fostering Full Access to Literacy by Including Information Books." *Language Arts* 68: 449–462.

Paul, R. 1976. "Invented Spelling in Kindergarten." *Young Children* 31: 195–200.

Perfetti, C. A., I. Beck, L. Bell, C. and Hughes. 1987. "Children's Reading and the Development of Phonological Awareness." *Merrill Palmer Quarterly* 33: 39–75.

Pinnell, G. S., and I. C. Fountas. 1997. *Help America Read: A Handbook for Volunteers.* Portsmouth, NH: Heinemann.

———. 1998. *Word Matters: Teaching Phonics and Spelling in the Reading/Writing Classroom.* Portsmouth, NH: Heinemann.

Pinnell, G. S., and A. McCarrier. 1994. "Interactive Writing: A Transition Tool for Assisting Children in Learning to Read and Write." In *Getting Reading Right from the Start: Effective Early Literacy Interventions*, edited by E. Hiebert and B. Taylor. Needham Heights, MA: Allyn and Bacon.

Pinnell, G. S., J. J. Pikulski, K. K. Wixson, J. R. Campbell, P. B. Gough, and A. S. Beatty. 1995. Listening to Children Read Aloud: Data from NAEP's Integrated Reading Performance Record (IRPR) at Grade 4. Report No. 23-FR-04, prepared by the Educational Testing Service. Washington, DC: Office of Educational Research and Improvement, U.S. Department of Education.

Pressley, M. 1998. *Reading Instruction That Works: The Case for Balanced Teaching.* New York: The Guilford Press.

Read, C. 1970. Children's Perceptions of the Sounds of English: Phonology from Three to Six. Ph.D. diss., Harvard University.

———. 1971. "Pre-School Children's Knowledge of English Phonology." *Harvard Educational Review* 41: 1–34.

Reutzel, D. R., P. M. Hollingsworth, and J. L. Eldredge. 1994. "Oral Reading Instruction: The Impact on Student Reading Development." *Reading Research Quarterly* 29: 41–59.

Rogoff, Barbara. 1990. *Apprenticeship in Thinking: Cognitive Development in Social Context.* New York: Oxford University Press.

Smith, F. 1988. *Understanding Reading: A Psycholinguistic Analysis of Reading and Learning to Read.* 4th ed. Hillsdale, NJ: Erlbaum.

———. 1983. Reading Like a Writer. *Language Arts,* 60, 558–567

———. 1992. "Learning to Read: The Never-Ending Debate." *Phi Delta Kappan* 74 (2): 432–441.

Snow, C. E., M. Burns, and S. Griffin, eds. 1998. *Preventing Reading Difficulties in Young Children.* Washington, DC: Committee on the Prevention of Reading Difficulties in Young Children, Commission on Behavioral and Social Sciences and Education, National Research Council.

Stanovich, K. E. 1991. "Word Recognition: Changing Perspectives." In *Handbook of Reading Research,* Vol. II, edited by R. Barr, M. L. Kamil, P. Mosenthal, and P. D. Pearson. New York: Longman.

Stauffer, R. 1980. *The Language Experience Approach to the Teaching of Reading.* 2d ed. New York: Harper and Row.

Tierney, R. J., and T. Shanahan. 1991. "Research on the Reading-Writing Relationship: Interactions, Transactions, and Outcomes." In *Handbook of Reading Research,* 2d ed., edited by P. D. Pearson, R. Barr, M. Kamil, and P. Mosenthal. New York: Longman.

Treiman, R. 1985. "Onsets and Rimes as Units of Spoken Syllables: Evidence from Children." *Journal of Experimental Child Psychology* 39: 161–181.

Treiman, R. A.1992. "The Role of Intrasyllabic Units in Learning to Read and Spell." In *Reading Acquisition,* edited by P. B. Gough, L. C. Ehri, and R. Treiman. Hillsdale, NJ: Lawrence Erlbaum.

Treiman, R. A., and J. Baron. 1981. "Segmental Analysis Ability: Development and Relation to Reading Ability." In *Reading Research: Advances in Theory and Practice,* Vol. 3, edited by E. E. MacKinnon and T. G. Walker. New York: Academic Press.

Vellutino, F. R., and M. B. Denckla. 1991. "Cognitive and Neuropsychological Foundations of Word Identification in Poor and Normally Developing Readers." In *Handbook of Reading Research,* Vol. II, edited by R. Barr, M. L. Kamil, P. Mosenthal, and P. D. Pearson. New York: Longman.

Vellutino, F. R., and D. B. Scanlon. 1987. "Phonological Coding, Phonological Awareness, and Reading Ability: Evidence from Longitudinal and Experimental Study." *Merrill Palmer Quarterly* 33: 321–363.

Venezky, R. 1970. *The Structure of English Orthography.* The Hague: Mouton.

Walsh, D. J., G. G. Price, and M. G. Gillingham. 1998. "The Critical but Transitory Importance of Letter Naming." *Reading Research Quarterly* 23: 108–122.

Williams, Jane (1998). Research Report on the Early Literacy Learning Initiative. Columbus: The Ohio State University.

Wood, D. 1988. *How Children Think and Learn.* Oxford: Basil Blackwell.

Zutell, J. 1996. "The Directed Spelling Thinking Activity (DSTA): Providing an Effective Balance in Word Study Instruction." *The Reading Teacher* 50 (2): 98–108.

Zutell, J., and T. V. Rasinski. 1991. "Training Teachers to Attend to Their Students' Oral Reading Fluency." *Theory into Practice* 30: 211–217.

Index